To Love
My Daughter
Joan
    Sept 7-1994
    From
    Mom
Nina M. Felkins

The
FAMILY
COOK BOOK

by

GERTRUDE WILKINSON

formerly home editor
Liberty Magazine

1962 EDITION

The Standard

FAMILY

COOKBOOK

Gertrude Wilkinson
formerly home editor
Liberty Magazine

INTRODUCTION

Among the great, unsung heroines of today's world is the homemaker who is called upon to produce three meals a day plus a constant succession of snacks for her husband and children. In addition to her role as cook, she must also be guardian of the family health, with a keen understanding of nutritional values. And since food accounts for the lion's share of the family earnings, she must be a budgeteer par excellence, running her kitchen just like someone in the restaurant business, with ever an eye on the till.

On the less practical but highly important side, she must further assume the responsibility for her family's enjoyment of food. Hers is the task of deciding what to serve and how to prepare it . . . and to make each meal an event to look forward to, whether it be a birthday celebration or a Thanksgiving dinner or just a meal for an average day. It is for her to make each mealtime one that will instill in her children an understanding of the sociability that should be part of food. Finally, it is up to her to do this in such a way that she never regards food preparation as a dreary chore, but rather an achievement that not only her family but she herself can enjoy.

Among the vast number of cookbooks now on the booksellers' shelves, The Standard Family Cookbook was carefully planned as a basic guide to help the homemaker in this complex assignment. In this new, modern cookbook you will find food phases from menu planning to table service, all presented in a simple, straightforward way, and indexed for handy, quick reference. Acknowledging the importance of the visual appeal to food, The Standard Family Cookbook is abundantly illustrated in appetizing full color and includes, as well, black-and-white photographs of the steps in the preparation of literally hundreds of dishes.

Service is the watchword throughout the 640 pages of The Standard Family Cookbook, whether the reader be a novice in the kitchen . . . a new bride in trepidation at the thought of her husband's first meal at home . . . or a seasoned "pro" who knows her range and mixing bowls like the palm of her hand. It is beamed at the epicure with a penchant for the glamor of foreign foods, at the woman who works and has a whole unique set of marketing and preparation problems, at the hasty gourmet who strives beaverishly to build a repertoire of budget casseroles. In addition, it gives special consideration to the dietary requirements of religious groups . . . and it takes into account the situation of those who must plan meals for invalids.

To own The Standard Family Cookbook is like having a whole shelf of cookbooks in one huge volume. It *tells* how and *shows* how to make cooking real fun. It is a book that was planned and written to help you cook better, avoid disappointments, prevent waste, shop more wisely and SAVE YOU TIME AND MONEY. Whether you have cooked for years, or are just learning, the new, revised edition of The Standard Family Cookbook will help make you a better cook.

The Publishers

CONTENTS

1.

PLANNING MEALS—
THE MODERN WAY

THE dinner table is the center of the family's leisure time together. At the end of the day when the tasks are done, every member of the family looks forward to this hour of congenial companionship, relaxation and rest. There is no more pleasant spot than a cheerfully lighted dining room, with a good table, appetizing fragrances, and the companionship of one's own family. This atmosphere —so well worth creating—has its foundation in a practical knowledge of food and nutrition.

Science and art have finally joined hands in our complex civilization. Experts in the chemistry of foods and nutrition are steadily advancing our knowledge in these fields. Today every housekeeper is interested in the preparation of meals which are nourishing, which yield dividends in health and vitality, and which are pleasing to the senses of sight, taste, and smell.

Scientists have taught the tense, keyed-up businessmen of America that when the dinner hour arrives business worries must be set aside, mind and body must gradually relax. These scientists are devoting their lives to laboratory experiments in order that the latest findings in nutrition may be made available to everyone. Women learn from them that it is important to choose a well-balanced diet—but many ask, "What *is* a well-balanced diet?" The scientists reply, "A well-balanced diet is one which provides all the essential materials that the body needs." It is vital, therefore, that the housewife should understand the elements of an adequate or well-balanced diet—these "essential materials." This is easily learned from the eating plans which were developed by nutritionists

13

during World War II, called the "Basic Seven," and, more recently, the newly developed daily food plan, called the "Basic Four," with the purpose of helping homemakers prepare and serve well-balanced meals including all the essential nutriments. Both these basic plans are given in the following:

THE BASIC SEVEN

Eat some food from each of these seven basic groups every day:

Group 1. Green and Yellow Vegetables (raw, cooked, frozen or canned).
Group 2. Oranges, Tomatoes, Grapefruit, Raw Cabbage, Salad Greens.
Group 3. Potatoes and other Vegetables and Fruits (raw, dried, cooked, frozen or canned).
Group 4. Milk and Milk Products (fluid, evaporated, dried milk, Cheese).
Group 5. Meat, Poultry, Fish, Eggs, Dried Beans, Peas, Nuts, Peanut Butter.
Group 6. Bread, Flour and Cereal (natural whole-grain, enriched or restored).
Group 7. Butter and Fortified Margarine.

A detailed explanation of the BASIC SEVEN FOOD GROUPS is outlined below:

Group 1. Includes string beans, beet greens, kale, asparagus, sweet potatoes, yellow turnips, broccoli, okra, green peppers, dandelion greens, carrots, cabbage, yellow corn, spinach, pumpkin, all raw salad greens, and all squash except white squash. These vegetables supply Vitamin A; also in lesser degrees, Vitamins B1, C and G, as well as iron and calcium.
Group 2. Includes citrus fruits, such as oranges and grapefruit, as well as pineapple, tomato, salad greens, raw cabbage. The fruits and tomatoes may be eaten canned or fresh. They supply a good deal of Vitamin C and a smaller amount of Vitamin B1.
Group 3. Includes all vegetables and potatoes, with the exception of those vegetables listed under Group 1. It also includes all fruits, with the exception of those listed under Group 2. These vegetables and fruits may be fresh, dried, quick-frozen or canned. They supply, in differing amounts, all the vitamins.
Group 4. Includes in every form, fresh, dried skim milk, or evaporated milk. A good way to get milk in daily diet is to include it in scalloped dishes, cream soups, ice cream and milk desserts. Cheese is also included in this group, and it can be eaten raw or in cooking, as a dessert and in salads. These products supply calcium, protein, and Vitamins A, B1 and G.
Group 5. Includes meat, poultry, fish, eggs, dried beans and peas, nuts and peanut butter. In the meat group are all cuts of beef, pork, lamb, veal; also, varieties such as heart, kidney, liver, sweetbreads, which are rich in food value and should be used once or twice during the week. In the poultry groups are all varieties—fresh, frozen, canned, dried. Eggs can be served in a hundred

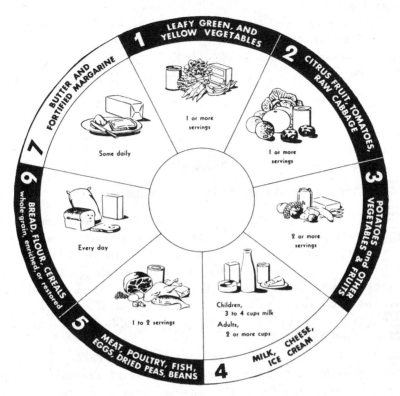

The basic seven food groups should be familiar to every homemaker who wishes to assure her family a well-balanced diet. Be sure that you and your family eat something every day from each of these seven groups.

ways. All these products supply iron and protein as well as Vitamins B1 and G. In addition eggs are a good source of Vitamin A.

Group 6. Includes bread and cereals which are made from the whole grain of wheat, corn, oats, rye; also breads from enriched white flour and cereals with restored whole grain values. These products supply Vitamin B1 and iron.

Group 7. Includes butter and fortified margarine. These products supply calcium and iron; butter and fortified margarine also supply Vitamin A.

GUIDE TO SERVINGS

MILK: 2 or more glasses daily for adults. 3 to 4 or more glasses daily for children. *Milk Equivalents:* 1 qt. milk equals 17 oz. evaporated milk, or 3½ oz. dried skim milk plus 1 oz. butter, or 4½ oz. dried whole milk, or 5 oz. American cheese.

VEGETABLES: 2 or more servings daily besides potato. 1 green or yellow; "greens" often.

FRUIT: 2 or more servings daily. At least 1 raw; citrus fruit or tomato often.

EGGS: 3 to 5 a week; 1 daily preferred.

CEREAL AND BREAD: 2 or more servings daily. Whole-grain value or enriched.

MEAT, CHEESE, FISH, FOWL: 1 or more servings daily. Dried beans, peas, peanuts occasionally.

BUTTER: 2 or more tablespoons daily.

THE BASIC FOUR

Food requirements from each of these four groups every day.

Group 1. Milk. Daily for children, at least 3 cups. Teen-agers, at least 4 cups. Adults, at least 2 cups. Pregnant women, at least 4 cups. Nursing mothers, at least 6 cups. (Cheese and ice cream may replace part of the milk.)

Group 2. Meat. 2 or more servings daily. (Includes beef, veal, pork, lamb, variety meats, poultry, fish, and eggs. As alternates you may use dried beans, peas, lentils and nuts.) One serving amounts to: 2-3 oz. lean cooked meat, poultry, or fish without bone; 2 eggs; 1 cup cooked beans, peas, or lentils; 4 Tbsp. peanut butter.

Group 3. Vegetable-fruit. 4 or more servings daily. (One dark-green or deep-yellow vegetable at least every other day. One citrus fruit or other Vitamin C-rich fruit daily. Other fruits and vegetables including potatoes.) One serving amounts to: ½ cup of vegetable or fruit, or medium-sized whole fruit.

Group 4. Bread-cereals. 4 or more servings daily. (Includes bread or cereals, whole grain, enriched or restored. Cereals, crackers, macaroni, spaghetti, noodles, rice, quick breads, and other baked goods if made with whole-grain or enriched flour.) One serving amounts to: 1 slice of bread, 1 oz. ready-to-eat cereal, ½ to ¾ cup cooked cereal, macaroni, noodles, etc.

These four groups form the foundation of a good balanced diet. Additional food energy will be furnished by other foods added to round out the eye- and taste-appeal of the meals.

DIETS AND FOOD VALUES

These are given in specific detail in Chapters 2, 27 and 28.

Using these basic groups as a guide to marketing, it is a matter of simple arithmetic to make out a nutritionally balanced market order. The following is an example of how two different families, one with only two adults, the other with two adults and two children, could make marketing plans for the week:

Careful marketing is the prelude to good eating. Buy foods when they are in season. Watch advertisements and week-end and special sales. Buy only in quantities which suit your needs, purse, and storage facilities.

WEEKLY MARKET ORDERS

	TWO ADULTS	TWO ADULTS AND TWO CHILDREN
Green leafy vegetables..................	6-7 lbs.	15 lbs.
Oranges, tomatoes, grapefruit	4 lbs.	8 lbs.
Other vegetables and fruits	8 lbs.	25 lbs.
Potatoes, including sweet	1½-2 lbs.	13 lbs.
Dried peas, beans	½ lb.	1 lb.
Milk	8-10 qts.	19 qts.
Cheese	½ lb.	1 lb.
Meat, poultry and fish	5 lbs.	12 lbs.
Eggs	1 doz.	2 doz.
Bread, flour and cereal	6 lbs.	13 lbs.
Butter or fortified margarine............	1 lb.	2 lbs.
Fats and oils	1½-2 lbs.	3 lbs.
Sugars, syrups, molasses, jams and jellies...	2 lbs.	4 lbs.

After meals are planned and a market order is made up, the housewife may make a further check on groceries purchased for their nutrition value, by dividing up food costs as outlined here:

One-fifth of food budget for milk and cheese.

One-fifth for fruits and vegetables.

One-fifth for meat, poultry, fish and eggs.

One-fifth for breads, cereals, pastries, cakes, potatoes and rice.

One-fifth for fats, oils, sugar, syrups and preserves.

Leafy, Green, and Yellow vegetables

Citrus Fruit, Tomatoes

Potatoes, Sweetpotatoes

Other Vegetables and Fruit

2 heads lettuce
1½ lb. snap beans
2 bunches carrots
2½ lb. spinach
1 lb. squash
1 head of cabbage (small)
1 No. 2 can green peas
1 pkg. green lima beans (frozen)

4½ to 5 lb. oranges
2 grapefruit
1 46-oz. can tomato juice
2 or 3 lemons or 1 small can lemon juice

2 lb. sweet potatoes
6 lb. potatoes

2 lb. apples
1 No. 2 can applesauce
1 No. 2½ can peaches
1 lb. prunes
½ lb. raisins
3 lb. other fruit in season or canned
1 bunch celery
1 lb. beets
1 lb. onions

A week's food supply for a family of four—two adults, two children. Some of the staple foods listed may be purchased in larger quantities to save time and money and stored away or frozen, if possible.

And finally, to complete the food picture, take into consideration:

1. CONTRAST OF COLOR

There is an old saying, "We eat with our eyes." This has been proved time and time again. A good rule to follow is to choose a group of foods in com-

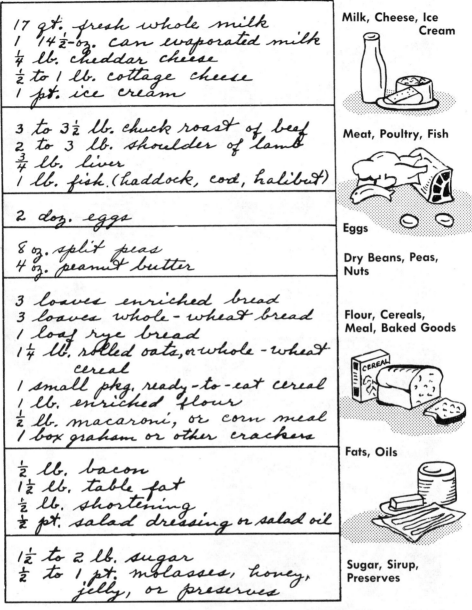

17 qt. fresh whole milk 1 14½-oz. can evaporated milk ¼ lb. cheddar cheese ½ to 1 lb. cottage cheese 1 pt. ice cream	**Milk, Cheese, Ice Cream**
3 to 3½ lb. chuck roast of beef 2 to 3 lb. shoulder of lamb ¾ lb. liver 1 lb. fish (haddock, cod, halibut)	**Meat, Poultry, Fish**
2 doz. eggs	**Eggs**
8 oz. split peas 4 oz. peanut butter	**Dry Beans, Peas, Nuts**
3 loaves enriched bread 3 loaves whole-wheat bread 1 loaf rye bread 1¼ lb. rolled oats, or whole-wheat cereal 1 small pkg. ready-to-eat cereal 1 lb. enriched flour ½ lb. macaroni, or corn meal 1 box graham or other crackers	**Flour, Cereals, Meal, Baked Goods**
½ lb. bacon 1½ lb. table fat ½ lb. shortening ½ pt. salad dressing or salad oil	**Fats, Oils**
1½ to 2 lb. sugar ½ to 1 pt. molasses, honey, jelly, or preserves	**Sugar, Sirup, Preserves**

Coffee, tea, salt, flavorings, and dessert mixes may be bought as needed. With fresh vegetables and fruits, the oftener the better; shop daily for some seasonal produce.

binations which please the eye. A dinner plate, for example, which has the tender pink of a slice of ham, the deep gold of a candied sweet potato, and the succulent green of tender peas is an appealing picture. Three different colors are used. Avoid two foods of the same color, such as beets and ham, or tomatoes and corned beef, or boiled codfish and mashed potatoes. Constantly

Contrast color, flavor, and texture in the daily menus. And above all, keep menus simple.

strive for contrast in the colors of the food, not only for one course, but for the entire meal, and try to avoid two of the same colors during the meal.

2. CONTRAST OF TEXTURES

The appeal to appetite is greater, and the charm of the meal is enhanced, when contrast in texture is employed. The dinner plate as outlined above offers an example of pleasing contrast in texture; the firm slice of meat, the soft potato, the skin of the green peas. Other textures which are classic in their appeal are familiar to everyone:

Ice cream and cake.
Hot soup and crisp crackers.
Chicken fricassee and steamed rice.
Corned beef and cabbage.

3. CONTRAST OF FLAVOR

This is the ultimate test of a good meal. The best food in the world may be purchased, but if it is ruined in the cooking, all is lost. Flavor is the priceless ingredient of good food. It is achieved by study and experiment; but here again we have fundamental rules to guide us. Experience has taught us that these contrasts please the palate:

Mild and tart—Roast duckling with orange sauce.
Hot and cold—Ice cream with hot fudge sauce.
Mild and strong—Corned beef and cabbage.
Sweet and sour—Beets with vinegar.

4. CONTRAST OF TEMPERATURE

Here the appeal is to man's capricious appetite. Offer a completely cold meal, even on a scorching hot day, and the stomach rebels at all this cold food. But balance hot and cold foods such as:

Sliced cold chicken—Stuffed tomato salad
Potatoes au gratin
Hot tea—Lemon sherbet

Immediately the contrast between hot and cold pleases, the gastric juices begin to flow and the food is eaten with zest.

GETTING DINNER ON THE TABLE

After the housekeeper has made out her menu and studied the meal she has planned, her next problem is the actual food preparation.

How to cook the main dish, potatoes, a sauce and one or two vegetables and have everything properly cooked and completed at the same minute—these are the young housekeeper's first lessons. When learned, they distinguish the expert from the amateur.

1. Plan to use the stove so that the cooking is divided between the top of the stove and the oven.
2. Cook simple dishes while getting the hang of things.

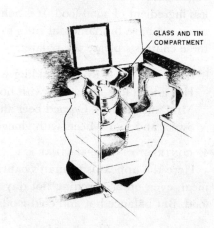

GLASS AND TIN COMPARTMENT

Planning helps in preparing, serving, cleaning up.

(1) Large room divided by a partial wall into kitchen proper and dining room saves steps, takes less space in house than would a kitchen with some eating space and a separate dining room.

(2) The modern kitchen can have a built in garbage-and-trash disposal unit, shown here in cross section.

(3) Workroom planned for kitchen-related jobs that might interfere with carrying out of regular meal-time chores helps to keep kitchen in order.

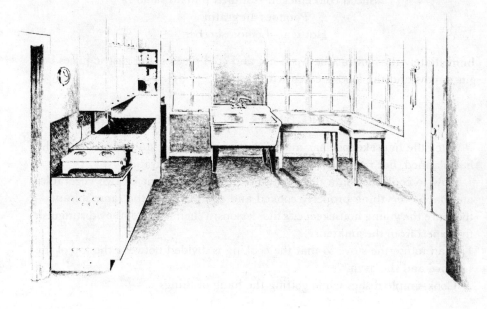

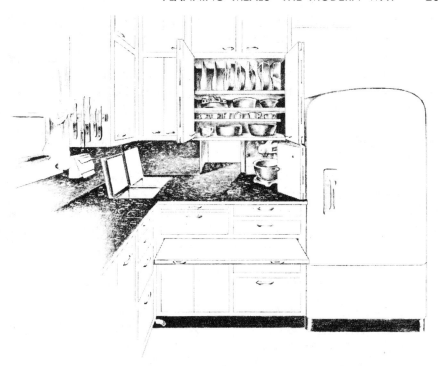

Food-mixing center, showing the pass door, storage for food mixer, pull-out board, and unit for disposal of garbage and trash. Time is saved by having supplies and utensils handy.

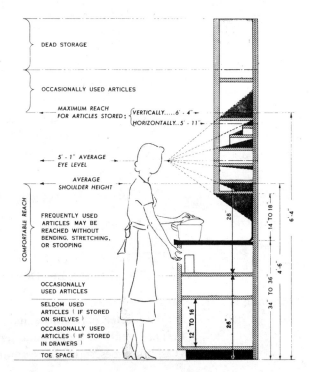

DEAD STORAGE

OCCASIONALLY USED ARTICLES

MAXIMUM REACH
FOR ARTICLES STORED : { VERTICALLY.....6' - 4"
                        HORIZONTALLY..5' - 11"

5' - 1" AVERAGE
EYE LEVEL

AVERAGE
SHOULDER HEIGHT

COMFORTABLE REACH

FREQUENTLY USED
ARTICLES MAY BE
REACHED WITHOUT
BENDING, STRETCHING,
OR STOOPING

28"

14" TO 18"

6'-4"

4'-6"

34" TO 36"

OCCASIONALLY
USED ARTICLES

SELDOM USED
ARTICLES (IF STORED
ON SHELVES)

OCCASIONALLY USED
ARTICLES (IF STORED
IN DRAWERS)

12" TO 16"

26"

TOE SPACE

Proper storage heights for supplies for an average-height woman. Standing normally, worker cannot see shaded areas.

3. Write your own special notes about the recipe in the margin of the book, to keep a record for future reference.

Different methods of cooking insure a variety of texture and flavor interest. Avoid an all-boiled dinner, or an all-fried dinner, or an all-baked dinner. Choose rather a roast of meat with mashed potatoes, a crisp raw green salad, fresh fruit and homemade cake, in order to include contrast of color, flavor and texture.

4. Seek variety during the week. Do not repeat the same dish twice in one week.
5. Seek variety over a period of a month. Do not serve the same menu on the same day each successive week.
6. Seek variety in recipes. Try out new ones to add to files of tested recipes.
7. Seek variety in methods of cookery, try out new combinations of foods. Every branch of cookery offers appealing possibilities.
8. And above all, keep menus simple. As one famous cook expresses it, "Better a few dishes well cooked, than a wealth of food prepared indifferently."

A FAMILY DINNER

Dinner—6:30 P.M.
Broiled meat cakes
Creamed potatoes
Spinach with hard-cooked egg
Tomato wedges—carrot strips
Hot rolls—butter—jam
Gingerbread—applesauce
Tea or coffee
Milk for children

PLAN OF WORK

A Time Schedule for Dinner Preparation

TASKS TO BE DONE

Morning Hours: Scrub, cook, cool potatoes.
Wash, quarter, core apples; make applesauce.
Prepare cream sauce for potatoes.
Wash tomatoes, scrub carrots; place in refrigerator.

5:15—6:30 P.M.: Slice carrots lengthwise; plunge in ice water to curl.

Shape meat balls; set in refrigerator.

Peel, dice potatoes; add to cream sauce; heat in double boiler over low flame.

Cook eggs.

Bake gingerbread.

Prepare spinach and put on to cook.

Cut tomatoes in sections.

Light broiler flame of oven.

Cook meat cakes under broiler flame; heat rolls in oven.

When meat is cooked and rolls hot, turn off heat.

6:25—6:30 P.M.: Carry food into dining room on tray.

Serve hot food in covered dishes.

Cover rolls with linen napkin.

Serve carrots and tomatoes in bowl of chopped ice.

Serve hot foods on warm plates.

Serve cold foods on cold plates.

The experienced cook always keeps in mind the adage, "Tomorrow is another day." Plan to cook a double amount when such foods as potatoes, rice or macaroni are prepared, but allow one full day to go by before introducing the same food in a new dish. Whenever possible, serve it a different way the second time it appears.

Save all liquids from canned, fresh and quick-frozen vegetables. Use them in soups, gravies or sauces. Save a bone from a ham for split pea soup. Save bits of meat and bones and leftover vegetables for the soup pot to give added flavor.

2.

GOOD EATING
AND GOOD HEALTH

THE goal of the nutrition expert is to teach every man, woman and child that the food eaten, day in and day out, determines the health of mind and body. There are many ancient sayings which express the idea of good nutrition. Among the most famous of these is the adage, "What you eat today will walk and talk tomorrow."

In the preceding chapter we discussed the Basic Seven Food Groups and their relation to the problem of menu planning for the average person, but there are many instances where the normal mixed diet is unsuitable. For example, in the case of illness a physician prescribes special diets; when a food allergy is indicated, a physician orders the highly specialized diet for that specific allergy. Prevalence of food allergies is now recognized as one of our great dietary problems. In all such instances the advice of a qualified physician should be sought.

One great American habit is to go on a diet to take off excess weight—often freak or fad diets which are dangerous to health. The only intelligent procedure is to consult a physician before embarking on a reducing diet.

JUDGING ONE'S WEIGHT

This is a matter for personal medical advice. During childhood and youth, a certain amount of extra weight is desirable; but by the time middle age arrives, it is usually far better to maintain the body weight which was ideal for the individual at the age of thirty.

As the individual grows older, there is a normal tendency to slow down on physical activities. But the appetite for food remains the same and thus the body accumulates fat.

CHECKING ONE'S WEIGHT

When it becomes apparent that the body is gaining weight, see a physician. Buy a set of reliable scales, and follow the doctor's orders. Weigh in each morning, and count the calories prescribed by your own doctor for your own needs.

COUNTING THE CALORIES

The unit used for measuring the amount of energy in food is called the calorie. All foods furnish calories, but in widely varying amounts. The human body is usually defined as a machine, because, whereas a machine burns gasoline or coal for fuel, the human body burns food. Just as a machine converts its fuel into other forms of energy, so does the body convert its fuel (food) into muscular energy.

The three chief sources of body energy are: fats, carbohydrates, and proteins. These words are translated into everyday use as butter, cream, oil for fats; sugar, bread, cereal for carbohydrates; meat, fish, eggs for proteins.

The foods which build and repair body tissue are the proteins and minerals, and water. These are the essential elements for building and repairing bone, muscle, blood and other fluids, but only part of the proteins yield energy.

The foods that yield energy are carbohydrates (starches and sugar), fats and proteins. This energy is measured in terms of calories or heat units. The carbohydrates are used entirely as fuel or are stored as fat.

Vegetable soup offers unparalleled nourishing goodness. Colorful, tender vegetables and liquid, with or without meat, can make a meal-in-itself dish at lunch time or lead into a heartier meal at dinner.

Fat is the most concentrated fuel of all the three sources, and yields more energy per unit than either the carbohydrates or proteins.

Body-regulating foods are minerals, vitamins, water and roughage. Minerals aid in all body processes.

We now see that food—for growth and repair, for yielding energy, for storing fat—comes from one of three great sources: protein—fats—carbohydrates. But the body has other functions and processes which are described under the general term—body regulating. Here the vitamins, minerals and water come into daily use.

WATER

Water is an essential for the proper functioning of the body. It provides the liquid medium for the blood and the digestive juices, and for elimination of waste. Water aids digestion, but should never be taken while food is still in the mouth.

MINERALS

The number of minerals in the body add up to nineteen; but the important ones are: calcium, phosphorus, iron, iodine.

Calcium and phosphorus build strong bones and teeth. The best food sources for calcium are milk and cheese.

Iron is essential in the formation of hemoglobin, which is responsible for the blood's red color and carries oxygen to the cells. The best food sources for iron are egg yolks, liver, kidney, heart, lean meat, green leafy vegetables, whole-grain cereal, molasses, apricots, prunes.

Iodine plays an important part in the normal functioning of the thyroid gland. The best food sources for iodine are fish-liver oils, fish, and shellfish.

VITAMINS

Modern science is responsible for our knowledge of vitamins and their necessity in the diet. Years of scientific research proved that experimental foods containing purified mixtures of proteins, carbohydrates and fats were not sufficient. The unknown substance had to be included. The name vitamin was soon given to this invisible ingredient. We now know what foods contain vitamins and what methods of food preparation and cooking affect them favorably and unfavorably.

Vitamin A is essential for growth. The best food sources are leafy green vegetables, carrots, yellow fruits such as peaches and apricots, milk, butter, cream, fish-liver oils and others.

Vitamin B1 (Thiamin) is essential for growth and general well-being. The

KNOW YOUR VITAMINS FOR GOOD HEALTH

Check shows vitamins in foods listed	A	Thiamine	Riboflavin	Niacin	C	D
DAIRY PRODUCTS, EGGS						
Butter	✓					✓
Cheese	✓		✓			
Cream	✓					✓
Eggs, whole	✓	✓	✓	✓		✓
Egg yolk	✓	✓	✓	✓		✓
Milk, whole	✓	✓	✓	✓		✓
MEAT, POULTRY, FISH						
Beef, lean		✓	✓	✓		
Chicken		✓		✓		
Codfish		✓	✓			
Fish-liver oils	✓					✓
Haddock				✓		
Kidney	✓	✓	✓	✓	✓	
Liver	✓	✓	✓	✓	✓	✓
Mutton, lean		✓	✓	✓		
Pork, lean		✓		✓		
Roe, fish	✓	✓	✓			
Salmon	✓	✓		✓		✓
Sardines	✓	✓				✓
FRUIT						
Apples		✓	✓		✓	
Apricots	✓	✓	✓		✓	
Avocados	✓	✓	✓		✓	
Bananas	✓	✓	✓	✓		
Blackberries	✓	✓				
Blueberries	✓					
Cantaloup	✓	✓	✓		✓	
Cherries					✓	
Cranberries					✓	
Currants, black	✓				✓	
Dates	✓	✓				
Figs		✓	✓			
Gooseberries					✓	
Grapefruit		✓	✓		✓	
Lemons					✓	
Oranges	✓	✓	✓		✓	
Olives, green and ripe	✓					
Peaches	✓				✓	
Pears		✓	✓			
Pineapples	✓	✓			✓	
Plums	✓	✓				
Prunes	✓	✓	✓			
Raspberries		✓			✓	
Strawberries	✓		✓		✓	
Tangerines	✓	✓	✓		✓	
Watermelon	✓	✓			✓	
VEGETABLES						
Asparagus, green	✓				✓	
Beans, lima		✓	✓			
Beans, navy		✓	✓			
Beans, snap	✓	✓	✓		✓	
Beet greens	✓		✓			
Broccoli	✓	✓	✓		✓	
Brussels sprouts	✓	✓	✓		✓	
Cabbage	✓	✓	✓	✓	✓	
Carrots	✓	✓	✓			
Cauliflower		✓	✓		✓	
Chard	✓					
Collards	✓	✓	✓	✓	✓	
Corn, sweet	✓					
Cowpeas	✓	✓		✓		
Dandelion greens	✓				✓	
Dock	✓	✓			✓	
Eggplant	✓					
Endive	✓	✓	✓		✓	
Kale	✓	✓	✓	✓	✓	
Kohlrabi		✓			✓	
Leeks		✓				
Lettuce, green	✓	✓	✓			
Mushrooms						
Mustard greens	✓	✓	✓	✓	✓	
Okra	✓					
Onions		✓			✓	
Parsnips		✓			✓	
Peanuts		✓	✓	✓		
Peas, dried		✓	✓	✓		
Peas, green	✓	✓	✓	✓	✓	
Peppers, sweet	✓	✓			✓	
Potatoes		✓			✓	
Radishes					✓	
Rhubarb					✓	
Rutabagas					✓	
Soybeans		✓	✓	✓		
Spinach	✓	✓	✓	✓	✓	
Squash, yellow	✓	✓			✓	
Sweet potatoes	✓	✓	✓	✓	✓	
Tomatoes	✓	✓	✓	✓	✓	
Turnip greens	✓	✓	✓		✓	
Water cress	✓	✓	✓		✓	
CEREALS						
Corn meal, yellow	✓	✓	✓			
Whole grains		✓	✓			

best food sources are whole-grain cereals, legumes, tomatoes, pork, lean meat, liver, kidney and others.

Vitamin C increases resistance to infection and helps maintain firm gums and sound teeth. The best food sources are the citrus fruits: oranges, grapefruit, lemons; tomatoes, also pineapple, strawberries, cabbage and others.

Green vegetable salad is vitamin-packed, refreshing, and pleasing to the eye as well. Tuck sliced tomatoes, onion rings, celery strips among shredded lettuce leaves. Add diced raw or left-over cooked vegetables when available. Complete the picture with slivers of cold meat, cheese, or chilled cubes of deviled ham.

Vitamin D is popularly known as the sunshine vitamin. It is essential in the prevention of rickets in young children. The best food sources are fish-liver oils, liver, egg yolk and others. Many commercial foods are "irradiated" with this vitamin.

Vitamin G (Riboflavin) promotes growth, steps up the digestive system. The best food sources are milk, green leafy vegetables, liver, whole-wheat cereals and others.

POINTERS ON REDUCING DIETS

1. Your physician will advise you that any low ealorie diet must still provide the necessary protein, vitamins and minerals. Bulk in the diet is especially important when the calories are reduced. The flavor of the food takes on added importance, as does variety.
2. Serve meats roasted, broiled, or pan-broiled, but omit the fat in the pan, or on the meat.
3. Omit all cream. Use buttermilk or skim milk.
4. Drink tea or coffee as desired, but omit cream and sugar. Many dieters find the use of saccharin tablets of benefit.
5. Eggs for breakfast or luncheon may be soft, hard-cooked or poached. Use salt lightly.
6. Avoid mayonnaise. Use a little lemon juice on green salads. If olive or

salad oil is prescribed by the physician, measure it carefully by table-spoons.

7. Drink plenty of water between meals when following a diet.
8. Be sure the essential foods are eaten daily.

AVOID THESE HIGH CALORIC FOODS

Beverages: Cream, beer, cocoa, soda fountain drinks.
Soups: Cream soups, thick vegetable soups (choose consommés).
Fruits: Canned fruits in heavy syrups, jams, preserves, sugared fruits.
Cereals: Macaroni, spaghetti, oatmeal, farina.
Pastries: Mustn't touch!
Sweets: Sugar, honey, rich candies.
Fats: Olive oils (unless prescribed), gravies, sauces, mayonnaise.

PURPOSE OF LOW CALORIE DIET

The low calorie diet causes the patient to utilize his own excess body fats, thereby reducing his body weight. The amount of food eaten, however, must be sufficient to furnish body requirements, with the exception of energy requirements. It is important that bulky foods, such as raw vegetable and mixed green salads, should be taken to satisfy hunger. Physicians are emphatic in their belief that no one diet can be made up to suit the needs of everyone. Diet lists are, at the most, simply suggestions of low calorie foods. The physician will modify any list to best suit each patient.

NUMBER OF CALORIES IN EVERYDAY FOODS

FRUITS	100 CALORIE PORTION
Apples	1 large
Apricots, Stewed and Sweetened	¼ cup
Bananas	1 medium
Grapefruit	½ medium
Orange	1 large
Pineapple	1 slice and juice
Prunes, Stewed and Sweetened	2 prunes and juice
Strawberries	1⅓ cups
VEGETABLES	
Asparagus	5 large stalks
Beets	4 medium
Broccoli	4 stalks
Cabbage, Raw	2½ cups
Carrots, Fresh Cooked	4 cups

VEGETABLES *(continued)*   100 CALORIE PORTION

Corn, Canned	⅓ cup
Green Beans	1⅙ cups
Lettuce	2 large heads
Lima Beans, Dried	⅙ cup
Potato	1 medium
Spinach	2½ cups
Sweet Potato	½ medium
Tomato	3 medium

DAIRY PRODUCTS

Butter	1 Tbsp.
Cheese, American	1⅛ inch cube
Cream, 20%	3 Tbsp.
Egg	1⅓ eggs
Milk, Whole	⅝ cup

MEAT, POULTRY, AND FISH

Bacon	4-5 slices
Fish, Lean	1 slice
Lamb	1 chop
Lean Beef	1 slice
Lean Pork	½ chop
Liver	1 slice
Poultry	3 slices
Salmon, Canned	⅝ cup

MISCELLANEOUS

Cereal, Cooked	¾ cup
Cereal, Dry	1 cup
Macaroni and Spaghetti	¾ cup
Cake, Plain	2 x 2¼ x 1 inch piece
Candy, Fudge	1 inch piece
Cookies, Sugar	2 medium
Jelly	1¾ Tbsp.
Peanuts	20-24 peanuts
Sugar	2 Tbsp.

SUBSTITUTIONS OF CALORIES

1 slice of bread may replace 1 glass skim milk.

1 serving of butter (one square) may replace 1 tablespoon cream (20% cream).

Non-fattening wafers on the relish tray team up happily with a cheese dip in a pineapple shell.

SUGGESTED 1500 CALORIE DIET

(Upon advice of physician)

MORNING:

Toast—1 slice

Butter—1 square

Milk—1 glass buttermilk or skim milk

Fruit—1 serving, choice of:

    1 orange

    1 very small apple

    ½ grapefruit

    ½ cup strawberries or berries

    1 peach

    1 slice watermelon

    1 slice pineapple

    1 very small pear

Coffee—black, no sugar or cream

NOON:

Meat—lean, 1 average serving; or fish—no gravy or rich sauces

Choice of:

    Bread—1 slice, whole-wheat or rye preferred, or

    Potato—baked, boiled or mashed, 1 average serving or

    Rice—noodles, spaghetti or macaroni, plain boiled, 1 average serving

Butter—1 very small square

Vegetable—2 average servings—hot or in salad

Fruit—1 serving (refer to breakfast list)

Milk—1 glass buttermilk or skim milk

Dessert—1 small serving

Coffee or Tea—plain, no sugar or cream

NIGHT:

Vegetables—1 medium serving—hot or in salad

Choice of:

Bread—1 slice, whole-wheat or rye preferred

Potato—(or potato substitute), 1 average serving

Butter—1 square

Choice of:

Meat—lean, 1 average serving

Fish—1 average serving

Cheese—1 small serving

Eggs—2

Fruit—1 serving (refer to breakfast list)

Broth—Clear, fat free

Coffee—plain, or Tea if desired

PUTTING ON WEIGHT

People suffering from underweight often find the problem of gaining weight a difficult one. Here, again, the advice of a physician must be sought before a campaign is mapped out to gain weight. If extra calories are indicated after medical consultation, then the patient will eat generously of foods prescribed. As a rule, foods which are included are low in bulk, but high in caloric food value.

These are whole milk, cream, butter, cereals, breads, root vegetables, rich desserts, gravies, mayonnaise. In-between meals are often prescribed, as well as a full quart of milk a day. Extra sleep, a quiet life, longer sleeping hours and, in the case of heavy smokers, a cutting down on cigarettes or cigars.

POINTERS ON GAINING WEIGHT

1. A glass of warm milk at bedtime is often restful and soothing.
2. Add extra cream to each glass of milk.
3. Drink an eggnog which contains milk.
4. Drink a chocolate milk shake.
5. Eat butter crackers or peanut butter with in-between meal bites.
6. Eat a substantial, hearty breakfast.
7. Spread butter with a generous hand; or if cost is excessive, use fortified margarine.
8. Enjoy rich desserts at luncheon and dinner. Be generous with the gravy and mashed potatoes.
9. Take vitamins under a doctor's directions.
10. Eat wheat germ on cereal, or in milk, or in cooking.

3.

TABLE OF MEASURES—
FOOD EQUIVALENTS—
TEMPERATURES

"A HEAPING cup of this . . . a scant cup of that . . . a piece the size of a walnut . . . cut out the size of a silver dollar . . ." These quaint directions appear in many an old cook book, and we enjoy their reminiscent flavor of by-gone days. But a modern housewife scorns such vague directions in following recipes.

The entire scheme of life is different now, and the art of cookery is no exception. Today's home cook, or a professional chef in cap and apron, demands unfailing accuracy in recipes, correctly balanced measuring utensils in the kitchen, and thermometers to determine the exact degree of doneness of sugar syrups, roasts, cakes and pies.

SIX STEPS TO RECIPE EFFICIENCY

1. Read recipe carefully before starting to prepare it.
2. Assemble all utensils needed before starting to work.
3. Assemble all ingredients needed to prepare recipe.
4. Always sift flour before measuring.
5. Measure or weigh all ingredients.
6. Practice cookery techniques such as creaming, beating, folding (see Chapter 4).

TABLE OF ABBREVIATIONS

In studying recipes, it will be noted that the measurements most frequently used are abbreviated for convenience, as shown here:

teaspoon	—	tsp.	quart	—	qt.
tablespoon	—	Tbsp.	ounce	—	oz.
cup	—	cup	pound	—	lb.
pint	—	pt.	square	—	sq.

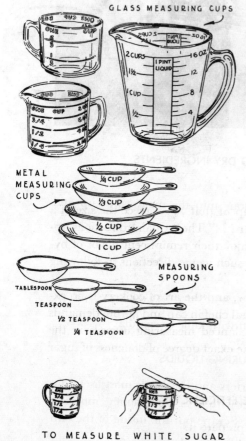

GLASS MEASURING CUPS

METAL MEASURING CUPS

¼ CUP
⅓ CUP
½ CUP
I CUP

MEASURING SPOONS

TABLESPOON
TEASPOON
½ TEASPOON
¼ TEASPOON

TABLE OF EQUIVALENTS

few grains	—	less than ⅛ tsp.
3 teaspoons	—	1 Tbsp.
4 tablespoons	—	¼ cup
8 tablespoons	—	½ cup
16 tablespoons	—	1 cup
1 cup	—	½ pt.
2 cups	—	1 pt.
4 cups	—	1 qt.
4 qts.	—	1 gal.
16 oz.	—	1 lb. (dry weight)
16 oz.	—	1 pt. (liquid measure)

STANDARD MEASURING EQUIPMENT

Glass Cups
  1 cup for liquids
  1 cup for dry ingredients
  1 pt. for dry or liquid ingredients
Metal Cups
  1 nest of cups consisting of:
    1 cup
    ½, ⅓, ¼ cups
Spoons
  1 set of spoons consisting of:
    1 Tbsp.
    1, ½, ¼ tsp.

TO MEASURE WHITE SUGAR

PRESS DOWN

TO MEASURE BROWN SUGAR

TO MEASURE CONFECTIONERS' SUGAR

SIFT

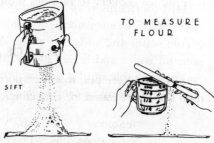

TO MEASURE FLOUR

SIFT

Measuring utensils are indispensable aids in following recipes. Accurate measurements will result in tastier, more tempting dishes.

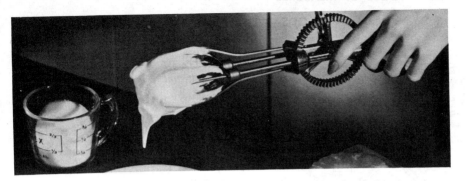

DIRECTIONS FOR MEASURING DRY INGREDIENTS

1. Flour
   Sift before measuring, pile the sifted flour into the measuring cup and level off with a knife. Do not pack down.
2. White Sugar
   Fill cup and level off with knife.
3. Brown Sugar
   Pack into cup and level off with knife.
4. Confectioner's Sugar
   Sift and pile lightly into cup and level off with knife or spatula.

DIRECTIONS FOR MEASURING LIQUIDS

Glass measuring cups marked off in quarters and thirds are most useful for measuring liquids. Hold the cup on a level with eyes. Pour honey, molasses or syrup into cup rinsed out in hot water. Scrape out the inside of the cup with a rubber spatula to obtain the last drops.

DIRECTIONS FOR MEASURING SHORTENINGS
(Butter, Margarine, Cooking Fats)

Hard shortening may be measured by the water displacement method. For example, if the measurement needed is ½ cup shortening, fill the cup ½ full of cold water and add shortening. When the water reaches the one cup mark, pour off water and ½ cup shortening remains. Or shortening may be placed on kitchen table until it softens and measured by packing into tablespoon or cup, then leveling off with knife.

2 cups fat or shortening	— 1 lb.
1 cup fat or shortening	— ½ lb.
½ cup fat or shortening	— ¼ lb.
8 Tbsp. fat or shortening	— ¼ lb.

FAMILIAR FOODS—WEIGHT AND BULK EQUIVALENTS

FOOD	PURCHASING UNIT	EQUIVALENT PER LB.
Cheese (grated)	1 lb.	4-4½ cups
Cottage cheese	1 lb.	2 cups
Chocolate	1 oz.	1 square
Cocoa	1 oz.	3 Tbsp.
Coconut (shredded)	1 lb.	5 cups
Coffee (ground)	1 lb.	5-5½ cups
Cornmeal	1 lb.	3 cups
Eggs (whole)	1	4 Tbsp.
Eggs (whites only)	10-12	1 cup
Flour (all purpose)	1 lb.	4 cups
Flour (cake)	1 lb.	4½ cups

FRESH FRUIT—WEIGHT AND BULK EQUIVALENTS

FRUIT	PURCHASING UNIT	EQUIVALENT PER LB. (approximately)
Apples.....................	1 lb.	2½-3 cups, diced 1½ cups sauce
Apricots	1 lb.	2½-3 cups, cooked
Bananas	1 lb.	2 cups, sliced
Berries....................	1 pt.	2 cups
Cherries	1 lb.	3 cups, stemmed
Grapefruit.................	per fruit	¾-1 cup juice 1-1¼ cups pulp
Oranges	1 lb.	3-4 1-1¼ cups pulp
Peaches	1 lb.	2-2½ cups, sliced
Pears	1 lb.	2-2½ cups, cooked
Pineapple	per fruit	2½-3 cups, diced
Plums	1 lb.	2 cups, cooked
Rhubarb..................	1 lb.	2 cups, cooked

SUBSTITUTIONS
MILK

1 cup fluid fresh milk may be replaced by any one of the following mixtures:

Evaporated milk....................½ cup plus ½ cup water

Sour milk or buttermilk ....1 cup plus ½ tsp. baking soda

CHOCOLATE

1 sq. chocolate (1 oz.) may be replaced in baking by ¼ cup (4 Tbsp.) cocoa. Increase shortening by 1½ tsp. For hot chocolate 2 to 3 Tbsp. cocoa will equal 1 sq. chocolate.

SUGAR

1 cup granulated sugar may be replaced by any one of the following ingredients:
    1 cup brown sugar
    ¾ cup honey, reduce other liquid in recipe
    1 cup molasses, reduce other liquid in recipe
    It is best, wherever possible, to use syrups in recipes especially developed for them.

SHORTENING

1 cup butter may be replaced by any one of the following ingredients:
    1 cup hydrogenated fats
    1 cup lard
    1 cup margarine

TIME TABLE FOR ROASTING MEAT, POULTRY, FISH

OVEN TEMPERATURE CHART

Slow...............	250° to 325° F.
Moderate	350° to 375° F.
Hot	400° to 450° F.
Very Hot..........	475° to 500° F. and above

KIND	TEMPERATURES Degrees Fahrenheit	TIME PER POUND Minutes
Beef, rare	300°-350°	18-20
Beef, medium...............	300°-350°	22-25
Beef, well done..............	300°-350°	27-30
Beef, rump	300°-350°	30-35
Lamb	350°	20-30
Pork	300°-350°	30
Cured Pork.................	300°-350°	25-30
Veal	300°	30
Chicken	350°	20-30
Duck	325°	20-25
Goose	350°	20-25
Turkey	350°	20-25
Fish	350°-400°	15-20

Stuffed Roasted Capon

MEAT THERMOMETER

The most accurate method of roasting meat is to use a meat thermometer. Insert thermometer through fat side of meat before it is put in oven, using a skewer to make a space first. Let pointed end reach center of roast. Don't let it touch bone. The following temperatures are indicated on the meat thermometer:

MEAT	DEGREES-FAHRENHEIT
BEEF	
Ribs	
Rare	140°
Medium	160°
Well done	170°
Sirloin	
Medium	160°
Well done	170°
Tenderloin	160°-170°
Rump	170°
PORK	
Fresh	185°
Cured	185°

LAMB
Medium . . . .   175°
Well done. . . . .   182°
VEAL . . . .   170°

OVEN TEMPERATURES FOR BAKING

FOOD	TEMPERATURE Degrees Fahrenheit	TIME (APPROXIMATE) Minutes
CAKE		
Angel	325°-350°	45-60
Sponge	325°	60
Butter		
Cup	375°	20
Layer.	350°	25-35
Loaf	350°	50-60
Sheet	350°-375°	30-40
Fruit	250°-325°	1-4 hours
Gingerbread	350°	45-50
COOKIES		
Brownies.	350°	30
Drop	350°	10-15
Rolled.	400°	8-10
PUDDINGS		
Custards	325°	25-30
Cottage.	350°-375°	30-40
Bread.	300°-350°	40-50
SCALLOPED DISHES	350°-400°	20-60
PASTRY		
Pastry shell	425°-450°	15
One-crust pie with cooked filling	425°-450°	20-30
Two-crust pie with cooked filling	425°-450°	35
Two-crust pie with uncooked filling	425°-450° for	10
	then 350° for	35-45
Custard pie.	450° for	15
	then 325° for	25
Meringue	350°	15

TEMPERATURE AND TIME TABLE FOR DEEP-FAT FRYING

KIND OF FOOD	TEMPERATURE OF FAT Degrees Fahrenheit	COOKING TIME Minutes
Uncooked Mixtures		
Doughnuts	360°-370°	2-3
Fritters	350°-365°	2-3
French fried potatoes	370°-380°	3-5
Oysters, clams	370°-380°	2-5
Cooked Mixtures		
Codfish balls	365°-380°	1-5
Croquettes	365°-380°	1-5

If a fat thermometer is not available, drop a 1-inch cube of stale bread into hot fat. If bread turns golden brown in 1 minute, it is just right for uncooked mixtures; if it browns in ¾ of a minute, it is right for cooked mixtures.

SYRUPS AND FROSTINGS

PRODUCT	STAGE	TEMPERATURES Degrees Fahrenheit	DESCRIPTION
Syrup	Thread	228°-234°	Spins a thread when dropped from spoon.
Fudge, Frosting	Soft ball	236°-240°	Soft ball in cold water, flattens on removal.
Caramels	Medium ball	244°-248°	Firm ball in cold water.

4.

COOKERY TERMS
AND METHODS

MANY a new cook is baffled by terms which she has never heard before, and wonders why recipe directions can't be given in words she understands. The following pages are devoted to just such simple explanations, for the benefit of the beginner in cookery.

Every type of recipe calls for its own particular characteristics in the dish to be prepared. It may be a light and delicate texture, or it may be a thick, smooth, creamy consistency. No matter what the finished product is to be, the results are achieved by exact, precise methods of handling the raw or partially cooked ingredients.

So it is essential for the beginning cook not only to learn what the various methods of blending ingredients are called, but also to perfect herself in the technique of each method.

MIXING TERMS

Creaming: for batters and doughs, consists of combining fats and sugar together by rubbing the two ingredients against the side of the bowl. The back of a mixing spoon is used, and the mixture is rubbed until it is as smooth as cream.

Cutting: incorporates fat into dry ingredients by finely dividing the mixture with a pair of knives or a pastry blender.

Beating: introduces air into the mixture by briskly turning the ingredients over and over. It may be accomplished with a mechanical or rotary beater or by using a spoon. A rotary movement at the wrist is the correct technique.

Beating eggs: introduces air, usually by means of a rotary egg beater or an electric beater. If eggs are to be beaten slightly, a fork is best. When yolks alone are beaten until they are thick, the color gradually changes to a light yellow. If egg whites are to be beaten stiff, there must be no speck of yolk remaining in the whites, and a rotary beater or electric mixer should be used. They are beaten until erect peaks are formed in the mass when the beater is withdrawn—but not until dry and flaky.

Folding: is the process of lifting ingredients over, and cutting down to prevent air already beaten in from escaping. This is accomplished by lifting the mass from one side of the bowl to the other.

Stirring: combines ingredients and insures smoothness of cooking mixtures. It is done by moving the spoon round-and-round the mixture until all lumps disappear.

COOKERY METHODS

Baking: cooking in an oven, heated to the desired temperature. When applied to meat it is called roasting. (A thermometer on the outside of an oven, set to the desired temperature, helps to insure more perfect results. If there is no thermometer on the oven, one can be purchased to place inside the oven to regulate the heat.)

Basting: pouring small quantities of fat or other liquid over food to prevent burning and to increase flavor.

Boiling: cooking in boiling water (212° F.) at sea level. Boiling need not be rapid; slow boiling is just as effective.

Braising: cooking meat or vegetables on all sides in a small amount of hot fat. A small amount of liquid is added, the pan covered and the food cooked over low heat, either in oven or on top of stove.

Broiling: cooking by exposing food directly to the heat.

Pan-broiling: cooking in a pan on top of the stove by dry heat, with just enough heat to keep food from sticking to pan.

Frying: cooking in fat, enough to cover bottom of pan.

French frying or deep-fat frying: cooking in deep fry kettle in enough hot fat or salad oil to float food. A temperature of 390° F. for cooked mixtures such as croquettes, 370° F. for uncooked mixtures such as fritters and doughnuts.

Poaching: cooking below the boiling point in enough hot liquid to cover food.

Parboiling: cooking food partially but not entirely in liquid.

Preheating: turning on heat in oven and heating to the desired temperature before putting in food to bake or roast.

Roasting: cooking by dry heat, usually in oven.

Sautéing: cooking in a small amount of fat in a pan over direct heat.

Scalding: heating to just below the boiling point.

Scalloping: baking food with sauce and crumbs.

Searing: subjecting raw meat to intense heat, browning the surface, usually in hot pan or hot oven.

Different cooking methods. Stew (top left), roast (top right), cooking in steam (bottom left), and steaming over boiling water (bottom right).

Simmering: cooking in liquid just below the boiling point.

Steaming: cooking in steam or over boiling water. A double boiler or steamer is ordinarily used.

Steeping: letting stand in hot liquid, as is done with tea leaves.

Sterilizing: killing bacteria by intense heat.

Stewing: cooking gently in liquid.

Toasting: browning in an oven or by direct heat.

COOKERY AIDS

BUTTER

Creaming: letting it stand in room temperature (62°-72° F.) until soft, and then using spoon or fork to get creamy consistency.

Clarifying: heating in a small pan, and removing froth as it forms at the top. Butter is poured off, leaving sediment in pan.

Cutting: dividing with knife blade, preferably covered with fold of waxed paper to make clean cuts.

Butter molds: small molds for individual servings. After scalding, they are chilled, packed solidly with butter, leveled off with knife, pressed down and chilled.

SUGAR

Brown sugar: should be stored in a tight glass or jar, preferably in a warm place. It can be softened by setting in oven and heating gently.

Caramelizing: melting over moderate heat in heavy shallow pan, stirring constantly until sugar melts and turns caramel in color.

Making caramel syrup: done by caramelizing 1 cup sugar, slowly adding ½ cup boiling water and simmering for 10 minutes.

Dredging: best done by placing powdered sugar in paper bag, adding food to be sugared, and gently shaking bag up and down until article is covered.

CRUMBS

Soft bread crumbs: made by removing sides and crust from soft bread and grating or crumbling loaf into small pieces.

Dry bread crumbs: made by drying stale bread in slow oven until crisp, then grating or rolling into crumbs.

MISCELLANEOUS

To extract onion juice: cut a slice from root end of onion, scrape juice from center with edge of teaspoon.

To chop or mince: cut off a small slice and cut the surface in ⅛ inch squares, cutting as deeply as needed. Hold firmly on a cutting board and slice off with a sharp knife, ⅛ inch at a time.

To dice: use the same method as to chop or mince, but cut in larger squares.

To cut dough: dip knife into flour frequently.

To cut or chop sticky foods (raisins, etc.): use scissors or knife dipped into cold water.

To cut parsley: hold firmly on cutting board and cut with other hand.

To chop ice: place in a canvas bag and strike with mallet.

To melt chocolate: melt over hot water in double boiler.

TERMS FREQUENTLY USED IN COOKING

À la king: a food served in rich cream sauce.

Au gratin: a food creamed or moistened with white sauce, milk, eggs or stock, covered with bread crumbs, butter or cheese and baked in oven or broiled under broiler flame.

Barbecue: meat or fowl roasted over coals or on a spit.

Batter: a mixture of flour and other ingredients thin enough to pour.

Bisque: a thick cream soup.

Blanch: to pour boiling water over a food, or to dip into boiling water, drain and rinse with cold water.

Blend: to mix thoroughly two or more ingredients.

Boil: to cook in liquid, usually water, in which bubbles constantly rise to the surface.

Bouillon: a clear soup made from lean beef, chicken or other meats.

Charlotte: a gelatin dessert with flavored whipped cream, molded in a form lined with cake or lady fingers.

Cobbler: a form of pie. Sometimes a deep layer of fruit covered with pastry or biscuit dough.

Compote: sweetened stewed fruit.

Condiments: various food seasonings such as herbs, vinegar, salt, pepper and spices.

Consommé: a highly seasoned clear soup made from meat or a combination of meat and vegetables.

Croquettes: a mixture of chopped or ground cooked meat, cereal or cheese, bound together by eggs or a thick sauce, then shaped and dipped into egg, then into crumbs and fried.

Croutons: cubes of bread toasted or fried and served on soups.

Cube: to cut into squares.

Demitasse: a small cup of coffee served after dinner.

Deviled: food to which a large amount of seasoning has been added.

Dice: to cut into small pieces.

Dissolve: to melt or liquefy a solid food.

Dredge: to coat with flour or sugar.

Entrée: the main dish of an informal meal, or less important dish served before the main course.

Fat: shortening, as butter, margarine, lard, or vegetable fats.

Fillet: cuts of boneless or boned meat or fish.

Fondue: a baked dish similar to a soufflé but including bread or cracker crumbs.

Frappé: sweetened fruit juices frozen until of a mushy consistency.

Fricassee: meat or poultry cooked in liquid or stock.

Fritters: a thin batter, to which has been added meat, fish, vegetables, fruit or cereal, fried in deep fat.

Frosting: a sweetened mixture used to cover or decorate cakes.

Garnish: to decorate one food with another food of a different color.

Giblets: heart, liver and gizzard of poultry.

Glaze: to coat with a thin cooked sugar syrup.

Grate: to rub on a grater until small particles appear on under side.

Julienne: food cut into long narrow strips.

Knead: to work dough with a pressing motion of the palm of the hand, stretching the food and then folding it over itself again.

Marinate: to soak in a liquid as vinegar, sour cream or French dressing.

Melt: to liquefy by heat.

Meringue: a mixture of stiffly-beaten egg whites, sugar and flavoring used as a decorative topping for pies and desserts.

Mousse: a mixture of sweetened whipped cream and other ingredients frozen without stirring, sometimes thickened with gelatin.

Pare: to cut off the outside skin.

Parfait: a frozen dessert made with eggs and hot syrup and combined with whipped cream, or a mixture of ice cream, fruit and whipped cream.

Pasteurized: to kill bacteria by use of a high degree of heat.

Pâté de foie gras: a paste made from liver.

Peel: to take off the outer cover.

Petits fours: small iced cakes.

Purée: to press fruit or vegetables through a sieve.

Deviled

Scored

Ramekins: individual baking dishes.

Render: to free fat from connective tissue by heating slowly until fat melts away from the tissue.

Roe: fish eggs.

Roux: to rub flour and butter together until smooth.

Score: to make light cuts in the surface of food, usually in squares, as on a ham.

Sherbet: fruit juice, sugar, egg whites combined with milk or water and frozen.

Shortening: any kind of fat suitable for cooking; butter, margarine, lard, and vegetable fats.

Shred: to cut into very fine slices or strips.

Skewer: a long pin of wood or metal on which food is placed and held in shape while cooking.

Soak: to keep in a liquid for a long time.

Stock: the liquid in which meat, fish, vegetables or fruits have been cooked.

Truss: to tie a fowl or other meat so that it will hold its shape.

Whip: to beat an ingredient rapidly, so as to incorporate air in the food and increase its volume, such as whipping egg whites, or heavy cream.

5.

CEREALS

AFTER many years of brushing aside breakfast cereals as unimportant, the modern world is beginning to realize what valuable and precious foods the cereals are. They provide some of our most inexpensive and nutritious foods, as well as a tremendous variety for all three meals of the day. We can enjoy wheat, oats, rye, barley, corn and rice in every conceivable form and in all sorts of combination dishes. For the sake of pleasing variety, we can choose uncooked bulk cereals for breakfast, or ready prepared cereals. The former are more appealing in cold weather, and the latter require no cooking— which makes them an asset in the early morning hours. There are also many quick-cooking cereals.

GENERAL DIRECTIONS FOR COOKING CEREALS

Place upper part of double boiler over direct heat. Measure boiling water according to directions on package of cereal. Bring water to full rolling boil, add salt. Measure cereal, and sprinkle or sift slowly into water, stirring constantly to prevent lumps forming. As soon as cereal begins to thicken, place upper part of double boiler over boiling water. Reduce heat, place cover on top, and cook covered until done. Cereals may be cooked in water or milk, or half and half.

CEREAL POINTERS

1. If more water is needed while cereal is cooking, add boiling water, not cold.
2. Do not stir cereal after it is placed over lower part of double boiler.
3. Cereal is most appetizing when liquid is entirely absorbed.
4. If, when cereal is nearly cooked, too much water remains, remove cover and finish cooking uncovered.
5. Cereal cooked in milk is enriched in nutritional value.

COOKING CHART

1 CUP CEREAL	WATER	SALT	COOKING TIME
Whole grained or ground Oats, Rice, Corn, Wheat ..	3 cups	1 tsp.	1 to 3 hours
Finely ground Wheat, Corn	3 cups	1 tsp.	Quick cooking, 3 to 10 minutes Non-processed, ½ to ¾ hour
Flaked Wheat, Oats	3 cups	1 tsp.	Quick cooking, 3 to 10 minutes Non-processed, ½ to ¾ hour
Coarse Cracked Wheat, Grits, Oatmeal.	3-4 cups	1 tsp.	1 to 3 hours

Farina, served with milk and sugar, provides a hearty send-off to school or office.

Oatmeal, fluffy and warm with plenty of cream and sugar, gets the day off to a satisfying start.

CEREALS FOR CHILDREN

Very often mothers find it a problem to persuade the children to eat their cereal. First-rate cooking is usually the answer; when trying any new food, tiny servings are best until a young child becomes accustomed to a new taste.

The addition of fruit often makes the difference between a dish of cereal that is enjoyed and one that is disliked. Such dried fruits as dates, figs, or raisins are attractive when cooked with a hot cereal. Prepared cereals are often liked if bananas, berries or sliced peaches are added as a topping.

Crisp, dry cereal and sliced bananas, nourishing duet for summer breakfasts.

6.

MACARONI, SPAGHETTI,
NOODLES, RICE,
DRIED BEANS

PACKAGED macaroni, spaghetti and noodles usually come with complete directions for cooking printed on their labels. When you purchase them in bulk, allow about 4 qts. of rapidly boiling water and 4 tsp. salt for 2 to 3 cups of the uncooked spaghetti, noodles or macaroni. Drop macaroni, spaghetti or noodles into boiling water. If the macaroni or spaghetti is overly long, break it in pieces before putting it in water. Keep at an active boil 9 to 12 minutes. Drain and rinse with hot water.

Each one of these recipes will make approximately *4 servings*.

BAKED MACARONI AND CHEESE

½ pkg. elbow macaroni
¼ lb. American cheese, grated
1 pt. medium white sauce

Cook macaroni in boiling water until tender, rinse in boiling water. Grease a casserole, cover bottom of casserole with layer of macaroni, add a layer of white sauce, sprinkle with cheese. Continue until macaroni and sauce are used. Cover top of dish with layer of cheese. Bake in moderate oven (350° F.) 15 minutes or until cheese is golden brown on top.

An old-fashioned way to make this dish is to cook the macaroni as above. Omit the white sauce. Slice the cheese in thin slices and cover each layer of macaroni with sliced cheese. Sprinkle lightly with flour, salt and pepper after addition of cheese. When dish is filled, pour milk over and around so it runs down to bottom of dish. Finish with layer of cheese on top and bake as above.

MACARONI LOAF

2 cups cooked macaroni	½ Tbsp. chopped parsley
½ cup bread crumbs	½ Tbsp. chopped onion
½ cup grated cheese	½ tsp. salt
3 Tbsp. butter	½ cup milk
	1 egg, beaten

Place a layer of cooked macaroni in a greased baking dish. Sprinkle bread crumbs, cheese, parsley, onions, salt and butter, between each layer. Repeat until all ingredients are used. Pour egg and milk over mixture. Bake in moderate oven (350° F.) 30 minutes or until it is set.

MACARONI AND TOMATOES

2 cups cooked macaroni	1 Tbsp. minced green pepper
2 Tbsp. butter	1 cup stewed tomatoes
1 onion, diced	¼ cup grated cheese
	½ tsp. salt

Melt butter in a skillet, add onion and pepper and fry until tender. Add tomatoes, green pepper, salt, and simmer gently. Place cooked macaroni in a greased casserole. Pour sauce over it and sprinkle grated cheese on top. Bake in moderate oven (375° F.) 30 minutes.

SPAGHETTI

"In spaghetti it's the sauce"—so a famous slogan goes. Cook spaghetti as directed. Prepare any of the following sauces. Place the cooked spaghetti on a hot plate and add sauce. Toss with 2 forks. Serve with grated cheese.

ITALIAN SAUCE

2 Tbsp. butter
2 Tbsp. olive oil
1 Tbsp. chopped parsley
2 cloves of garlic, peeled and minced
2 chopped onions
1 small can tomato purée
2 cans tomato paste
2 tsp. Worcestershire sauce
⅔ lb. ground meat

Melt butter in skillet. Add olive oil, parsley, garlic and onions. Cook until onions are soft. Add tomato purée, tomato sauce and Worcestershire sauce. Bring to a boil. Fry meat until well-browned and add to tomato sauce. Simmer over low heat for 1½ hours. Pour over spaghetti.

Curried shrimp or sliced hard-boiled eggs in creamy sauce are delicious poured over spaghetti or shredded wheat biscuits. Garnish with crisp dark green watercress or green pepper strips for color contrast.

NEAPOLITAN SAUCE AND MEAT BALLS

Sauce

¼ cup olive oil
¼ cup minced onion
¼ cup chopped mushrooms
2 peeled cloves of garlic, minced

1 cup tomato paste
3 cups canned tomatoes
1 tsp. salt
¼ tsp. pepper
2 bouillon cubes

Heat oil in skillet. Add minced onion, mushrooms and garlic. Fry until onions are tender. Add tomato paste, canned tomatoes, salt, pepper and bouillon cubes. Simmer over low heat for 1½ hours, stirring occasionally.

Meat Balls

1 lb. chopped steak
1 egg, beaten
2 peeled cloves of garlic, minced
2 Tbsp. chopped parsley

1 tsp. salt
½ tsp. pepper
½ cup bread crumbs
½ cup grated Parmesan cheese
2 Tbsp. melted fat

Combine all ingredients except the fat. Mix well and shape into balls about 2 inches in diameter. Melt fat in skillet and brown meat balls on all sides. Then add to Neapolitan sauce and let simmer for ½ hour before sauce is done. Pour over spaghetti.

NOODLES

NOODLE RING

2 cups cooked noodles
2 Tbsp. butter
1 tsp. salt

¼ tsp. pepper
½ cup hot milk
3 egg yolks, well-beaten
3 egg whites, beaten

To cooked noodles, add other ingredients in order, folding in the egg whites last. Pour into a buttered 1½ qt. ring mold, set in pan in hot water and bake in slow oven (325° F.) 30 minutes. Turn onto creamed chicken or creamed fish.

SCALLOPED TUNA FISH AND NOODLES

2 cups cooked noodles
1 cup tuna fish (other sea food may be used)

1 cup medium white sauce
1 tsp. onion, chopped
½ cup buttered crumbs

Prepare medium white sauce. Arrange noodles and tuna fish and onion in layers in greased casserole. Cover with white sauce. Top with bread crumbs. Bake in moderate oven (375° F.) 20 minutes or until browned.

RICE

BOILED WHITE RICE

1 cup raw white rice
2 qts. water
3 tsp. salt

Boiled white rice ring is an excellent partner for spicy, economical curried eggs. Garnish with parsley and shiny black olives.

Place rice in strainer, under running water, and rub between hands until clear. Slowly add rice to salted boiling water. Boil gently without stirring 15 to 20 minutes or until tender. Drain into sieve, rinse with hot water. Cover with cloth and set sieve over hot water to separate grains. Makes 3 cups when cooked.

BOILED BROWN RICE

Follow directions for Boiled White Rice

SPANISH RICE

3 slices of bacon
¾ cup raw white rice
1 tsp. salt
1 clove garlic

½ cup onions, diced
1 green pepper
1¼ cups stewed tomatoes
½ tsp. salt
1 tsp. paprika

Fry bacon until brown and chop fine. Wash rice, dry, add to bacon fat and cook, stirring constantly for 10 minutes. Add garlic, onion and chopped green pepper. Continue cooking until onion is lightly browned. Add tomatoes and

Spanish rice, a delicious tomato-rice mixture studded with nuggets of green pepper, garlic, onion, and bacon or chicken, lends itself easily to decorative casserole or pan-to-table service. With it serve a tossed salad of tender young greens and chilled French dressing.

seasoning. Cover and simmer slowly for 25 minutes. Sprinkle with grated cheese.

DRIED BEANS

BAKED BEANS

1½ cups dried pea beans
2 Tbsp. onion, chopped
¼ lb. salt pork
¼ lb. dark molasses
2 Tbsp. catsup
½ Tbsp. dried mustard
1 tsp. salt

Boston baked beans and pork swimming in rich brown liquid are a traditional New England supper favorite but have found overwhelming popularity elsewhere as well. Be sure to serve with the also traditional brown bread. For unexpected supper guests a quick trick is to add molasses, prepared mustard, and minced onion to canned baked beans.

Wash beans, put in kettle and cover with boiling water. Let them soak overnight or for 12 hours. Drain and cover with boiling water. Cook slowly for about 1½ hours. Drain. Scald pork and scrape, remove ½ inch slice and put in bottom of bean pot. Put beans in the pot. Mix salt, molasses, mustard, catsup and 1 cup boiling water and pour over beans. If necessary add enough water to just cover the beans. Put piece of salt pork on top, cutting edges every inch or two so it won't curl. Put cover on bean pot and bake in slow oven (250° F.) 6 to 8 hours. During the last hour, remove cover and let bake so that pork becomes brown and crisp.

CANNED BAKED BEANS AND BACON

1 No. 2 can baked beans	2 Tbsp. brown sugar
¼ cup catsup	2 Tbsp. bacon drippings
2 Tbsp. molasses	4 strips of bacon

To can of baked beans add catsup, molasses, brown sugar and bacon drippings. Place in a shallow oven-proof baking dish. Over the top lay strips of bacon. Bake in moderate oven (375° F.) 30 minutes.

CHILI CON CARNE

1 Tbsp. bacon drippings or butter	1 No. 2 can kidney beans
¼ cup chopped onion	1 Tbsp. chili powder
½ lb. ground beef	½ tsp. salt

Fry chopped onion in bacon drippings or butter. Add ground beef and fry it until it is well done. Add beans, chili powder and salt. Cook slowly for 1 hour.

BAKED LIMA BEANS AND SAUSAGE

2 cups dried lima beans
½ Tbsp. finely chopped onion
2 Tbsp. butter
½ tsp. salt
1 lb. link sausage

Baked lima beans and cheese achieve a hearty dish chock-full of nutrients and mouth-watering goodness.

Soak lima beans overnight in sufficient water to cover, or for about 12 hours. When the beans are soaked, add chopped onion, butter, salt, and cook until beans are tender. Pour in greased casserole, add just enough liquid to cover the beans. On top lay links of sausage. Bake beans in slow oven (300° F.) 30 minutes.

7.

SOUPS

SOUPS may be thin, clear, hearty, savory, rich jellied consommés, or foreign cold fruit soups—each one serves its own purpose, has its own special function in the parade of good meals.

The thin delicate consommés stimulate appetite and aid digestion. The cream soups, hearty bisques, and chowders contribute valuable nourishment to luncheon or dinner.

SOUP STOCKS

Soup stock is exactly what its name implies; the foundation for the soup. It may be made from meat or a combination of two meats, or meat and poultry, or fish. Soup stock is described as Brown stock or White stock. For many generations, soup stock was made at home and the pot simmered on the stove for hours. Surveys of modern American homes show that the old-fashioned stock pot has largely been replaced by a variety of excellent commercially canned or condensed soups.

For example, beef consommé usually replaces brown stock and clear chicken consommé replaces white stock. But for thrift and economy, leftover bones from poultry or roasts, and bits of unused vegetables, with spices and herbs, may be put to good use in the preparation of homemade beef or chicken stock.

SOUP STOCK FROM LEFTOVER BONES

Leftover bones from steak, chops or roasts, with scraps of meat	¼ cup onion, chopped
	1 bay leaf
2 qts. water	2 peppercorns
1 cup carrots, diced	1 sprig parsley
1 stalk celery, chopped	1 tsp. salt
	½ tsp. pepper

Combine all ingredients in cold water. Cover and let simmer 2 to 3 hours. Strain, cool, reheat when ready to use. *8 servings.*

TO STRAIN SOUP STOCK

Pour the hot soup through a colander and cool quickly. When ready to use, remove any fat on surface. Place a folded cheese cloth in strainer over a bowl. Pour soup through cloth. Season soup with finely cut cooked vegetables or small portion of cooked rice or noodles. Or it may be served clear with thin slice of lemon floating on top of each portion.

CHICKEN STOCK

4-5 lb. fowl, cut up	1 cup onion, chopped
3 qts. water	1 sprig parsley, chopped
1 cup carrots, diced	1 bay leaf
1/3 cup celery, chopped	2 tsp. salt

Wash fowl, place in kettle of cold water. Cover, bring slowly to boil. Remove froth. Add vegetables, bay leaf and salt. Cover and simmer slowly for 3 hours. Strain, chill, remove fat and strain again through several layers of cheese cloth. This makes about 2 qts. of stock.

SOUPS WITH STOCK

Bouillon

Canned bouillon is sold in tins in liquid form. It is also sold in concentrated form: cubes, pastes or liquids. Boiling water is the only addition needed.

Tomato Bouillon

Clear soup stock, or canned bouillon, or concentrated bouillon may be blended with tomato juice in equal parts to make tomato bouillon.

Jellied Bouillon

Sometimes this product is sold in the jellied form in tins, and only requires chilling in the refrigerator to bring it to a "jell." If gelatin is needed, allow 1 tsp. gelatin to 1/2 pt. of consommé or bouillon. Dissolve gelatin, add hot bouillon, stir well, chill.

Consommé

Canned, condensed or dehydrated consommés have become the accepted practice in place of the tedious slow cooking needed to prepare homemade consommé.

VEGETABLE SOUP

1½ qts. soup stock	1 cup canned tomatoes
2 Tbsp. shortening	1 bay leaf
1 onion, chopped	1 tsp. salt
1 cup celery, chopped	½ tsp. pepper
1 cup carrots, diced	1 cup string beans or peas or lima
1 cup potatoes, diced	beans

Measure stock, bring to boil. Melt shortening, add onions, celery, and cook until soft and yellow. Add other vegetables and seasonings. Simmer over low heat 30 minutes. *8 servings.*

RICE OR NOODLE SOUP

1 qt. soup stock	½-1 cup cooked noodles or rice

Heat stock, add rice or noodles. Heat well, serve at once. *4 to 6 servings.*

CHICKEN OR TURKEY BONE SOUP

Bones from cooked turkey or chicken	1 onion, chopped
	2 Tbsp. parsley, chopped
2-3 qts. cold water	1 tsp. salt
½ cup celery, chopped	¼ tsp. pepper

Break up carcass; place in kettle with cold water to cover; add celery, onion, seasonings. Cover and simmer gently 2 to 3 hours. As the water heats a light foam forms on surface. Skim off occasionally with long-handled spoon. Half an hour before soup is cooked, add parsley. Strain, cool. Reheat. *8 servings.*

CHICKEN CORN SOUP
(Pennsylvania Dutch Recipe)

Wings, back, neck of uncooked chicken	1 Tbsp. onion, chopped
	½ tsp. salt
6 cups water	3 cups canned or fresh corn
1 cup celery, chopped	2 hard-cooked eggs, chopped

Place chicken in kettle with cold water to cover; add celery, onion and salt. Cover and simmer gently 2 to 3 hours. Remove chicken from broth, cool and chop chicken meat in fine pieces. Replace in broth, add corn, simmer 15 minutes. Add eggs. *6 to 8 servings.*

OLD-FASHIONED BEAN SOUP

1 cup navy beans	½ cup celery, chopped
2 qts. water	½ tsp. salt
Ham bone	1 bay leaf
1 onion, chopped	¼ tsp. pepper
	1 tsp. parsley, chopped

Wash, soak beans in water overnight. Add ham bone, onion, celery and seasonings. Cover, bring slowly to a boil and simmer gently for 2 hours. Remove ham bone. Garnish soup with parsley and serve hot. *8 servings.*

LENTIL SOUP

1 cup lentils	¼ cup onions, diced
3 cups water	½ cup celery, chopped
1 ham bone, fat removed	¼ cup carrots, chopped
6 cups water	1 tsp. salt
	¼ tsp. paprika

Soak lentils in 3 cups water 4 to 6 hours. Drain and place in deep kettle. Add ham bone and water. Simmer 2 hours. Add remaining ingredients, simmer 1 hour longer. Remove the bone, rub soup through colander. Add salt, paprika. *8 or more servings.*

Chilled buttermilk soup is quick and easy to make, and a refreshing first course on a hot summer night. Beat 5 oz. softened chive cream cheese and blend gradually with 2 cups cold buttermilk. *4 servings.*

POTATO SOUP

4 potatoes	Stalk of celery
3 cups milk, scalded	1 tsp. salt
1 Tbsp. butter	¼ tsp. pepper
1 Tbsp. flour	1 bay leaf
1 sliced onion	Minced parsley

Peel potatoes, add enough boiling water to cover them. Boil until tender. Measure water to 1 cup. Set aside. Cook butter and flour together until smooth and bubbly. Scald milk with celery, onion and seasonings. Strain, add potato water and mix with cooked butter and flour. Rub potatoes through sieve. Gradually beat into milk. Season to taste. Garnish with parsley. *4 servings.*

OXTAIL SOUP

2 Tbsp. fat	¼ cup parsley, minced fine
1 split oxtail, cut in small pieces	½ cup carrots, diced
2 qts. water	1 cup celery, diced
1 to 2 tsp. salt	2 to 3 peppercorns
½ cup onions, diced	1 bay leaf
	½ cup tomato purée

Wash and dry oxtail, dust lightly with flour. Heat fat in deep kettle, add oxtail, cook until well-browned. Add water and seasonings. Simmer gently 2 to 3 hours. Remove meat, set aside. Add vegetables, simmer 20 minutes longer. Remove meat from oxtail, cut in pieces, add to soup. Serve hot. *8 servings.*

OYSTER STEW

½ pt. raw oysters, removed from shell	¼ tsp. pepper
	1 pt. hot milk
¼-½ cup butter	or
½ tsp. salt	1 cup hot milk and 1 cup thin cream
¼ tsp. paprika	

Turn oysters into strainer over bowl, save liquor; remove any bits of shell clinging to oysters. Melt butter in saucepan, add oysters, cook gently over low heat until edges of oysters begin to curl. (This is the real secret of good oyster stew.) Slowly add hot liquid, stirring all the while. Pour into hot tureen or bowls. Serve at once. *4 servings.*

Note: Oyster liquor may be added to milk.

CHICKEN GUMBO FILÉ

1 chicken, disjointed	2 onions, finely minced
3 Tbsp. vegetable oil or lard	1 tsp. salt
3 Tbsp. flour	½ tsp. pepper
½ lb. slice raw ham, cut in cubes	1 bay leaf
1 pt. raw oysters and liquor	Stalk of celery, diced
	1 to 2 Tbsp. powdered filé

Melt lard in deep pan until hot. Brown each portion of chicken separately. Remove from pan and set aside. Heat ham in pan, brown lightly, set aside. If fat is not then sufficient, measure to quantity of 3 Tbsp. Add flour, stir until bubbly. Add 1 cup boiling water, stir until smooth and thickened. Add chicken, ham, onion, celery, salt, pepper and bay leaf. Add enough boiling water to cover. Cover tightly, simmer gently until tender. Remove bones from chicken. Cut meat in pieces, return to pan, add liquor and oysters, simmer until edges curl. Add filé, stir well, serve at once on hot steamed rice. *4 to 6 servings.*

Important: Do not cook after addition of filé.

CREAM OF VEGETABLE SOUPS

Cream of vegetable soups offer a variety of flavors, either alone or in combination with other vegetables. They are rich in food value as well, and are a good source of milk in the diet. Some of the cream soups are improved in flavor by a bit of salt pork or sliced onion or bay leaf. A pinch of dried herb adds interest, too.

The basic recipe for cream soups is thin white sauce seasoned with whatever vegetable is chosen. There needs to be enough of the vegetable pulp and liquid to give the soup the vegetable's own distinctive flavor. The onion may be sliced and added to the milk. The milk is scalded and onion removed before the milk is stirred into the butter and flour (Method I). Or the onion may be added to the melted butter, cooked until soft and then removed before flour is added (Method II).

Each one of these recipes will make approximately *4 servings.*

BASIC THIN WHITE SAUCE FOR CREAM SOUPS
Method I

2 Tbsp. butter	½ tsp. salt
2 Tbsp. flour	¼ tsp. pepper
2 slices raw onion	1 cup milk

Place milk and onion in upper part of double boiler over hot water. Scald milk, remove onion. Melt butter in skillet, add flour and seasonings. Stir until bubbly, add milk slowly, stir until sauce is smooth and thickened. Mix with hot vegetable pulp.

Method II

Melt butter in skillet, add onion, cook until soft, discard onion. Add flour and seasonings, stir until bubbly, add cold milk slowly, proceed as above.

VEGETABLE PULP

Cook soft vegetables, such as asparagus, broccoli, cabbage, carrots, peas, potatoes or string beans in boiling water, salted, until tender. Force vegetable pulp through a sieve.

BASIC CREAM OF VEGETABLE SOUP

1 cup basic thin white sauce for soups

1 to 1½ cups sieved vegetable pulp and liquid

Prepare sauce as directed by Methods I or II. Blend thoroughly with heated vegetable pulp. Mix well and serve in warmed soup plates.

Variations

Cream of Asparagus Soup: Use 1 to 1½ cups sieved asparagus pulp as the vegetable; reserve the tips as a garnish.
Cream of Broccoli Soup: Use 1 to 1½ cups sieved broccoli pulp as vegetable.
Cream of Carrot Soup: Use 1 to 1½ cups sieved carrot pulp as vegetable.
Cream of Green Pea Soup: Use 1 to 1½ cups sieved green peas as vegetable.
Cream of Celery Soup: 1 cup celery cut in 1 inch lengths. Cook with milk or cook separately. Use ½ celery water and ½ milk for sauce. Do not press celery through sieve.
Cream of Corn Soup: Use 1½ cups cream-style canned corn as vegetable. Do not press corn through sieve.

CREAM OF MUSHROOM SOUP

1 pt. milk
2 Tbsp. butter
2 Tbsp. flour

2 slices raw onion
¼ lb. mushrooms
½ tsp. salt
¼ tsp. pepper

Wipe mushrooms, do not peel. Slice caps and stems. Melt butter, add onion and cook until soft, but not brown. Remove onion, add mushrooms, cook gently for 5 minutes. Add flour and seasonings, stir well and add milk. Stir constantly and cook until smooth and thickened.

CREAM OF TOMATO SOUP

2 cups fresh or canned tomatoes	3 whole cloves
½ cup water	1 bay leaf
½ tsp. salt	⅛ tsp. soda
	1 pt. medium white sauce

Cook tomatoes for 15 minutes with water, salt, cloves and bay leaf. Strain through a fine sieve, add soda. Stir well, add slowly to the hot white sauce.

Cream of tomato soup dresses up for company with a topping of whipped cream.

SPLIT PEA SOUP

1 cup dried split peas	1 tsp. salt
2 qts. cold water	¼ tsp. pepper
1 onion	1 ham bone or ⅛ lb. ham
1 celery stalk	2 Tbsp. shortening
1 bay leaf	1 Tbsp. flour

Soak peas in cold water for 30 minutes. Place peas, water, ham bone or ham in soup kettle, bring to boil. Add vegetables and seasonings, stir occasionally. Cook slowly until peas are tender, 1½ to 2 hours. Remove bone, press vegetables through sieve. Melt shortening in saucepan, add flour, stir until bubbly. Add a small portion of hot soup, stir well and add to soup in kettle. Cook 5 minutes longer. If a thinner soup is desired, 1 cup of milk or thin cream may be blended with hot soup.

CHOWDERS

NEW ENGLAND CLAM CHOWDER

1 pt. raw clams, removed from shell	1 Tbsp. flour
	1½ cups cubed potatoes
1 pt. water	1 tsp. salt
⅛ lb. salt pork, diced	¼ tsp. pepper
2 Tbsp. onion, minced	1 pt. milk
	½ tsp. thyme

Wash clams in water; place in strainer over bowl. Cut soft parts of clam away from hard, set aside in refrigerator. Chop hard parts finely, add water, simmer gently for 20 minutes. Fry pork in skillet until crisp, add onion and cook until soft, lift out pork and onion, add to stewed clams. Add flour to fat remaining in pan and cook until bubbly. Mix with stewed clams and stir until smooth. Add potatoes, salt and pepper and cook until tender. Add soft parts of clams, milk and thyme. Cook for 5 minutes. Serve at once.

MANHATTAN CLAM CHOWDER

Omit milk and substitute 1 pt. fresh or canned tomatoes. Add to clam chowder with potatoes and seasonings.

SEA CAPTAIN'S CORN CHOWDER

2 slices salt pork, diced	1 can kernel corn
1 large onion, sliced	½ tsp. salt
3 potatoes, cubed	¼ tsp. pepper
1 pt. boiling water	1 qt. milk

Fry pork until crisp. Add onion and cook gently until yellow. Add potatoes and water. Cover, and cook slowly until potatoes are tender. Add drained corn, milk and seasonings. Bring to scalding point. Serve at once.

JELLIED CONSOMMÉ
Madrilène

1 Tbsp. plain unflavored gelatin	1 carrot, sliced
3 Tbsp. cold water	1 stalk celery, chopped
1 cup canned clear chicken broth	½ tsp. celery seed
1 cup canned bouillon	½ tsp. salt
1 cup canned tomatoes	1 bay leaf
1 small onion, sliced	2 whole cloves
	1 tsp. lemon juice

Jellied consommé presents a new flavor treat with 2 Tbsp. chives and ¾ tsp. Angostura aromatic bitters added to the contents of each 12-oz. can.

Soften gelatin in cold water, set aside. Combine all ingredients, except lemon juice. Simmer, covered, 30 minutes. Strain through cheesecloth, add hot liquid to gelatin and lemon juice. Stir until thoroughly dissolved. Chill until stiff, beat with a fork. If color isn't a deep enough red, add a few drops of red vegetable coloring to hot soup. When ready to serve jellied soup, beat it with a silver fork, pile it into bouillon cups with thin slice of lemon on top.

GARNISHES FOR SOUPS

CROUTONS

Cut 2 slices of stale bread into cubes ⅓ inch. Melt 2 Tbsp. butter in a small frying pan. Add the cubes of bread and brown delicately. Turn frequently.

GARNISHES FOR CLEAR SOUPS

Thin slice of lemon; tiny sprig of parsley in center.
Thin slices of stuffed olive.
Slivers of cooked carrot.

GARNISHES FOR JELLIED SOUPS

Finely minced olives.
Hard-cooked egg yolk rubbed through sieve.
Hard-cooked egg white rubbed through sieve.
Minced parsley or onion.
Slice of lemon.

GARNISHES FOR CREAM SOUPS

Croutons.
Grated cheese.
Buttered Popcorn.

Salted whipped cream.
Broiled bacon, crumbled into pieces.
Paprika.

Finely minced parsley.

8.

VEGETABLES

NOT so many years ago, housewives depended upon locally grown vegetables for their entire variety of table vegetables; in the long winter months every family living in the country or in a town had an old-fashioned root cellar where the "hard" vegetables such as potatoes, carrots, turnips, parsnips and squash were stored for use all winter long. For extra luxury, the housewife canned vegetables from her own garden.

CANNED AND QUICK-FROZEN VEGETABLES

Nowadays, American families regard canned foods as a major source of their food supply. In recent years, commercially prepared foods have gone ahead so rapidly, and the quality is so uniformly good, that canned foods are welcome in practically every corner of the globe. Food chosen to be canned is supervised through every step of the extensive process of manufacture. The labels on the tins and glass jars tell such a descriptive story of the contents, that the shopper who reads her labels knows exactly what she is buying. To this tremendous variety of commercially canned foods, modern industry now adds packaged quick-frozen foods. For best results, the directions for cooking on every package should be carefully followed.

GENERAL DIRECTIONS FOR USING CANNED VEGETABLES

These directions have been published by the canning companies to teach the housewife the best method of preparing canned vegetables in order to preserve the flavor and the valuable vitamin and mineral salts in the liquid. "The liquid of the canned vegetable should be drained off and placed in a saucepan over a low heat, to simmer until it is reduced to half the original quantity. The canned vegetable is then added and heated through." Salt, pepper and butter to taste is added last.

BUYING FRESH VEGETABLES

Modern means of rapid transportation, including the airplane, have revolutionized the fresh vegetable industry. Vegetables travel in refrigerator cars the length and breadth of the continent. Such delicacies as fresh asparagus and tomatoes are flown from California to New York. To be at their best, vegetables must be crisp, free from blemishes or any sign of decay. They need to be young and tender. Vegetables scrubbed clean before they are delivered to the market are rapidly gaining in favor with the housewife. It is a wise woman who checks the market report in her daily newspaper or on the radio before she starts out to market. Market reports name the most plentiful vegetables; as well as those which are scarce and therefore high in price. Armed with this accurate information, the shopper is able to make her purchases intelligently.

STORING VEGETABLES

A small family needs to buy in small quantities. A metal vegetable bin with perforated holes to permit the circulation of air is the most practical method for storing fresh vegetables for the average household. This bin may hold potatoes, onions, winter carrots and turnips, as well as oranges and lemons. Fresh vegetables which are to be cooked the day of purchase should be cleaned, wrapped in food bags or waxed paper, and stored in the proper storage space in the refrigerator. Quick-frozen vegetables should be stored in the freezing unit of the refrigerator until ready for cooking.

MAKING VEGETABLES POPULAR

Well-cooked vegetables make a real contribution to good health. It is right, therefore, for the young housewife to study the fundamental rules for cooking vegetables to preserve their flavor and nutrition values. The newer methods of cookery show clearly that vegetables should be cooked just long enough to render them palatable. Over-cooking and cooking at too high temperatures produce unpleasing odors in such vegetables as cauliflower, cabbage and onion. The use of an uncovered saucepan for such vegetables as these tends to preserve their whiteness and to make their flavor more pleasing.

A covered saucepan is regarded as better for the more delicate vegetables. Old-fashioned cooks often add a pinch of soda to keep the green color of vegetables, but scientists have proved that the precious vitamin content of the vegetables is destroyed by the soda. No modern cook would dream of spoiling the health value of the vegetable for the sake of the color. It is an established fact, also, that some of the most valuable vitamins are soluble in water, so it is important to use the liquid in which the vegetable is cooked. Raw vegetables are a valuable addition to the diet, as their mineral salts and vitamins are preserved intact.

HIGHLIGHTS ON FRESH VEGETABLES

Nowadays the best authorities say that fresh vegetables, either out of the garden or from market, should be cooked in one of the following ways:

Covered saucepan: Pour boiling water ½ to 1 inch in depth into a saucepan, depending upon amount of vegetable to be cooked. Place vegetable into boiling water, cover with lid, and as soon as boiling point is reached again, add salt. Keep water at boiling point until vegetable is tender but still crisp. Turn off heat; if any liquid remains in pan, remove vegetable, boil liquid down and pour over vegetable. Or if a cream sauce is to be made, add liquid to scalded milk. Or save liquid for soup or gravy or sauces.

Steaming: Pour boiling water in bottom of steamer. Place perforated inset over water, add cleaned vegetable, sprinkle lightly with salt. Cover lightly and steam until crisp but tender. Good for asparagus, spinach, other greens.

Baking: This has proved to be a delightful method for such vegetables as potatoes, sweet potatoes, squash, tomatoes, turnips, onions, green peppers and eggplant.

Pan cooking: This is fine for such vegetables as squash, kale, spinach, cabbage. Melt 2 Tbsp. drippings or salad oil or bacon fat in large skillet, add vegetables. If squash, slice thin, but do not peel. Cover, and cook slowly over low heat. Stir occasionally. If it gets dry a small amount of boiling water may be added. Season, serve at once.

OTHER VEGETABLE IDEAS

There are many combinations of vegetables which are pleasing. Cook them separately, then combine with a rich cream sauce for serving. Good combinations are: carrots and peas; string beans and corn; mushrooms and peas; celery and peas.

Creamed vegetables, either separately or together, may be placed in greased casserole and baked in oven with a topping of grated cheese or buttered bread crumbs.

The flavor of vegetables may be varied by the use of such sauces as Lemon, Hollandaise, Vinaigrette (see Sauces, Chapter 13).

Vegetables add flavor, as well as vitamins and minerals, to a well-balanced diet. Canned, fresh, frozen, or dried, they provide the wherewithal for tasty combinations. Add Ac'-cent and salt, whether they are broiled, panned, boiled, or baked.

Tender cauliflower prettied up with cream sauce nestles among green peas. These two are excellent running mates; service together saves on dishes.

TIME TABLE FOR COOKING FRESH VEGETABLES

VEGETABLE	PREPARATION	APPROXIMATE TIME
	Wash all vegetables thoroughly before cooking. Use ½ tsp. salt to 1 cup water.	Depends on age of vegetable. Younger the vegetable, the shorter the time required.
Artichoke	Remove stems, discard outside leaves.	30-45 minutes. Plenty of water.
Asparagus	May be boiled or steamed, tied in bunches.	15-30 minutes.
Beans (Green Lima)	Shelled.	20-30 minutes. ½ inch boiling water in saucepan, covered tightly.
Beans, String (Green or Wax)	Remove strings, cut lengthwise or in diagonal pieces.	20-40 minutes. ½ inch boiling water, same as above.
Beets, young	Left whole, with 2 inches of stem left on.	15-30 minutes. ½ inch boiling water, same as above.
Broccoli	Remove large outer leaves, lower part of stalk. Tie broccoli in bundle.	30-45 minutes. Stand upright in boiling water. Add 1 Tbsp. salad oil if desired.
Brussels Sprouts	Leave whole, discard wilted leaves, slice off end of stem. Soak in salted water ½ hour.	15-30 minutes. Cook uncovered in plenty of salted water.
Cabbage	Shred or cut in thin strips, or in eighths.	7-15 minutes. Cook uncovered in plenty of salted water.
Carrots	Scrub well, slice any style.	10-30 minutes. Cook uncovered in ½ inch boiling water.
Cauliflower	Stand upside down ½ hour in cold salted water (1 tsp. salt to 1 qt. water). Rinse, drain, cook whole or separate into flowerets.	20-30 minutes. Cook with head up, uncovered, in plenty of salted water. Drain.
Celery	Cut in pieces.	15-20 minutes. ½ inch boiling water in saucepan. Cover tightly.
Corn on Cob	Husks and silk removed.	7-12 minutes (no salt). Water to cover, reduce heat and simmer.
Kale	Pick over, remove coarse stems, change water until all sand is removed. Lift out of water.	7-15 minutes.
Onions	Peel under cold water. Leave whole.	20-30 minutes. Cook uncovered in plenty of salted water.

VEGETABLE	PREPARATION	APPROXIMATE TIME
Parsnips	Scrub, peel, cut in strips lengthwise or in round slices.	7-15 minutes. ½ inch boiling water in saucepan. Cook uncovered.
Peas..................	Shelled.	8-15 minutes. Cook as above in 1 inch water.
Potatoes	Scrub, left whole, peeled or not.	20-30 minutes. Cook as above.
Potatoes (Sweets or Yams)	Scrub, left whole.	30-45 minutes. Cook in boiling salted water.
Spinach...............	Roots, tough stems, wilted leaves removed. Wash in fresh water until all sand and dirt is removed. Don't pour water off, but lift spinach out of each panful. Lukewarm water is best.	10-15 minutes. Use no water at all. Sufficient water clings to leaves. Cook covered.
Squash, Summer	Scrub, cut in ½ inch slices.	15-20 minutes. ½ inch boiling water in saucepan, cover tightly.
Turnips (White or Yellow)	Scrub well, peel, cut in small pieces.	20-25 minutes. Cook as above.
Zucchini	Scrub well, do not peel, cut in pieces.	15-20 minutes. Cook as above.

Broccoli and asparagus look appetizing if served partially covered by sauce, with extra sauce at hand.

FRENCH ARTICHOKES

Remove discolored outer leaves, cut off stem about ½ inch below base of leaves. If ends of each leaf are hard and horny, snip off with sharp scissors. Wash artichokes by standing upside down in pan of cold water for half an hour. Boil in salted water until leaf pulls off easily (30 to 40 minutes). Some cooks add a spoonful of salad oil and a bay leaf to cooking water for added flavor. Drain upside down in strainer so excess water will run out. Serve with Hollandaise or melted butter. Place the artichokes upright on separate plate, with small dish of sauce by side. Each leaf is pulled off by hand, dipped in sauce and pulled between teeth to obtain fleshy portion of each leaf. The discarded leaves are piled at side of artichoke. As the leaves are pulled off, gradually the "choke" or thistle-like center appears. This is not edible. It is cut away, and only the tender heart is eaten. Artichokes served cold as a salad are highly regarded.

ASPARAGUS

Break upper stalk of asparagus from lower, woody portion. Stalk snaps off easily. Stalks may be scrubbed with stiff vegetable brush to remove any sand which may cling to them. With sharp paring knife, remove scales from upper part of stalk. Asparagus may be tied in bunches and placed upright in deep saucepan of boiling water, so tips are not immersed in water. The bunches may be tipped on side during last five minutes of cooking. However, the steaming method is preferable. Asparagus is delicious with cream sauce, butter sauce, Hollandaise or cheese sauce.

BEANS—GREEN AND WAX

Buttered: Wash well, remove ends and strings, if any. Beans may be left whole (for salads) or slit lengthwise or sliced thin on a slant. Cook in covered saucepan or in pressure cooker. Boil down any leftover liquid, add seasonings, butter, pour over beans.

Creamed: Prepare as above, add to medium cream sauce.

Succotash: Cut beans in pieces on a diagonal slant, cook, season, add equal quantities of cooked corn, and a generous amount of milk and butter, cook over low heat until corn is heated through. If fresh corn is available, it may be cut off cob before cooking, added to beans and cooked in milk until tender. Quick-frozen corn is excellent when cooked, added to cooked beans and seasoned with milk and butter.

String Beans with Mushrooms: Cook beans. Just before serving, garnish with piping hot sautéed mushrooms (fresh or canned).

BEETS

Boiled: Scrub well, cut off tops, leaving on 2 inches of the stem end. Put ½ to 1 inch boiling water in saucepan, add ½ tsp. salt, add beets, cover tightly and cook 30 to 60 minutes. Drain, plunge beets in cold water for a minute, slip off skins. Season with salt, pepper, butter, little vinegar.

Buttered: Cook as above, dice or slice or cut in slivers, add butter.

Harvard Beets: Cook as above, dice and add to Harvard Sauce.

HARVARD SAUCE

¼ cup sugar	½ cup vinegar
½ tsp. salt	2 Tbsp. butter
	1 Tbsp. cornstarch

Blend dry ingredients, add vinegar, mix to smooth paste. Cook 5 minutes, add salt, pepper, beets. Simmer over low heat, add butter, serve hot.

Oven-Baked Beets: Bake by same method as Oven-Baked Carrots.

Pickled Beets: Cook beets, slip off skins, slice thin. Place in deep bowl, cover with pickling mixture.

PICKLING MIXTURE

½ cup vinegar	1 Tbsp. sugar
¼ cup beet juice (water in which beets are cooked)	½ tsp. salt
	½ tsp. dry mustard
	½ clove of garlic

Cover bowl with plate, place in refrigerator for several hours. Remove garlic, serve as a relish.

Young Beet Greens: Use fresh, tender beet tops. Wash thoroughly in several waters. Cook in covered saucepan. 1 Tbsp. of boiling water will be sufficient. When tender, drain well. Add salt, pepper, butter. Cut finely with sharp knife or leave whole, as desired. Allow about ½ lb. per person.

CARROTS

Buttered: Scrub carrots well, scrape lightly, cut in julienne strips or quarters, or diced or round slices. Cook by covered saucepan or pressure cooker method. Remove carrots as soon as tender. Boil down any remaining liquid, season with butter, salt and pepper. Pour over carrots, serve at once. Takes about 20 minutes.

Creamed: Prepare as above, add to medium cream sauce. Use liquid from carrots as part of liquid for sauce.

Glazed: Scrub carrots well and scrape. Cut in half lengthwise and across, making 4 sections of each carrot. Cook as above. Melt 2 Tbsp. butter and 2 Tbsp. brown sugar in skillet, add cooked carrots and simmer gently, basting with spoon so each piece of carrot is completely covered by syrup.

Oven-Baked Carrots: Scrub vegetable well. Place in pan. Add ½ cup boiling water, 1 tsp. salt, 2 Tbsp. butter, margarine or salad oil. Place cover on pan securely. Bake in moderate oven (375° F.) 40 to 60 minutes.

Carrot Ring: Cook carrots by covering saucepan or pressure cooker method. Drain well, season with salt, pepper, press through a sieve. Grease a ring mold and fill with sieved carrots. Place mold in pan of hot water until ready to serve, turn out on platter and fill with creamed vegetables or chicken.

CORN "OYSTERS"

2 cups canned corn (whole kernel)	½ tsp. salt
1 egg	½ tsp. sugar
1 Tbsp. flour	¼ cup butter

Drain corn, add well-beaten egg, seasonings and flour. Mix well. Should be thin batter. Drop by spoonfuls into moderately hot pan in which butter has been melted. Brown carefully on both sides. Reduce heat and cook gently on both sides until center is cooked. May be served with meat course, or as a dessert with powdered sugar. Fresh corn cut off cob is delicious when used for the "oysters."

Baked cheese and rice croquettes make a satisfying no-meat meal. Add a green vegetable, such as the Frenched green beans pictured here, or asparagus or broccoli. A real mayonnaise sauce adds the finishing touch.

EGGPLANT

STUFFED EGGPLANT

Parboil a medium sized eggplant about 20 minutes, or until easily pierced with a fork, but not squashy. Remove to platter, and when cool enough slice in half lengthwise. Scoop out the pulp into a bowl, leaving ½ inch shell of eggplant.

Stuffing

2 Tbsp. olive oil	1 egg or ½ lb. ground round beef
½ cup soft bread crumbs	1 clove garlic
½ tsp. salt	1 small onion
6 ripe olives	4 Tbsp. grated cheese

Herbs

1 Tbsp. minced parsley	½ tsp. thyme
	1 tsp. sweet marjoram

Add the bread crumbs and salt to the eggplant pulp. Scrape the onion for juice and also add. Sauté the garlic in the olive oil. Remove the garlic, and add the eggplant mixture, which has been well mixed. Simmer gently for ten minutes. Remove from the fire, cool. Add the sliced olives and the well-beaten egg, 2 Tbsp. grated cheese, and herbs if desired. Refill the shells, sprinkle with remainder of cheese, and top with buttered crumbs. Bake in moderate oven (350° F.) 30 to 45 minutes. (Ground round beef, omitting the egg, may be used, browning it with the garlic.) Serve with garlic bread or rolls and a green salad.

Garlic Bread

Cut thick slices of french bread. Peel one clove of garlic, place in bowl and crush thoroughly with handle of knife. Discard coarse pieces of garlic. Add piece of butter to garlic in bowl and cream well. Spread the garlic-seasoned butter on each slice of bread. Toast lightly under flame of broiler oven.

EGGPLANT IN CASSEROLE

1 eggplant	2 cups thin white sauce (use 1 cup
1 7-oz. tin mushrooms	milk and 1 cup liquid from
1 7-oz. tin minced clams	mushrooms and clams)
½ cup grated cheese	½ cup buttered bread crumbs

Cut raw eggplant into 1 inch cubes. Grease a casserole and cover bottom of dish with layer of eggplant, cover with a layer of mushrooms, clams and grated cheese. Continue until all ingredients are used. Pour cream sauce over all, sprinkle bread crumbs on top. Bake in moderate oven (375° F.) ½ hour.

MUSHROOMS

Many arguments go on as to the proper method of cleaning mushrooms; experts say "wash thoroughly," others say "brush thoroughly." If the mushrooms are tender you do not need to peel them—simply cut off a thin slice from the stem end. If the stems are full and plump they may be cooked right along with the mushroom cap. But if stems tend to be tough they can be peeled, cut up and cooked in water to be used for sauce, soup or gravy.

CREAMED MUSHROOMS

Peel mushrooms, slice in ⅛ inch slices lengthwise. Melt 2 Tbsp. butter in saucepan, add sliced mushrooms, cover and sauté over medium heat for 10 minutes, stirring occasionally. Prepare a thin or medium cream sauce, add sautéed mushrooms. (Use the melted butter from the sautéed mushrooms as the base for the sauce. Remove mushrooms, add flour, cream or milk. When sauce is ready, replace mushrooms in pan.)

GRILLED MUSHROOMS

Wash or brush mushrooms; if tough, peel skins. Cut off stems, lay mushrooms on broiler, rounded side up. When well-heated, turn over and place a piece of butter in each cap (as much as cap will hold—½ to 1 tsp.). Sprinkle with salt and pepper, replace under broiler flame and grill for 7 to 8 minutes. Serve on hot buttered toast at once. Serve with wedge of lemon.

SAUTÉED MUSHROOMS

Melt butter in skillet, add whole mushrooms or peeled and sliced mushrooms. Cover and cook over low heat for 10 minutes or until mushrooms are tender. Stir occasionally. Allow 2 to 3 Tbsp. butter to ½ lb. mushrooms.

OKRA

1 pt. young okra pods	1 Tbsp. onion juice
¼ cup butter	Salt, pepper
	Dash of cayenne

Wash pods, dry, cut off both ends. Cut pods into pieces, fry rapidly in butter, until pieces are delicately browned. Add seasonings, reduce heat and cook slowly until tender, but not dried out.

GREEN PEAS

This delicate, popular vegetable must be cooked as soon as possible after picking, or as soon as brought home from market. Peas are as good as can be when treated with respect. The same general directions given for cooking vegetables are right for peas.

BUTTERED GREEN PEAS

Shell peas, add just enough boiling salted water to cover saucepan to depth of 1 inch. Allow ½ tsp. salt to ½ cup boiling water. Cover pan tightly and simmer until tender (8 to 15 minutes). Add butter or a little cream. Serve in saucers so that every bit of flavor in liquid is enjoyed. 1 lb. of peas in pod makes about 1 cup shelled peas.

BAKED POTATO

Baked potatoes have become a specialty dish in many homes, due to the development of the "baking" potato by the growers. Both the States of Maine and Idaho have featured these mammoth potatoes—thin-skinned, mealy and dry.

Steaming baked potatoes call for plentiful butter and seasoning. Jackets, filled with nourishment themselves, lock in inner goodness.

One such potato apiece is all anyone with an average appetite could consume, but smaller potatoes may also be baked. The method is the same in each instance.

The potatoes should be well-scrubbed, and dried with a soft cloth or paper toweling. Any melted fat may be used for brushing the entire surface of the raw potato. This coating of fat insures a soft, pliable skin.

Preheat the oven for 15 minutes to 425° to 450° F. Bake the potatoes in this hot oven until tender to the touch when squeezed with a dry towel. A small baking potato requires about 30 minutes, the mammoth ones 60 minutes.

Hold potato in a towel, cut gash in top—squeeze from bottom. Slip a square of butter in top, sprinkle with paprika and serve at once.

STUFFED BAKED POTATOES

4 baked potatoes	½ tsp. salt
2 Tbsp. butter	1 tsp. pepper
2 Tbsp. scalded milk or cream	1 tsp. minced parsley

Cut potatoes in half lengthwise. Scoop out and whip together with other ingredients. Beat until fluffy. Replace in shells, sprinkle with parsley. Replace in oven and bake until tops begin to brown. One half potato is usually regarded as a serving at a party.

Variations

1. Add 1 to 2 Tbsp. finely chopped onion to the potatoes.
2. Add ½ cup sautéed mushrooms.
3. Add 1 to 2 Tbsp. finely chopped chives or parsley.

FRENCH FRIED POTATOES

Pare potatoes and cut in long thin slices. Let stand 30 minutes in salted ice water (1 Tbsp. salt to 1 cup water). Drain and dry potatoes. Heat lard or vegetable shortening to 380° F. in deep saucepan. Cover the bottom of a wire frying basket with potatoes, immerse in hot fat until potatoes are cooked, then let stand on paper to drain off excess fat. Sprinkle with salt. Repeat same process until all potatoes are fried. Serve at once.

PUFF POTATOES

Prepare potatoes as directed above. Fry potatoes in hot fat (370° F.) until soft and just beginning to brown. Remove from fat and drain on paper. When ready to serve, immerse in deep hot fat (390° F.) and cook until golden brown. Drain on paper and sprinkle with salt. Serve hot.

FANCY POTATO BALLS

Use a ball cutter to cut potatoes into balls, or use small uniform sized potatoes. Cook in boiling salted water 15 to 20 minutes, or until tender. Drain, roll in melted butter, sprinkle with paprika or chopped parsley.

CREAMED POTATOES

Boil as directed for boiled potatoes. Pare and dice in cubes, or use cooked sliced or diced potatoes to make potato balls. Prepare thin white sauce. Add potatoes to sauce. (If potatoes are cold, reheat in sauce.) Sprinkle with chopped parsley or paprika.

MASHED POTATOES

3 cups sieved boiled potatoes	3 Tbsp. butter
⅓ cup hot milk	½ tsp. salt

Boil potatoes (old ones, not new) in boiling salt water until soft. Heat gently over a low heat to evaporate water. Mash or press through a sieve or ricer. Add hot milk. Add butter and salt. Beat until fluffy and white. Serve with a bit of butter on top.

SCALLOPED POTATOES

4 cups thinly sliced potatoes	¼ cup grated onions
	2 cups thin white sauce

Wash, pare potatoes and slice thin. Place one layer of potatoes in greased casserole. Sprinkle onion over them. Continue until casserole is filled. Pour thin white sauce over them. Bake uncovered in moderate oven (350° F.) 45 minutes. Serve hot.

POTATOES AU GRATIN

Prepare scalloped potatoes, sprinkle grated cheese between each layer, and continue until casserole is filled. Bake as directed.

HASHED BROWNED POTATOES

3 Tbsp. shortening	2 Tbsp. flour
3 Tbsp. chopped onion	¼ cup milk
3 cups diced, cooked potatoes	1 tsp. salt
	¼ tsp. pepper

Fry onions in shortening for 5 minutes. Turn all ingredients into pan with

For a welcome variation on the potato theme add 1 Tbsp. chopped fresh dill and 2 Tbsp. butter or margarine to 1½ lb. cooked new potatoes. Grind a bit of black pepper over them, toss them lightly, and serve them hot.

onion. Press down firmly into a flat round cake. Cover and cook 10 minutes, on one side. Turn and cook on other side 10 minutes or longer.

SWEET POTATOES AND YAMS

Sweet potatoes and yams resemble each other closely in appearance. The cookery methods are the same, but the devotees of yams claim they are superior to sweets in flavor and texture.

BOILED SWEET POTATOES OR YAMS

Scrub the skins thoroughly until all loose dirt is washed away. Rinse in cold water and cover with boiling salted water. Allow 1 tsp. salt to 1 qt. of water. Cook covered until tender (20 to 30 minutes). Drain, lift each potato from pan with silver fork. Peel quickly and serve in any one of the following ways.

CANDIED SWEETS

4 boiled sweet potatoes or yams	½ cup boiling water
½ cup brown sugar	¼ cup butter

Cut potatoes in half lengthwise. Place in shallow greased baking dish. Cook sugar and water together to make a syrup. Pour syrup over potatoes, dot with butter, and place in preheated hot oven (400° F.). Bake 15 to 20 minutes.

Variations

1. Substitute 1 cup maple syrup for the brown sugar.
2. Substitute 1 cup drained crushed pineapple and ¼ cup brown sugar, for ½ cup brown sugar.
3. Sprinkle 1 tsp. cinnamon over potatoes before cooking.

SCALLOPED SWEETS WITH APPLES

4 boiled sweet potatoes	½ cup brown sugar
2 raw tart apples	1 to 2 Tbsp. boiling water

Grease a round casserole on bottom and sides. Peel potatoes and slice in thick round slices. Peel, core and cut apples in thick, round slices. Place apples and potatoes in alternate layers in baking dish. Sprinkle each layer with sugar. Add water if apples are not juicy, or if ingredients dry as they bake.

Variations

Sweets with Oranges: Substitute thick, round slices of peeled oranges for tart apples. Proceed as above.

Sweets with Pecan Nuts: Substitute 1 cup nut meats for apples. Proceed as above.

MASHED SWEET POTATOES OR YAMS

4 sweet potatoes	½ tsp. salt
¼ to ½ cup hot milk	¼ cup butter

Boil potatoes as directed in previous recipe. Peel, return to hot saucepan. Mash well with potato masher. Add milk gradually, beat well with spoon, add seasonings and butter. Beat until light. Serve at once.

Variations

Sweet Potatoes with Sherry Wine: Substitute sherry for hot milk. Scald wine, but do not bring to boil.

Sweet Potatoes in Orange Shells: Cut navel oranges in half crosswise. Scoop out pulp and mix with mashed potatoes. Fill shells with mixture. Place lump of butter on top and bake in moderate oven (350° F.) 30 minutes. Garnish with a candied cherry.

BAKED SWEET POTATOES

When putting a panful of potatoes in the oven to bake, it is always better to choose potatoes of uniform size. Baked sweet potatoes are a good choice when a meat loaf or an all-oven dinner is planned, such as baked acorn squash, or stuffed eggplant. Scrub potatoes well, rinse in cold water and dry. They may be brushed with melted fat for a soft, pliable skin. Bake in hot oven (400° F.) until soft to touch when squeezed; 30 to 40 minutes depending on size.

BAKED STUFFED SWEET POTATOES

Bake potatoes as directed in above recipe. Cut in half lengthwise and proceed as for stuffed white potatoes.

Variations

Sweet Potatoes with Pineapple: Add ¼ cup of canned crushed pineapple to 4 baked sweet potatoes. Beat until light and fluffy. Season with butter. Reheat in oven.

Sweet Potatoes with Sausages: Prepare stuffed sweet potatoes as directed above. Replace in shells, place partially cooked link sausage on top of each potato half. Bake in oven until sausage is golden brown.

SPINACH

In many communities spinach is brought to market already cleaned and neatly packaged in cellophane bags. If your community lacks this up-to-the-minute blessing, it is still necessary to clean the spinach in the time-honored method, as follows: Purchase 2 qts. for a family of two. Pick it over carefully, discard any wilted leaves, cut off roots and any tough stems. Place two big pans in sink, fill each with lukewarm water. Toss spinach in first pan and swirl around with hands. Lift spinach from water and toss into second pan. Throw away water in first pan. Then lift spinach from second pan and replace in first pan which now has fresh water. It takes several washings in alternate pans to remove all sand and dirt. As spinach is washed in successive waters, let water continue to run colder, until final 2 or 3 waters are very cold.

BOILED SPINACH

Shake water off leaves, pack spinach into deep kettle. Add ½ tsp. salt to 2 qts. spinach. Cover tightly and cook over low heat. As leaves on bottom wilt from heat, turn over with fork until all leaves have been turned. Cook without adding any extra water. This method produces bright green spinach with all the flavor and vitamins intact.

Spinach may be served just as it comes from fire, with additions of butter and a garnish of hard-cooked egg. But there are also other ways to serve this vegetable:
1. Place spinach in wooden bowl, chop fine and season, then return to fire to heat again.
2. Chop as above, return to fire, and add a little heavy cream.
3. Spinach may be puréed through a sieve, and heated with heavy cream.
4. Many food authorities like to add a little grated nutmeg to this dish.

OVEN-BAKED SQUASH

2 acorn squash	4 Tbsp. melted butter
4 Tbsp. brown sugar	½ tsp. salt
	⅛ tsp. pepper

Scrub squash, cut in half, remove seeds. Sprinkle center cavity of each half with sugar, add butter. Place in oven. Bake in hot oven (400° F.) 1 hour. Remove cover at end of 30 minutes of baking. When tender, remove from oven, stir pulp lightly with fork, sprinkle with salt and pepper. Serve right in shell. A small amount of water may be poured in baking dish when placed in oven. *4 servings.*

TOMATOES

Tomatoes are such a versatile vegetable that chapters on tomato cookery alone could easily be written.

SCALLOPED TOMATOES

2 cups tomatoes (canned or fresh)	½ tsp. salt
2 Tbsp. butter	¼ tsp. pepper
2 slices buttered bread, cut in small cubes	Bay leaf, well-crumbled
	Paprika

Grease baking dish well, line with layer of tomatoes, cover with bread cubes, sprinkle with seasonings and butter. Add layer of tomatoes, repeat bread and seasonings and dabs of butter. Top off with bread cubes. Bake in moderate oven (375° F.) 20 minutes. *4 servings.*

STUFFED TOMATOES

4 tomatoes	¼ tsp. pepper
1 cup soft bread crumbs	Paprika
1 tsp. salt	½ tsp. thyme or savory
	1 onion, minced

Cut a slice from stem end of tomato. Remove center of pulp. Place in bowl with a mixture of soft bread crumbs and seasonings of salt, pepper, paprika, thyme or savory. Add minced onion, mix well. Refill tomatoes with mixture. Cover with buttered crumbs and bake in moderate oven (375° F.) until shell is tender, but holds its shape. *4 servings.*

Variations

Bread crumbs may be replaced by any one of following:
   1 cup cooked rice.
   1 cup cooked elbow macaroni.
   1 cup cooked fresh or canned whole kernel corn.

STEWED TOMATOES

1 pt. fresh tomatoes	Slice raw onion
1 tsp. salt	Bay leaf
¼ tsp. pepper	1 Tbsp. butter
	1 Tbsp. flour

Wash tomatoes. Cut out stem end, cut tomatoes in pieces. Place in enamel saucepan, add seasonings. Simmer gently until well cooked down. Rub flour and butter together until smooth (commonly known as *roux*). Pour a little of tomato on flour mixture to make a paste, stir well, return mixture to saucepan and cook 5 minutes longer. *4 servings.*

SAUTÉED TOMATOES

4 raw tomatoes	½ tsp. salt
¼ cup fine bread crumbs	4 Tbsp. bacon fat

Wash tomatoes and cut in thick slices. Melt fat in heavy frying pan; dip tomatoes in salted bread crumbs. Place each carefully in hot fat. Brown on one side and then on other. Reduce heat and fry until golden brown, about 10 minutes. *2 to 4 servings.*

SOUFFLÉ

Practically any vegetable may be used to make this party dish. For the baking of the soufflé use a greased ring mold. When done, the soufflé is turned out on a dish and the center filled with any creamed mixture, such as chicken, crab meat, salmon or tuna fish. This dish is handsome in its appearance. Serve on a large dish, garnish with a wreath of parsley all around the edge. Either asparagus, carrots, peas, spinach or string beans may be used to prepare this dish.

VEGETABLE SOUFFLÉ

2 cups cooked vegetables	1 Tbsp. minced onion
1 cup medium white sauce	1 Tbsp. lemon juice
3 egg yolks, beaten	½ tsp. salt
3 egg whites, beaten until stiff	⅛ tsp. pepper
	Dash of paprika

Drain well, press through sieve. Combine vegetables, sauce, egg yolks, seasonings, fold in egg whites. Turn into greased ring mold. Bake in pan of hot water in moderate oven (375° F.) until firm, about 30 minutes. *4 to 6 servings.*

9.

EGGS
AND
CHEESE

WELL over fifty years ago, a little book was published with the eloquent title "100 Ways to Cook Eggs." But when we look over those pages today, we find that the simple addition of paprika, or curry powder, or some other such triviality was considered sufficient to justify listing recipes as separate items. Modern cooks scorn such recipes, and call them "stuff and nonsense."

Information on the basic methods of cooking eggs is what the busy, active woman wants—she supplies her own touch of genius in developing a hundred adaptations. The newer knowledge of nutrition has given the use of eggs a valuable position in the planning of weekly meals. If meat is scarce or expensive, an entrée of eggs at luncheon or dinner may very well take the place of meat, at the same time giving a pleasant variety to the week's routine.

Eggs are a valuable source of protein, and also contribute important amounts of minerals and vitamins. The egg yolk is rich in fat. A simple way to compare the food value of eggs with meat is to figure that 1 doz. large eggs equals 1¼ lbs. of meat. If the cook plans 2 eggs apiece—when eggs take the place of meat, fish or poultry in the menu—that is about the right proportion.

BUYING EGGS

Brown shelled eggs are the equal of the white ones both as to taste and quality, and size has no relation to the quality of the egg. Good eggs may be either large or small, but size does make a difference in value received for money expended. Of course, you get more edible food in a dozen large eggs than in a dozen small eggs; but if the small eggs are enough lower in price, they may be the better "buy."

It is pretty hard to tell much about the quality of an egg's contents by the appearance of the shell. However, it is true that eggs are usually better when the shell has a dull appearance, since that means that the natural "bloom" is still on the egg. When this bloom, or covering, is rubbed off, air can more readily go through the shell, and this may cause the egg to lose moisture more rapidly.

The most practical guide for the homemaker in selecting eggs is the grading system based on the way an egg looks on the outside as well as on the inside. The inside quality is judged by a test called "candling," which is simply putting the egg in front of a bright light, which makes it possible to see the contents inside the shell.

It is well worth your while to learn the different grades, and buy according to your needs. The top—and best—grade is the Grade "A." The next, Grade "B," is a good usable egg for most purposes. Grade "C" eggs are suitable for use in cooking where delicacy of flavor is not so important.

Eggs in all grades are wholesome. However, if you intend to cook and serve "as is," the better grades are advisable. For most other cooking purposes, the less expensive grades will serve just as well.

CARE OF EGGS

1. Keep eggs in the refrigerator. Buy only a week's supply at a time.
2. If a bit of egg yolk gets in raw egg white when separating eggs for cooking, scoop it out with edge of shell. Yolk will adhere to shell, and can be easily removed. Egg whites will not beat up stiff if egg yolk is in whites.
3. Stir water a few times when eggs are boiling for deviled eggs. This tends to keep yolk in center, and the white at even thickness.
4. Always wash egg beater immediately after using.
5. Always rinse egg dishes in cold water before putting them in with the other dishes for washing.

Bacon and eggs turn out perfect every time when you use the new thermostatically controlled gas burner.

TO SEPARATE EGGS

One bad egg can spoil the lot, so separate each egg alone, first. Then add single white or yolk to quantity in larger bowl.

6. When separating whites and yolks of eggs, separate each egg in cup or small bowl and then add the single white or yolk to the quantity in larger bowl. One bad egg will spoil the whole lot.

7. If making a custard or cooked egg dish where hot liquid is used, slowly pour the hot liquid onto the beaten eggs, stirring constantly. This creates a smooth mixture, with no curdling.

8. Are there any leftover egg yolks? Cover with cold water, cover dish and place in refrigerator. These may be added to scrambled eggs or may be hard-cooked and used for garnishes or salads. Leftover egg whites? Cover tightly and place in refrigerator. And don't forget the witticism: "Never throw away good food. Wait until it spoils!" There is both irony and truth in that old saying.

WAYS TO PREPARE EGGS

HARD-COOKED

Place required number of eggs in saucepan, cover with cold water, heat slowly to simmering point, and cook 20 minutes. Drain, plunge into cold water. Crack shell lightly at rounded end and it will slip off easily. If eggs are to be saved for use at a later date, leave shells on and place eggs in refrigerator.

DEVILED EGGS

Deviled eggs are beloved by picnickers. Use the recipe for hard-cooked eggs, then slice the eggs in half, lengthwise. Remove the yolks, season with mayonnaise, a dash of good vinegar, salt, pepper, paprika. A bit of curry powder or dry mustard adds a dash of zippiness. Mash the yolks with other ingredients until smooth. Refill the whites with this mixture. A garnish of parsley, a slice of stuffed olive or a bit of pimiento adds color. The seasoning needs to be sharp enough to be noticeable. Bland deviled eggs are no good to anyone.

CREAMED EGGS

1 pt. medium white sauce
8 hard-cooked eggs
4 slices buttered toast
Paprika

Creamed ham and eggs top buttermilk waffles, in place of toast.

Cut toast in triangles. Slice eggs in half lengthwise. Heat eggs in white sauce and pour over toast, sprinkle with paprika. Serve hot.

Variations

1. Add 1 cup of cooked green peas to sauce.
2. Add 1 cup minced ham to sauce.
3. Serve eggs on bed of cooked rice in place of toast.

POACHED EGGS ON TOAST

Cooked properly, this dish is one of the most delightful of egg styles. Grease a frying pan lightly. Pour in boiling water; add ½ tsp. salt, 1 tsp. vinegar. Lower heat so water doesn't boil. Carefully break egg into a shallow saucer and slip it from there into water. Water must completely cover egg. Let stand over low heat until white is firm, and thin film covers the yolk (3 to 5 minutes). Use a long-handled perforated skimmer or griddle cake turner to insert under egg. Lift out onto prepared toast (see below).

TOAST FOR POACHED EGGS

To have perfect poached eggs, the toast needs special attention. Prepare toast as usual, but place small saucepan on stove with boiling salted water. Hold toast, one slice at a time, between thumb and forefinger. Dip each of four sides into the water. Place toast on hot plate, lift out egg, add dab of butter, sprig of parsley. Rush to table!

Special metal egg poachers, or metal rings, are available in many stores. Ring is placed under water and egg slipped in. This is easier for an inexperienced cook to use. Poached eggs are often served with vegetable dinners, or corned beef hash, or fried ham.

EGGS BENEDICT

2 English Muffins (split and
  toasted)
½ lb. boiled ham (cut in 4
  slices)
1 Tbsp. butter
4 poached eggs
1 cup Hollandaise sauce (Chapter 13)

Grease four individual casseroles. Melt the butter in skillet and broil the ham 1 minute on each side. Place ½ muffin in each casserole, cover muffin with a slice of ham. Carefully place egg on ham and cover with sauce. Dust lightly with paprika.

CODDLED EGGS

To cook eggs to suit every member of the family buy an hourglass with a fine trickle of sand running through which is timed for 3 minutes. It is an excellent egg watcher. Pour boiling water in deep saucepan, then lower the eggs into water with a long-handled spoon. Be sure eggs are completely covered by water. Cover saucepan tightly, remove from heat, let stand until desired degree of firmness is reached. 6 minutes soft- -8 to 10 minutes medium cooked.

BACON AND EGGS

Cook bacon, keep hot. Drain excess bacon fat from pan, crack each egg on side of pan with a light sure touch. Slip egg into pan. Turn heat low. With large spoon dip up bacon fat and baste top of egg with fat until yolk and white are firm but tender.

BAKED EGGS—A GOOD LUNCHEON DISH

Individual casseroles are a godsend to the small family. They may be greased with butter, margarine or salad oil. Each casserole will hold one egg.

Eggs are a valuable source of protein. What's more, they are adaptable to every meal. Be sure to prepare correctly in order to gain greatest goodness from this basic food.

Scrambling eggs? Go easy on the heat. Stop cooking as soon as eggs are thickened; overcooked eggs have an unpleasant way of "weeping."

Fluffy egg dishes profit by slow baking. Low heat permits air cells to expand and set, prevents collapse.

Carefully crack egg, slip in center of dish, season to taste. Eggs should be baked in casserole in moderate oven (350° F.) 15 minutes or until eggs are set.

Variations

Season with salt, pepper, paprika, pour in little cream, dot with butter.
Sprinkle minced ham on bottom of dish.
Sprinkle cheese over top.
Lay slice of thin cooked ham on bottom of dish.
Lay slice of ham on bottom, add finely chopped spinach, add egg.

SCRAMBLED EGGS

Allow 1 or 2 eggs per person   ¼ tsp. salt for every 2 eggs
1-2 Tbsp. light cream or milk per   Dash of pepper for every 2 eggs
    egg   Butter, margarine, or bacon fat

Heat fat in bottom of frying pan. Beat eggs lightly with silver fork, add milk and seasonings. (Eggs should be beaten just enough to make smooth consistency.) Reduce heat under pan, pour in eggs and let them stand untouched for a minute, then with a fork start to stir until the eggs are a creamy, golden mass, soft but firm enough to eat with fork.

Another popular method is to cook the eggs in the upper part of a double boiler. Melt butter, add beaten eggs, cook over hot water until thick and creamy, stirring constantly.

Variations

Allow 1 Tbsp. of any one of the following ingredients to 4 beaten eggs:

Finely minced parsley   Grated cheese
Curry powder   Chili sauce
Grated onion   Minced ham
    Crumbled, broiled bacon

PLAIN OMELET (FRENCH OMELET)

Allow 1 or 2 eggs per person   Allow ¼ tsp. salt to every 2 eggs
Allow 1 to 2 Tbsp. milk per egg   ⅛ tsp. pepper to every 2 eggs

Melt butter or salad oil in pan. (A heavy iron frying pan or an aluminum omelet pan with smooth surface is essential.) Beat eggs just enough to blend well—use hand egg beater for small omelet. Add liquid and seasonings. Heat fat in pan, turn and twist pan so fat covers sides also. Pour eggs into pan and turn heat low. Let eggs stand for a minute; as soon as a bubble or two forms, take spatula and lift omelet at edge so uncooked portion of egg runs down to bottom of pan and is cooked. Repeat this process of lifting cooked egg at edge and allowing uncooked portion to run down until the whole thing is a creamy, rather smooth mass. When omelet is nearly cooked, roll one half of it over onto other half. Let stand a minute. Turn onto hot dish.

If a number of people are to be served, it is better to make a few small omelets rather than to attempt a large one. Many cooks like to vary the omelet by adding a different ingredient at the last minute, just before the omelet is rolled over to the other half. Jelly, cheese, grated or minced ham, bits of broiled bacon, are all pleasing additions.

A double omelet pan may be purchased in many stores. Many cooks prefer this type of pan.

PUFFY OMELET
(Basic Recipe)

This style of omelet is regarded by large numbers of people as being the last word in fancy cookery. Its appearance is elegant, its taste is delightful, and to the uninitiated it looks as if it is a work of art. Actually it is an extremely simple dish and is in high favor as a party dish for "brunch." ("Brunch" is usually thought of as a meal too late for breakfast and too early for lunch, good for holiday and party meals.)

Allow 1 to 2 eggs per person
Allow 1 Tbsp. cold water to every egg
Allow ⅛ tsp. salt to every egg
Dash of pepper to every egg
Butter or salad oil to melt in pan

The puffy omelet invariably excites an admiring chorus of "oh's" and "ah's." A good sauce will lend enchantment.

Separate the eggs. Beat the whites until stiff. Set in refrigerator. Beat the egg yolks until thick and lemon-colored; add salt, pepper, water. Remove whites from refrigerator, carefully pour yolks over whites. Using a folding motion, fold yolks into whites. Heat fat in pan, tip and turn pan so fat covers sides as well as bottom. Turn mixture into pan. Turn heat to low and cook until omelet is puffed up and firm on underside. Spatula may be carefully slid under edge

Luncheon Onion Pie

Appetizer Salad Platter

Basket Picnic

Cook 'n' Eat Picnic

Cook 'n' Carry Picnic

of omelet to test firmness of bottom. Place omelet in oven at moderate heat (350° F.) and cook for about 5 to 8 minutes. To test "doneness" carefully thrust a clean silver knife directly through center, right down to bottom. If no uncooked egg clings to knife, omelet is done.

Remove from oven. Some cooks turn omelet out in original shape and pour sauce over top. Other cooks make a deep cut through the center of the omelet, without cutting to bottom, then fold omelet, and turn out. Sauce is an asset to a puffy omelet.

Good sauces for omelets are cheese, tomato, and mushroom, or a melted tart jelly such as currant. If jelly is used, it is usually added before omelet is folded over. Omit pepper and add a dash of sugar for sweet omelets.

SPANISH OMELET

Use the basic recipe for Puffy Omelet for the eggs. Serve with Creole Sauce, for which recipe is given in Chapter 13. If you prefer a sauce which is quicker to prepare, eliminate from that recipe the olives, consommé and mushrooms.

CHEESE

Cheese is a prima donna food and it has the temperament of one. But what a grand versatile food it is! From grated cheese, on toasted squares of bread floating gayly on onion soup, right up to a wedge of cheese served with apple pie. Bread and cheese have made many a meal for a weary traveler. Cheese soufflés have built fine reputations for plain cooks.

It's a budget food, too—2 oz. of whole milk cheese, such as American Cheddar, being equal to the protein in an average serving of meat. It is rich in calcium, and other minerals and vitamins. It is rich in fat and high up in flavor appeal. It enhances the flavor of dried beans, macaroni, rice and cereals.

CHEESE PRECAUTIONS

1. *Bulk Cheese and Processed Cheese*

Keep cheese in refrigerator. Cover with wax paper and place in dish with tightly fitted cover. Processed cheeses may be kept in their original wrapper until used.

2. *Cottage Cheese and Cream Cheese*

These are cheeses which should be used almost immediately after purchasing as they spoil rapidly. Place in refrigerator, in covered container or original wrapper.

Cheese, crackers, and fruit are a versatile trio ready to serve as dessert, buffet item, or snack.

Cheese canapé mold, chilled and elegant, permits guests to help themselves.

3. *Leftover "Nubbins" of Cheese*

Don't toss these away. Save until dry and grate for sauces, spaghetti or soup. For dry cheese use a fine grater, for soft cheese a coarse grater. For processed cheese do not grate, but slice off what you need, wrap remainder of package tightly, and keep in refrigerator.

RECIPES FOR USE OF CHEESE

CHEESE SUPPER DISH

6 slices buttered bread	1 pt. milk
½ lb. Cheddar cheese	½ tsp. salt
3 eggs, well-beaten	¼ tsp. pepper
	½ tsp. paprika

Grease a round casserole on bottom and sides. Cut cheese in 6 thin slices. Remove crusts from bread, slice, cover each slice with cheese. Cut slices of bread in quarters. Fit quarter slices of bread into casserole, pressing down lightly. Sprinkle with seasonings. Mix eggs with milk, pour over bread and cheese. Let stand for 30 minutes. Place in pan of hot water and bake in moderate oven (350° F.) until a silver knife thrust down into center comes out clean with no milky substance clinging to it. *4 to 6 servings.*

CHEESE SOUFFLÉ

2 Tbsp. shortening
2 Tbsp. flour
½ tsp. salt
Few grains pepper
¾ cup milk
¼ lb. sharp cheese
2 eggs, separated

A cheese soufflé, golden and gleaming, is truly a work of art. Serve immediately after it leaves the oven, plain, or with sauce as tomato.

Melt shortening, add flour, salt and pepper. Blend well, stir in milk and cook over low heat until mixture thickens. Grate or cut cheese in pieces. Add cheese and stir until melted. Stir into slightly beaten egg yolks. Fold in stiffly beaten egg whites. Pour into a quart-size greased baking dish or individual casseroles. Set into pan of hot water. Bake in slow oven (300° F.) 1 hour, or until knife, when inserted in center, comes out clean. Serve at once. *4 servings.*

CREAMY WELSH RAREBIT

This recipe dates back a good many years. Changes are made by each generation, but the following recipe is an all-time favorite.

1 lb. American cheese
3 eggs
½ cup light cream

½ tsp. salt
¼ tsp. cayenne
½ tsp. dry mustard
¼ tsp. Worcestershire sauce

Cut cheese in small pieces. Place cheese in upper part of double boiler. Add the unbeaten eggs, cream, and dry seasonings. Cook over hot water, but not boiling water. Stir constantly until well-blended. Remove from heat, add Worcestershire sauce. Serve on fresh toast. *4 to 8 servings.*

TOASTED CHEESE SANDWICHES

4 slices cheese or	4 slices buttered bread
8 Tbsp. grated cheese	Paprika

Preheat broiler oven. Remove bread crusts. Place slices of bread on greased cookie sheet. If sliced cheese is used, trim it to fit bread exactly. If grated cheese is used, spread it lightly over entire slice. Place under broiler heat at distance of 3 inches from flame. Cook gently until cheese melts. *4 servings.*

Creamy welsh rarebit over fresh golden-tan toast, unequalled as a Sunday night supper when you've had a heavy midday meal. Serve with colorful fresh salad and beverage.

Colorful cheese ball with crackers and fruit makes a good party-time tempter.

10.

MEATS AND CARVING

AMERICA is a nation of meat lovers. From the lowly "hot dog" to that aristocrat among meats—the rib roast of beef—we enjoy the texture, flavor, aroma and appeal of meat. As meat is the largest single item of expense in the food budget, the homemaker will be well advised to learn everything possible about the buying and care of meat, as well as how to cook it.

GRADING MEAT

The United States Department of Agriculture has set up standards for all fresh meat sold from one state to another. A round purple stamp, marked on the meat itself, assures the shopper that the meat is wholesome. It is sold according to grades, and stamped to indicate these grades.

The Government grades are:

U. S. Prime
U. S. Choice
U. S. Good
U. S. Commercial
U. S. Utility

In addition to the official stamp which the government puts on the meat, packers may add their own private brand name right along with the government's grade stamp.

PRACTICAL HINTS—BUYING BEEF

1. Beef of good quality has clear red flesh. The fat is well "marbled" or streaked, and is smooth, fine-grained and cream-colored. The muscle tissue is firm, the bones clear and hard.
2. Learn the cuts of meat from your butcher. He is invaluable in pointing out the differences in various cuts. The more tender cuts of meat—and therefore the more costly—are more desirable for roasting and broiling. But, for stews and casserole dishes, the less tender—and less expensive—cuts are preferable. The cheapest cuts of all, made up mostly of bone, are still the

best buy for soup-making. Don't forget, meat is weighed before it is trimmed. Take the trimmings home for soup.

CARE OF MEAT

Place uncooked meat in the storage space in the refrigerator as soon as you have it in the house. Remove outer paper, but keep a layer of waxed paper loosely wrapped around meat. When ready to cook, wipe outer surface with clean, damp cloth. Outer skin, or fat, may need to be scrubbed with clean vegetable brush. Never soap meat, nor wash in quantity of water (with the exception of smoked ham). Quick-frozen meats should be allowed to thaw out before outer paper is removed. (See Chapter 24.)

For kosher meat, separate instructions are given in Chapter 29.

BEEF CUTS AND THEIR USES

Tender cuts of beef from the ribs and loin—that is, roasts or steaks—should be cooked by dry heat. Tender beef is served rare, medium or well-done. Less tender cuts of beef should be cooked by moist heat until well-done—that is, pot roasts, braised steaks, stews, and boiling meat. Slow cooking for all cuts of beef will result in more juicy, tender meat.

QUICK COOKING—DRY HEAT

Club Steak	Sirloin Steak
Porterhouse Steak	Standing Rib Roast
Rolled Rib Roast	

SLOWER COOKING CUTS—MOIST HEAT

Round Steak	Stew Meat
Rump Roast	Short Ribs
Flank Steak	Chuck Roast
Brisket	

A standing rib roast of beef. Juicy and tender, served with rich brown gravy, will be a sure success at Sunday dinner or company meals.

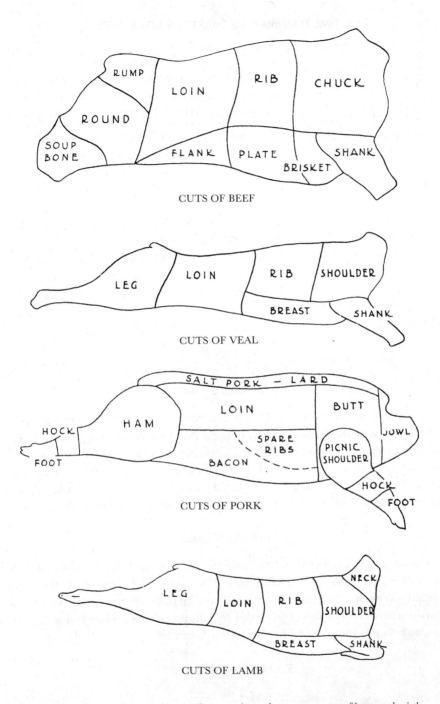

CUTS OF BEEF

CUTS OF VEAL

CUTS OF PORK

CUTS OF LAMB

Meat is no mystery when you know the cuts. Cuts vary in tenderness, amounts of bone and gristle, according to the part of the animal from which they come. These items are reflected in prices. For that reason it will pay you to learn the cuts so that you can name them when you see them. Try to shop at an hour when your butcher is not too busy and can take the time to help you familiarize yourself with meat cuts.

TIME-TEMPERATURE CHART FOR ROAST BEEF

CUT	WEIGHT (in lbs.)	OVEN TEMPERATURE (Fahrenheit)	INTERIOR TEMPERATURE OF FINISHED PRODUCT (Internal Thermometer)		APPROXIMATE TIME PER LB. (in minutes)
Boned and Rolled Ribs.	6-8	300°-325°	140°	rare	32
			160°	medium rare	38
			170°	well done	48
Rib (Standing)	2-8	300°-325°	140°	rare	18-20
			160°	medium rare	22-25
			170°	well done	27-30
One Rib	2-2½	325°-350°	140°	rare	33
			160°	medium rare	45
			170°	well done	50
Tenderloin		300°	140°	rare	20-22
			160°	medium rare	25
Top Round		300°	160°	medium rare	20-25
			170°	well done	30-35

BROILED STEAK

Any cut of tender steak may be selected, preferably cut 1½ to 2 inches thick. Wipe steak with damp cloth and lay on greased rack of broiling oven. Preheat the broiler for 5 to 10 minutes before placing steak under heat. If oven has temperature control set it at 500° F. When steak is seared on top side, sprinkle with salt and pepper. Turn, sear on second side, and sprinkle with salt and pepper. Reduce heat to 350° F. and continue broiling to desired degree of doneness.

MINUTE STEAKS

Minute steaks are cut very thin, and the process used is pan-broiling. Heat the frying pan until sizzling, drop in 1 Tbsp. fat (not butter). Sear the steak quickly on each side; sprinkle with salt and pepper after searing. As soon as steak is seared, reduce heat and cook 1 to 3 minutes longer on each side. Transfer steak to hot plate, add lump of softened butter.

STANDING RIB ROAST

2 or 3 rib roast

Wipe with damp cloth. Place (fat side up) in a roasting pan, in slow oven (300°-325° F.). Do not add water. Roast to the desired doneness, using the previous chart for correct timing, or the internal thermometer.

TIME CHART FOR BROILING BEEF STEAKS

CUT	THICK-NESS (Inches)	WEIGHT in lbs.	APPROXIMATE COOKING TIME IN MINUTES Rare	Medium	ACCOMPANI-MENTS FOR BROILED STEAKS
Club Steak or Delmonico	1	1	15	20	Drawn Butter
	1½	1¼	25	30	
	2	1½	35	45	
Rib Steak	1	1½	15	20	Mushroom
	1½	2	25	30	Sauce
	2	2¼	35	45	
Porterhouse Steak	1	2	20	25	Broiled Mush-
T-Bone Steak	1	2	20	25	rooms
	1½	2½	30	35	
	2	3	40	45	
Sirloin Steak	1	3	20	25	Butter, Pars-
	2	4¼	30	35	ley Garnish
	3	5¾	40	45	
Chuck Steak (good quality)	1	2⅓	25	30	
	1½	4	40	45	
Ground Beef Patties		¼	15	25	Broiled Onions
Filet Mignon or Tenderloin	1½	½	8	10	

ROLLED BEEF ROAST

Select rib, sirloin, or chuck roast; have it boned and rolled at the market. Wipe with damp cloth, rub with 1 tsp. salt and place fat side up on rack in open pan. If the roast has little fat lay a piece of suet or a couple of pieces of salt pork over the top. Process as for standing rib roast, following the previous chart for correct timing and temperature.

RICH BROWN GRAVY

Remove the roast from the pan and place in another pan to stay warm. Skim the fat from the pan. For each cup of gravy required measure 2 Tbsp. of fat. To each 2 Tbsp. of fat add 2 Tbsp. of flour. Blend well until it is a rich brown color. Stir constantly. Stir in 1 cup of cold water (or it may be vegetable juice or part water and part stock). Season with salt and pepper. Return to heat and cook until smooth. Strain through fine sieve.

Three-way pot roast: Using a sharp knife, cut a boneless piece from the round end of the roast for stew meat. (2) From the center, cut a chunky pot roast with the round bone included. (3) Grind the boneless piece left for meat balls or patties.

BROILED BEEF STEAK

The tender cuts are the best for broiling. Sirloin, T-Bone, Porterhouse, Club, and Tenderloin are the most successful. They should be cut approximately 1 to 2 inches think, nicely browned on one side for half the broiling time. Turn and broil on the other side.

POT ROAST

4 lbs. beef—round, chuck or heel	½ tsp. pepper
½ cup flour	¼ cup suet or meat drippings
1 tsp. salt	1 onion, sliced
	1 cup water or vegetable juices

Have butcher tie meat with strong cord to hold it in place. Mix flour, salt, pepper. Wipe meat with cloth and rub well with flour mixture. Heat the fat in a heavy skillet or Dutch oven; brown meat on all sides. Add onion and water. Cover and simmer gently 3 to 4 hours. Turn the meat occasionally. Add more liquid if necessary. Remove meat to hot platter. Remove liquid from pan and skim off excess fat. Make brown gravy as directed.

PHILADELPHIA POT ROAST

4 lbs. beef	4 potatoes
8 onions	8 carrots

Scrub and peel vegetables. Fix meat as for regular pot roast. An hour before meat is finished add onions, potatoes, and carrots. Remove pot roast and vegetables from hot pan and prepare gravy as directed. This method of cooking gives vegetables a delicious flavor, saves fuel and dishwashing.

BRAISING

Cuts of meat that are neither tough nor tender are excellent for braising. The neck, brisket, chuck, plate, rump, heart, liver, and short ribs are all excellent. To braise, brown the meat evenly on all sides in an open skillet on top of the stove before adding liquid. Moderate heat is best for browning, as it preserves the flavor and also keeps the meat from drying out. The meat should be floured before it is braised, for flavor and richness.

BRAISED SHORT RIBS OF BEEF

2 lbs. short ribs of beef, cut	1 onion, sliced
¼ cup flour	¼ tsp. thyme
1 tsp. salt	1 Tbsp. vinegar
1 Tbsp. shortening	2 Tbsp. catsup
½ tsp. pepper	⅓ cup water

Dust each piece of beef with flour seasoned with salt and pepper. Brown in shortening in a heavy skillet. Remove meat to casserole. Place onion, thyme, vinegar, catsup and water in skillet and stir until well-blended. Pour over meat and cover tightly. Roast in slow oven (325° F.) about 2 hours. Potatoes, carrots, onions may be added to taste at end of first hour.

SWISS STEAK

1½ lbs. beef, cut 1 inch thick	1 tsp. salt
¼ cup flour	⅛ tsp. pepper
	2 Tbsp. shortening

Mix flour, salt, and pepper. Pound into both sides of steak with the edge of a saucer. Brown both sides of steak in shortening. Cover with boiling water or meat stock; and simmer slowly on top of stove until tender. Keep tightly covered.

CREOLE SWISS STEAK

1½ lbs. beef, cut 1 inch thick
¼ cup flour
1 tsp. salt
⅛ tsp. pepper

2 cups tomatoes (cooked or canned
3 whole cloves
2 slices onion
Bay leaf

Prepare meat as for Swiss Steak. Pour tomatoes over steak, add boiling water to cover. Add spices and simmer slowly on top of stove until tender. Keep tightly covered.

CASSEROLE OF BEEF

1 lb. beef, cut in inch cubes
4 Tbsp. flour
4 Tbsp. bacon fat
4 potatoes, diced
Boiling water

¾ cup diced carrots
3 slices onion
½ cup turnips, diced
1 tsp. salt
¼ tsp. pepper

Roll the meat in flour, brown in bacon fat; cover with water and simmer slowly 1½ hours, or until almost tender. 30 minutes before meat is done, add vegetables and seasonings and cook slowly until vegetables and meat are tender. Keep tightly covered. Make gravy.

BEEF STEW WITH DUMPLINGS

Proceed as in recipe for Lamb Stew with Rice, with the same quantity of meat and other ingredients. Omit rice. At the end of the simmering period, see that the liquid does not cover the meat, as the dumplings must not be in the stew. They steam on top.

DUMPLINGS

Sift 1½ cups all-purpose flour with 3 tsp. baking powder and ½ tsp. salt. Blend in 2 Tbsp. shortening. Add only sufficient cold water so that dough will hold together. Place on top of stew mixture in large spoonfuls, allowing space between for rising. Boil tightly covered for exactly 12 minutes. The dumplings will be light and just sufficiently flavored with the stew.

GRAVY FOR BEEF STEW

Allow 2 Tbsp. flour for each cup of liquid in the pot. Blend flour with ¼ cup cold water to make a thin paste. Pour the flour paste gradually into the

Beef stew (above left) is the perfect do-ahead one dish meal that simply needs reheating in a handsome chafing dish. Serve it over noodles and accent it with spiced cherries. Plenty of piping hot, strong coffee makes the perfect accompaniment.

Meat pie (above right) appears impressive but is actually nothing more than casserole of beef (or beef stew) covered with dough, and baked to a luscious brown. Flavorful Cheddabits make this tender, easy, and foolproof crust.

Savory sour cream sauce (right) makes distinctive beef rolls. Lay them on a bed of rice and mushrooms, and accompany them with deviled eggs.

stew liquid, stir briskly to avoid lumping. Bring to a boil, cook until thick and smooth.

MEAT PIE

Make casserole of beef; pour into baking dish; cover with crust made of biscuit dough. Bake in hot oven (450° F.) until crust is brown, or about 15 minutes.

ROLLED STUFFED FLANK STEAK

2 lbs. flank steak	¼ tsp. pepper
1 tsp. salt	2 Tbsp. shortening
	½ cup water or tomato juice

Score the steak by cutting it across the grain every inch or two. Wipe meat with a cloth; sprinkle with salt and pepper. Fill with Lancaster stuffing. Roll lightly and fasten with skewers or tie with a string. Melt shortening in iron skillet. Brown the meat on all sides. Place in roasting pan, add liquid, cover and roast in slow oven (300° F.) about 2 hours or until tender.

MEAT LOAF

2 lbs. ground beef
½ lb. ground pork
1 egg, beaten
½ cup milk
1 cup bread crumbs
1 onion, finely chopped
2 tsp. salt
¼ tsp. pepper

Meat loaf, hot or cold, is a star standby for economy meals, also serves as a well-seasoned sandwich meat. Ac'cent improves the flavor. Grinding makes tough meat tender and delicious.

Combine meat, egg, milk, crumbs, seasonings. Mix lightly. Shape into loaf. Bake in greased oblong pan in moderate oven (350° F.) about 1 hour.

CORNED BEEF AND CABBAGE
(New England Boiled Dinner)

2-3 lbs. corned brisket of beef   4 potatoes, peeled
4 carrots   1 medium-sized head of cabbage

Wash corned beef in cold water. Place in a pot, cover with cold water. Simmer until tender, allowing 45 minutes to a lb. About 30 minutes before beef is done, skim off excess fat and add carrots and potatoes, cover and boil. Cook for 10 minutes, add cabbage cut in wedges. Cook uncovered 20 minutes. Place meat on hot platter, drain vegetables, arrange around meat.

BEEF PATTIES
(Hamburger)

1½ lbs. ground meat   ¼ tsp. pepper
2 Tbsp. shortening   1 Tbsp. diced onion
1½ tsp. salt   1 egg, well-beaten

Blend all ingredients together. Form into patties ½ to ¾ inches thick. Melt shortening in skillet. Brown patties on each side, reduce heat and cook slowly until done. Or, place on greased broiler rack, turning only once. Beef patties, like steak, may be served rare, medium or well-done.

BRAISED OXTAIL

2 oxtails, cut at joints	¾ cup canned tomatoes
4 Tbsp. shortening	¾ cup water
½ tsp. salt	8 onions, peeled
¼ tsp. paprika	½ cup celery, diced
½ cup flour	¼ cup carrots, diced

Wipe oxtails with damp cloth. Melt shortening in kettle. Combine salt, paprika and flour. Roll pieces of oxtail in flour. Brown each piece in melted shortening. Bring tomatoes and water to boil. Add vegetables. Pour over browned oxtails in a greased casserole. Cover and simmer slowly for 3 hours. If a thickened gravy is desired, blend 2 Tbsp. flour and 3 Tbsp. cold water for each cup of gravy. Return meat to casserole and serve hot.

STUFFED PEPPERS

4 green peppers	1 Tbsp. olive oil
1 cup beef, ground	1 tsp. butter
1 cup canned tomatoes	Bread crumbs
	Salt and pepper to taste

Cut stems, remove seeds, parboil 2 minutes and drop into cold water. Combine tomatoes and meat with enough crumbs to make a thick stuffing. Heat

Stuffed peppers belong high on the list of quick dishes easily concocted from left-over or canned meat. In addition stuff tomatoes and cabbage, to make a novel stuffed vegetable platter.

stuffing in frying pan with oil and butter, and season to taste. Fill peppers and put into pan just large enough to hold them upright. Pour in 1 cup hot water and bake 20 to 30 minutes.

STUFFED CABBAGE ROLLS

4 large uncooked cabbage leaves
Boiling water

Mixture for Filling

½ lb. beef, ground
¼ cup well-seasoned gravy

1 cup cooked rice
½ tsp. salt
¼ tsp. pepper

Pour the boiling water over the leaves. Let stand for 5 minutes. Drain, smooth out each leaf until it lies flat on wax paper. Combine ingredients for filling. Form into 4 rolls or balls. Place each one on cabbage leaf and roll up. Fasten with toothpicks.

Mixture for Cooking

1 cup canned tomatoes
1 cup consommé

1 or 2 onions, sliced
1 cup sour cream

Line bottom of saucepan with sliced onion. Place cabbage rolls on top, add tomatoes and consommé. Cover tightly. Place over low heat on top of stove and simmer gently until leaves are tender, turn leaves once or twice. Lift out on hot dish. Add sour cream to mixture in saucepan, cook for 1 or 2 minutes. Pour over cabbage rolls.

VEAL

Veal is the meat from young calves. It is light pink in color, firm to the touch and fine-grained, with little fat. Thin strips of salt pork may be used on a veal roast to add the necessary fat. Veal should not be broiled, or pan-fried, or hurried in the cooking. It is a lean meat, and the tissues are apt to be made less tender by high heat. These facts form the basis for veal cookery.

As to veal roasts, 4 to 5 lbs. shoulder, loin or leg cuts make fine roasts—if the meat is given a thorough cooking at a low temperature. Most veal roasts are not cooked enough. It is safer and more satisfactory to roast to an internal temperature of 180° F., instead of the 170° F. indicated on some roast meat thermometers. Since heavy veal resembles beef, 170° F. will mean well-done, but 180° F. will always result in thoroughly cooked veal roast, even when lighter weight veal is used.

Steaks or cutlets from the leg and shoulder, and chops from the loin, should be sliced from ¼ to 1 inch thick. A protective covering of flour or sifted cracker or bread crumbs is called for. Often directions call for "breading" the veal chops. This term means dipping the chops into sifted crumbs, then into a mixture of milk-diluted egg (say 2 Tbsp. of milk per egg). Next, dip the chops into sifted crumbs again. Note should be taken of the term "sifted." Coarse, hard pieces of bread crumbs or flakes of cracker crumbs will never make a fine breaded veal chop or cutlet.

TIME TABLE FOR ROASTING VEAL

ROAST	WEIGHT in lbs.	OVEN TEMPERATURE CONSTANT —Fahrenheit	INTERIOR TEMPERATURE WHEN REMOVED FROM OVEN	APPROXIMATE TIME PER LB. —in minutes
Leg Roast	7-8	300°	180°	25
Loin..........	4½-5	300°	180°	30-35
Rack	2½-3	300°	180°	30-35
Shoulder	7	300°	180°	25
Shoulder, rolled..	5	300°	180°	40-45

TIME TABLE FOR BRAISING VEAL

CUT	AVERAGE WEIGHT OR THICKNESS	APPROXIMATE COOKING TIME
Breast—Stuffed	3-4 lbs.	1½-2 hours
Breast—Rolled........	2-3 lbs.	1½-2 hours
Birds	½ in. x 2 in. x 4 in.	45-60 minutes
Chops	½-¾ inch	45-60 minutes
Chops—Breaded	½-¾ inch	45-60 minutes
Steaks or Cutlets	½-¾ inch	45-60 minutes
Shoulder Chops	½-¾ inch	45-60 minutes

BRAISED VEAL CHOPS

1½ lbs. veal chops (cut ½-¾ inches thick)
¼ cup flour

1 tsp. salt
½ tsp. pepper
4 Tbsp. shortening

Blend flour, salt and pepper together, roll veal chops into flour mixture. Melt shortening in skillet. Add chops and brown on both sides. Reduce heat, add small amount boiling water, cover, and simmer slowly until tender, about 45 minutes.

BREADED VEAL CUTLETS

1½ lb. slice of veal steak	1 Tbsp. water
1 cup cracker crumbs	¼ cup melted shortening
1 tsp salt	½ tsp. celery salt
¼ tsp. pepper	1 tsp. Worcestershire sauce
1 egg, well-beaten	1 cup tomato sauce

Add salt and pepper to crumbs. Beat egg and water together. Dip steak into crumbs, then into egg, and back again into crumbs. Melt shortening in skillet, add veal steak and brown on both sides. Reduce heat. Combine celery salt, Worcestershire sauce and tomato sauce, pour over veal. Cover, and simmer slowly until tender, about 45 minutes.

STUFFED BREAST OF VEAL

2-3 lb. boned veal breast (with pocket cut at market)	Parsley stuffing
	4 strips bacon or salt pork
	1 cup boiling water

Stuff pocket of breast of veal with parsley stuffing. Close opening with skewers or by sewing. Place on rack in roasting pan. Lay strips of bacon or salt pork over the top. Add 1 cup boiling water and bake in moderate oven (325° F.) allowing 35 minutes per lb. Make gravy from drippings.

VEAL BIRDS

1 slice veal (1½ lbs., cut thin)	4 Tbsp. shortening
Parsley stuffing	1 cup boiling water

Pound veal very thin and cut into pieces approximately 4 inches long by 2 inches wide. Spread a spoonful of stuffing in the center of each slice of cutlet. Roll up meat and fasten each roll with string. Roll birds in flour. Melt shortening in heavy skillet and brown meat on all sides. Add water, cover and simmer slowly 40 to 50 minutes. Remove to hot plate and make brown gravy.

JELLIED VEAL

2 lbs. shoulder veal	2 cups celery, diced
1 knuckle of veal	1 green pepper, diced
1 bay leaf	2 hard-cooked eggs, diced
2 Tbsp. vinegar	1 cup cooked peas
1 tsp. salt	1 Tbsp. gelatin
	¼ cup cold water

Put veal and knuckle, bay leaf, vinegar and salt in kettle. Cover with cold water. Simmer until tender, strain. Measure 1 pt. stock. Dice meat, add celery, pepper, eggs, peas, and arrange in rinsed ring mold. Soften gelatin in cold water and add to hot meat stock. Pour carefully over ingredients in mold and chill until firm. Unmold and serve with mayonnaise on crisp lettuce.

BLANQUETTE OF VEAL

1 lb. shoulder veal	1 Tbsp. flour
½ tsp. salt	¼ lb. fresh mushrooms
1 small onion, stuck with 2 cloves	8 small onions (parboiled)
½ carrot	1 egg yolk
¼ tsp. thyme	Juice of ½ lemon
2 sprigs parsley	Dash of pepper
2 Tbsp. butter	¼ tsp. nutmeg
	1 cup white rice

Cut meat in small pieces and trim off gristle and bone. Cover with cold water, add salt, and bring slowly to a boil. Skim. Add onion, carrot, thyme, parsley. Cover, simmer 1½ hours. Melt butter, add flour. Cook until bubbly, add stock from meat. Cover over low heat 5 minutes. Slice mushrooms and add to sauce. Add onions, meat and seasonings. Cook 15 minutes. Add small amount of gravy to slightly beaten egg yolk, mix well. Return to meat mixture, add lemon juice, pepper, nutmeg. Boil rice, drain, and arrange in ring around edge of platter. Fill center with meat and sauce.

VEAL-HAM LOAF

2 lbs. raw veal	1 cup fine cracker crumbs
1 lb. smoked raw ham	2 Tbsp. prepared mustard
2 eggs, unbeaten	¼ tsp. pepper

Grind meats together three times. Add other ingredients and mix thoroughly. Place in greased oblong casserole. Bake in moderate oven (350° F.) 2 hours. Strips of bacon may be added to top of loaf before baking. Serve with cream of mushroom sauce.

LAMB AND MUTTON

Lamb is the flesh of the young sheep; mutton is the flesh of the mature sheep. Mutton is firmer and deeper in color than lamb, but both are fine-grained and reddish pink in color. The fat is firm and white, but mutton fat is darker. "Spring lamb" is the meat from lambs 3 to 5 months old.

LAMB CUTS

Roasting: Choose leg, loin of lamb, or rack. Shoulder may be roasted if it is boned and rolled.

Braising: Shoulder, breast, neck.

Broiling: Loin and rib lamb chops are more popular selections, but shoulder lamb chops are good value.

Stew: Shoulder, shank, breast, neck.

Lamb is NEVER served rare.

TIME TABLE FOR ROASTING LAMB

ROAST	WEIGHT in lbs.	OVEN TEM- PERATURE CONSTANT —Fahrenheit	INTERIOR TEMPERATURE WHEN REMOVED FROM OVEN	APPROXIMATE TIME PER LB. —in minutes
Leg	6½-7½	300°	175°-180°	30-35
Shoulder (rolled)	3-4	300°	175°-180°	40-45
Shoulder	4½-5½	300°	175°-180°	30-35

TIME TABLE FOR BROILING LAMB

CUT	WEIGHT in lbs.	TEMPERATURE Fahrenheit	APPROXIMATE COOKING TIME (Minutes)
Shoulder chop			
1 inch	3 oz.	350°	12
1½ inches	6 oz.	350°	18
2 inches	10 oz.	350°	22
Rib chop			
1 inch	2 oz.	350°	12
1½ inches	4 oz.	350°	18
2 inches	5 oz.	350°	22
Loin chop			
1 inch	3 oz.	350°	12
1½ inches	5 oz.	350°	18
2 inches	6 oz.	350°	22
Ground meat patties			
(1x3 in.)	4 oz.	350°	18

Broiled lamb chops, especially when flavored with Ac'cent, are favorites with all the family; both at home and on a picnic.

BROILED LAMB CHOPS

Choose:
    Loin chops
      or
    Rib chops
      or

Shoulder chops
    or
French chops
Salt
Pepper

Have chops cut 1-2 inches thick. (If loin chops are used, wrap flank end around tenderloin, and fasten with a toothpick.) Preheat broiling oven (350°

F.). Place chops on center of broiler rack so that top of meat comes 3 inches below flame or electric element. Broil on one side and turn to broil on the other side. Follow broiling chart.

IRISH STEW

2 lbs. lamb diced in 2 inch sq.
  (forequarter of lamb or neck)
1 onion, diced
2 Tbsp. shortening
3 cups potatoes, diced

1 cup carrots, diced
1 cup turnips, diced
¼ cup flour
¼ cup cold water
1 tsp. salt
⅛ tsp. pepper

Fry onion in shortening. Wash and dry meat; brown meat in pan with butter and onion. Put in a kettle with boiling water and cook slowly for 1½ to 2 hours. ½ hour before serving add potatoes, carrots, turnips and cook slowly. Make a thickening of flour and water. Pour a bit of the hot juice into the flour thickening, and pour this over the stew. Season with salt and pepper.

Roast leg of lamb, with its outside moist and brown, and with thin slivers of garlic tucked into the fat, is sure to give eating pleasure.

ROAST LEG OF LAMB

6 to 7 lb. leg of lamb
1 tsp. salt

½ tsp. pepper
1 clove of garlic

Choose leg of lamb according to size and quality. Leave the fell (thin parchment-like cover) on leg of lamb. Wipe meat with damp cloth. Sprinkle with salt and pepper. Leg may be rubbed with cut clove of garlic for extra flavor, and thin slivers of garlic inserted into fat. Place, fell side up, on rack in roasting pan. Roast uncovered in moderate oven (350° F.). Allow 30 minutes per lb. Fell may be removed before serving.

STUFFED SHOULDER OF LAMB

3 to 4 lb. shoulder of lamb	1 tsp. salt
1 to 2 cups parsley stuffing	½ tsp. pepper

Have shoulder of lamb boned at market, and fell removed. Wipe meat with damp cloth, sprinkle with salt and pepper. Prepare stuffing. Fill cavity of lamb with stuffing. Skewer edges together. Place on rack in roasting pan. Roast uncovered in moderate oven (350° F.). Allow 30 minutes per lb.

LAMB EN CASSEROLE

3 cups cooked diced lamb	8 small cooked onions
2 Tbsp. shortening	1 cup water
1 cup cooked diced carrots	1 cup leftover gravy
1 cup cooked potato balls	1 tsp. salt
	¼ tsp. pepper

Brown lamb in shortening, then put it in baking dish. Add carrots, potato balls and onions. Add leftover gravy and water to moisten. Season with salt and pepper. Cover and bake in hot oven (400° F.) 20 to 25 minutes.

SHEPHERD'S PIE

Chop cold leftover lamb into small pieces, and moisten with leftover gravy. Dot with small pieces of butter, and cover with hot mashed potatoes. Spread top with beaten egg yolk mixed with 2 tsp. of cold water. Bake in hot oven (400° F.) 20 minutes or until brown. This is an excellent way to use the leftover leg of lamb from Sunday's dinner.

LAMB STEW WITH RICE

2½ lbs. shoulder of lamb	3 stalks celery, chopped
3 Tbsp. flour	1 onion, sliced
3 Tbsp. salad oil	½ cup raw rice
	1 Tbsp. parsley, minced fine

Cut the meat in 1½ inch cubes, roll lightly in salted flour, and sauté in the oil in a large kettle. Leave the meat in the kettle, add celery and onion. Add boiling water to cover, simmer 2 hours, adding salt any time after the first

A stuffed pork shoulder roast changes flavor and appearance with a creamy piquant sauce.

half hour. Keep covered tightly. Turn up the heat to boiling point, add the rice, stir thoroughly, cover and boil gently for 20 minutes. At the end of that time the rice should be done, and will have absorbed practically all the liquid. Serve as one-dish meal. Garnish with parsley. Diced carrots and peas may be cooked separately and placed on top of dish before serving.

PORK

Pork is the meat from hogs, and is selected from comparatively young animals. The flesh is fine-grained, firm to the touch and well-covered with fat. Pork requires long cooking, at low temperature, to develop its best flavor. High temperature melts the fat. Pork is more versatile than the other meat animals. Some of the cuts are desirable cooked fresh, but other cuts are best when smoked. For example: smoked ham, bacon, picnic shoulder, ham butt.

FRESH PORK CUTS

Roasting: Ham, tenderloin, loin shoulder and spareribs are excellent roasting cuts.
Pan-frying: Chops from shoulder, rib and loin.
Braising: Chops, tenderloin and spareribs are all good braising cuts.

TIME TABLE FOR ROASTING PORK

ROAST	WEIGHT in lbs.	OVEN TEMPERATURE Fahrenheit	INTERIOR TEMPERATURE WHEN REMOVED FROM OVEN	APPROXIMATE TIME PER LB. minutes
Fresh Pork Loin				
Center............	3-4	350°	185°	35-40
Whole...........	12-15		185°	15-20
Ends	3-4		185°	45-50
Shoulder				
Whole...........	12-14	350°	185°	30-35
Boned and rolled...	4-6		185°	40-45
Cushion	4-6		185°	35-40
Butt................	4-6	350°	185°	45-50
Ham	10-12	350°	185°	30-35
Smoked Pork				
Ham				
Whole..........	10-12	300°	185°	25
Half............	6	300°	170°	30
Tendered	6	300°	160°	20
Shank end	3	300°	170°	40
Butt end	3	300°	170°	45
Cottage butt.......	2-4	300°	170°	35
Picnic	3-10	300°	170°	35

TIME TABLE FOR BROILING PORK

MEAT	WEIGHT in lbs.	APPROXIMATE TIME PER LB. minutes
Ham slice		
½ inch	¾ to 1	20-well done
1 inch	1½ to 2	25-30
Ham sliced (tendered)		
½ inch	¾ to 1	10-12
1 inch	1½ to 2	16-20
Bacon		4-5

ROAST FRESH PORK

4 to 5 lbs. boneless loin roast or   1 tsp. salt
    roast with rib ends "Frenched"   ½ tsp. pepper

Season with salt and pepper and place in open roasting pan—the boneless roast on rack, or the French style roast with rib ends down. Roast uncovered in moderate oven (350° F.) 35 minutes per lb., or to an internal temperature of 185° F.

BONED STUFFED SHOULDER OF PORK

3 to 4 lb. shoulder of pork   ½ cup raisins
1 to 2 cups bread stuffing   2 tsp. prepared mustard

Have shoulder of pork boned at market. Prepare stuffing, add raisins and mustard. Fill cavity of pork with stuffing. Skewer edges together. Place on rack in roasting pan. Roast uncovered in moderate oven (350° F.). Allow 35 minutes per lb.

BROILED PORK CHOPS

Pork chops (cut ¾ to 1 inch thick)

Preheat broiling oven (350° F.). Cut edge of pork chops in 2 or 3 places to prevent curling. Place on broiler rack 3 inches below direct heat. Broil 10 minutes on one side and 10 minutes on the other side.

STUFFED PORK CHOPS

4 double-thick pork chops (with pocket)
1 cup parsley stuffing

Have butcher cut loin pork chops 1½ inches thick and slit each chop to bone to form pocket for stuffing. Fill each pocket with parsley stuffing. Fasten edges with skewers. Broil as above.

RITZY PORK CHOPS

4 double-thick pork chops
1 14-oz. tin cream of mushroom soup

Have butcher cut loin pork chops 1½ inches thick. Place in well-greased round baking pan. Cover with soup and bake covered in slow oven (300° F.) 3 hours. Chops will absorb flavor of soup. (For a planned oven meal, bake potatoes in oven at same time, also a pan of apples.)

PORK CHOPS WITH CORN STUFFING

4 rib or loin pork chops, cut 1 inch thick	½ tsp. salt
	¼ tsp. pepper
	Corn stuffing

Make a pocket in each pork chop by cutting into the chop along the bone. Chops cut from this side hold the stuffing better. Fill the pockets with corn stuffing. Brown chops on both sides, cover and finish cooking slowly on top of the range for about 1 hour. Make cream gravy from drippings.

CORN STUFFING

1 cup whole kernel corn	½ tsp. salt
½ cup cracker crumbs	¼ tsp. pepper

Combine corn, cracker crumbs and seasonings. Mix well, and stuff chops with mixture.

BROILED BACON

Place bacon on cold broiler rack, and brown under flame (350° F.) about 4 minutes, turn once.

PAN-BROILED BACON

Place bacon in cold heavy iron skillet. Cook over low flame until browned and crisp, pouring off fat as it accumulates. Do not let bacon smoke. Drain slices on paper toweling and serve.

BARBECUED SPARERIBS

2 lbs. spareribs	½ tsp. paprika
1 onion, sliced	¼ tsp. red pepper
1 Tbsp. vinegar	¼ tsp. black pepper
1 Tbsp. Worcestershire sauce	1 tsp. chili powder
2 tsp. salt	⅓ cup catsup
	⅓ cup water

Place spareribs in roaster with sliced onion. Make a sauce of vinegar, Worcestershire sauce, salt, paprika, red pepper, black pepper, chili powder, catsup and water. Pour over spareribs. Cover and bake in moderate oven (350° F.) about 1½ hours. Baste occasionally. Turn spareribs once or twice. During the last 15 minutes remove the cover and brown the spareribs.

BAKED SPARERIBS AND SAUERKRAUT

2 lbs. spareribs	1 tsp. salt
1 qt. sauerkraut and juice	½ tsp. pepper

Put sauerkraut in center of baking dish. Place spareribs in baking dish. Sprinkle with salt and pepper. Add water if necessary, to keep spareribs and kraut moist. Bake in hot oven (400° F.) until nicely browned. Baste spareribs frequently with sauerkraut juice. Turn spareribs so they brown on both sides.

Baked ham with cloves is breathtakingly good.

SMOKED HAM

BAKED SMOKED HAM—REGULAR

Tenderized hams are branded, and directions for preparing them are printed on labels. If the ham is not tenderized—or if it is home-cured ham—it is wise to soak it overnight, or for several hours, in cold water to cover. Drain. Cook, covered, in simmering water to cover until tender, approximately 25 to 30 minutes per lb. Remove skin, score fat, rub with sugar, decorate with cloves. Brown in oven.

To bake tenderized or regular ham, place fat side up on rack in open roasting pan and roast in moderate oven (350° F.) until done (internal temperature

160° F. for tenderized ham or 170° F. for regular ham), allowing 25 minutes per lb. About 45 minutes before ham is done, take from fire and carefully remove skin. Score the surface in squares or diamonds. Cover with one of these glazes for baked ham:

1.	1 cup honey	¼ cup brown sugar
	¼ cup fruit syrup	½ tsp. cinnamon

Blend honey, sugar, cinnamon, fruit syrup together. Pour over scored ham. In each square place a whole clove. Continue baking for 30 minutes.

2.	1 cup brown sugar	2 Tbsp. flour
		1 cup fruit juice or cider

Cover scored ham with blended sugar and flour. Baste with fruit juice. Continue baking for 30 minutes.

Each one of the following recipes makes approximately *4 servings.*

HAM CUTLETS WITH APPLE RINGS

2—½ inch slices of smoked ham	½ cup pineapple juice
4 Tbsp. brown sugar	2 apples, unpeeled
2 Tbsp. bread crumbs	2 Tbsp. shortening
	1 cup water

Cut each slice of ham in half. Parboil in simmering water 10 minutes. Arrange in baking pan and cover each piece with brown sugar and bread crumbs. Pour pineapple juice over all. Bake uncovered in moderate oven (350° F.) 25 minutes. Fry cored red apple in slices in fat until light brown in color. Serve on top of each slice of ham.

ESCALLOPED HAM AND POTATOES

1 slice smoked ham cut about 1 inch thick	1 tsp. salt
	½ tsp. pepper
4 large potatoes, pared and sliced thin	½ grated onion
	2 Tbsp. butter or margarine
	2 cups milk

Place in greased pan one layer of thinly sliced potatoes. Sprinkle with salt and pepper and a bit of onion. Dot with butter or margarine. Add another layer of potatoes, seasoning, shortening and repeat until all the ingredients are used. Pour milk over the top. Lay ham on top. Bake in moderate oven (350° F.) about 1 to 1½ hours, or until potatoes are tender.

HAM LOAF

⅔ lb. smoked ham, ground	2 eggs, beaten
1⅓ lbs. fresh pork, ground	1 cup milk
1 cup fine cracker crumbs	⅓ cup brown sugar
¼ tsp. pepper	1 Tbsp. mustard (dry)
	¼ cup vinegar

Combine meat, cracker crumbs, pepper, eggs, milk. Mix thoroughly and form into a loaf. Put on a rack in open roasting pan. Mix sugar, mustard and vinegar into a paste and spread over loaf. Bake in moderate oven (350° F.) 1 hour. Ham loaf sliced cold is an excellent sandwich filling.

Another covering for ham loaf: Cover loaf with sliced lemon, pour over 2 cups canned tomatoes, 1 cup tomato catsup, bake as directed.

CASSEROLE OF HAM AND RICE

1 cup cold cooked ham, minced	1 tsp. dry mustard
2 cups cold cooked rice	¼ cup soft bread crumbs
1 cup thin white sauce	Butter for topping

Grease a round casserole on bottom and sides. Cover bottom with alternate layers of rice and ham. Add mustard to white sauce and stir until well-blended. Add to ingredients in casserole. Sprinkle top with bread crumbs and dabs of butter. Bake in a moderate over (375° F.) 15 to 20 minutes.

PAN-FRIED SAUSAGE PATTIES

Shape sausage meat into patties. Preheat a heavy frying pan, place patties in pan. Reduce heat to moderate and cook for about 15 minutes or until nicely browned on both sides. Pour off excess fat. Serve hot.

SAUSAGE WITH APPLE

1 lb. sausage meat	2 Tbsp. sugar
2 lbs. tart apples	¼ tsp. cinnamon
	¼ tsp. salt

Pan-broil sausage as usual in little cakes. Then remove from the pan to the upper part of a double boiler. Cover closely and keep water in lower part simmering gently. If fat in pan is more than ¼ inch deep, pour off and save for drippings. Quarter and core unpeeled tart apples. Lay apples in the sausage pan, sprinkle with the sugar, cinnamon and salt; add 1 Tbsp. water. Stir the

Ham banana rolls bring taste variety to your menu. Wrap each banana in boiled ham slice lightly touched with mustard. Brush banana tips with golden melted butter. Place rolls in shallow baking dish and add cheese sauce. Baking time: 30 minutes in moderate oven (350° F.).

apples carefully, scraping up any brown crumbs from the pan, then blend the fat and the seasonings with the fruit. Cover closely and steam over a low fire until the apples are tender, adding a little more water if necessary. This will usually be about ½ hour. Stir occasionally. Serve on a hot plate with the sausage—which will delight you after its extra cooking.

SAUSAGE CASSEROLE

4 apples	1 cup water
16 cloves	¼ tsp. cinnamon
¼ cup white sugar	¼ tsp. nutmeg
¼ cup brown sugar	1 No. 2 can hominy
	16 to 20 sausages

Wash apples, core, cut in half crosswise. Stick 2 cloves in each. Place in baking pan. Mix sugar, water, spices, bring to a boil and pour over apples in hot oven. Bake (400° F.) 15 minutes before putting in sausages and hominy. Place drained canned hominy in greased casserole. Set a wire cake rack over it, lay sausages on the rack. Reduce heat (350° F.) and bake 30 minutes, until sausages are brown. Sausages should be turned once during baking. Serve on a platter with sausages on the hominy in the center, and apples around the edge.

LIVER AND BACON

¼ lb. bacon	¼ cup flour
1 lb. liver	1 tsp. salt
	½ tsp. pepper

Fry bacon in heavy skillet. Pour off excess fat. Combine flour, salt and pepper. Dust liver in flour and brown slowly on both sides in bacon drippings. Serve with slices of bacon on top of liver.

BEEF KIDNEY STEW

2 beef kidneys	1 small onion, diced
2 Tbsp. flour	2 cups carrots, diced
2 tsp. salt	1 tsp. Worcestershire sauce
¼ tsp. pepper	3 medium-sized potatoes, diced
2 Tbsp. shortening	1 cup stewed tomatoes
2 cups water	½ tsp. paprika

Wash kidneys in cold water. Soak 1½ hours, drain. Pour boiling water over them to blanch. Remove tubes, skins and any hard pieces. Sprinkle with flour, salt and pepper. Sauté kidneys in shortening in heavy skillet until brown. Add water, onions and carrots. Cover and cook slowly 30 minutes. Add Worcestershire sauce, potatoes, tomatoes, salt, paprika. Cover and cook until tender.

STUFFED HEART

1 heart (preferably beef or veal, large enough for 4 people)	1 tsp. salt
Lancaster or mushroom stuffing (Chapter 11)	½ tsp. pepper
	1 Tbsp. shortening
½ cup flour	¼ cup water
	½ cup wine

Wash heart thoroughly under warm running water. Soak in wine or vinegar for ½ hour. Stuff with dressing, fasten with skewers. Mix flour, salt and pepper together. Brown evenly on all sides in fat. Put the heart on a rack in the roaster, add liquid. Cover tightly and cook in slow oven (325° F.) until tender, about 2 to 3 hours.

TONGUE

Tongues are used fresh, corned, smoked or pickled. They are always cooked in water. Scrub the tongue, and if it is corned or smoked, soak it 2 hours in cold water. If tongue is fresh, add 1 tsp. salt for each qt. of water, and put it in kettle with sufficient water to cover. Cover the kettle, and simmer until tongue is tender (3 to 4 hours). Remove tongue from hot water, plunge into cold water to loosen skin, then remove skin and cut away roots. Cool tongue in the cooking water. Tongue may be served hot with currant jelly, and cold tongue makes an excellent meat for sandwiches.

SWEETBREADS

Sweetbreads are the thymus glands of lamb or calf—but in cookery we consider only the sweetbreads of the calf. To prepare, plunge into cold water

For special occasions use a variety of breads and rolls and serve the sandwiches on colorful plates.

For indoor and outdoor parties the "big" loaf lends itself to infinite variations. For a hot sandwich, wrap in foil and heat in the oven or over outdoor grill.

For Ghost 'Burgers, cut faces from cheese slices and place one over each hamburger, then heat in a moderate oven until cheese starts to soften.

and let stand for 1 hour. Drain, put into salted boiling water. To each qt. of water, add 2 Tbsp. lemon juice or vinegar. Cook slowly 20 minutes. Drain and plunge into cold water.

CREAMED SWEETBREADS

1 pair sweetbreads	1 tsp. salt
1 can cream of mushroom soup	¼ tsp. pepper

Prepare sweetbreads as directed. Cut up into small pieces. Add cream of mushroom soup, salt and pepper. Heat thoroughly and serve on buttered toast.

BRAINS

Soak brains in cold water for ½ hour. Remove all membrane. Simmer in water to cover for 15 minutes, adding 1 Tbsp. vinegar or lemon juice and 1 tsp. salt for each qt. of water. Cool, and prepare in one of following ways:

1. Combine with medium white sauce
2. Dip in egg and bread crumbs. Sauté in hot fat or deep fat (355° to 375° F.).
3. Brush with melted butter and broil.
4. Combine with chicken, or veal, in medium white sauce to which mushrooms have been added.

CARVING—A FINE ART

The dictionary says, "Carve: to cut, especially in an artistic manner; to shape by cutting." But the art of carving a roast is much more important than cutting "in an artistic manner." We have learned, through centuries of civilization, that the appearance of food is important, and that properly cut meat tastes immeasurably better than hacked-up pieces.

The art of carving is simple. The requirements for success are only a few essential tools and a few basic serving pieces. For example, the carver needs to have the roast on a platter large enough so that he can cut the meat efficiently. Incidentally, elaborate garnishes, large ornamental fruit or vegetable displays are out of place on a meat platter, no matter how pretty they may look in a picture. The platter may be china or silver, but it should be heated before the appetizing hot roast is placed on it. The cook should see to it that skewers and cords are removed before the roast is carried to the table. The exception is a rolled roast where skewers are needed to keep it in shape. The dinner plates, also preheated, are placed at the carver's right. Arguments wax hot and furious as to whether the host should stand or sit when he carves. The majority of men prefer to stand. And after all, why shouldn't they? A carver who knows his cut of meat presents an impressive picture of dignity and hospitality as he stands at the head of the table.

When the original carving set is purchased, let its quality be of the best. The knife should have a curved point. The carving fork has one mission in life, and only one: to hold the juicy roast in place so it doesn't go skittering off onto the table cloth. The sharpening steel included in a carving set gives the knife its fine edge just before the roast is carved. Above all, use the carving knife for carving—and for nothing else. And take the job of carving calmly, as if it were an everyday occurrence.

CARVING A STANDING RIB ROAST

The meat market usually removes the short ribs when the roast is purchased, in order to simplify carving. For this process, the roast is placed on a large platter, with rib sides to left of carver.

1. Plunge fork between two top ribs. Insert carving knife at the far outside edge and slice across grain towards ribs.
2. Still holding fork in place, cut close along rib with tip of knife blade to release slice.
3. Lift each slice after cutting, and place on hot serving plate at side.

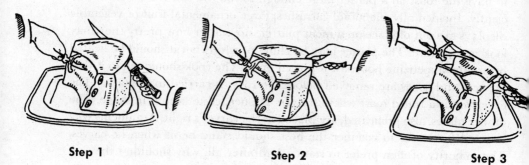

Step 1   **Step 2**   **Step 3**

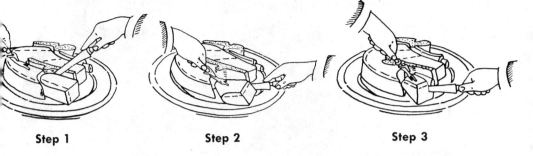

Step 1   **Step 2**   **Step 3**

CARVING BLADE POT ROAST

The blade of beef contains part of one rib and a portion of the blade bone. As pot roasts are cooked by long, moist heat, bones slip out easily before roast is served.

1. Plunge fork into pot roast at the left, and run carving knife between two muscles.
2. Turn section just separated, so that grain of meat is parallel with platter, in order to cut slices across grain.
3. Hold the section of meat firmly with fork and cut slices ¼ inch thick.

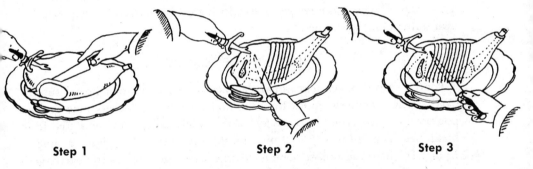

Step 1   **Step 2**   **Step 3**

CARVING ROAST LEG OF LAMB

Place the leg of lamb so that the shank bone is at the right of carver, and the cushion or thick meaty section is on the far side of platter.

1. Plunge carving fork into large end of leg. Carve a few lengthwise slices from the near thin side.
2. Turn roast onto surface just cut, with shank bone upwards. Insert fork in left of roast. Start at shank end and cut each slice clean down to leg bone. (Lamb slices are more appetizing if cut thin, about ¼ inch thickness.)
3. Do not remove fork, but continue to grasp it firmly, and at the same time run the carving knife along the leg bone until slice of meat is free.

11.

POULTRY

AND

STUFFINGS

"A CHICKEN in Every Pot" was coined as a political slogan in our country. Poultry is such a versatile food that the slogan could easily be changed to read "A Chicken, Duck, or Turkey in Every Pot, Roaster, or Casserole." The variety of dishes which may be made from one kind of bird is infinite. This chapter offers basic recipes from which each homemaker may create her own individual "specialties."

SELECTION OF POULTRY

Poultry is no longer a seasonal delicacy, dependent upon heavy supply. Cold storage methods, quick-freezing, and deep-freeze lockers now give us poultry the year 'round. Look for birds which are plump and free from blemishes. Young birds (5 to 9 months old) are best for roasting, broiling or frying. In these the breast bone is flexible when pressed, as the cartilage is soft; the skin is smooth; the feet are soft. For birds still young but beyond the roaster stage, braising in a casserole is best. For birds full grown, long slow cooking in water or steam is the only way to insure tenderness right through to the bone. Always ask poultry man to remove leg tendons if bird is to be roasted.

PREPARATION OF POULTRY

The farm home which is lucky enough to enjoy its own fresh-killed poultry also has to dress and draw the poultry. City dwellers find that poultry is sold already dressed and drawn, but the weight is figured before the vital organs are removed. This is termed "drawing." The head and feet are then

132

cut off, and the bird split or disjointed, if the type of cooking to be employed calls for that.

The following steps in the preparation of poultry may differ in some respects from the preparation used in kosher cooking. For those who observe the kosher dietary rules, see Chapter 29 in addition to the general procedure given here.

Singeing: The first step in preparation is to examine for hairs. Hold the bird over direct heat, and turn so that hairs are burned off.

Cleaning: Hold bird under cold running water, then wipe thoroughly with paper toweling. Remove lungs, also tiny oil sac which lies directly above tail. Pull out any large pinfeathers with knife blade or tweezers. If bird is left whole for roasting, stuff cavity with paper toweling to absorb any excess moisture.

Stuffing: After the preliminary steps of singeing and cleaning the bird are carried out, the neck is cut off and set aside to be cooked with giblets. The stuffing is prepared according to your favorite recipe, and the neck cavity is filled loosely, then the body cavity. The stuffing expands during cooking, so it is important to allow room for swelling during the roasting process. A heavy needle and coarse thread are necessary to sew up the openings at the neck and vent, or the loose skin may be folded over and fastened with metal skewers.

Trussing: The bird is trussed to keep it in neat shape while cooking. Fold the tip of each wing under the wing joint, or cut off the tip and fasten the wing flat with skewers. Tie the wings down, then pull back the skin of the neck and fasten it with toothpicks. Tie ends of legs together with stout twine, bring twine down beneath body and up over tips of wings, tie across back in any method that is satisfactory, just so wings and legs are held securely in place.

Giblets: The giblets are the liver, gizzard and heart. Near the liver is a green ball known as the gall bladder. Remove it whole from the liver, because if its contents come in contact with the meat, they will give it a bitter flavor. Remove all the fat from the gizzard, then cut through the thick outer muscle and turn the gizzard inside out, discarding the inner sack. Remove the fat, cut arteries and veins from it, and wash in cold water. Place gizzard in saucepan, cover with cold water, simmer 10 minutes; add heart, cook 10 minutes longer; add liver, pinch of salt, part of bay leaf, bit of onion. Cook until liver is tender. Strain, use for gravy; chop heart and liver and add to gravy.

PRINCIPLES OF MODERN POULTRY COOKING

Use only a moderate temperature to cook birds of all kinds and ages, because poultry is toughened by intense heat. Though it takes longer to cook

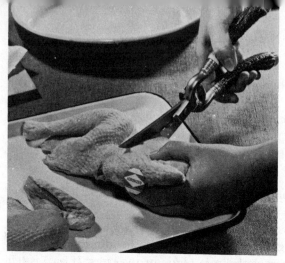

Poultry shears with serrated blade and notched cutter for tackling bones make quick work of disjointing a fowl.

at moderate temperature, the bird shrinks less and so there is actually more meat to serve—also more juice and flavor. Vary the cooking method according to the age and fatness of the bird.

CARVING A ROAST BIRD

A carver should study the anatomy of the bird before he even starts. Provide a large platter for him, and avoid garnishes and trimmings. See that his knife is sharp, and that he is equipped with a fork, sharpener, and serving spoon. He should then proceed as follows:

Plunge carving fork directly through breastbone, grasping it firmly in left hand. Hold knife in right hand, and carve second joint and leg away from body. Place on a separate plate. Separate leg from second joint. Cut wing away from body and place on plate. Now slice the breast meat down close to bone, in neat lengthwise slices. Next, turn bird and carve other side in same manner.

TIPS ON ROASTING

A shallow, uncovered pan is best for roasting a young bird. Place a rack under the bird, in order to keep it from sticking to pan and allow hot air to circulate. Steaming breaks the skin and forces juice out of the meat, so do not add water to pan. Begin the cooking, breast down, so that the fat on the back will melt, ready for basting. For even browning, turn the bird occasionally, placing it breast up part of the time. The parts standing highest in the oven cook more quickly than those next to the rack. Baste frequently. Many cooks prefer to cover the exposed parts of the bird with a double layer of cheesecloth which has been dipped in melted butter. If this is kept moist with butter or pan-drippings, it is necessary to turn the bird only once, about ¾ hour before it is finished. At this point, turn it breast-side up, and put the cloth over the breast, moistening well with fat. Remove cloth ten minutes before taking bird from oven. The skin will be delicately browned, the meat deliciously juicy and tender.

ROAST CHICKEN OR CAPON

A capon is an unsexed male, 6 to 10 months of age. Select a chicken or capon of the size desired. Singe, clean, stuff and truss. Figure about 1 cup of stuffing to 1 lb. of poultry.

1 chicken (3½-4 lbs.)	1 tsp. salt
3 Tbsp. butter	½ tsp. pepper

Rub outside of bird with butter. Sprinkle with salt and pepper. Roast in moderate oven (350° F.). Cook poultry until it is tender and done to the bone. When done, the thick portions of the flesh and thigh do not show pink juice when carefully speared with fork. The joints move easily. The time table suggested is average. Small birds require more minutes per lb. than do larger birds.

ROAST TURKEY

Roast turkey is prepared and cooked in precisely the same manner as roast chicken. See time table for roasting.

A traditional Thanksgiving feast focuses on a tender, golden-brown turkey with cranberry garnish.

TIME TABLE FOR ROASTING YOUNG BIRDS

BIRD	DRESSED WEIGHT OF BIRDS (lbs.)	OVEN TEMPERATURE Fahrenheit	TIME hours
Capon	4-5	350°	1½-2
Chicken............	4-5	350°	1½-2
Duck	5-6	350°	2-2½
Turkey.............	6-9	325°	2½-3
	10-13	300°	3½-4½
	14-17	275°	5-6
	18-23	250°-275°	6½-7½
	24-20	250°	8-9

TIPS ON STEWING

Old birds may be stewed or steamed, either whole or in pieces. To stew whole, place the bird on a rack in a kettle, and add boiling salted water to cover. Turn the bird occasionally to insure even cooking, and simmer—do not boil. To steam whole, place the bird breast side up, and add water only to level of rack. The meat is juicier if allowed to cool in the broth for 1 hour or more. Cool quickly, because warm broth spoils easily. Save liquid, usually called "stock," for gravy or sauce.

TIME TABLE FOR BROILING

BIRD	DRESSED WEIGHT OF BIRD (lbs.)	TIME minutes
Chicken......................	2	35-45
Turkey......................	4	60-75
Squab	¾-1	30-40
Duckling	2-2½	35-45

BROILED CHICKEN

Choose young, tender, well-fatted birds. They may be split down the back only, and cooked whole. Larger birds are split down the back and breast-bone, so that each half makes one serving. Keep heat of broiler moderate for consistent, even cooking, and keep the bird several inches away from heat. Wipe chicken dry, brush skin side with melted shortening or salad oil. Sprinkle with salt and pepper. Place chicken on rack of broiler pan, skin side down. As chicken begins to brown, baste with melted fat as it collects in bottom of pan. Turn several times during cooking process. Or chicken may be started under broiler, and at end of 15 minutes placed in moderate oven (350° F.) to finish cooking. The average young bird requires about 35 to 45 minutes cooking.

Herbed chicken and olive mousse is a special party recipe (given below) for important summer occasions.

HERBED CHICKEN AND OLIVE MOUSSE

2 envelopes unflavored gelatine	Dash ground cayenne pepper
½ cup cold water	2 tsp. fresh lemon juice
2½ cups hot chicken stock	2 tsp. salt
⅛ tsp. garlic powder	⅓ cup diced black olives
1 tsp. onion powder	2½ cups diced cold chicken
½ tsp. ground thyme	1 cup heavy cream
1¼ tsp. powdered dry mustard	Salad greens, tomato wedges, and cucumber slices for garnish.

Sprinkle gelatine over cold water. Stir in chicken stock until gelatine is dissolved. Blend in herbs, lemon juice, and salt. Chill until mixture begins to thicken. Fold in black olives and chicken. Whip cream until it stands in soft peaks and fold into gelatine mixture. Turn into a 1½ qt. mold. Chill until firm and ready to serve. Unmold onto a serving plate. Garnish with greens, tomato wedges and cucumber slices or decorative seasonal fruit. *8 servings.*

PAN-FRIED CHICKEN

For frying, select a plump young chicken weighing between 2½ and 3½ lbs. dressed. Other young birds can be fried the same way as chicken.

CHICKEN FRIED IN SHALLOW FAT

To pan-fry chicken, disjoint and cut it into portions suitable for serving. Wipe the pieces of chicken dry, season with salt and pepper, and roll in flour. Have ready a thick frying pan with ½ inch or more of hot fat, but not smoking. Put the thickest pieces of chicken in the pan first. Cover the pan to keep the fat from spattering. Cook at moderate heat, and turn when brown. For a tender finished crust, brown each piece in uncovered pan; then put cover on pan and complete frying. Pan-fried chicken requires 20 to 25 minutes to cook completely.

MARYLAND CHICKEN

Fry chicken as directed above, remove from pan. Measure fat in pan and allow 1 Tbsp. of flour for 1 Tbsp. of fat. Return to pan, stir and scrape until all bits of browned fat and flour are well-blended, but not browned. Pour milk or thin cream over mixture (1 cup to 1 Tbsp. flour) and cook until thickened, add more salt if necessary. Pour over chicken. Do not strain.

CHICKEN MARENGO

1 4-lb. chicken	1 tsp. salt
¼ cup flour	½ tsp. pepper

Cut up chicken. Dust with flour, salt and pepper, and sauté in butter.

Sauce

¼ cup melted butter	1 cup canned tomatoes
¼ cup flour	1 tsp. salt
1½ cups boiling water	⅛ tsp. pepper
1 small onion, diced	½ lb. mushrooms, cut fine

Melt butter, add flour, blend together. Add boiling water, onion, tomatoes, salt, pepper and mushrooms. Cook slowly for 10 minutes. Pour over chicken, and cook until meat is tender.

CHICKEN LIVERS EN BROCHETTE

4 chicken livers	Salt and pepper
8 short slices bacon	2 metal skewers
	Lemon wedges

Wash livers well, cut in half, dry. Sprinkle lightly with salt and pepper. Wrap each portion of liver in raw bacon, place on skewer. Place under broiler heat

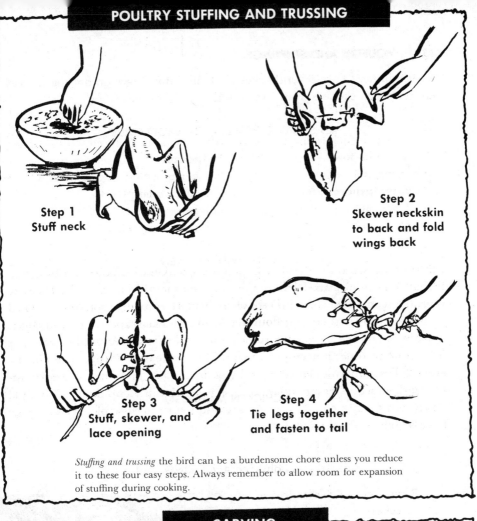

Step 1
Stuff neck

Step 2
**Skewer neckskin
to back and fold
wings back**

Step 3
**Stuff, skewer, and
lace opening**

Step 4
**Tie legs together
and fasten to tail**

Stuffing and trussing the bird can be a burdensome chore unless you reduce it to these four easy steps. Always remember to allow room for expansion of stuffing during cooking.

CARVING

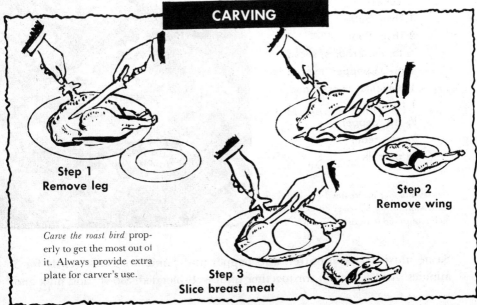

Step 1
Remove leg

Step 2
Remove wing

Step 3
Slice breast meat

Carve the roast bird properly to get the most out of it. Always provide extra plate for carver's use.

for 10 minutes. Turn several times while broiling. Serve on hot toast. They may be left on skewers, with lemon wedges as garnish.

CASSEROLE FOWL WITH VEGETABLES

4 to 5 lb. fowl	3 carrots
½ tsp. salt	1 turnip
¼ tsp. pepper	1 bunch celery
1 bay leaf	1 onion
Flour	1 cup boiling water
2 Tbsp. butter	1 cup milk

Cut up fowl, season with salt and pepper, sprinkle with flour and brown in the fat in a frying pan. Remove the browned pieces to a casserole. Dice the vegetables, and pour them into the frying pan to let them absorb the browned fat. Then transfer them to casserole with the chicken, add water and cover. Cook in a slow oven 3 to 4 hours, or until the bird is tender. Add more water from time to time, if necessary. Skim off and measure fat in casserole. To every 2 Tbsp. allow an equal quantity of flour. Cook in a small saucepan until well-blended. Measure liquid in casserole. Mix in 1 cup liquid with milk, slowly add to saucepan. Cook until smooth, return to casserole. Serve at once in casserole. *4 to 6 servings.*

CHICKEN À LA KING

2 cups cooked chicken (cut in
  cubes)
4 Tbsp. butter
2 Tbsp. flour
½ lb. mushrooms, sliced
1 green pepper, minced fine
1 pimiento, minced fine
1 tsp. salt
½ tsp. pepper
½ pt. cream
½ pt. milk

Chicken à la king or creamed chicken is an ideal solution for left-over chicken. Serve on hot buttered toast or on noodles.

Sauté mushrooms in butter, add pepper and pimiento. Cook gently for 5 minutes. Add flour and stir together until well-blended. Slowly add milk and

Curried chicken, Indian style, is an easy-to-prepare company meal that can be cooked and served with a minimum of utensils. Cook chicken with onion and season with pepper and curry powder. Onion rings, peanuts, coconut strips, and raisins can surround the fowl on the platter.

cream. Bring to boil and stir until smooth. Reduce heat, add chicken and heat through. Serve at once, on hot buttered toast. Garnish with parsley. *4 servings.*

CHICKEN IN RAMEKINS

2 Tbsp. butter

1 Tbsp. flour

1 cup cooked chicken, minced fine

1 cup cold boiled rice

1 cup chicken broth

1 tsp. salt

¼ tsp. pepper

4 Tbsp. soft bread crumbs

4 tsp. butter

Melt butter in saucepan, add flour and seasonings. Stir until well-blended. Add chicken broth and cook until smooth and thickened. Add chicken and heat through. Grease 4 individual casseroles. Divide mixture evenly into dishes. Cover with rice, sprinkle with bread crumbs. Dot with butter, bake in moderate oven (350° F.) 15 minutes. *4 servings.*

FRICASSEED FOWL

Disjoint a fowl into pieces for serving. Place the pieces in a kettle, add salted water to cover, partly cover the kettle, and cook the fowl until tender. Many cooks add an onion, a carrot, a stalk of celery and a bay leaf. Simmer —do not boil. When done (3 to 4 hours) remove from the broth and keep hot in warm, covered dish.

There should be from 3 to 4 cups of broth in kettle. Skim off the fat and measure the broth. For each cup of broth mix 2 Tbsp. of the fat with an equal quantity of flour. Stir several spoonfuls of the hot broth into the blended fat and flour and then, stirring constantly, pour the mixture into the broth in the kettle. Cook the gravy until it is slightly thickened, pour through a strainer. Add more salt if necessary.

BRUNSWICK STEW IN CASSEROLE

1 chicken, disjointed	Uncooked
Boiling water	1 cup green peas
Bay leaf	1 cup diced carrots
Salt and pepper	1 cup diced celery
	1 cup lima beans

Wipe pieces of chicken with damp cloth. Place in deep kettle, cover with boiling water, add seasonings. Cover tightly and simmer until tender. Remove chicken from kettle, cool, remove skin and bones. Cut chicken in good-sized pieces. Set aside. Bring chicken broth to boil (there should be 2 qts. of liquid). Slowly add vegetables, simmer 5 minutes. Pour into deep casserole, cover and bake in moderate oven (350° F.) until tender. Add chicken and cook until heated through. Serve with boiled potatoes or rice. *4 to 6 servings.*

CHICKEN AND NOODLE CASSEROLE

1 8-oz. package noodles	1 can condensed mushroom soup
2 cups cooked chicken, cut in neat pieces	(1½ cups)
	⅔ cup milk
1 No. 2 can green peas, drained	½ cup buttered crumbs
1 Tbsp. onion, grated	⅛ tsp. paprika

Cook noodles, drain and rinse. Grease casserole. Arrange noodles, chicken and peas in alternate layers. Combine soup and milk, pour over mixture. Top with buttered crumbs and paprika. Bake in moderate oven (375° F.) 25 minutes. *4 to 6 servings.*

SAVORY GRAVY

The quantity of well-flavored gravy that can be made from a roasted bird depends on how much juice, or stock, cooks out of the bird into the dripping pan and the amount and strength of broth obtained from the giblets. With a 4 lb. chicken a reasonable yield of gravy is 1 to 1½ cups; with a 10 lb. turkey the yield is 3 to 4 cups.

To make gravy, pour the drippings out of the roasting pan and let the fat rise to the top of the brown stock. Skim off the fat and set it aside. For each cup of liquid (brown stock and giblet broth, with or without added water) measure 1½ to 2 Tbsp. of flour and place in a roasting pan. Blend with the flour an equal quantity of the fat skimmed from the brown stock. Add the cool or lukewarm liquid to the smooth mixture, slowly stirring over a low fire. Cook the gravy until thickened and strain through a sieve. Allow ½ tsp. salt and ¼ tsp. pepper for every cup of liquid. Add chopped giblets.

STUFFINGS

PLAIN POULTRY STUFFING

3 Tbsp. onion, finely minced	¼ tsp. pepper
½ cup shortening, melted	½ tsp. poultry seasoning
½ tsp. salt	4 cups bread crumbs

Sauté onion in shortening until soft, but not brown. Add seasonings, pour over bread crumbs, stir well.

Variation

Chestnut stuffing: Boil and peel ½ to 1 lb. chestnuts. Chop coarsely. Add to plain stuffing.

MUSHROOM STUFFING

1 cup mushrooms, sliced	1 tsp. salt
½ cup butter	½ tsp. pepper
	3 cups soft bread crumbs

Sauté mushrooms in butter, add seasonings. Pour over bread crumbs, stir well.

Herb fried chicken adds up to a company dinner when it is served with garlic French bread, tossed salad, and iced cokes.

Vary the stuffings to make them a surprise treat hidden within the turkey.

LANCASTER STUFFING

2 Tbsp. onion, minced fine	½ tsp. pepper
½ cup celery, chopped	½ tsp. poultry seasoning
½ cup shortening, melted	1 tsp. celery seed
1 tsp. salt	2 Tbsp. parsley, chopped
	3 cups bread crumbs

Sauté onion and celery in shortening until soft, but not brown. Remove from stove, add seasonings. Pour over crumbs, stir well.

BREAD STUFFING

1 qt. bread crumbs	½ tsp. sage or thyme
½ cup boiling water	½ tsp. salt
½ cup chicken fat or salad oil or	¼ tsp. pepper
butter or margarine	¼ cup onion, minced fine

Mix ingredients together lightly with fork, adding water in small amounts until consistency is moist, but not too wet.

CELERY STUFFING

Add 1 cup of finely minced celery to basic Bread Stuffing.

Two birds can have two different kinds of stuffing.

CORN BREAD STUFFING

Use 1 pt. of corn bread crumbs in place of bread crumbs. It is customary to omit boiling water when corn bread crumbs are used.

PARSLEY STUFFING

1 qt. bread crumbs, toasted
½ cup butter or margarine

2 Tbsp. parsley, minced fine
½ tsp. salt
1 tsp. sage

Remove crusts from bread 2 days old. Toast until golden brown. Grate on coarse grater. Add seasonings.

OYSTER STUFFING

1 cup raw oysters, drained
2 Tbsp. shortening, melted
1½ tsp. salt

¼ tsp. pepper
2 Tbsp. oyster liquor
1 cup coarse cracker crumbs

Sauté the oysters in shortening until edges curl. Add salt, pepper and oyster liquor. Pour over crumbs. There should be just enough oyster liquor to hold mixture together. It should be moist, but not soggy.

12.

FISH AND SHELLFISH

OF ALL the foods which are valuable sources of protein and suitable, therefore, to serve as the main course at luncheon or dinner, fish seems to be the least popular and least understood. For many years, it was "fish on Friday" —and ignored the rest of the week.

However, the introduction of quick-freezing has given a great impetus to the popularity of fish. The small family may now enjoy the convenience of salmon steaks, slices of halibut, fish fillets, and many other sea food delicacies. Salt fish and canned fish are also good sources of food values.

In flavor, texture, and treatment in cooking, fish is so strikingly different from meat—its chief competitor—that housewives need to study its fine points. Fish needs the accompaniment of crisp raw vegetables: cole slaw, cucumbers, or a tossed green salad with a sharp French dressing. It also needs the tang of lemon or lime. Baking, boiling, broiling, and pan-frying are good ways to cook fish.

BUYING FRESH FISH

A fresh fish has clear red gills; the eyes are bright and bulging; the scales shine and lie closely together; it feels firm to the touch, with nothing soft or flabby about it.

CARE OF FISH

Fresh fish is highly perishable. It should be wrapped closely in waxed paper, kept in the coldest compartment of the refrigerator, and used as soon as possible after purchasing. Before cooking, wash thoroughly, both inside and out, and dry with a paper towel.

PREPARATION OF FISH

It is a good plan to ask questions of the fish dealer before you make your

146

selection. He will explain that such fish as the bluefish, mackerel, herring, shad, and salmon are known as fat fish, so that little extra oil or melted butter is necessary in the cooking. Whereas cod, haddock and flounder, which are the lean fish, are dry, and a slice of salt pork—or extra oil—will add to their palatability.

The table on page 148 presents a list of the common varieties of fish, and the most advantageous methods of preparation. Fish requires a shorter period of cooking time than many meat dishes, and the inexperienced cook is often puzzled about how to know when the fish is fully cooked.

WHEN COOKED

A silver fork may be used to lift up a small portion of the fish. If it separates easily, or flakes when the fork touches it, the fish is cooked. If still somewhat uncooked, the fish clings to the main piece.

COOKING GUIDES

Leave fish in the refrigerator until last possible moment before preparation for cooking.

When ready for cooking, fish should be at room temperature.

Allow frozen fish to thaw to room temperature before cooking.

Fish requires a short cooking period, or low temperature. Do not overcook fish.

When using oil in pan-frying, never let the fat reach the smoking point.

Steam fish whenever possible, instead of "boiling." To boil, place the fish in a strainer, tie in cheesecloth or muslin, or wrap in parchment. Then the

Broiled South African lobster tails (right) is a colorful bit of seafare adored by many. Provide warm melted butter or a supply of mayonnaise on the side for dipping chunks of luscious lobster meat.

fish may be lifted out of the container and served in one piece without break-ing.

When steaming, use a small quantity of water, and cover tightly. More flavor and nutritive value are retained in fish cooked by this method.

Never throw cooking water (fish stock) away. Use it in place of milk as a basic liquid for sauce to serve over fish.

COMMON VARIETIES OF FISH AND METHOD OF COOKING

FISH FOR BAKING	FISH FOR BOILING (Poaching)	FISH FOR SAUTÉEING	FISH FOR BROILING
Bass	Cod	Bass	Same as Fish for Bak-
Bluefish	Flounder	Butterfish	ing and Boiling.
Brook trout	Haddock	Cod	Swordfish
Cod	Hake	Flounder	Quick-frozen or fresh
Haddock	Halibut	Haddock	fish fillets are an ex-
Halibut	Perch	Hake	cellent choice for
Mackerel	Pickerel	Halibut	broiling.
Perch	Salmon	Mackerel	
Salmon steak	Sole	Perch	
Shad		Pickerel	
Smelts		Pompano	
Weakfish		Salmon	
Whitefish		Smelts	
		Sole	
		Swordfish	
		Whiting	

TO BAKE FISH

Fillets, slices and steaks are all adaptable to easy baking. Both dry and fat fish turn out well with this method. The fat fish, such as bluefish, salmon, mackerel or shad, require little basting. But dry fish, such as cod or haddock, need strips of salt pork laid across the top of the fish, or melted shortening or salad oil brushed over the top before baking.

BAKED FISH FILLETS

Allow one fillet per person. Brush fish with salad oil so that every bit of fish is covered by a film of oil. Sprinkle with salt, pepper, paprika. Place in

Frozen fish sticks are quickly dressed up for company. Add a spicy tomato sauce seasoned with molasses, vinegar, and mustard and you will have a dish called Fish Sticks Louisiana.

greased shallow pan. Bake uncovered in a moderate oven (350° F.) 15 to 30 minutes. Break off a piece with silver fork. If it flakes away from body of fish easily, it is cooked sufficiently.

In Florida, fish is prepared for the oven as above and 1 Tbsp. of lime juice is sprinkled over each piece. It is very good!

Fish is much more delicious if served right in the dish in which it was baked. The less cooked fish is handled, the more attractive its appearance.

Always serve a wedge of lime or lemon with fish, together with a garnish of watercress or parsley.

BAKED FISH FILLETS IN MILK

4 fillets of fish	¼ tsp. pepper
2 cups milk	1 cup dry bread crumbs
½ tsp. salt	2 thin slices of onion
	1 bay leaf

Roll fillets in crumbs seasoned with salt and pepper, and lay fillets in greased baking dish. Cover with milk, and bake uncovered in moderate oven (350° F.) 30 minutes. Serve in baking dish. Milk may be poured off and thickened by mixing with 2 Tbsp. flour blended with 2 Tbsp. cold water. Cook in saucepan until smooth and thickened. Pour over fish.

BAKED FISH FILLETS—STUFFED

Allow one fillet per person. Sprinkle each fillet with lemon or lime juice, salt and pepper. Prepare fish stuffing (at end of this chapter). Spread stuffing on fillet. Place second fillet on top of stuffing. Brush top fillet with salad oil. Skewer together with metal skewers, or tie firmly with string. Place fillets in greased baking dish, bake in moderate oven (375° F.) 40 minutes to 1 hour. Cut in half when serving. Cole slaw, and steamed potatoes with parsley garnish, go well with this dish.

BAKING WHOLE FISH

Either fat or lean fish may be used for baking. Set oven at 400° F., and bake the fish according to its weight. Fish for baking should be cleaned, scaled, fins and tail removed. The most important fact to know is the weight of the dressed fish, ready for baking. Be sure to read the scales at the store for the final weight.

Fill the fish two-thirds full with stuffing. Close the opening by sewing with a needle and thread, or inserting toothpicks or metal skewers and lacing it closed with string. The toothpicks or metal skewers will support the fish in an upright position while baking.

Place the fish on oiled brown paper in a shallow baking pan. Allow 11 minutes per lb. for baking halibut or salmon. Allow 16 minutes per lb. for striped bass, carp or whitefish. Spanish mackerel will take 19 minutes per lb. for baking. Bake all fish in a hot oven (400° F.). Regardless of the variety, be sure to note the dressed weight of the fish—with the head on or off as you intend baking it.

Broil small fish or fillets. Serve
with lemon slices.

Broiled fish on alcoa wrap teams
up with broiled tomatoes, a fine
sauce, and heated soft rolls.

BAKED FISH

4 lbs. fish (weight after cleaning)	Cooking oil
4 strips fat salt pork	Fish stuffing

Clean fish, remove backbone. Wash fish in cold salted water. (Allow ½ cup
salt to 1 qt. water.) Let stand for 5 minutes. Drain fish, slit skin in several
places, brush fish with oil. Stuff fish according to directions above. Lay in
baking pan and place strips of salt pork across top of fish. Bake in hot oven
(400° F.). Length of time depends upon type of fish. *6 to 8 servings.*

TO BROIL FISH

Small fish are especially good when broiled. Smelts, butterfish, porgies are
usually broiled whole, with heads and tails left on. Larger fish, such as blue-

fish, mackerel and shad are split down the back, opened, and broiled, skin side down. The steaks, such as salmon, halibut or swordfish, should be about ½ to ¾ inch thick for best results in broiling.

BROILED MACKEREL—SPLIT

Grease baking sheet with a piece of bacon or salt pork. Wash fish, dry with paper toweling. Brush with salad oil. Open fish, place on sheet skin side down. Place the pan so that the flame of broiler oven is as close as possible without flame touching fish. Broil 10 minutes, or until surface is nicely browned. Sprinkle with salt and pepper. Add lime juice, if desired. Turn fish with pancake turner and brown on other side. Repeat salt and pepper. Place pan in baking oven for 5 to 6 minutes to complete cooking throughout. (Many housewives keep special pan for broiling fish.)

BROILED SHAD ROE

This dish has long been regarded as one of the seasonal delicacies in the fish kingdom. It requires careful attention in cooking, even though the method is simple. Allow 1 pair of roe for 2 servings. Dust lightly with flour. Preheat the pan and oven compartment for 10 minutes at full heat (550° F.). Spread the top of the roe evenly with soft butter. Place on the preheated broiling pan, 3 inches from the heat, and broil 3 minutes on the first side. Season and turn. Spread other side with butter, and broil 5 minutes longer. Baste once again during the broiling period. Season and remove from broiling pan. Sprinkle with finely chopped parsley, and serve immediately on a hot dish. Shad roe is at its best when it weighs 12 oz. to 1 lb.

TO BOIL FISH

A perfectly boiled slice of fillet or solid piece of fish is the basis for a number of delightful fish dishes. Essential kitchen equipment for this method of fish cookery is simple—a square of cheese cloth and a perforated tin plate. (Keep for cooking fish.) Cod, haddock, flounder are good choices for boiling. Wash fish and place on the clean cheesecloth, tie loosely. Fill a deep saucepan with boiling water, add ½ tsp. salt and 1 Tbsp. vinegar to 1 qt. water. (The vinegar preserves color, keeps flesh firm.) Place pan in water, bring to boiling point, reduce heat to simmering, cover and cook until fish flakes. This is about 6 to 8 minutes per lb.

For added flavor, a slice of onion, a piece of bay leaf, a sprig of thyme are possibilities. Especially good if fish is to be used to make a fish salad.

Lift fish out of water with long-handled fork, drain. If used as entrée, serve on hot platter with egg sauce or cream sauce. But if used for salad, serve with French dressing.

BOILED SHRIMP

1 lb. green or raw shrimp (shelled or unshelled)
1 cup water

½ stalk celery or celery leaves
Piece of bay leaf
2 peppercorns
1 tsp. salt

Shrimp may be shelled and cleaned prior to cooking. Prepare stock in 1 qt. saucepan by adding water, celery, bay leaf, peppercorns, salt and vinegar. Cover and simmer 5 minutes. Add raw shrimp to boiling stock; cover and simmer 5 minutes more. (Count cooking time after shrimp returns to boiling.) Remove from heat; strain stock and reserve. Stock may be used in fish sauces or in molded food salads. Leftover cooked shelled shrimp may be placed in a jar, covered with stock, and stored in refrigerator.

BOILED LOBSTER

3 Tbsp. salt

12 cups water
1 live lobster (1 lb.)*

Bring salt and water to boiling, in 4 qt. saucepan. Add live lobster, head first, to water. Cover and simmer 5 minutes. (Count cooking time after water returns to boiling.) Remove lobster from water. With sharp knife cut lobster on abdominal side, full length. Meat can then be easily extracted. *1 or 2 servings.*

* Allow 3 minutes additional cooking time for each lb. of lobster over the first pound.

BOILED SALMON

Allow about 10 minutes per lb. This is good served hot as an entrée, or chilled and served on a bed of lettuce with mayonnaise as a cold entrée.

FRIED SHRIMP

Shrimp may be dipped in light batter and sautéed in fat.

SHRIMP OMELET

Just as omelet begins to set, add diced cooked shrimp to omelet.

CREAMED SHRIMP

Shrimp may be added to rich cream sauce and served with steamed rice or on toast.

CURRIED SHRIMP

The simplest recipe is to season a rich cream sauce with 1 to 2 Tbsp. curry powder and add shrimp. Serve with rice. Chutney is a good accompaniment.

CRABS

Crabs should be alive and kicking when purchased. Plunge hard-shell crabs into rapidly boiling water. Boil for 5 minutes, add 1 Tbsp. salt to every qt. of water. Continue boiling 20 to 30 minutes longer. Break off tail, pull shell open. The edible crabmeat is in the compact part of the shell, and in claws. (A nutcracker is an essential tool.)

DEVILED CRABMEAT

2 cups cooked or canned crabmeat
1 cup medium white sauce
¼ tsp. dry mustard
½ tsp. paprika
Dash of cayenne
1 to 2 Tbsp. lemon juice
¼ cup buttered crumbs
1 Tbsp. parsley

Deviled crabmeat served in the shell shows up dramatically on the buffet table.

Add seasonings to white sauce. Pick over crabmeat to remove cartilage. Add crabmeat to sauce and pack lightly in clean clam or crab shells. Sprinkle lightly with parsley and crumbs. Bake in hot oven (400° F.) 10 minutes. Fills 4 shells.

CRABMEAT CASSEROLE

1 can crabmeat
2 eggs, separated

1 cup medium white sauce
¼ cup sherry wine
¼ cup grated cheese

Remove contents of tin of crabmeat, separate into pieces, remove thin cartilage. Drain crabmeat, add to sauce and heat over low heat. Add sherry wine

Curried shrimp, in its rich sauce, made by blending 1 cup medium white sauce with 1 Tsp. curry powder, likes crisp accompaniment, perhaps cucumber rings and watercress.

and stir constantly for a few minutes. Turn into well-greased casserole. Sprinkle with cheese and place under broiler to brown. Serve at once. *4 servings.*

TO PAN-FRY OR SAUTÉ FISH

Whole small fish, fillets, or thin slices of fish steak are ideal for this method of cooking. Sole, halibut, swordfish, salmon are all good choices.

1 fillet or fish steak per person	¼ tsp. salt
1 egg	⅛ tsp. pepper
2 Tbsp. cold water	2 Tbsp. vegetable shortening or
¼ cup fine dry bread crumbs	salad oil

Beat egg with cold water. Dip fish into egg, then into crumbs seasoned with salt and pepper. Melt fat in skillet until moderately hot but not smoking. Brown fish on both sides quickly. Reduce heat and cook slowly until well-done. (Fish is cooked through when it flakes away from main portion.) Drain fish on paper towel. Serve with lemon wedges.

OYSTERS AND SCALLOPS

Oysters are considered at their best in the "R" months, September to April. But the introduction of quick-frozen packaged oysters has made them an all-year-round food. Bits of shell may cling to the oysters, so it is always advisable to strain the oysters through a fine sieve, then pick each one up in turn, examine it, and remove any trace of shell.

CREAMED OYSTERS

1 pt. oysters	2 Tbsp. butter
1 cup light cream	2 Tbsp. flour
1 cup milk	¼ tsp. salt
	⅛ tsp. pepper

Heat oysters in their own liquor. As soon as edges curl, oysters are sufficiently cooked. (Over-cooking makes oysters tough and flavorless.) Scald milk and cream, skim oyster liquid, add to scalded milk. Melt butter in saucepan, add flour, seasonings. Stir constantly until bubbly, slowly add liquid, bring to boil, reduce heat. Add oysters to sauce. Serve on buttered toast. *4 servings.*

SCALLOPED OYSTERS

1 pt. oysters	Milk and oyster liquid, equal parts
1 cup cracker crumbs (soda crackers)	½ tsp. salt
	¼ tsp. pepper
¼ cup butter	⅛ tsp. paprika

Drain oysters, remove any bits of shell. Roll crackers out on board until they are in coarse pieces. (They do not need to be fine.) Lay a thick layer of crumbs on bottom of dish, add layer of oysters, sprinkle with seasonings, add generous dabs of butter. Repeat process of alternate layers of crumbs and oysters until all are used. Finish off with crumbs as top layer. Mix milk with oyster liquor, slowly add at sides until moisture shows at top of dish. Bake in hot oven (450° F.) 20 to 30 minutes. Top should be crisp and brown, and the center moist, buttery and succulent. *4 servings.*

FRIED OYSTERS

1 pt. oysters	½ cup fine dry crumbs
1 egg, slightly beaten	½ tsp. salt
2 Tbsp. water	¼ tsp. pepper

Drain oysters, dry on paper toweling. Dip in crumbs seasoned with salt and pepper. Dip in egg mixed with water, dip in crumbs again. Fry in deep hot fat (375° F.) until golden brown. If deep-fat thermometer is not available, drop a cube of bread into hot fat, and if bread browns in 1 minute the fat is about right. *4 servings.*

FRIED SCALLOPS

Scallops are prepared as above. Some chefs recommend that the scallops stand in salted water for 5 minutes before being drained and prepared for frying.

SALTED OR SMOKED FISH

New England has given the country these classic recipes. They are old-timers, and as good today as they ever were, though modern methods have simplified their preparation. Codfish cakes are put up in tins, ready to heat and serve.

CREAMED CODFISH

1 cup salt codfish
1 cup medium white sauce

blended with 1 hard-cooked
egg, chopped
(Omit salt when preparing sauce)

Soak codfish in boiling water to cover. Let stand 5 to 10 minutes. Pour off water and repeat process. Cool and tear codfish into shreds. If too salty, repeat process. Add to sauce, heat thoroughly.

Codfish is probably the most popular of the dried, salted fishes. But haddock, whole mackerel and herring are also well-liked.

Kippered herring is sold in cans, but salted smoked haddock (commonly called Finnan Haddie) is prepared by soaking in hot water for 5 minutes to remove skin and bones. If the fish has been filleted, this preliminary soaking is unnecessary. *2 to 4 servings.*

PAN-COOKED FINNAN HADDIE

½ to 1 lb. fillet of finnan haddie
4 Tbsp. butter

Wipe fillet with damp cloth. Melt butter in skillet and brown fish for 2 minutes on one side and 3 minutes on the other side. Sprinkle with parsley and lemon juice. *2 servings.*

SALT MACKEREL

Allow 1 salt mackerel fillet per person. Soak in cold water, skin side down, for 12 hours or more. Drain, wipe dry with paper toweling, and brush with salad oil. Cook as per directions for broiled mackerel.

BAKED FISH FLAKES IN FLUTED SHELLS

1½ cups medium white sauce
1 cup flaked cooked fish (cod,
   haddock, sole, tuna, salmon)

⅛ tsp. dry mustard
½ tsp. Worcestershire sauce
1 Tbsp. grated Parmesan cheese
1 tsp. finely minced parsley

Grease shells with salad oil or butter. Mix sauce with mustard and Worcestershire sauce, add fish. Blend well and fill shells with mixture. Sprinkle with grated cheese. Brown under broiler flame of oven. Garnish with parsley. *3 to 4 servings.*

Salmon mold is irresistible. Note how this salmon mold rides on the crest of a cottage cheese wave.

SHRIMP AND OLIVE CASSEROLE

3 Tbsp. butter
3 Tbsp. flour
Pepper
1½ cups milk
¼ tsp. Worcestershire sauce

1 cup diced celery
1¾ cups cooked or uncooked
   shelled shrimp
1 cup soft fresh bread, cut into
   ¼ inch cubes
¾ cup sliced stuffed olives

Blend butter, flour and pepper. Gradually add milk, Worcestershire sauce and celery; blend well. Cook for 10 minutes; add shrimp. Cook 3 minutes longer. Pour into casserole with olives and bread. Bake in hot oven (400° F.) 16 minutes. *4 to 6 servings.*

TUNA FISH SUPREME

1 7-oz. can tuna fish
1 cup medium white sauce
¼ lb. cheddar cheese

1 can condensed mushroom soup
¼ cup chopped pimiento
½ cup buttered bread crumbs

Break tuna fish into flakes. Add to cream sauce, in which cheese has been melted. Add soup and pimiento. Put in buttered baking dish, sprinkle with crumbs. Bake in moderate oven (350° F.) 15 minutes. *4 servings.*

SEAFOOD À LA NEWBURG

To the amount of one recipe of Newburg Sauce, allow 2 cups cooked seafood.

Lobster: Cut in small pieces. Add to sauce.
Crabmeat: Pick over, remove slender strands of cartilage, but leave large flakes. Add to sauce.
Shrimp: Clean, cut in pieces. Add to sauce.
Mixed Seafood: Any leftover cooked fish. Flake in pieces. Add to sauce.

LUNCHEON SALMON RING

1 cup canned salmon or tuna	1 Tbsp. chopped parsley
½ cup hot milk	1 tsp. salt
1 cup soft bread crumbs	¼ tsp. mustard
	2 eggs, slightly beaten

Drain oil from salmon, and flake. Combine milk, bread crumbs, parsley, salt and mustard. Add eggs. Stir into salmon. Pour in a well-buttered mold; bake in moderate oven (350° F.) about 35 minutes, or until mixture is firm. Unmold, and serve hot or cold. If it is served cold, fill the center with tomato cucumber salad. If served hot, fill center with hot green peas. *4 servings.*

STUFFING FOR FISH

1 cup soft bread crumbs	⅛ tsp. pepper
¼ cup shortening, melted	1 Tbsp. onion, minced fine
¼ tsp. thyme	1 tsp. parsley, minced fine
¼ tsp. salt	¼ cup boiling water

Mix all ingredients except water. Add just enough water to hold mixture together. It should be moist, but not soggy.

13.

SAUCES—FOR ENTRÉES

SAUCES should be smooth, of the right consistency, seasoned to the exact degree of perfection, delicate enough in flavor to accentuate the foods with which they are served. That kind of sauce-making is an art in cookery which goes back to the sixteenth century! Today sauces are held in high esteem by all lovers of good food, but the mumbo-jumbo of elaborate preparation has been simplified by the American housewife. The classic sauces which are known to the gourmets, the chefs and other experts, are still known by their original names, and the recipes are fundamentally the same—even though they have been changed in minor details by many people.

Sauces for everyday cooking need to be simple, not too highly seasoned, and made from ingredients of modest price. Such liquids as canned beef bouillon, chicken consommé, concentrated bouillon cubes, together with bottled sauces such as Worcestershire, and tomato sauce, all have their place as materials to be used from time to time. The use of domestic wine as an ingredient in sauce-making has greatly increased in this country during the past few years, and wine may replace part of the liquid in recipes which use consommé or bouillon. In cream sauces, sherry wine may be added slowly after the sauce is made; it is then simmered gently until the alcohol has evaporated.

Occasionally, a more elaborate meal than the usual family lunch or dinner is served, and then a richer sauce may be used. Cream may replace milk, beaten eggs may be added to the recipe, wine may replace the chicken or beef stock. It may be noted that the word "stock" is ordinarily used to describe the well-seasoned liquid used in sauce making.

FOR MEAT—FISH—VEGETABLE

BASIC WHITE SAUCE

(Cream Sauce)

White sauce, or cream sauce as it is more usually called, is a basic sauce of the utmost simplicity. Made properly, so that the finished sauce is smooth, well-seasoned and rich, it is the foundation for a whole list of special sauces—

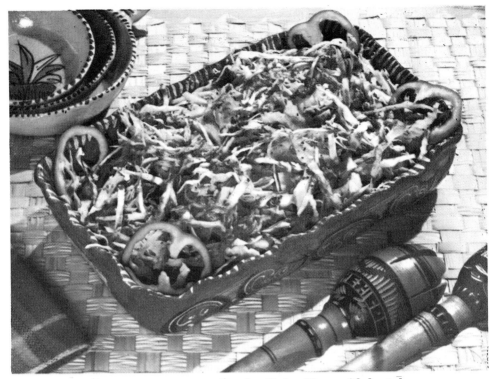

Make barbecue slaw in-a-jiffy by tossing shredded cabbage with heated canned barbecue sauce.

Garnish and serve vegetables attractively.

especially the "medium" consistency. Thin white sauce is used as a basis for cream soups as well as for other sauces.

A special recipe for cream soups made with thin white sauce is in Chapter 7 on Soups. In preparing creamed dishes, medium white sauce is more commonly used. A creamed egg recipe, for example, calls for 2 hard-cooked eggs to be sliced and added to 1 cup of sauce, with other cooked foods (such as chicken, tuna fish, salmon, macaroni or rice); the proportions are 1 cup of cooked food to 1 cup of medium white sauce.

WHITE SAUCE

	BUTTER	FLOUR	LIQUID	SALT	USES	PROPORTIONS
THIN	1 Tbsp.	1 Tbsp.	1 cup milk or ½ milk and cream	½ tsp.	cream sauces	1 to 1½ cups cooked, strained vegetable pulp to 1 cup sauce.
MEDIUM	2 Tbsp.	2 Tbsp.	1 cup	1 tsp.	creamed dishes	2 hard-cooked eggs or 1 cup cooked food to 1 cup sauce.
THICK	4 Tbsp.	4-6 Tbsp.	1 cup	½ tsp.	soufflés and croquettes	1 to 3 cups cooked food to 1 cup sauce.

Melt butter in saucepan, add flour and seasonings. Stir well until bubbly. (Do not allow mixture to brown.) Add milk slowly and stir constantly until sauce is smooth and thickened. *For pictures see page 163.*

Variations of White Sauce

ALLEMANDE SAUCE

1 cup thin white sauce	½ cup cream
2 slightly-beaten egg yolks	1 tsp. lemon juice or pinch of rosemary

Mix egg yolks with cream. Slowly pour a little of the hot sauce over mixture, stir well and return to saucepan set in pan of hot water. Cook until sauce is smooth and thickened. Serve with egg dishes.

BÉCHAMEL SAUCE

Another name for medium white sauce, usually one in which a portion of the milk is replaced with cream or chicken stock or fish stock. Serve with chicken or fish.

CHEESE SAUCE

1 cup medium white sauce	½ cup grated cheese
	¼ tsp. Worcestershire sauce

Prepare sauce, add cheese and Worcestershire sauce, stirring constantly until cheese is melted. Serve with vegetables.

CURRY SAUCE

Blend 1 cup medium white sauce with ½ to 1 tsp. curry powder.

EGG SAUCE

To 1 cup medium white sauce add 2 chopped hard-cooked eggs. Serve with fish.

SUPREME OR VELOUTÉ SAUCE

For medium white sauce, substitute 1 cup chicken stock or consommé for milk. Serve with chicken croquettes or hash.

TOMATO SAUCE

Substitute 1 cup canned tomatoes for milk. Add bay leaf, parsley, slice of onion. Cook until soft, press through sieve. Serve with beef dishes.

BASIC BROWN SAUCE

2 Tbsp. butter	1 Tbsp. tomato purée
2 Tbsp. flour	1 bay leaf
1 Tbsp. grated onion	½ tsp. salt
1 Tbsp. grated carrot	¼ tsp. pepper
	1 cup beef consommé

Melt butter in saucepan, add onions and dry seasonings, cook gently until onions are yellow. Add flour and stir constantly until flour begins to brown. Add carrots and tomato purée, cook a few minutes longer. Add consommé and stir until smooth and thickened. Strain and serve with roast beef.

Creamed eggs on toast (*top*) play a welcome role at luncheon.

Creamed kidneys (*left*) are extra good when served on warm, fluffy waffles. Accompany them with grapefruit halves and a cold soup-and-milk drink for a refreshing summer brunch.

Variations of Brown Sauce

PIQUANT SAUCE

Add 1 Tbsp. capers to basic brown sauce. Serve with tongue.

ORANGE SAUCE

Substitute ½ cup orange juice for ½ cup consommé. Add 1 Tbsp. grated orange rind. Serve with duck.

CURRANT JELLY SAUCE

Add 2 to 4 Tbsp. currant jelly. Serve with roast lamb.

MUSHROOM SAUCE

Add ½ cup chopped cooked mushrooms. Serve with meat or poultry.

HOLLANDAISE SAUCE

(Simplified)

Many a dinner has been spoiled because the Hollandaise curdled. To prevent curdling, cook in upper part of double boiler and don't let the water in the lower part come to a boil. If sauce does curdle, slowly add 1 Tbsp. boiling water and stir until smooth.

½ cup butter	Salt to taste
2 egg yolks	Juice of 1 lemon
	⅓ cup boiling water

Melt butter over hot water, remove from heat, add egg yolk and beat thoroughly. Add other egg yolk and beat again. Add salt, lemon juice, stirring constantly. Add the boiling water slowly. Replace over hot water and cook until mixture coats a silver spoon; the consistency will be that of a thick custard. This sauce may be prepared in advance and reheated. Leftover sauce will keep in refrigerator. More lemon juice may be added if a sharper tang is liked.

HORSERADISH SAUCE (NO. I)

To 1 cup medium white sauce add 1 Tbsp. grated horseradish and pinch of cayenne.

HORSERADISH SAUCE (NO. II)

To 1 cup whipped cream (sweet or sour) add 1 to 2 Tbsp. grated horseradish, with vinegar or dry mustard to taste.

CREOLE SAUCE

2 Tbsp. onion, chopped	2 Tbsp. olives, chopped
2 Tbsp. green pepper, chopped	1 cup tomato paste
1 clove garlic	½ cup chicken or beef consommé
4 Tbsp. olive oil	½ cup mushroom pieces

Cook onion, pepper and garlic in olive oil until soft. Discard garlic, add other ingredients and simmer until thick. Sprinkle with finely minced parsley.

NEWBURG SAUCE

¼ cup butter	½ tsp. salt
2 Tbsp. flour	Dash of cayenne
2 egg yolks, well-beaten	1 cup thin cream
	¼ cup sherry

Melt butter, add flour and seasonings. Cook over low heat until thick and bubbly. Add cream slowly, and cook until sauce is smooth. Pour over eggs, return to saucepan over hot water. Cook 1 minute longer. Add fish and pour wine over it. Serve at once.

MINT SAUCE

4 Tbsp. fresh mint leaves   2 tsp. sugar
                                   ½ cup vinegar

Wash a bunch of fresh mint in cold water. Strip the leaves from stems. Place leaves in bowl, add sugar and crush thoroughly. Add vinegar, stir well. Serve with hot or cold roast lamb.

PENNSYLVANIA DUTCH SAUCE

½ cup water   ¼ cup butter
½ cup vinegar   1 Tbsp. flour
5 Tbsp. sugar   ½ tsp. salt
                                   2 eggs, well-beaten

Heat water, vinegar, sugar and salt in upper part of double boiler, over hot water. Rub butter and flour together until smooth. Slowly pour hot liquid onto paste. When well-blended, add slowly to eggs. Place over hot water, stir constantly and cook until sauce thickens.

DRAWN BUTTER SAUCE

4 Tbsp. butter   ¼ tsp. salt
2 Tbsp. flour   ⅛ tsp. paprika
1½ cups boiling water or seasoned 1 Tbsp. lemon juice
   boiling water in which fish has
   cooked

Melt 2 Tbsp. butter in saucepan, add flour, stir constantly until well-blended. Slowly add liquid. Bring to boiling point, reduce heat and simmer gently for 1 to 2 minutes. Add seasonings and remaining piece of butter. Beat well, pour over fish or serve in sauce bowl.

Variations

Anchovy Drawn Butter: Add 1 Tbsp. of anchovy paste to sauce.
Egg Drawn Butter: Add 2 hard-cooked eggs, sliced thin.

14.

SALADS AND SALAD
· DRESSINGS

SALADS were looked upon as "sissified" in the early years of 19th century America. Strong men refused to eat such "rabbit" food—it was meat, potatoes and pie for them. But eventually the knowledge that raw green vegetables give us our precious vitamins and minerals in abundance awakened the nation to their importance. Once experienced, their crisp texture, their appealing colors, and their manifold flavors made them popular to the point where men now order them as a matter of course. ·

Salad masterpieces, created by famous chefs, often serve as the main entrée at luncheons. Chef's salads are usually prepared and brought to the table in a huge wooden bowl filled with a variety of crisp greens. They are often seasoned with highly-flavored cheese, or strips of smoked tongue, ham or chicken, and the whole thing is blended with a well-seasoned French dressing.

For the feminine side of the restaurant clientéle, salads known as "Ladies Luncheon Salads" have been created. These are elaborate affairs of fruit, vegetables, poultry or shell fish.

Salads really fall into two categories: (1) the mixed green salad, which is served at luncheon or dinner to give color and flavor to the meal, as well as to pep up the vitamin content of the diet; and (2) the hearty salad which has become popular as the main course at luncheon or supper.

166

TRICKS TO KNOW ABOUT SALADS

Buy greens that are fresh.

Wash them immediately, preferably under cold running water.

Separate the leaves, shake well, and drain on paper toweling.

Store in covered container or wrap lightly in clean bag. Place in refrigerator until ready to use.

See that greens are dry and crisp before mixing. Wet lettuce ruins a salad.

For a "tossed" green salad, rub wooden salad bowl with a cut clove of garlic. (A mixed green salad is commonly called "tossed".)

Keep a variety of vinegars in the pantry; different vinegars change dressings. Some popular kinds are listed here.

Cider Vinegar—Red currant   Garlic Vinegar
Malt Vinegar   Herb Vinegar
Tarragon Vinegar   Red Wine Vinegar
                              Raspberry Vinegar

Make salad dressing just before mixing salad.

WHAT TO DO WITH RAW VEGETABLES

The part which crisp, raw vegetables play in this scheme of things has brought the raw vegetable platter into a prominent place as a salad course. The brilliant colors, the firm texture, the low calorie content have combined to give raw vegetables a place of honor. The varieties of dressings are so enormous that the hostess can always serve something different.

A large platter, with an indentation in the center to hold a bowl of dressing, is all that is needed in the way of equipment. Then choose vegetables for color: tomatoes, carrots, lettuce wedges, and celery make a good color combination. Avoid two foods of the same color.

The dressings may be: Thousand Island Dressing, Cucumber Mayonnaise, Sour Cream Dressing, Cottage Cheese Dressing.

CARROTS JULIENNE

Scrub tender young carrots, scrape lightly, lay on board and cut in thin, lengthwise strips. Plunge into ice water for an hour or more until they curl. Wrap in clean, dry towel and place in refrigerator until ready to use.

CELERY, HOTEL STYLE

Wash celery hearts in cold water without separating stalks. Trim root ends down to a point, then cut hearts lengthwise from root to top. Plunge in bowl of ice until crisp. Serve on platter separately, or arrange with other raw vegetables on combination platter.

CELERY CURLS

Cut single stalks of celery into 3 or 4 inch lengths, then cut each individual length into narrow strips and plunge into bowl of ice water with spoonful of salt. When curled, wrap in dry towel and place in refrigerator until ready to use. If prepared at last minute, simply drain and serve.

CUCUMBER WEDGES

Peel cucumber, taking off a thick peel so that no bitter green is left on cucumber. Cut lengthwise in four strips, cut crosswise once, and remove seeds. Plunge in ice water with a spoonful of salt. When crisp, drain and lay in pan covered with damp cloth.

RADISH ROSES

Select fresh, crisp radishes. Cut off root end so it is flat. With a sharp knife, start at tip and carefully cut peel down from tip almost to stem end. Place in ice water until peel curls back, thus resembling petals of roses.

STUFFED CELERY STALKS

The hearts of celery may be used Hotel Style and the clean outer stalks saved for stuffing. The whole length may be used, or shorter lengths may be cut. Many prefer to stuff entire stalk, and cut it into 2 inch lengths for simple handling. The following mixtures are good for stuffing:

1. Equal parts of cottage and cream cheese seasoned with chopped chives, salt and pepper.
2. Equal parts of Blue cheese and cream cheese with dash of curry powder.
3. Cream cheese mixed with finely chopped pimiento.
4. Cream cheese mixed with finely minced cucumber and seasoned with onion juice.
5. Cream cheese mixed with finely chopped stuffed olives.

MIXED GREEN SALAD

(Tossed Salad)

Any greens which are in season may be mixed in a salad bowl, and blended with French dressing. Celery, celery cabbage, cabbage, chives, chicory, dan-

Salad maker, molds, cruets, salt and pepper grinder, salad fork and spoon, and vegetables are all important in the making of a delicious salad.

Cruets of vinegar and oil, 1 cup of sour cream, and ¼ cup crumbled American blue cheese go into this piquant salad dressing.

Three different shaped molds were used to make these dairy dishes.

A shamrock mold and a can of crushed pineapple are necessary for this St. Patrick's day treat.

Salad-making is an art in which you may indulge to your heart's content, when you have at your disposal all the tricks of the trade.

delion greens, lettuce, escarole, endive, parsley, romaine, spinach, watercress and radishes are basic greens and any combination of these may be tossed together lightly to yield a pleasing green salad.

An attractive salad with a kraut juice dressing is a good warm-weather choice. Serve macaroni and cheese as the one hot dish, and complete the meal with slices of cold roast beef, ham, or chicken.

MIXED RAW VEGETABLE SALAD

Any vegetables which make up an attractive color scheme in the salad bowl may be mixed with raw greens. Flowerets of cauliflower, chopped spinach leaves, diced tomatoes, provide a good example of blending colors. So does a combination of diced cucumbers, sliced radishes and julienne carrots.

MIXED COOKED VEGETABLE SALAD

Here again, any combination of cooked vegetables which are pleasing in color and texture may be used for attractive salads. The trick to making a first rate vegetable salad is to cook the vegetables properly, then drain off excess liquid and cover each separate vegetable with French dressing. Chill vegetables in refrigerator for 1 hour. When ready to serve, lift vegetables out with perforated spoon. Arrange on crisp greens. Garnish with hard-cooked egg, parsley, watercress. Serve mayonnaise or cooked salad dressing in separate bowl.

ASPARAGUS SALAD

Fresh-cooked, quick-frozen or canned asparagus stalks are all equally good for a popular salad. Drain asparagus, place in shallow dish, cover with French dressing. Chill well. Serve as above. Garnish with thin strips of pimiento. Vinaigrette dressing is preferred for this salad.

WALDORF SALAD

Combine equal parts of peeled, diced apples and celery with mayonnaise

Cucumber salad boats are easily made by filling scooped-out cucumber halves with diced pulp, shrimp, gherkins, green pepper, radishes, and onion. Add an Ac'cented French dressing, chill, and serve.

dressing to moisten. Garnish with chopped walnut meats. Serve on lettuce.

SPRING SALAD

A salad made with fresh greens, such as new lettuce, combined with young scallions and tiny radishes is usually called Spring Salad. Use French dressing seasoned with dry mustard to taste. Finely chopped hard-cooked eggs are used as a garnish. Instead of French dressing, some people prefer a generous serving of sour cream or a heaping dab of cottage cheese on the mixed greens.

CUCUMBER SALAD

Slice cucumber as thinly as possible, and stand in salted ice water for 30 minutes. Allow 1 tsp. salt to 1 qt. water. Drain well, add French dressing or sour cream dressing. Garnish with minced parsley or watercress.

TOMATO SALAD

A ripe red tomato is undoubtedly one of the most popular salad ingredients. Practically any type of vegetable salad may be made with good, firm tomatoes. Tomatoes may be sliced, or diced, or cut in wedges, marinated in French dressing, and added to any vegetable salad. They may be stuffed with meat or fish or vegetable salad, or served with mayonnaise, or cut in fancy shapes.

To Peel: Pour boiling water into bowl, carefully lower tomatoes into water, one at a time. Let stand a minute, lift out with perforated spoon. Place next tomato in water. Cut stem end from tomato and peel. Skin slips off easily. Repeat process until all tomatoes are used.

To Stuff: Scald, peel tomatoes, remove top. Scoop out center pulp, set aside and sprinkle inside of tomatoes with salt. Stand upside down on plate, chill in refrigerator 30 minutes. Stand right side up, fill with any desired stuffing. Serve on crisp lettuce.

OLD-FASHIONED POTATO SALAD

12 cold cooked medium-sized po-tatoes (allow 2 per person)	1 cup mayonnaise
2 cups celery, diced	1 cup French dressing
1 cup cucumbers, diced	3 hard-cooked eggs
	1 head lettuce

Scrub potatoes, cook unpeeled in boiling salted water until tender, but not broken. Drain and cool, then peel and dice potatoes. Add French dressing and blend lightly with two forks, handling potatoes carefully in order not to crush pieces. Place bowl of potatoes in refrigerator for 5 to 6 hours. Peel cucumbers, dice and soak in salted ice water. Dice celery. Just before serving salad, drain cucumber and celery, dry on paper towel, add to potatoes. Add mayonnaise to taste. Blend all ingredients together lightly. Line salad bowl with lettuce, fill with potato salad, garnish with sections of hard-cooked egg.

The above and each of the following recipes will make approximately *6 servings.*

COLESLAW

2 cups cabbage	2 Tbsp. French dressing
1 Tbsp. onion, minced fine	½ cup boiled salad dressing
	1 tsp. celery seed

Remove outer leaves from small, firm head of cabbage. Cut in quarters, and let stand in ice water 30 minutes. Drain, remove core.

The texture of cole slaw depends upon the knife, cutter, or grater which is used to cut the cabbage. The usual method is to shred the cabbage with a sharp knife, or with a regular cabbage cutter. But many fine cooks prefer a coarse grater in a large bowl, as the grated cabbage makes a far more delicate and attractive slaw than shredded cabbage. Mix the prepared cabbage with French dressing and cooked salad dressing. Arrange on crisp lettuce, garnish with celery seed.

GOOD HEALTH SALAD

½ lb. cottage cheese	1 Tbsp. chives, chopped
½ cup sour cream	Romaine
½ cup mayonnaise	½ tsp. salt
	1 tsp. lemon juice

Whip sour cream, add mayonnaise. Combine with cottage cheese, chives, salt and lemon juice. Press the mixture into individual small molds (first rinsed out with cold water) and place in refrigerator to chill. Place salad plates in refrigerator to chill also. Turn out on the individual salad plates, garnish with romaine.

CLUB DAY SALAD

1 cup sliced tongue	1 cup artichoke hearts
1 cup chicken	French dressing
1 head lettuce	Black olives
	Mayonnaise

Shred tongue and chicken into fine thin strips, with a sharp knife. Place tongue and chicken in covered bowl and leave in refrigerator. Drain artichoke hearts and marinate with French dressing. Rub wooden salad bowl with clove of garlic. Tear lettuce into small pieces, blend lightly with artichoke hearts, cover with chicken and tongue. Garnish with black olives. Serve mayonnaise separately in sauce boat.

SPORTSMEN'S SALAD

Heart of romaine, shredded fine	1 cup celery, diced
Heart of Chinese cabbage,	1 clove garlic
shredded fine	1/4 tsp. dry mustard
1 cup Chinese bean sprouts	1/2 cup French dressing

Mince clove of garlic to a fine paste in bottom of wooden salad bowl. Add mustard and 1 Tbsp. French dressing. Beat vigorously. Add celery, bean sprouts, Chinese cabbage and romaine. Add balance of French dressing slowly, and blend all ingredients lightly with two silver forks.

GROWING GARDEN SALAD

Raw celery with tops on	Raw shoestring beets
Raw carrot	Garnish of olives
Endive	1/2 cup mayonnaise
Raw cucumber	Chili sauce

Fill glass bowl with finely-chopped ice. Arrange in upright form (around the outer rim of the bowl) well-washed, crisp stalks of celery, carrot, endive, cucumber, beets. Make a slight indentation in center of bowl, and press into the indentation a cup filled with a combination of mayonnaise and enough chili sauce to give a deep rich color to the mayonnaise. Garnish with olives.

FISH SALADS

(Basic Recipe)

Canned or fresh crabmeat, lobster, salmon, shrimp or tuna fish can be used most effectively for fine salads.

2 cups cooked fish, flaked or cut in pieces	1 Tbsp. lemon juice
	½ tsp. salt
1 cup celery, diced	¼ tsp. pepper
	½ to 1 cup mayonnaise

Blend ingredients together, mix well. Serve in nest of crisp lettuce. Garnishes: stuffed olives, capers, hard-cooked egg, watercress, parsley, lemon wedges.

PICNIC TUNA SALAD

2 lbs. potatoes	½ cup French dressing
1 cup tuna fish	½ cup mayonnaise
1½ cup celery, diced	2 Tbsp. sweet pickle, chopped
Juice of ½ onion	1 Tbsp. parsley, minced
1 clove garlic	½ tsp. salt

Boil the potatoes in their skins. When cool, peel and dice into a large bowl which has been well-rubbed with a cut clove of garlic. Sprinkle with salt. Add onion juice and French dressing, mix lightly and let stand in refrigerator for an hour or more. Drain fish and flake into bits. Combine potatoes, tuna, celery, sweet pickle and mayonnaise. Cover top with minced parsley. Serve very cold. (The longer this stands, the better it is.) Wonderful for a main super dish, or for a picnic.

EASY ASPIC

1 Tbsp. gelatin	1 bay leaf
2 Tbsp. cold water	1 sprig parsley
2 cups chicken consommé	1 stalk celery
	1 sliced onion

Soften gelatin in water. Place consommé in a saucepan and add seasonings, simmer 5 minutes. Strain and pour over gelatin mixture. Set aside to thicken enough to pour.

A colorful variety of cooked vegetables, or diced chicken, or a combination of the two, may be arranged in any fashion and allowed to "set" until firm. An oblong mold is often lined with sliced stuffed olives, arranged in a simple design. A small amount of aspic is carefully ladled over olives. When the layer has become firm, a layer of chicken is added and more aspic added. Diced carrots and green peas are attractive when arranged in an aspic, in layers, separated by sliced egg.

SUNDAY SUPPER SALAD

1 Tbsp. gelatin	⅛ tsp. salt
2 Tbsp. cold water	⅛ tsp. pepper
1½ cups tomato juice	½ Tbsp. onion, minced
1 bay leaf	1 cup celery, chopped fine
2 peppercorns	½ Tbsp. parsley, minced
2 whole cloves	½ Tbsp. lemon juice
	½ Tbsp. vinegar

Soften gelatin in cold water. Heat tomato juice with seasonings, cover and simmer gently for 15 minutes. Strain, add to gelatin, and stir until dissolved. Pour into ring mold, chill until firm. At serving time, turn out on large round platter garnished with crisp lettuce. Fill center of mold with chicken or tuna or vegetable salad.

DEVILED EGGS IN CHICKEN ASPIC

2 cups clear chicken broth	4 hard-cooked eggs
1 Tbsp. gelatin	2 Tbsp. mayonnaise
2 Tbsp. water	4 stuffed olives, sliced

Soften gelatin in cold water. Heat chicken broth in saucepan, pour over gelatin. Cook eggs, cool, remove shell. Slice eggs in half lengthwise, remove yolks and combine with mayonnaise. Replace yolks in egg white cases, press

Shamrock salad mold is made with 1 can grapefruit sections, 1 package lime flavored gelatine, 2 Tbsp. lemon juice, ¼ tsp. salt, 1 cup evaporated milk, ½ cups each chopped nuts and diced celery, and ¼ cup finely chopped green pepper. This mold can be made a day ahead of time.

yolk down until smooth. Rinse out individual molds in cold water. Arrange olive slices in bottom of mold. Carefully place 1 Tbsp. of gelatin broth mixture over bottom of each mold to set olive mixture in place. When mixture has set enough to hold eggs upright, place egg halves in mold and pour remaining mixture equally into the four molds. Set in refrigerator to chill. Turn out either on individual salad plates or on a round plate. Garnish with crisp lettuce and serve mayonnaise with it. *4 servings.*

Cucumber stuffed tomato salad is perfect warm-weather dish. Looks pretty on crisp greens. Smooth avocado dressing tastes good with this crunchy salad, gives texture contrast.

GOLDEN GATE CHICKEN SALAD

1 cup chicken, cooked	3 hard-cooked eggs
1 cup celery, sliced thin	¼ cup French dressing
½ cup almonds, blanched	½ cup mayonnaise

Cut chicken in small neat pieces, add French dressing, blend lightly with two forks taking care not to break pieces of chicken. Cover dish and place in refrigerator, preferably for several hours. When ready to serve, add crisp celery, and fold in mayonnaise (combine with ½ cup of whipped cream if desired). Serve extra mayonnaise in salad dressing boat. Arrange salad on a platter of lettuce, garnish sides of salad with sections of hard-cooked eggs, and garnish top of salad with almonds.

GUACAMOLE

(Mexican Butter)

Avocado pears (1 pear for 3 servings)	1 Tbsp. onion, minced
	Few drops of lime juice
1 head lettuce or romaine	Ripe tomatoes (1 tomato for 3
French dressing	servings)
Dash of cayenne	Yolk of 2 hard-cooked eggs (press
Dash of chili powder	through sieve)

Slice an avocado pear. Beat in French dressing drop by drop in order to make a butter. When the pear and dressing are the consistency of heavy cream add seasonings to taste. Arrange slices of tomato on bed of lettuce leaves and pile the pear butter lightly in center. Dust with yolk of hard-cooked egg.

Note: Delicious with squares of Swiss cheese on crisp crackers.

RICE PIMIENTO AND OLIVE HONOLULU

2 cups rice, cooked	¼ cup stuffed green olives,
¼ cup mayonnaise	chopped

Combine cold rice, olives and enough mayonnaise to hold ingredients together. Pack individual molds with the rice. Place in refrigerator for several hours. Turn out just before serving. Good to serve with a platter of assorted cold meats. Garnish with watercress.

FRUIT SALAD

Fruit salads are the glamour salads. Their sun-kissed colors, their natural sweetness, their juiciness and texture, make them the Queen of the Meal. Fresh fruits, peeled and chilled, may be served alone or in combination with canned fruits. All fruits for salads must be well-drained. Any salad dressing which is free of sharp flavors is suitable for fruit salads. The artistic arrangement of fruits on a nest of lettuce leaves is an important element in a fruit salad. Avoid fancy shapes or heavy garnishes. Avoid masking fruits in mayonnaise.

GRAPEFRUIT SALAD

Cut grapefruit. Arrange segments on lettuce. Segments may overlap. Garnish with thin crescent-shaped slices of maraschino cherry.

Variations

1. Arrange with alternate slices of orange.

2. Arrange with alternate slices of avocado pear.
3. Arrange with alternate slices of fresh pear.

MELON SALAD

Cut any melon in season in balls (using French cutter), or cut in neat cubes. Any combination is good. Watermelon, cantaloupe, and honeydew blend well. Chill in refrigerator with honey dressing. Sprinkle liberally with lime juice. Garnish with sprig of fresh mint.

AVOCADO PEAR SALAD

Cut a ripe avocado pear in half, lengthwise. Remove seed. Fill cavity with French dressing. Serve on crisp lettuce.

Variations

1. Pear half may be scooped out with French cutter, pear balls added to mixture of diced orange and grapefruit. Pecan halves may be used as garnish.
2. Pear half may be filled with diced orange or grapefruit.
3. Pear half may be filled with chicken salad.

ROMAINE AVOCADO SALAD

1 head romaine	1 ripe avocado pear
¼ lb. French endive	¼ cup French dressing
	Paprika

Tear romaine and endive into coarse pieces, mix lightly with dressing. Peel avocado pear, cut in slices with sharp knife. Arrange on top of greens. Dust lightly with paprika.

FRUIT SALAD

1 head lettuce	2 cups pineapple chunks
6 peach halves	1 pkg. cream cheese (3 oz.)
6 pear halves	¼ cup pecan nut meats, chopped
	1 Tbsp. red cinnamon drops

Chill 6 salad plates in refrigerator. Wash, drain and chill lettuce until crisp and dry. Open cans of fruit and drain. Save juices for a fruit juice cocktail. (Pineapple juice plus a dash of lemon juice is a delicious hot weather beverage.) Lift pear halves carefully from can, place in shallow dish. Pour pear juice into saucepan, add cinnamon candies, and simmer gently until pear juice

Ham and apple salad is a delicious combination of frosty deviled ham and crisp, red skinned, fall apples. This is a treat to delight your first fall luncheon guests.

turns a brilliant red. Pour over pear halves and let cool. Moisten cream cheese with enough milk or cream to soften and mash with silver fork. Form cheese into 6 small balls, roll in the chopped nut meats. Arrange lettuce on chilled salad plates. Arrange fruit in the following manner: place peach half with rounded side up, then a mound of pineapple chunks, then pear half. In center of the plate, place a little lettuce cup filled with mayonnaise, and top with cream cheese.

BLACK HEART SALAD

(Dessert)

1 cup black bing pitted cherries	1 Tbsp. lemon juice
1 Tbsp. plain gelatin	2 Tbsp. sugar
¼ cup cold water	2 large navel oranges, sliced
1 cup cherry juice	½ cup mayonnaise
½ cup boiling water	½ cup whipped cream

Dissolve gelatin in cold water, add boiling water, cherry juice and sugar. Stir until dissolved. Add lemon juice. Rinse a mold in cold water. Pour in one-half of gelatin mixture and as it begins to thicken, add cherries. When mixture is firm, arrange orange slices on top and add remainder of syrup. (Orange slices to be free from membrane.) When ready to serve, turn out on round platter, garnish with lettuce. Serve with whipped cream and mayonnaise blended together.

SALAD DRESSINGS

MAYONNAISE

(Basic Recipe)

½ tsp. mustard	3 egg yolks
1 tsp. salt	¼ cup vinegar
Pinch of pepper	1 pt. salad oil

Beat egg yolks with dry ingredients until light and thick. Set bowl in pan of ice cubes while beating. Oil should be chilled, but not thick. Add oil a few drops at a time until dressing becomes very stiff. Then oil may be added more rapidly. When mixture is too thick so egg beater is difficult to turn, add small amount of vinegar. Continue to add oil and vinegar alternately until thick. Place in cool place at once.

Variations

Cucumber mayonnaise: Add ¼ cup finely minced cucumber to 1 cup mayonnaise. Good for vegetable salad.

Pineapple mayonnaise: Add ¼ cup whipped cream and ¼ cup drained crushed pineapple to 1 cup mayonnaise. Beat well. Good for fruit salad.

Russian dressing: Add ½ cup chili sauce, ¼ cup tomato ketchup and 1 Tbsp. minced onion to ½ cup mayonnaise.

THOUSAND ISLAND DRESSING

1 cup mayonnaise	1 Tbsp. stuffed olives, chopped
1 Tbsp. onion, minced	1 Tbsp. tarragon or wine vinegar
1 Tbsp. parsley, minced	1 Tbsp. lemon juice

Mix all ingredients together. Beat well, chill.

COTTAGE CHEESE DRESSING

½ cup mayonnaise	1 cake cream cheese
1 cup cottage cheese	1 Tbsp. lemon juice
	¼ tsp. salt

Beat all ingredients together until well blended. Chill and serve.

Variations

Add 1 Tbsp. onion juice, or minced chives, or minced parsley, or minced cucumber, for sake of variety.

ASPIC MAYONNAISE

1 cup clear consommé	1 cup mayonnaise
1½ tsp. plain gelatin	1 tsp. lemon juice
1 Tbsp. cold water	¼ tsp. salt

Soften gelatin in cold water. Add boiling hot consommé, stir well until dissolved. Add lemon juice, cool and chill until mixture thickens. Beat in mayonnaise. Chill. Use as dressing for jellied salads.

FRUIT JUICE (HONEY) DRESSING

½ cup salad oil	2 Tbsp. lemon juice
2 Tbsp. orange juice	1 tsp. strained honey
	¼ tsp. salt

Mix all ingredients and beat thoroughly with silver fork. Suitable for any fruit salad.

FRENCH DRESSING

(Basic Recipe)

1 tsp. salt	1 cup olive or salad oil
1 Tbsp. sugar	1 clove garlic
½ tsp. paprika	1 Tbsp. onion juice
¼ tsp. dry mustard	3 Tbsp. lemon juice
	Vinegar to taste

Mix the dry ingredients, blend with oil, add onion juice. Individual tastes vary, so beat in the lemon juice and vinegar to taste. Cut garlic in pieces and let it stand in the dressing. Remove garlic before serving.

This twelve-month summer salad is made of crisp salad greens, 1 cup each blueberries and strawberries, ⅔ cup salad oil, ¼ cup lemon juice, 1 tsp. each salt and paprika and the following, julienne style: 4 pear halves, 1 peeled avocado, and 1 package Switzerland Swiss cheese.

Variations

Add ½ tsp. Worcestershire sauce to 1 cup of dressing.

Add 1 tsp. thyme to 1 cup of dressing.

Add 2 Tbsp. chili sauce to 1 cup of dressing.

VINAIGRETTE DRESSING

1 cup French dressing	1 Tbsp. parsley, chopped fine
1 Tbsp. sweet pickle, chopped fine	1 Tbsp. hard-cooked egg white, chopped fine

Mix French dressing with other ingredients, and beat well. Excellent with asparagus.

BOILED SALAD DRESSING

1 Tsp. oil	1 Tbsp. sugar
1 tsp. salt	3 eggs
¾ Tbsp. mustard	1 cup vinegar
	1 cup milk

Stir oil, salt, mustard and sugar in a bowl until perfectly smooth. Add the eggs, and beat well; then add the vinegar and finally the milk. Place the bowl over boiling water and stir the dressing until it thickens like a soft custard.

SOUR CREAM DRESSING

Sour cream is available at nearly every grocery store in ½ pt. containers. It is an unusually good dressing for hot weather salads.

1 cup heavy sour cream	¼ tsp. paprika
½ tsp. salt	1 Tbsp. lemon juice
	1 Tbsp. cucumber, minced fine

Beat cream until stiff, add other ingredients. Place in refrigerator to chill. Dust lightly with paprika as garnish.

Variation

Add 2 Tbsp. fresh tomato pulp.

15.

YEAST BREADS—
QUICK BREADS

THERE is no branch of cookery which gives a homemaker greater satisfaction than baking—no sight more gratifying than a fine, light loaf of homemade bread, a pan of fluffy biscuits, of sky-high popovers. There is something about baking which satisfies that creative urge deep inside every human being. To simplify home baking, the novice needs to know the difference between the various flours offered for sale, since each flour has specified characteritics and qualities which determine the type of the finished product. The most widely-used flour is made from wheat; it contains starch and protein. The latter is commonly called gluten, because its two proteins form gluten when liquid is added. This gluten is elastic, and holds the air as it is beaten in; or if yeast or other leavening agents are used, it holds the gas released by these ingredients, thus producing a light product. Wheat flour may be classified as:

Bread flour. From "hard" or spring wheat, high in gluten. Used chiefly by bakers.

Pastry and cake flours. From "soft" or winter wheat. Contains more starch, less gluten than bread flour, and the gluten is more delicate.

Cake flour. Usually a specially milled fine flour.

All-purpose flour (sometimes called "family flour"). From a blend of hard and soft wheat. Can be used for practically all home baking with the exception of fine cakes.

Whole wheat and graham flour. From the whole wheat grain, richer in minerals and vitamins than white flour. A good choice for muffins and quick breads, it is usually blended by the homemaker with all-purpose flour and used for special recipes.

Other flours and cereals available at stores include rye, buckwheat, cornmeal, oatmeal, rice, rice flour, and soybean flour.

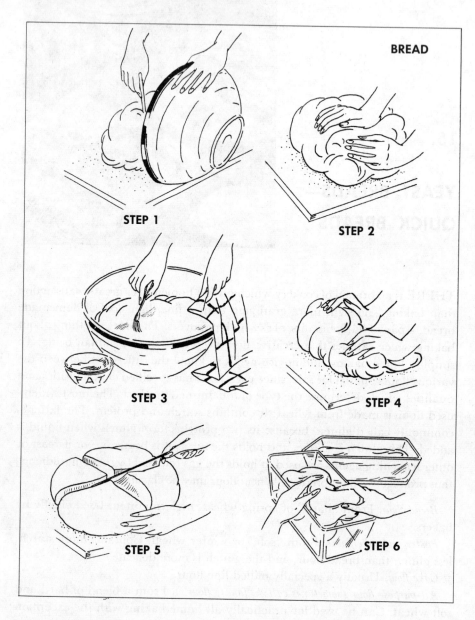

Self-rising flour is a packaged product containing salt and a leavening agent. Directions on each package should be carefully followed for best results.

INGREDIENTS FOR BREAD AND ROLLS

Liquids: Milk or water, or water in which peeled potatoes have been boiled. Potato-water tends to keep bread moist for a longer period of time.

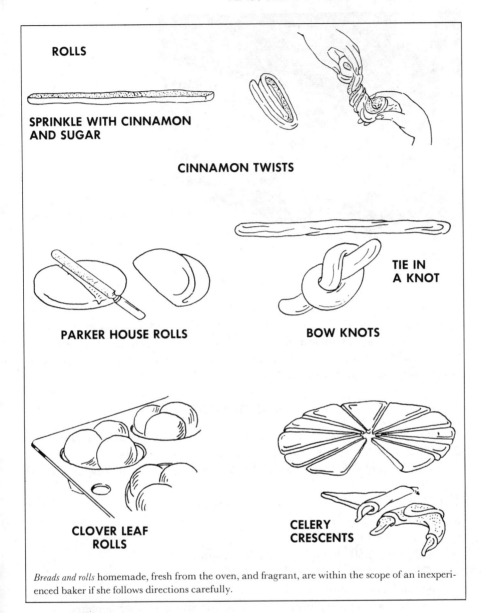

ROLLS

SPRINKLE WITH CINNAMON
AND SUGAR

CINNAMON TWISTS

TIE IN
A KNOT

PARKER HOUSE ROLLS

BOW KNOTS

CLOVER LEAF
ROLLS

CELERY
CRESCENTS

Breads and rolls homemade, fresh from the oven, and fragrant, are within the scope of an inexperienced baker if she follows directions carefully.

Fats: Fats improve texture, flavor and keeping qualities of finished product. Fine cakes require sweet butter or margarine or prepared commercial shortenings.

Sweetening Agents: Used for flavor and browning quality; may be sugar, or a combination of sugar with either honey, molasses, corn syrup or corn sugar.

Eggs: Beaten egg yolks or whole eggs may be added for rolls or rich bread.

Ready for Baking—after the dough has been shaped and allowed to rise. Both glass and aluminum pans are suitable for baking bread.

BREADS

Breads may be described as yeast breads and quick breads. Yeast breads are made light and spongy by the use of yeast. Quick breads depend upon baking powder, baking soda with sour milk or molasses, air or steam for their lightness. A batter or dough is named according to the proportion of liquid to flour used; a batter uses more liquid, a dough less.

BREAD BAKING

1. An even temperature of 80° to 85° F. is essential while dough is rising.
2. Milk is scalded in order to melt fat and dissolve sugar and salt.
3. Liquid is cooled before yeast is added, so yeast plants will grow and bread will rise.
4. Dough is kneaded to develop elasticity of gluten.
5. Time schedule for bread in oven:
     First 10 minutes—400° F.
     Reduce to 350° F. and bake for 10 minutes.
     Reduce to 250° F. and finish the baking.
   The total baking time should be approximately 1 hour.
   If oven does not have thermometer, buy portable oven thermometer.
6. Remove loaves from pans as soon as removed from oven.
7. Place loaves upside down on wire rack, away from drafts.
8. Brush tops of hot loaves with butter to keep moist.
9. When bread is thoroughly cool, put away in a newly-scalded, thoroughly dried and well-aired bread box.
10. Grease pans with a fat other than butter, and loaves will turn out easily when baked.

WHY FAILURES OCCUR IN BREAD BAKING

Below are listed the possible causes of common bread-baking failures which may be encountered, not only by the "beginner" housekeeper but often by an experienced one also:

THE RESULT	THE CAUSES
Loaf uneven shape	Dough molded incorrectly. Pan not turned—during early stages of baking.
Heavy weight	Flour of poor grade. Dough too heavy.
Crackled crust	Cooled too rapidly in a draft.
Bulges and cracks in crust	Dough not sufficiently soft. Heat inconsistent.
Thick crust	Baked too slowly.
Tough crust	Dough too heavy. Excess of salt. Flour of poor grade. Dough handled too much.
Pale crust	Oven heat too low. Excess of salt. Dough not sufficiently moist.
Dark crust	Dough too light. Oven temperature incorrect.
Streaked crumb	Flour added during molding of dough. Top dough allowed to dry before shaping.
Crumbly crumb	Poor grade flour. Dough too light.
Coarse crumb	Dough too light. Oven temperature incorrect.

PREPARED DOUGHS AND BATTERS

Each year sees new labor-saving methods developed in food preparation. There are biscuit mixes and muffin mixes; ready-prepared pie crusts; cake, gingerbread and cookie ready-mixed products. These commercial mixes are made of fine ingredients, blended with the utmost skill in factories. They are weighed, measured and controlled by rigid laboratory formulas.

How shall the inexperienced housewife choose? Shall she prepare all these products in her home kitchen, or shall she take advantage of modern packaged goods? The intelligent approach is to weigh the advantages between the two types of baked foods. If biscuits, muffins and cakes are made from ingredients in her own kitchen, she undoubtedly gains a more homelike flavor, and saves a few pennies. But she also spends a great deal more time in preparation. If her time is limited, if her other activities and duties consume a great deal of her energy, then she might well consider spending the few extra cents for the commercial products.

However, there is another consideration—the hidden values. The satisfaction an artist feels when he creates a beautiful picture is no different from the satisfaction of the cook who creates a beautiful cake. And if there are small children in the home, they dearly love to watch their mother making homemade cookies; they like to feel they are "helping mother" by sifting the flour and doing any other little tasks she can entrust to them. It can't be improved upon as a method of creating a home!

YEAST BREADS

WHITE BREAD

3 cups all-purpose flour	1 Tbsp. sugar
1 yeast cake	½ tsp. salt
2 Tbsp. lukewarm water	1 cup milk, scalded
	1 Tbsp. shortening

Sift; measure flour. Crumble yeast cake in large bowl, add water, stir until dissolved. Add sugar and salt to scalded milk; cool to lukewarm. Stir in shortening and ½ of flour. Beat until smooth. Add remaining flour and mix well. Turn onto a lightly-floured board and knead until smooth and elastic. Place in a greased bowl, brush the surface with fat, and let rise until double in bulk (2 to 4 hours) keeping dough covered. Knead, shape into loaf and put in greased bread pan. Again let rise until doubled in bulk (1 to 2 hours) and bake in hot oven (400° F.) 20 minutes; reduce heat to moderate (350° F.), and bake 40 minutes longer.

Variations

Rye Bread: Substitute equal quantity of sifted rye flour for white flour. 1 to 2 Tbsp. caraway seeds may be sprinkled over dough.

Graham Bread: Substitute 1½ cups of whole wheat flour for 1½ cups white flour in above recipe.

Whole Wheat Bread: Follow recipe for white bread; but substitute 3 cups whole wheat flour for 3 cups white flour. Replace 1 Tbsp. white sugar with 1 Tbsp. brown sugar.

During the kneading process add 1 cup of nuts or fruits to the above mentioned ingredients to make any of the following breads:

Whole Wheat Nut Bread
Whole Wheat Prune Bread
Whole Wheat Fig Bread
Whole Wheat Raisin Bread

BUCHTA COFFEE CAKE

(From an old cook book)

3¼ cups flour	½ cup sugar
2 cakes yeast	1 tsp. salt
¼ cup warm water	¼ cup shortening
1 cup milk, scalded	1 egg, well-beaten

Topping

⅓ cup sugar	¼ cup cinnamon
	¼ cup chopped nut meats

Sift; measure flour. Crumble yeast in lukewarm water. Scald milk, add sugar, salt and shortening. Let cool to lukewarm temperature. Add egg, 1 cup flour, and yeast mixture. Beat thoroughly. Add remaining flour to make a stiff batter. Beat well. Pour into greased angel food pan, sprinkle with topping. Let rise 1 hour. Bake in moderate oven (375° F.) 35 to 40 minutes. (Makes 1 coffee cake about half the depth of an angel food cake pan.) Mix topping ingredients together and sprinkle on cake.

PLAIN ROLLS

Yeast dough may be shaped into rolls and baked same day, or it may be stored in the refrigerator for 2 to 3 days before being baked. When ready to use, dough is taken from refrigerator, kneaded and shaped into rolls. It is then allowed to stand at room temperature until rolls double in bulk. Rolls are always baked in a very hot oven.

4-5 cups flour	1 tsp. salt
2 yeast cakes	1 cup milk, scalded
¼ cup sugar	¼ cup shortening
	1 egg, well-beaten

Sift; measure flour. Crumble yeast cakes in large bowl, add water, stir until dissolved. Add sugar and salt to scalded milk. Let cool to lukewarm temperature. Stir in yeast mixture. Add ½ of shortening, egg, and ½ of flour. Beat until smooth. Add remaining flour and shortening. Mix well. Knead on floured board until smooth. Place dough in greased bowl, cover, set in warm place, and let rise until doubled in bulk. When light, punch dough down, form into various shapes. Place on greased baking sheets, brush with melted shortening, and let rise again until double in bulk. Bake in hot oven (400° F.) 15 to 20 minutes.

Variations

Cloverleaf Rolls: After dough has risen once, divide dough into small balls. Roll in melted shortening and place 3 balls together in muffin tin. Let rise and bake as for Plain Rolls.

Parkerhouse Rolls: Follow Plain Rolls recipe. Four Tbsp. each of sugar and shortening added give excellent results. When light, roll dough ¼ inch thick. Cut with biscuit cutter, brush each circle with melted fat and crease through the center of each roll with the dull edge of a knife. Fold each roll over double. Place on a well-greased pan 1 inch apart, brush with melted fat and when very light bake in hot oven as for Plain Rolls.

SWEET ROLLS

Double the amount of sugar, shortening, and eggs called for in recipe for plain rolls. Otherwise, use the same ingredients and method.

QUICK YEAST BREADS

QUICK LUNCHEON ROLLS

⅔ cup milk	⅔ cake yeast
⅓ Tbsp. sugar	1½ to 2 cups sifted flour
½ tsp. salt	1⅓ Tbsp. shortening, melted

Scald milk; add sugar and salt; cool to lukewarm. Crumble in yeast and stir until dissolved. Add half of the flour and beat until perfectly smooth. Add melted shortening and remaining flour, or enough to make a soft dough. Place in greased bowl. Cover and set in warm place, free from draft. Let rise until doubled in bulk, about 1 hour. Fill well-greased muffin pans half full. Cover and let rise again about 45 minutes. Bake in hot oven (425° F.) about 20 minutes.

CHEESE BREAD

1 Tbsp. sugar	1 cake yeast
1 tsp. salt	1 egg
⅔ cup lukewarm water	1⅓ cups grated American cheese
	2⅓ cups sifted flour

Dissolve sugar and salt in lukewarm water. Crumble in yeast and stir until dissolved. Add well-beaten egg, grated cheese and flour to make easily-handled dough. Knead dough quickly and lightly until smooth and elastic. Shape into loaf and place in greased bread pans. Cover and let rise in warm place, free from draft, until doubled in bulk, about 1¾ hours. Bake in moderate oven (375° F.) 45 minutes.

Waffles for dessert, not just breakfast and lunch. Serve chilled pineapple, cream topping and coconut to go over warm waffles.

QUICK CELERY CRESCENTS

½ cup milk	½ cup lukewarm water
2 Tbsp. sugar	3 cups flour, sifted
1½ tsp. salt	3 Tbsp. melted butter
1 cake yeast	½ tsp. salt
	1 tsp. celery seeds

Scald milk; add sugar and salt; cool to lukewarm. Dissolve yeast in lukewarm water and add to lukewarm milk. Add 1½ cups flour and beat until perfectly smooth. Add melted shortening and remaining flour, or enough to make easily-handled dough. Knead well. Roll dough into circular shape about ½ inch thick. Cut into 12 pie-shaped pieces. Brush lightly with melted butter, beginning at wide end, roll up to pointed end. Shape into crescents and place on well-greased baking sheet with pointed end underneath. Brush with melted butter; sprinkle with the salt and celery seeds. Cover and set in warm place, free from draft. Let rise until light, about 1 hour. Bake in hot oven (425° F.) 20 minutes.

SWEDISH TEA RING

Dough Mixture

⅓ cup milk	1½ cakes yeast
¼ cup sugar	1½ Tbsp. sugar
½ tsp. salt	⅓ cup lukewarm water
3 Tbsp. butter	2 eggs
	3 cups flour, sifted

Filling Mixture

½ cup brown sugar	½ cup raisins
	½ tsp. cinnamon

Scald milk; add sugar, salt and shortening; cool to lukewarm. Dissolve yeast and 1½ Tbsp. sugar in the lukewarm water; add lukewarm milk mixture. Add beaten eggs and half of the flour; beat until smooth. Add remaining flour, or enough to make an easily-handled dough. Knead dough quickly and lightly until smooth and elastic. Place in greased bowl, cover and set in warm place, free from draft. Let rise until doubled in bulk, about 1 hour. When light, punch dough down and form into a smooth ball. Roll out into oblong piece ¼ inch thick. Brush generously with melted butter. Sprinkle with filling mixture. Roll up as for jelly roll; place on greased baking sheet. Shape into ring, sealing ends together. Cut 1-inch slices almost through with scissors. Turn each slice partly on its side, pointing away from the center. Cover and set in warm

place, free from draft. Let rise until doubled in bulk, about 30 minutes. Brush with 1 egg yolk beaten with 2 Tbsp. milk. Bake in moderate oven (350° F.) about 30 minutes.

HONEY PECAN BUNS

Bun Mixture

½ cup milk	3 yeast cakes
¼ cup sugar	1 Tbsp. sugar
½ tsp. salt	½ cup lukewarm water
3 Tbsp. butter	1 egg, well-beaten
	3½ cups flour, sifted

Filling Mixture

6 Tbsp. brown sugar	6 Tbsp. finely-cut pecan nuts
	3 Tbsp. butter, melted

Syrup Mixture

½ cup brown sugar	3 Tbsp. butter
½ cup honey	Pecan nut halves (3 to a tin)

Cook sugar, honey and butter together until it forms a syrup. Place nut halves in bottom of each tin. Pour syrup over nut meats.

Scald milk, add sugar, salt and butter. Cool to lukewarm temperature. Dissolve yeast and 1 Tbsp. sugar in water; add to milk mixture. Add egg and 1 cup flour; beat until smooth. Add remaining flour and knead dough quickly and lightly. Place in greased bowl, cover and set in warm place, away from drafts. Let rise until doubled in bulk, about ½ hour. When dough has doubled in bulk, punch down. Turn out on lightly-floured board. Roll out to 12 inch length, about ½ inch thick. Brush with melted butter, sprinkle with sugar and nuts. Roll up as for jelly roll; cut in 1-inch slices. Place cut-side up in muffin tins on top of nuts and syrup mixture. Cover, let rise until doubled in bulk. Bake in hot oven (400° F.) 30 minutes.

QUICK ROLLS AND BREADS

Quick breads are usually called by that name because it takes such a short time to prepare them in comparison with yeast breads. No yeast at all is required in their preparation. For such delicacies as popovers, steam which develops during the baking is the only leavening agent. Liquids are added last, and mixture is stirred just enough to moisten the dry ingredients.

A good quick bread adds that little extra something which turns a fairly good plain meal into a special meal. The delicacy and lightness of quick breads endear them to young and old alike. A tender pancake, a hot muffin, a fluffy biscuit. How everyone cheers their appearance!

Here is a classification of quick breads from which the type of batter may be learned at a glance:

BATTERS AND DOUGHS—CLASSIFICATIONS

TYPE OF MIXTURE	RECIPE	PROPORTION OF LIQUID	BASED ON 2 CUPS FLOUR
Batters			
Thin or Pour	Popovers	2 cups	2 cups
	Griddle Cakes		
	Waffles		
Stiff	Muffins	1 cup	2 cups
	Cake		
Doughs			
Soft...........	Baking Powder	¾-⅔ cup	2 cups
	Biscuits		
	Doughnuts		
	Quick Breads		
	Cream Puffs		
Stiff	Pastry	¼-½ cup	2 cups

BAKING POWDER BISCUITS

2 cups flour

3 tsp. baking powder

1 tsp. salt

4 Tbsp. shortening

¾ cup milk

Sift; measure flour. Add dry ingredients to flour, sift again. Cut in shortening with two knives or pastry blender and blend until the mixture resembles coarse crumbs. Add milk and mix with fork until flour makes smooth dough. Turn out on floured board, knead lightly about ½ minute. Roll to thickness of ½ inch. Cut in rounds with floured biscuit cutter. Brush tops lightly with melted butter. Bake on ungreased baking sheet in hot oven (450° F.) 12 to 15 minutes.

Variation

Whole Wheat Biscuits: Substitute 1 cup unsifted whole wheat flour for 1 cup of white flour.

SOUR MILK BISCUITS

2 cups flour
1 tsp. baking powder
1 tsp. salt

4 Tbsp. shortening
¾ cup sour milk
½ tsp. soda

Follow directions for baking powder biscuits.

MUFFINS

Muffins can be made from nearly every pleasant ingredient that is on the pantry shelf. From one basic good recipe, an entire list of changes can be devised. Mixing and beating determine the quality of a muffin. The mixture should be rough, so stir just enough to hold the ingredients together. Have a good hot oven, fill the greased tins about ⅔ full, and bake at once. Eat as soon as possible; the sooner the better. Everyone loves hot muffins!

PLAIN MUFFINS

2 cups flour
3 tsp. baking powder
½ tsp. salt
2 Tbsp. sugar
1 cup milk
1 egg, beaten
3 Tbsp. shortening, melted

Muffins profit by the addition of blueberries.

Sift; measure flour. Add dry ingredients, sift again. Add egg and shortening to milk, stir this mixture quickly into the dry ingredients. Do not beat. Pour at once into greased muffin pans, filling ⅔ full. Bake in hot oven (400° F.) 20 minutes.

Variations

Blueberry Muffins: Add 1 cup fresh blueberries or huckleberries to sifted dry ingredients.

Cheese Muffins: Add ¾ cup grated cheese to sifted dry ingredients.

CORN MUFFINS

1 cup flour	3 Tbsp. sugar
¾ cup yellow cornmeal	1 egg, well-beaten
4 tsp. baking powder	1 cup milk
¾ tsp. salt	3 Tbsp. shortening, melted

Sift; measure flour. Add dry ingredients, sift again. Combine eggs, milk and shortening. Pour into dry ingredients and stir just enough to moisten dry ingredients. Do not beat. Fill greased muffin tins ⅔ full and bake in hot oven (400° F.) 20 minutes.

BRAN MUFFINS

1 cup flour	2 Tbsp. sugar
1 cup bran flakes	1 egg, well-beaten
3 tsp. baking powder	¾ cup milk
¼ tsp. salt	3 Tbsp. shortening, melted

Sift; measure flour. Add dry ingredients. Combine egg, milk and shortening. Pour into dry ingredients and stir just enough to moisten dry ingredients. Do not beat. Fill greased muffin tins ½ to ¾ full and bake in hot oven (400° F.) 20 minutes.

POPOVERS

The trick to popovers is the high temperatures at which they are baked. They'll increase to 4 times their size.

1 cup flour	2 eggs
1 cup milk	½ tsp. salt
	½ tsp. sugar

Sift; measure flour. Add dry ingredients, sift again. Beat eggs until very light, add milk. Pour half of this mixture on flour, beat 1 minute. Add remaining flour and beat again. Fill piping hot, heavy iron muffin tins ⅓ full with mixture. Bake in hot oven (450° F.) 20 minutes, reduce heat to moderate (350° F.) and bake 15 minutes more.

WAFFLES

1⅓ cups flour	2 eggs, separated
2 tsp. baking powder	1 cup milk
¼ tsp. salt	4 Tbsp. shortening, melted

Sift; measure flour. Add dry ingredients, sift again. Combine well-beaten egg yolks and milk; add shortening, beat just enough to mix together. Fold in stiffly-beaten egg whites. Bake on hot waffle iron 4 to 5 minutes.

Variations

Bacon Waffles: Cut bacon in small strips and fit on the hot waffle iron. Close cover and bake for a moment. Add batter and bake as usual.

Orange Waffles: Substitute ½ cup of milk for 1 cup, then add ½ cup of orange juice.

Griddle cakes—all-American dish. Keep a heavy griddle handy, use often. Vary milk for thick or thin batter. Add corn or berries or whatever you fancy.

GRIDDLE CAKES

An American delicacy that is second to none; golden brown, thin, tender, dripping with amber maple syrup. To achieve perfection a griddle cake needs only a thin batter and a heavy griddle, evenly heated. Crushed or chopped fruit, fresh or canned berries, drained canned or fresh corn may be added to the batter.

1 cup flour	1 tsp. sugar
1½ tsp. baking powder	¾ cup milk
¼ tsp. salt	1 egg, well-beaten
	2 Tbsp. shortening, melted

Sift; measure flour. Add dry ingredients, sift again. Combine eggs and milk, and stir into dry ingredients. Beat well, add shortening. Bake on both sides on ungreased hot griddle.

Note: Add more milk to make thinner cakes.

SOUR MILK GRIDDLE CAKES

1 cup flour	2 tsp. warm water
½ tsp. sugar	1 cup sour milk
½ tsp. salt	1 egg, well-beaten
½ tsp. baking soda	1 Tbsp. shortening, melted

Sift; measure flour. Add sugar and salt, sift again. Dissolve soda in water. Add sour milk. Stir into dry ingredients, add egg and shortening. Beat well and bake on both sides on ungreased hot griddle.

Variation

Cornmeal griddle cakes: One-half quantity of flour may be replaced by yellow cornmeal.

BUCKWHEAT CAKES

¼ cake yeast	1 tsp. salt
1 pt. milk, scalded	1 Tbsp. molasses
2 cups buckwheat flour	¼ cup warm water
½ cup cornmeal	½ tsp. soda

Crumble yeast into bowl. Cool milk to lukewarm temperature, add to yeast, stir well. Add salt and flour, beat well. Cover, let stand overnight. Before breakfast, add soda dissolved in warm water, add molasses. Beat thoroughly. Save ½ cup of mixture to use next time instead of using yeast. Bake on hot griddle

QUICK LOAF BREADS

DARK NUT BREAD

1 cup flour	¼ cup sugar
1 cup graham flour	1 egg, well-beaten
½ tsp. salt	¼ cup molasses
2 tsp. baking powder	¾ cup milk
	½ cup nut meats

Sift; measure flour. Add salt, baking powder and sugar. Sift again. Add egg, milk, molasses and nut meats, to dry ingredients. Beat vigorously. Pour into greased bread pan or into a cylindrical can. Bake in moderate oven (350° F.) 1 hour. Cool before cutting.

BANANA BREAD

½ cup butter

1 cup sugar

2 eggs, well-beaten

2 ripe bananas, well-beaten

2 tsp. sour milk

2 cups flour, sifted

1 tsp. soda

½ tsp. salt

Cream butter, add sugar. Mix in order given. Bake in 2 greased loaf pans in slow oven (300° F.) 1 hour.

HONEY COCONUT MUFFINS

Serve these special muffins at brunch.

For Pans

⅓ cup sugar

¼ cup honey

2 Tbsp. shortening

¼ cup coconut

Combine sugar, honey, and shortening in small sauce pan. Bring to boil slowly, over moderate heat, stirring constantly. Remove from heat. Measure 2 tsp. of this syrup into each muffin cup. Sprinkle 1 tsp. coconut into each cup on top of honey mixture. Set aside while preparing batter.

Batter

1½ cups sifted flour

2 tsp. baking powder

¼ tsp. salt

1 Tbsp. sugar

1 egg, beaten

⅔ cup milk

3 Tbsp. melted shortening

Sift together flour, baking powder, salt and sugar into a mixing bowl. Beat egg and add milk and melted shortening. Stir to mix. Add all at one time to flour mixture in bowl. Stir only until flour is well-moistened. (Batter may look a bit lumpy.) Spoon batter into muffin pans on top of honey-coconut mixture. Fill each cup ⅔ full. Bake in moderately hot oven (400° F.) 25-30 minutes. When done, loosen edges of muffins with spatula or knife tip and turn out at once. Drizzle any remaining honey-mixture in pan over muffins.

LIGHT NUT BREAD

2 cups flour	1 egg, well-beaten
2 tsp. baking powder	¾ cup milk
½ cup light brown sugar	½ cup nut meats
½ tsp. salt	½ cup raisins

Sift; measure flour, add dry ingredients, sift again. Stir in egg and milk. Add raisins and nut meats. Beat well. Bake in greased bread pan in moderate oven (350° F.) 45 minutes.

ORANGE BREAD

1½ cups flour	1 cup water
1 tsp. baking powder	1 cup sugar
¼ tsp. salt	1 Tbsp. butter
1 cup orange peel, chopped fine	¼ cup milk
	1 egg, well-beaten

Sift; measure flour. Add dry ingredients, sift again. Cook orange peel in water 15 to 20 minutes or until tender. Add sugar, cook until consistency of marmalade. Let cool a little, add melted butter, milk and egg mixed together. Add dry ingredients. Bake in greased loaf pan in moderate oven (350° F.) 1 hour.

SOUTHERN SPOON BREAD

1 pt. milk	2 eggs, separated
½ cup cornmeal	1 tsp. baking powder
½ tsp. salt	1 Tbsp. melted butter

Scald milk in double boiler. Stir in corn meal gradually. Add salt and cook 15 minutes. Cool slightly. Combine beaten egg yolks with this mixture, add butter. Fold in baking powder and stiffly-beaten egg whites. Bake in greased casserole in moderate oven (350° F.) 30 to 40 minutes. Serve immediately.

BOSTON BROWN BREAD

1 cup sour milk	1 tsp. soda
⅓ cup molasses	¾ tsp. salt
½ cup bran	½ tsp. cinnamon
½ cup whole wheat flour	½ cup raisins
½ cup cornmeal	1 Tbsp. sugar

Mix milk, molasses and bran together. Let stand 10 minutes. Combine dry ingredients and raisins. Fold gently into bran mixture. Pour into a 1½ qt.

Fruit and nut bread studded with raisins and citrons is superb fare for a comfortable afternoon tea. Ice and decorate.

greased mold. Cover with heavy waxed paper. Steam 3 hours. Uncover and bake in slow oven (250° F.) 20 to 30 minutes.

PEANUT BUTTER BREAD

(Makes 1 large loaf)

3 cups sifted flour	⅓ cup sugar
5 tsp. baking powder	½ cup peanut butter
1½ tsp. salt	1 egg, well-beaten
	1½ cups milk

Sift together flour, baking powder, salt and sugar. Add peanut butter. Mix in thoroughly with a fork until crumbly in appearance. Add beaten egg and milk; mix well. Place in greased loaf pan. Bake in moderate oven (350° F.) about 1 hour.

BRAN NUT BREAD

1 egg	½ cup bran
¾ cup sugar	2½ cups flour, sifted
1 cup milk	1 tsp. salt
2 Tbsp. melted butter	3 tsp. baking powder
	½ cup pecan nut meats, broken

Beat egg and sugar until light. Add milk, butter and bran. Sift flour with salt and baking powder; combine with nut meats; add to first mixture, stirring lightly, spread in greased loaf pan, waxed paper in the bottom. Bake in moderate oven (350° F.) about 1 hour.

CINNAMON TOAST

1 cup sugar	1 to 2 Tbsp. cinnamon
	Buttered toast

Mix cinnamon and sugar in small container with perforated top. Mixture keeps well indefinitely if wax paper is tied over top. Sprinkle mixture over hot buttered toast. Place under oven broiler. Heat until sugar bubbles and browns.

FRENCH TOAST

1 egg, slightly-beaten	¼ tsp. salt
1 cup milk	4 slices stale bread
	⅛ lb. butter or shortening

Combine egg, milk and salt. Dip each slice of bread in egg mixture. Melt butter in skillet and sauté bread on one side until brown. Turn on other side and brown. Use low heat.

MELBA TOAST

Use bread at least 1 or 2 days old. Cut in very thin slices. Remove crusts and cut in half. Place on baking sheet and bake in a slow oven (300° F.) 20 minutes or until slightly browned.

16.

CAKES

AND

CUP CAKES

"WHAT a delicious cake!" This is probably one of the compliments a good cake baker hears most often. And it's a remark she never tires of hearing.

Nearly everyone regards a dessert as the highlight of luncheon or dinner. After a meal which is rather plain, a slice of rich homemade cake appeals most to the appetite. But if the meal itself is rich, then an angel or sponge cake, with fresh fruit or a gelatin dessert, is preferable.

A good cake every time is the result of following exact rules, which are easily learned. Correct measuring, mixing the batter, and baking—each plays an important part in the final successful result, namely, a moist tender cake, of fine crumb.

BAKING THE CAKE

Many modern ranges are equipped with oven heat controls, but if such a regulator is absent, it is possible to buy a portable oven thermometer. If neither of these pieces of equipment is available, the following guide will show at a glance how the baking proceeds. Regulate heat so oven is correct temperature when cake is placed in oven. Divide the baking time into quarters:

    1st quarter—Cake batter rises.
    2nd quarter—Cake continues to rise and begins to brown.
    3rd quarter—Cake has risen to full volume and continues to brown.
    4th quarter—Cake "settles" and shrinks from edges of the pan.

When cake is done:

    (a) It will spring back when pressed lightly with the finger.
    (b) It shrinks from the sides of the pan.
    (c) A clean toothpick inserted in the center comes out clean and dry.

Remove the cake pan from the oven, but let cake remain in pan for 5 minutes. Then loosen the sides of the cake with a spatula and turn out of the pan onto a wire cake rack. Remove paper from the bottom of the cake and turn right side up on rack to finish cooling. When cold it is ready for filling and frosting.

TYPES OF CAKE

Cakes are divided into two groups—those made with shortening and those made without. Cakes in which shortening is used are usually baked in more shallow tins than unshortened sponge or angel food cake. Pans for cakes with shortening are greased, and to be sure cake slips out of pan easily, you should line bottom of pan with wax paper. Grease bottom of pan and paper well; grease sides of pan sparingly. Pans for cakes made without shortening do not need to be greased.

PREPARATION OF CAKE PANS FOR BAKING

Salad oils or vegetable shortenings are generally used to grease shallow cake pans for cakes made with shortening. Grease pans well, shake a spoonful of flour in pan, shake until inside of pan is lightly dusted with flour, then empty out extra flour. Another popular method is to line the bottom of greased tin with layer of wax paper as indicated above.

POSITION OF CAKE PANS IN OVEN

If only 1 cake or 1 layer is to be baked, place it in the center of a rack which is in the exact center of the oven. If 2 cakes or layers are to be baked at once, make sure tins do not touch each other, nor the sides of the oven. If there are 3 layers, use 2 oven racks, but alternate the position of pans so no pan is directly above another.

DO'S AND DON'T'S FOR GOOD CAKES

The first rule for good cakes is to follow the directions accurately.

Do use standard measuring cups and spoons.

Do use level measurements.

Do sift flour before measuring, and sift again after the baking powder has been added.

Do assemble all ingredients.

Do grease pan before mixing cake.

Do cream shortening and sugar together well; a good-textured butter cake depends upon this.

Do use proper-sized pans for batter. Don't fill too full.

Do have oven at correct temperature, and put cake in at once. Don't let cake batter stand around after mixing, as it will lose some of its rising action.

Do cool cake quickly on wire rack. But do not let it dry out.

Do frost cake as soon as it is cool.

MAKING CAKES WITH ELECTRIC MIXER

Assemble all ingredients for the cake on kitchen table, so all will be of uniform temperature.

BUTTER CAKES

(Electric Mixer)

Cream shortening on high speed for 2 minutes. Add sugar gradually, on high speed. Scrape down bowl with rubber scraper. Beat again on high speed for 1 minute. Then add eggs one at a time; beat on high speed for 1 minute for each egg. Scrape bowl down again, and add flour and milk alternately on low speed, for 2 minutes only. Scrape bowl down again and beat for 1 minute on low speed. Cake is then ready to be placed in buttered pan for baking. Do not overheat.

SPONGE CAKE

(Electric Mixer)

Beat egg whites on high speed for 3 minutes. Add sugar on low speed for 2 minutes. Scrape bowl down and then beat on low speed for 1 minute.

In another bowl, beat egg yolks for 5 minutes on high speed. Fold 2 mixtures together with wooden spoon, add flavorings, and cut and fold in sifted

Butter cakes are pretty as a picture at the tea table

flour and salt. Cake is then ready to be turned into ungreased tube for baking. Do not overbeat.

WHY FAILURES OCCUR IN CAKES WITH SHORTENING

It is well to acquaint yourself with the possible causes of the common failures in this type of cake, so you may benefit by the knowledge for your own good cake caking:

THE RESULT	THE CAUSES
Top split	Oven too hot at beginning of baking period.
	Batter not sufficiently soft.
Center raised to point	Batter not sufficiently soft.
	Oven too hot at beginning of baking period.
	Over-mixing.
Center cavity	Excess of shortening.
	Excess of sugar.
	Oven heat too low.
	Excess of leavening.
	Not baked long enough.
Crust or crumb tough	Insufficient shortening.
	Insufficient sugar.
	Excess of flour.
	Over-mixing.
Crust sticky	Excess of sugar.
	Flour not entirely dry.
	Not baked long enough.
Crust sugary	Excess of sugar.
	Excess of leavening.
	Mixed incorrectly.
Soggy texture	Cooling in moist hot air.
	Proportion of liquid to flour incorrect.
Flavor bitter	Excess of baking powder.

Heaviness	Insufficient leavening.
	Over-mixed.
	Excess of shortening.
	Excess of sugar.
	Excess of liquid.
	Not baked long enough.
	Oven temperature incorrect.
Crumbly and too light	Excess of leavening.
	Oven temperature too low.
Texture coarse	Excess of leavening.
	Not enough creaming of shortening and sugar.
	Use of liquid shortening.
Dryness	Insufficient shortening.
	Insufficient liquid.
	Excessive beating of egg whites.
	Overlong baking.
	Chocolate added, but no compensating increase in liquid made.
Large holes	Excessive beating of batter.
	Leavening agent not distributed evenly.
	Oven too hot.
	Air not expelled from tin when batter is put in.

CAKES WITH SHORTENING

(Basic Recipe)

2 cups cake flour	1 cup sugar
3 tsp. baking powder	2 eggs, separated
½ tsp. salt	⅔ cup milk
½ cup shortening	1 tsp. vanilla extract

Sift; measure flour. Add baking powder and salt, sift again. Cream shortening, add sugar slowly, and cream until fluffy. Add beaten egg yolks. Add ⅓ of flour mixture. Add ⅓ of milk and continue to add flour and milk alternately. Beat well after each addition. Add vanilla extract. Beat egg whites until stiff, and fold into batter. Bake in 2 well-greased 9-inch layer-cake pans, in moderate oven (375° F.) 25 to 30 minutes. (*Variation:* Whole eggs may be beaten until thick and fluffy and added to creamed shortening mixture.)

Variations of Basic Recipe

Chocolate: Reduce the flour to 1¾ cup. Add 1 sq. melted chocolate to cake batter, fold in stiffly-beaten egg whites last.

Cocoa: Reduce the flour to 1¾ cup. Add Tbsp. cocoa to flour and sift with other dry ingredients.

Spice: Add ½ tsp. cinnamon.

Double Spice: Add ¼ tsp. cinnamon, ¼ tsp. cloves and ⅛ tsp. nutmeg, and sift with other dry ingredients.

Fruit: Add ½ cup lightly-floured raisins or citron or currants before folding in stiffly-beaten egg whites.

LADY BALTIMORE CAKE

3 cups cake flour	1½ cups sugar
3 tsp. baking powder	1¼ cups milk
½ tsp. salt	1 tsp. vanilla extract
½ cup butter	4 egg whites, beaten until stiff

Sift; measure flour. Add baking powder and salt. Sift together 3 times. Cream butter thoroughly. Add sugar gradually and cream together until light and fluffy. Add dry ingredients alternately with milk, and beat after each addition. Add vanilla extract. Fold in egg whites. Bake in two 9-inch layer pans, in moderate oven (375° F.) 25 to 30 minutes.

Frosting

1 recipe of Seven Minute Frosting.

Filling

½ cup chopped nuts	½ cup chopped dates or figs
½ cup chopped raisins	1 tsp. lemon extract
	1 tsp. almond extract

Divide frosting in half. To one half add the filling. Mix well. Spread mixture between layers. Spread remaining half of frosting on top and sides of cake. Garnish with candied fruit.

WHITE CAKE

3 cups cake flour	1½ cups sugar
4½ tsp. baking powder	1 cup milk
½ tsp. salt	3 egg whites, stiffly-beaten
½ cup butter	1 tsp. vanilla extract

Sift; measure flour. Add baking powder and salt, sift again. Cream butter, add sugar slowly, and cream until fluffy. Add milk and flour alternately. Beat well after each addition. Add vanilla extract. Fold egg whites into mixture. Bake in well-greased pan (10x10x2 inches), in moderate oven (350° F.) 60 minutes. Ice with Seven-Minute Frosting.

BLACK WALNUT CAKE

1½ cups cake flour	2 eggs, separated
2 tsp. baking powder	½ cup cold coffee
⅓ cup shortening	1 tsp. vanilla extract
1 cup brown sugar	1 cup walnut meats, chopped

Sift; measure flour. Add baking powder, sift 3 times. Cream shortening, add sugar slowly, and cream until fluffy. Add egg yolks and vanilla extract. Beat well. Add coffee alternately with flour. Beat well after each addition. Add nut meats. Fold in stiffly-beaten egg whites. Bake in well-greased loaf pan, in moderate oven (350° F.) 30 to 40 minutes.

SPICE CAKE

2 cups cake flour
1 tsp. soda
¼ tsp. salt
1 tsp. cloves
2 tsp. cinnamon
½ tsp. allspice
½ cup shortening
2 cups brown sugar
2 eggs, well-beaten
1 cup sour cream

Spice cake becomes a banana layer cake with the addition of lavish amounts of whipped cream and sliced bananas.

Sift; measure flour. Add soda, salt, and spices and sift again. Set aside. Cream shortening, add sugar slowly, and cream until fluffy. Add eggs and beat well. Add sour cream alternately with sifted dry ingredients. Bake in well-greased 9-inch layer-cake tins in moderate oven (350° F.) 20 to 30 minutes.

ORANGE FRUITCAKE

3 cups cake flour	1 cup nut meats
1½ tsp. soda	1½ cups raisins
1 tsp. salt	¾ cup shortening
1½ oranges	3 eggs, well-beaten
2¼ cups sugar	1 cup sour milk
	1 tsp. vanilla extract

Sift; measure flour. Add soda, salt, and sift again. Squeeze oranges, pour juice over ¾ cup sugar. Set aside until cake is baked. Cut up orange skins, put through food grinder with nuts and raisins alternately. Cream shortening, add 1½ cups sugar slowly, and cream until fluffy. Add eggs, nuts and fruit. Beat well. Add milk and flour alternately. Beat well after each addition. Add vanilla extract. Bake in slow oven (300° F.) 1½ hours. Remove from pan. Pour orange mixture over warm cake.

APPLE SAUCE CAKE

2 cups cake flour	1 cup sugar
1 tsp. soda	1 egg, well-beaten
½ tsp. nutmeg	1 cup raisins
½ tsp. cloves	1 cup nut meats, chopped
½ cup shortening	1 cup apple sauce
	¼ cup milk

Sift; measure flour. Add soda, spices, and sift again. Cream shortening, add sugar slowly, and cream until fluffy. Add egg, raisins, nuts and apple sauce. Beat well, add milk and flour alternately. Beat well after each addition. Bake in a well-greased pan (10x10x2 inches), in moderate oven (350° F.) 1 hour.

PLANTATION MARBLE CAKE

2 cups cake flour	2 eggs, well-beaten
2 tsp. baking powder	½ cup milk
¼ tsp. salt	1 tsp. cinnamon
½ cup shortening	½ tsp. cloves
1 cup sugar	½ tsp. nutmeg
	2 Tbsp. molasses

Sift; measure flour. Add baking powder and salt, sift again. Cream shortening, add sugar slowly, and cream until fluffy. Add eggs, beat well. Add milk and flour alternately. Beat well after each addition. Divide batter into 2 parts. Add spices and molasses to 1 part. Drop a spoonful at a time, alternating between light and dark, into a well-greased pan (10x10x2 inches). Bake in a moderate oven (350° F.) 50 minutes.

GRAHAM CRACKER CAKE

3¼ cups graham cracker crumbs	½ cup butter
3 tsp. baking powder	¾ cup sugar
¼ tsp. salt	2 eggs, separated
½ tsp. cinnamon	1 cup milk

Sift; measure crumbs. Add baking powder, salt and cinnamon. Sift again. Cream butter, add sugar slowly, and cream until fluffy. Add egg yolks, beat well. Add crumbs alternately with milk. Beat well after each addition. Fold in stiffly-beaten egg whites. Bake in well-greased pan (10x10x2 inches), in moderate oven (350° F.) 45 minutes. Serve with a topping of sweetened whipped cream.

GOLD CAKE

3 cups cake flour	1½ cups sugar
3 tsp. baking powder	8 egg yolks, well-beaten
½ tsp. salt	1 cup milk
¾ cup butter	1 tsp. lemon extract

Sift; measure flour. Add baking powder and salt, sift again. Cream butter, add sugar slowly, and cream until fluffy. Add egg yolks. Beat well. Add milk and flour alternately. Beat well after each addition. Add lemon extract. Bake in 3 well-greased layer-cake pans (8x8x2 inches), in moderate oven (375° F.) 20 minutes.

Marble cake with rich icing makes a festive dessert for any occasion. Lovely silver platters and silver candelabras add an elegant note.

NO-EGG CHOCOLATE CAKE

1½ cups cake flour
1 tsp. soda
1 tsp. salt
1 cup sugar

2 sq. chocolate, melted
3 Tbsp. shortening, melted
1 cup sour milk
1 tsp. vanilla extract

Sift; measure flour. Add soda and salt, sift again. Mix sugar, chocolate and shortening. Add milk and flour alternately. Beat well after each addition. Add vanilla extract. Bake in a well-greased tube pan, in moderate oven (350° F.) 40 minutes. Ice with Uncooked Frosting.

RICH CHOCOLATE CAKE

1 cup sour cream
1 egg
1 cup brown sugar
1 tsp. vanilla extract

1 tsp. soda dissolved in ¼ cup
    boiling water
1½ cups sifted cake flour
1 sq. chocolate, melted

Combine ingredients in order named. Bake in well-greased square pan (10x10x 2 inches) in moderate oven (350° F.) 20 minutes. Ice with Mocha Frosting.

ONE-BOWL CHOCOLATE CAKE

1 cup sugar
1 egg
½ cup sour milk
½ cup cocoa
½ cup soft shortening

½ tsp. salt
1 tsp. vanilla
1½ cups sifted cake flour
1 tsp. soda
1 cup boiling water

Use one bowl only, add ingredients in order named. After water is added, beat well for 3 minutes. Bake in well-greased pan (10x10x2 inches) in moderate oven (350° F.) 30 minutes. Ice with Chocolate Frosting.

FUDGE CHOCOLATE CAKE

1¾ cups cake flour
4 sq. chocolate
4 Tbsp. butter
¾ cup boiling water

1½ cups sugar
2 eggs, well-beaten
⅜ cup sour milk
1 tsp. soda
1 tsp. vanilla extract

Sift; measure flour. Melt butter and chocolate, add boiling water. Beat until it thickens. Add sugar and eggs, beat well. Add milk and flour alternately. Beat well after each addition. Add soda and vanilla extract. Bake in well-greased pan (8x8x2 inches) in moderate oven (350° F.) 45 minutes.

RED DEVIL'S FOOD CAKE

1½ cups cake flour	2 eggs, well-beaten
1½ tsp. baking powder	½ cup sour milk
½ tsp. salt	½ cup boiling water
4 Tbsp. butter	2 sq. chocolate, melted
1 cup sugar	1 tsp. soda
	1 tsp. vanilla extract

Sift; measure flour. Add baking powder and salt, sift again. Cream butter, add sugar slowly, and cream until fluffy. Add eggs, beat well. Add milk and flour alternately. Beat well after each addition. Mix water, chocolate and soda. Stir until thick. Cool slightly, add to cake batter. Beat well, add vanilla extract. Bake in two well-greased 9-inch layer-cake pans, in moderate oven (375° F.) 25 to 30 minutes. Ice with Seven-Minute Frosting.

DE LUXE CAKE

3 cups cake flour	5 egg yolks
1½ tsp. baking powder	¾ cup milk
1 cup butter	1 tsp. lemon extract
2 cups sugar	3 egg whites, stiffly-beaten

Sift; measure flour. Add baking powder and sift again. Cream butter, add sugar slowly, and cream until fluffy. Add egg yolks, beaten until thick. Add milk and flour alternately. Beat well after each addition. Add lemon extract. Fold in egg whites. Bake in two well-greased 9-inch square cake pans, in moderate oven (375° F.) 30 minutes. Ice with Uncooked Lemon Frosting, using the 2 extra egg whites left over from cake.

QUICK COFFEE CAKE

2 cups cake flour	½ tsp. salt
2 tsp. baking powder	6 Tbsp. shortening
½ cup sugar	1 egg, well-beaten
	½ cup milk

Topping

2 Tbsp. melted butter	1 Tbsp. flour
4 Tbsp. sugar	½ tsp. cinnamon

Sift; measure flour. Add baking powder, salt and sugar; sift again. Cut in shortening. Mix milk and egg, add to flour mixture. Stir until well-blended. Pour in well-greased 9-inch square cake pan. Spread with Topping. Bake in hot oven (400° F.) 25 to 30 minutes.

CHOCOLATE MINT STICKS

2 eggs
1½ cups sugar
¼ lb. butter, melted
6 Tbsp. cake flour

1 sq. chocolate, melted
1 cup almonds, cut fine
¾ tsp. peppermint essence
2 sq. chocolate, separate from
above

Beat eggs and sugar until light. Add butter and flour, beat well. Add 1 sq. chocolate, nuts and peppermint essence. Bake in well-greased oblong baking pan (8x8x1 inches) in moderate oven (350° F.) 25 minutes. Ice with Uncooked Frosting, colored while still in pan with few drops of green vegetable coloring. When frosting is set, pour 2 sq. of melted chocolate over it and let set. Cut in strips 1x3 inches.

CHOCOLATE ICE BOX CAKE

2 sq. chocolate, melted
2½ Tbsp. water
2 Tbsp. sugar

1 tsp. vanilla extract
4 eggs, separated
24-30 lady fingers

Melt chocolate and water together. Add sugar and vanilla extract to chocolate mixture. Add yolks of eggs, one at a time. When chocolate is cool, add stiffly-beaten egg whites. Arrange a layer of lady fingers in the bottom of a round pan. Pour enough of the chocolate mixture over to cover them. Lay another layer of lady fingers over the top, and pour chocolate mixture on top of lady fingers. Continue until all is used. Stand in ice box 24 hours. Turn out on plate. Serve with whipped cream.

ORANGE ICE BOX CAKE

1 cup orange juice
Juice of 1 lemon
½ cup sugar

1 Tbsp. cornstarch
3 egg yolks
2 Tbsp. butter
3 egg whites, stiffly-beaten

Cook orange juice, lemon juice, sugar, cornstarch, egg yolks and butter in double boiler until thickened. Cool, fold in egg whites. Split sponge cake into three layers. Fill two layers with orange mixture, replace layers on top of each other, and place in ice box for 24 hours. Cover cake with whipped cream.

PINEAPPLE UPSIDE DOWN CAKE

1½ cups cake flour
1 tsp. baking powder
¼ tsp. salt
4 egg yolks, well-beaten

1½ cups sugar
½ cup boiling water
1 tsp. vanilla extract
4 egg whites, stiffly-beaten

Sauce

4 slices pineapple
4 maraschino cherries

4 Tbsp. butter
¾ cup brown sugar

Melt butter for sauce in skillet; add brown sugar and cook until sugar is dissolved. Place pineapple slices in sauce, place cherry in center of each slice. Sift; measure flour. Add baking powder and salt, sift again. Beat egg yolks and sugar together, add boiling water. Beat well, add flour and vanilla extract. Fold in egg whites. Pour cake batter over pineapple slices in skillet. Bake in slow oven (325° F.) 45 minutes. Serve with whipped cream.

Cheese cake with a zwieback crust is one of the richest and creamiest of dessert treats.

CHEESE CAKE

Crust

1 pkg. zwieback
1 cup sugar

1 tsp. cinnamon
½ cup butter, melted

Roll zwieback into fine crumbs. Mix with sugar, cinnamon and butter. Grease a 9-inch spring-form pan and spread ¼ of crumb mixture on bottom and sides.

Filling

6 eggs, well-beaten	Juice ½ lemon
1 cup sugar	¼ cup cake flour
¼ tsp. salt	1¼ lbs. cottage cheese
	½ pt. heavy cream

Beat eggs with sugar until light. Add salt, lemon juice and stir well. Add other ingredients and beat thoroughly. Rub through fine sieve. Pour into spring-form. Cover with remaining ¾ of crumb mixture. Bake in slow oven (300° F.) 1 hour, or until silver knife comes out clean when inserted in center. Let cake stand until cold in open oven after heat is turned off.

SOFT GINGERBREAD

3 cups cake flour	1 cup sugar
2 tsp. ginger	2 eggs, well-beaten
2 tsp. cinnamon	1 cup molasses
1 tsp. cloves	1 cup sour milk
¼ tsp. nutmeg	1 tsp. soda
¼ cup shortening	¼ cup boiling water

Sift; measure flour. Add spices and sift again. Cream shortening, add sugar slowly, and cream until fluffy. Add eggs and molasses. Beat well. Add milk and flour alternately. Beat well after each addition. Add soda dissolved in water. Bake in well-greased cake pan (10x10x2 inches), in moderate oven (350° F.) 30 minutes.

RICH GINGERBREAD

2¾ cups cake flour	½ cup shortening, melted
2 tsp. soda	1 cup sugar
½ tsp. salt	1 cup molasses
1 Tbsp. ginger	2 eggs, well-beaten
1 tsp. cinnamon	1 cup sour milk

Sift; measure flour. Add soda, salt, and spices. Sift again. Cream shortening and sugar together. Add eggs and molasses. Beat thoroughly. Add milk and flour alternately. Beat well after each addition. Bake in well-greased pan (10x10x2 inches), in hot oven (400° F.) 30 minutes.

SOUTHERN WHITE FRUITCAKE

1 lb. cake flour

2 tsp. baking powder

¼ tsp. salt

1 lb. butter

1 lb. sugar

1 lb. (1 doz.) eggs, separated

*1 lb. glacé pineapple

*1 lb. glacé cherries

1 lb. white raisins

*1 lb. glacé citron

*1 lb. almonds, blanched

1 tsp. rose extract

1 tsp. vanilla extract

1 cup Bourbon whiskey

Fruitcake at Christmas time is traditional.

Sift; measure flour. Add baking powder and salt. Sift again. Cream butter, add sugar slowly, and cream until fluffy. Beat egg yolks until light, add to mixture and beat well Add flour slowly. Beat well after each addition. Add the cut fruit, a little at a time (first flouring lightly and shaking off excess flour). Add the extracts and the Bourbon. Beat well. Fold in stiffly-beaten eggs whites. Pour into loaf pans lined with greased paper. Bake the cakes for 4 hours. Set the oven at slow (200° F.), bake for 1 hour. Increase heat to 275° F., bake 1 hour longer. Increase heat to 325° F., bake for final 2 hours.

Note: The pineapple, cherries and citron should be cut in thin strips, as fine as possible in length and width. Almonds should be cut in thin slivers.

CARE OF FRUITCAKES

Fruitcakes should be cooled on a wire rack; then removed from their pans and allowed to cool entirely before being wrapped. Clean linen napkins may be dipped in brandy, and each cake wrapped individually and placed in an air-tight container. The container should be well-lined with wax paper, then covered tightly. A few days before the holiday season, the fruitcakes may be iced with an uncooked frosting and decorated for display.

Frosted mince meat cup cakes spell out MERRY CHRISTMAS to add to the holiday cheer.

CUP CAKES

(Basic Recipe)

1⅔ cups cake flour	1 cup sugar
1½ tsp. baking powder	2 eggs, well-beaten
¼ tsp. salt	⅔ cup milk
½ cup shortening	1 tsp. vanilla extract

Sift; measure flour. Add baking powder and salt, sift again. Cream shortening, add sugar slowly, and cream until fluffy. Add eggs, beat well. Add milk and flour alternately. Beat well after each addition. Add vanilla extract. Fill well-greased cup cake tins ⅔ full. Bake in hot oven (400° F.) 15 to 18 minutes. Ice with Orange Butter Frosting.

PEANUT BUTTER CUP CAKES

2 cups cake flour	1½ cups brown sugar
2½ tsp. baking powder	½ cup peanut butter
½ tsp. salt	2 eggs, well-beaten
⅓ cup shortening	¾ cup milk
	1 tsp. vanilla extract

Sift; measure flour. Add baking powder and salt, sift again. Cream shortening, add 1 cup sugar slowly, and cream until fluffy. Add peanut butter and beat well. Stir eggs and ½ cup sugar together, add to mixture. Add milk and flour alternately. Beat well after each addition. Add vanilla extract. Fill well-greased cup cake tins ⅔ full. Bake in moderate oven (350° F.) 30 minutes.

SPICY CUP CAKES

2½ cups cake flour
½ tsp. salt
½ tsp. cloves
½ tsp. mace
1 tsp. cinnamon
½ cup shortening
1 cup brown sugar

1 egg, separated
¼ cup raisins
¼ cup currants
¼ cup nut meats, chopped
1 tsp. soda
1 Tbsp. boiling water
¾ cup sour milk

Sift; measure flour. Add salt, spices, and sift again. Cream shortening, add sugar slowly, and cream until fluffy. Add egg yolk, raisins, currants and nuts. Add soda dissolved in water. Beat well. Add milk alternately with flour. Beat well after each addition. Fold in stiffly-beaten egg white. Fill well-greased cup cake tins ⅔ full. Bake in moderate oven (350° F.) 15 minutes.

GOLDEN CUP CAKES

1 cup cake flour
¼ tsp. salt
1 tsp. baking powder
4 Tbsp. shortening

1 Tbsp. grated orange rind
½ cup sugar
4 egg yolks, well-beaten
¼ cup milk

Sift; measure flour. Add salt and baking powder. Sift three times. Cream shortening, add orange rind. Add sugar slowly, and cream until fluffy. Add egg yolks and beat well. Add milk alternately with flour. Beat well after each addition. Fill well-greased cup cake tins ⅔ full. Bake in moderate oven (350° F.) 18 minutes.

BLACK AND WHITE CUP CAKES

2 cups cake flour
2 tsp. baking powder
½ tsp. salt
3 Tbsp. sugar
3 Tbsp. water
1½ sq. chocolate

¼ tsp. soda
⅓ cup shortening
¾ cup sugar
2 egg whites
⅔ cup milk
1 tsp. vanilla extract

Sift; measure flour. Add baking powder and salt. Sift three times. Place sugar, water and chocolate in saucepan and cook over low heat until smooth and glossy. Add soda and cool slightly. Set aside, add sugar slowly, and cream until fluffy. Add egg whites, one at a time, and beat well after each addition. Add milk and flour alternately. Beat well after each addition. Add vanilla extract. Divide batter into 2 parts. Add chocolate mixture to 1 part, stir until well blended. Fill well-greased cup cake tins ⅔ full, alternating light and dark mixture. Bake in moderate oven (350° F.) 30 minutes. Ice with Chocolate Frosting.

DOUGHNUTS AND CRULLERS

Doughnuts are called by various names—doughnuts, crullers, or fried cakes. Raised doughnuts are made with yeast. Modern methods of deep fat frying have largely taken doughnuts into commercial production, and they are seldom made in the home kitchen.

If you do make them there, the fat should be tested by a thermometer and should reach 375° F. before doughnuts are cooked. Brown them on one side, then on the other, and lift them out of the hot fat with perforated spoon onto paper toweling.

DOUGHNUTS

¼ cup butter

½ cup sugar

2 eggs, well-beaten

2 cups flour, sifted before measuring

½ tsp. nutmeg

¼ tsp. salt

½ tsp. soda

¼ tsp. cinnamon

½ cup sour milk or buttermilk

Cream butter, add sugar slowly, and cream until fluffy. Add eggs. Sift dry ingredients together and add alternately with milk. Roll dough ½ inch thick on lightly-floured board. Cut with doughnut cutter, and fry in deep fat (375° F.).

CAKES WITHOUT SHORTENING

Cakes without shortening are the sponge cakes and angel foods, which depend for their leavening largely upon the amount of air beaten into the eggs. The pan used for sponge cakes, angel food cakes (also fruitcakes) is a deep pan with a hollow tube in the center.

The pan for the sponge cake is never greased, as the batter should cling to the sides of the pan, thereby helping the cake reach its full height. When the sponge cake or angel cake is removed from the oven, turn the pan upside down on a cake rack and let the cake hang in the pan for an hour. This gives time for the very delicate cell walls of the angel cake or sponge cake to be stiffened slightly by cooling. When the cake is cool, insert spatula between cake and sides of pan, and cut cake free from pan. Loosen cake around center tube. Tilt pan gently and draw cake out onto rack.

WHY FAILURES OCCUR IN SPONGE CAKES

To enable you to avoid the common failures which occur in baking sponge cakes, the possible causes are given below:

THE RESULT	THE CAUSES
Crust heavy and hard	Oven too hot at beginning of baking period. Over-baking.
Crust sticky	Excess of sugar. Flour not entirely dry. Baking time too short.
Split in crust	Mixture too stiff. Excessive beating of eggs. Oven too hot.
Crumb tough	Baking temperature too high. Excessive mixing.
Crumb coarse	Insufficient beating of eggs. Insufficient mixing. Oven too hot.
Dryness	Excessive beating of egg whites. Excess of flour. Insufficient sugar. Over-baking. Baking temperature too low.
Shrinkage	Baking temperature too low. Insufficient cream of tartar. Baking time too short.

SPONGE CAKE

1 cup cake flour	½ tsp. salt
6 egg yolks	1 Tbsp. lemon juice
1 cup sugar	1½ tsp. grated lemon rind
	6 egg whites

Methods of mixing:

METHOD I—Sift; measure flour. Beat egg yolks until thick. Add sugar gradually. Continue beating. Add flavoring. Beat egg whites (to which the salt has been added) until stiff but not dry, and fold one half of these into the yolk and sugar mixture. Sift in flour about ¼ at a time, and combine by cutting and folding. Fold in the remainder of the egg whites.

METHOD II—Add the salt to the egg whites, and beat until stiff but not dry. Add sugar gradually, continuing the beating. Beat egg yolks until thick and add flavoring. Sift in flour about ¼ at a time, and combine by cutting and folding.

METHOD III—Beat egg yolks until thick. Beat in gradually one half of sugar. Sift in flour about ¼ at a time, and combine by cutting and folding. Add flavoring. Add salt to egg whites, and beat until stiff but not dry. Add remainder of sugar gradually, with continued beating. Pour yolk mixture over white mixture and combine by cutting and folding.

Baking

Baking: Put sponge cake mixture in an ungreased shallow pan or tube pan. Bake in slow oven (300° F.) 30 to 60 minutes, depending upon size and shape of pan.

Testing: Cake, when done, feels firm and its surface rebounds at once when pressed with the finger.

Care after baking: Invert the pan on a cake cooler and remove cake when cold.

Sprinkle top with confectioner's sugar, or ice with Seven Minute Boiled Frosting.

SUNSHINE CAKE

1¾ cups cake flour	1 tsp. salt
4 egg yolks	1 tsp. vanilla
3 tsp. cold water	½ cup boiling water
1½ cups sugar	4 egg whites, stiffly-beaten
	½ tsp. cream of tartar

Sift; measure flour. Beat yolks of eggs with cold water. Add sugar, beat until light yellow. Add salt, vanilla, boiling water. Add flour and beat well. Add cream of tartar to egg whites and beat until stiff. Fold in egg whites. Bake in ungreased tube pan, in slow oven (325° F.) 1 hour. Ice with Lemon or Orange Frosting.

ANGEL FOOD

1 cup cake flour	¼ tsp. salt
1¼ cups sugar	1 tsp. cream of tartar
1¼ cups egg whites	1 tsp. vanilla
	½ tsp. almond flavoring

Fluffy angel food, disc-dotted, milk in decorated mugs, and a balloon banana bowl make an easy-to-prepare children's party.

Sift; measure flour. Sift sugar and flour together three times. Add salt to egg whites, beat until foamy. Add cream of tartar, beat until stiff. Sift in flour and sugar mixtures, about ¼ at a time, and mix by cutting and folding. Add flavoring just before completion of the mixing process. Place cake in cold oven. Bake in ungreased tube pan, in slow oven (325° F.), until cake feels firm on the surface. Invert pan and remove cake when cool. Ice with Seven-Minute Frosting.

HOT WATER SPONGE CAKE

1 cup cake flour	⅞ cup sugar
2 tsp. baking powder	½ cup boiling water
¼ tsp. salt	1 Tbsp. lemon juice
2 egg yolks, well-beaten	1½ tsp. lemon rind
	2 egg whites, stiffly-beaten

Sift; measure flour. Add baking powder and salt, sift again. Beat egg yolks with sugar until light and fluffy. Add water, lemon juice and rind, and beat thoroughly until well-blended. Fold in egg whites. Bake like Sponge Cake.

DAFFODIL CAKE

Yellow Part

¾ cup cake flour	6 egg yolks, well-beaten
1 tsp. baking powder	¾ cup sugar
¼ tsp. salt	¼ cup boiling water
	1 tsp. lemon extract

Sift; measure flour. Add baking powder and salt, sift again. Beat egg yolks and

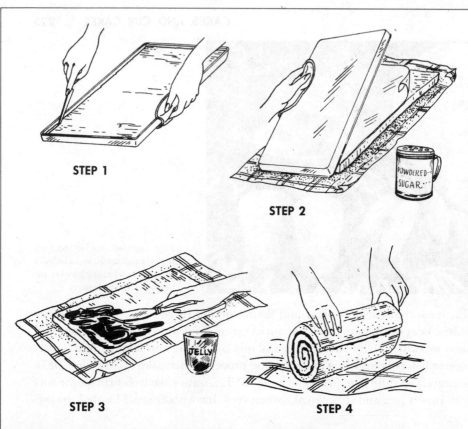

STEP 1

STEP 2

POWDERED SUGAR

STEP 3

JELLY

STEP 4

Intricate though the cake roll may seem when its slices are served up to you, its creation is not such a mysterious task. Speedy spreading of filling and rolling are the main tricks.

Golden Fish Sauce
Combine 1 cup mayonnaise with 2 tablespoons each A.1. Sauce and prepared mustard. Serve with fried, baked, or broiled fish. Makes 1¼ cups.

Planked Whitefish with Vegetables

Baked Trout with Dressing

sugar until thick and lemon-colored. Add water and flour alternately. Beat well after each addition. Add lemon extract.

White Part

¾ cup cake flour	6 egg whites, stiffly-beaten
½ tsp. cream of tartar	¾ cup sugar
¼ tsp. salt	½ tsp. vanilla extract

Sift; measure flour. Add cream of tartar and salt, sift again. Fold sugar into egg whites. Fold in flour. Add vanilla extract. Line a tube pan with waxed paper. Add yellow and white batter alternately by spoonfuls. Bake in moderate oven (350° F.) for 10 minutes. Reduce to low heat (300° F.) and bake 40 minutes longer.

JELLY ROLL

¾ cup cake flour	4 eggs
¾ tsp. baking powder	1 tsp. vanilla extract
¼ tsp. salt	¾ cup sugar
	1 cup tart currant jelly

Sift; measure flour. Mix baking powder, salt and eggs in bowl. Place over hot water and beat with rotary egg beater, adding sugar gradually until mixture becomes thick and light-colored. Remove bowl from heat, fold in flour and vanilla. Line greased pan (15x10 inch) with greased paper. Pour in mixture, and bake in hot oven (400° F.) 13 minutes. Remove from oven and quickly cut off edges. Turn out on clean towel, which has been covered with powdered sugar, and remove paper. Quickly spread with jelly and roll lengthwise into a roll. Wrap in a towel and cool on rack.

CHOCOLATE ROLL

¼ cup cake flour	4 eggs, well-beaten
½ tsp. baking powder	1 Tbsp. cold water
¼ tsp. salt	¾ cup sugar
6 Tbsp. cocoa	1 tsp. vanilla extract

Sift; measure flour. Add baking powder, salt and cocoa. Sift together three times. Add water and sugar to eggs. Beat until thick and lemon-colored. Add flour, stir in lightly and quickly. Add vanilla. Line well-greased pan (15x10x1 inch) with wax paper. Bake in hot oven (400° F) 13 minutes. Remove from oven and quickly cut off edges. Proceed as for Jelly Roll. Spread with Butter Frosting or whipped cream.

17.

COOKIES

COOKIES and cookie jars belong to "making a home." Cookie-baking spells fun to a child, and a mother finds companionship with the child when they carry out this pleasant task together. Many children have learned to appreciate good food while they passed happy hours helping in their mother's kitchen— and a happy childhood is a healthy childhood. So let's bake cookies! They keep, and are good to have ready for company.

DROP COOKIES

DROP SPICE COOKIES

2½ cups cake flour	1 cup shortening
1 tsp. cinnamon	1½ cups brown sugar
1 tsp. cloves	3 eggs, beaten
1 tsp. nutmeg	1½ cups nut meats, chopped
1 tsp. soda	1½ cups raisins
	½ cup hot water

Sift; measure flour. Add spices and soda, sift again. Cream shortening, add sugar gradually, add eggs, beat well. Add nuts and raisins. Beat again. Add dry ingredients alternately with water. Drop by teaspoonfuls on greased cookie sheet. Bake in moderate oven (350° F.) 8 to 10 minutes.

OATMEAL COOKIES

1 cup cake flour	½ cup sugar
½ tsp. soda	6 Tbsp. shortening, melted
1 tsp. baking powder	2 Tbsp. sour milk
½ tsp. salt	1 cup rolled oats
1 egg	½ cup raisins
	½ cup nut meats, chopped

Sift; measure flour. Add soda, baking powder and salt, and sift again. Beat egg and add sugar. Add melted shortening, milk and rolled oats. Add to first mixture and stir until well-blended. Stir in raisins and nut meats, and drop by teaspoonfuls onto greased cookie sheet. Bake in moderate oven (375° F.) 12 minutes.

MOLASSES COOKIES

2½ cups cake flour	½ cup sugar
1 tsp. cinnamon	1 egg, beaten
1 tsp. ginger	½ cup molasses
1 tsp. soda	½ cup raisins
⅓ cup shortening	½ cup sour milk

Sift; measure flour. Add spices and soda, sift again. Cream shortening, add sugar gradually, add egg and molasses. Beat well, add raisins, add milk and dry ingredients alternately. Drop by teaspoonfuls 2 inches apart on greased cookie sheet. Bake in moderate oven (350° F.) 8 to 10 minutes.

CAPE COD COOKIES

¾ cup cake flour	1 Tbsp. molasses
½ tsp. soda	2 Tbsp. milk
½ tsp. cinnamon	¾ cup rolled oats
1 egg, well-beaten	½ tsp. salt
½ cup sugar	¼ cup raisins
½ cup shortening, melted	¼ cup nut meats, chopped

Sift; measure flour. Add soda and cinnamon, and sift again. Combine egg, sugar and shortening. Beat well. Add molasses, milk, oats, salt, raisins and nut meats. Add dry ingredients. Beat well. Drop by teaspoonfuls 2 inches apart onto greased cookie sheet. Bake in moderate oven (350° F.) 10 minutes.

PRESSED AND CUT COOKIES

HONEYBOYS

1½ cups cake flour	2 egg yolks, beaten
1 tsp. baking powder	1 tsp. vanilla
½ cup shortening	2 egg whites
½ cup white sugar	1 cup brown sugar
½ tsp. salt	1 cup nuts, chopped

Sift; measure flour. Add baking powder and sift again. Cream shortening; add sugar, salt and egg yolks. Beat well. Add vanilla and flour. (This dough will be quite stiff.) Pat into ½ inch thickness on a cookie sheet. Press down with a fork. Beat egg whites until stiff. Add brown sugar gradually. Add nuts. Spread over cake mixture. Bake in moderate oven (350° F.) 20 minutes. Cool and cut into squares.

PEANUT BUTTER COOKIES

1 cup cake flour	¼ tsp. salt
1 tsp. soda	½ cup brown sugar
⅓ cup shortening	½ cup peanut butter
½ cup white sugar	1 egg

Sift; measure flour. Add soda, and sift again. Cream shortening; add sugar, salt, peanut butter and egg. Beat well. Add dry ingredients. Form dough into balls, the size of a walnut. Place on a greased cookie sheet 2 inches apart. Press dough down with a fork in one direction, and then press down again at right angles to form a cross. Bake in hot oven (400° F.) 10 minutes.

TOM THUMB COOKIE BARS

1 cup cake flour	2 eggs, beaten
½ tsp. baking powder	1 tsp. vanilla
½ cup shortening	2 Tbsp. flour
1½ cups brown sugar	1½ cups shredded coconut
	1 cup nut meats, chopped

Sift; measure flour. Add baking powder and sift again. Cream shortening; add sugar, eggs and vanilla. Beat well. Add dry ingredients. Spread batter in a greased baking pan (8x8x2 inches). Bake in slow oven (325° F.) 15 minutes.

Cookies are favorites with the young, reminiscent of childhood and "Mother's kitchen" for the not-so-young. Chocolate Easter cookies can be frosted a new, easy way with semi-sweet chocolate frosting.

Mix together flour, coconut and nut meats. Spread over baked mixture. Return to oven and bake 30 minutes. Cool and cut into rectangles.

BROWNIES

¾ cup cake flour	¼ tsp. salt
¼ tsp. baking powder	2 eggs, beaten
½ cup shortening	2 sq. chocolate, melted
1 cup sugar	½ cup nut meats, chopped

Sift; measure flour. Add baking powder and sift again. Cream shortening; add sugar, eggs and salt. Add chocolate, melted over hot water and cooled slightly. Add dry ingredients and chopped nut meats. Spread batter in a greased baking pan (8x8x2 inches). Bake in moderate oven (350° F.) 30 minutes. Cut in squares and remove from pan.

ROLLED AND CUT COOKIES

SUGAR COOKIES

1⅔ cups cake flour	⅛ tsp. salt
1½ tsp. baking powder	1 egg, beaten
⅓ cup shortening	1 Tbsp. cream
⅔ cup sugar	⅛ tsp. nutmeg
	¾ tsp. lemon extract

Sift; measure flour. Add baking powder and sift again. Cream shortening; add sugar, salt, egg and cream. Beat well. Add nutmeg, extract and dry ingredients. Chill thoroughly, roll thin on a lightly-floured board. Dip cookie cutters into flour, and cut dough into shapes. Place on floured cookie sheet ½ inch apart. Bake in moderate oven (350° F.) 6 to 7 minutes.

Variation

Chocolate Sugar Cookies: Substitute 2 Tbsp. cocoa for 2 Tbsp. flour.

REFRIGERATOR COOKIES

2 cups flour	½ cup shortening
½ tsp. cinnamon	½ cup brown sugar
½ tsp. cloves	½ cup white sugar
½ tsp. nutmeg	2 eggs, beaten
1 tsp. soda	½ tsp. salt
	½ cup nut meats, chopped

Sift; measure flour. Add cinnamon, cloves, nutmeg, soda and sift again. Cream shortening; add sugar, eggs and salt. Beat well. Add nut meats and dry ingredients. Shape into solid roll about 2½ inches in diameter. Roll in oiled paper and chill in refrigerator overnight. Remove dough from refrigerator and cut into thin slices with a sharp knife. Hold hand lightly on chilled dough. Place on a greased baking sheet, and bake in moderate oven (375° F.) 8 to 10 minutes.

PECAN CRESCENTS

2 cups cake flour	5 Tbsp. powdered sugar
½ cup butter	1½ cups pecan nuts, chopped
	2 tsp. vanilla extract

Sift; measure flour. Cream butter. Add sugar gradually. Work in flour, add nuts and vanilla. Take 1 Tbsp. of the dough, roll or pat it into a crescent with the fingers. Make crescent about 2 inches long and ½ inch wide. (Will show finger marks when baked!) Bake on a cookie sheet in moderate oven (350° F.) 30 minutes. While still hot, roll in confectioner's sugar. When cool, store in tin box, serve at holiday parties.

HERMITS

2½ cups cake flour	1 tsp. cinnamon
½ cup butter	½ tsp. soda
¾ cup brown sugar	1 Tbsp. milk
¼ tsp. cloves	1 egg, well-beaten
	½ cup currants

Sift; measure flour. Beat butter to a cream, gradually beat in sugar and spices. Dissolve soda in milk, and beat this into sugar and butter. Add egg, beat well, add flour and currants. Roll out about 1 inch thick and cut in squares. Bake in moderate oven (375° F.) 10 to 12 minutes.

Green maraschino cherries form the shamrocks on St. Patrick's day cookies.

SAND TARTS

2½ cups flour	2 cups sugar
½ tsp. baking powder	3 eggs, beaten
1 cup shortening	¼ cup milk
	1 cup nut meats

Sift; measure flour. Add baking powder and sift again. Cream shortening; add sugar and eggs, beat well. Add milk and dry ingredients alternately. Chill thoroughly. Roll thin on a lightly-floured board. Dip cookie cutters into flour and cut dough into shapes. Place a nut meat in center of each cookie. Place on floured cookie sheet ½ inch apart. Bake in moderate oven (350° F.) 8 to 10 minutes.

18.

CAKE FROSTINGS

CAKE frostings (or icings, as they are often called) may be thick or thin creamy or fluffy, cooked or uncooked. After all the recipes are read, it will be noted that there are only two chief varieties—cooked and uncooked—but that many changes are played on the basic recipes. The best known cooked frosting is boiled sugar syrup, beaten into stiffly-beaten egg whites. It requires a certain amount of practice and skill to make a perfect boiled frosting of this type but it's a favorite with most people. The use of a sugar thermometer is advised for all sugar syrup cookery.

SUGGESTIONS FOR FROSTINGS

1. Be sure the cake is cool.
2. In frosting a 2-layer cake, place the first layer with the top side down and spread frosting smoothly, then place the next layer on top, match the edges and finish frosting.
3. Brush off loose crumbs and trim loose edges with scissors.
4. Frost sides of cake first, spreading a short distance over the top edge, and down around the cake in sweeping strokes.
5. Then fill in center top and work out to edges, making swirls or folds with spatula.
6. Delicate-tinted frostings are a variation, and fit nicely into special occasions. Add a small amount of coloring to any white frosting, and blend evenly before spreading. Do not use too much coloring as highly-colored frostings look garish.

FROSTINGS AND CAKE FILLINGS

BOILED FROSTING I

1 cup sugar

⅓ cup water

1 egg white, beaten

1 tsp. vanilla extract

⅛ tsp. cream of tartar or

1 tsp. lemon juice

Combine sugar, water and cream of tartar. Bring quickly to a boil, stirring only until sugar is dissolved. Boil rapidly, without stirring, until small amount of syrup forms a soft ball in cold water, or spins a long thread when dropped from tip of spoon, or until the candy thermometer reaches 240° F. Beat the egg white until stiff, then pour the syrup over the egg white and beat constantly. Add vanilla, and continue beating until frosting stands in peaks. Spread on cake. Makes enough for top and sides of 1-layer cake.

BOILED FROSTING II

2½ cups sugar

5 Tbsp. corn syrup

½ cup water

2 egg whites

1½ tsp. vanilla extract

Cook together sugar, corn syrup and water until candy thermometer reaches 240° F., or until syrup spins a thin thread when dropped from tip of spoon. Beat egg whites until stiff, then pour syrup over egg whites and beat constantly. Add vanilla, and continue beating until frosting stands in peaks.

SEVEN-MINUTE FROSTING

2 egg whites, unbeaten

1½ cups sugar

5 Tbsp. water

1½ tsp. corn syrup

1 tsp. vanilla extract

Combine whites, sugar, water and corn syrup in top of double boiler. Place over rapidly boiling water and beat constantly with rotary egg beater. Continue cooking and beating for 7 minutes, or until frosting stands in peaks. Remove from boiling water, add vanilla, and beat until thick enough to spread. Makes enough frosting to cover top and sides of a 2-layer (8 inch) cake or 2 doz. cup cakes.

MOCK MAPLE FROSTING

¾ cup brown sugar

2½ Tbsp. water

1 egg white, unbeaten

¼ tsp. maple extract

Cook sugar, water and egg white in double boiler; beat constantly until frosting stands in peaks (about 7 minutes). Remove from heat and add flavoring. Makes enough frosting for top and sides of 1 layer.

FUDGE FROSTING

1 cup sugar	¼ cup milk
⅛ tsp. salt	¼ cup butter
½ cup cocoa	1 tsp. vanilla extract

Combine sugar, salt, cocoa and milk. Cook until it comes to boil. Boil 1 minute. Add butter, cool, and add vanilla. Beat until smooth, and thick enough to spread on cake. Makes enough frosting for tops and sides of 2 layers.

GLOSSY CHOCOLATE FROSTING

2 sq. chocolate, melted	5 Tbsp. water
2 tsp. butter	½ tsp. vanilla extract
	2 cups sugar

Melt chocolate and butter in top of double boiler over boiling water. Add water and vanilla. Add sugar and beat until thick enough to spread. Makes enough frosting for tops and sides of 2 layers.

BUTTER FROSTING

(Basic Recipe)

4 Tbsp. butter	Pinch of salt
2 cups 4x sugar	3 Tbsp. milk (about)
	1 tsp. vanilla

Cream butter, add 1 cup sugar gradually, blending after each addition. Add remaining sugar, alternately with milk, until thick enough to spread. Add vanilla and beat until smooth. For parties, a bit of color added makes a very festive icing. Makes enough frosting for tops and sides of 2 layers or 24 cup cakes.

Variations

1. *Coffee Butter Frosting:* Substitute strong hot coffee for milk.
2. *Lemon Butter Frosting:* Substitute 1 tsp. grated lemon rind and 3 Tbsp. lemon Juice for vanilla and milk.
3. *Chocolate Butter Frosting:* Add 2 sq. chocolate, melted.
4. *Mocha Butter Frosting:* Add 3 Tbsp. cocoa to sugar; substitute strong hot coffee for milk.

Seven-minute frosting is just right for devil's food cake.

POWDERED SUGAR FROSTING

1 cup powdered sugar
Pinch of salt

¼ cup cream
½ tsp. vanilla extract
½ tsp. almond extract

Place sugar, salt in bowl. Add cream until soft enough to spread. Add extract.
This is a good frosting for pastel tints of pure vegetable coloring.

ORNAMENTAL FROSTING

This is an ideal frosting when nut halves, candied cherries, or any ornaments are arranged on top. Frosting glazes over on top, but remains soft underneath, and, therefore, keeps well.

2 egg whites, unbeaten	1 tsp. vanilla, almond or lemon
1½ cups sugar	extract
	Pinch of salt

Place egg whites in bowl, and add salt. Add sugar gradually, beat until smooth. Flavor to taste. Following are interesting variations:

Variations

1. *Lemon Frosting:* Add 1 tsp. grated lemon rind, 1 tsp. or more of juice.
2. *Orange Frosting:* Same as lemon, using orange rind and juice.
3. *Chocolate:* Add 3 Tbsp. cocoa to sugar.
4. *Coconut:* Sprinkle ½ cup shredded moist coconut over top and sides before frosting has "set."

QUICK CHOCOLATE FROSTINGS

MAGIC CHOCOLATE FROSTING

2 sq. chocolate, melted	1⅓ cups condensed milk
	1 Tbsp. water

Melt chocolate in top of double boiler, over boiling water. Add condensed milk and stir until thickened. Remove from heat, add water and cool. Makes enough to cover tops and sides of 2 layers.

QUICK CHOCOLATE PEPPERMINT FROSTING

2 sq. chocolate, melted	8 marshmallows
1⅓ cups condensed milk	¼ tsp. oil of peppermint

Melt chocolate in top of double boiler, over boiling water. Add condensed milk, stir until thickened. Add 8 marshmallows, stir until they melt. Add peppermint. Makes enough to cover top and sides of 2 layers.

CHOCOLATE GLAZE (RAFFETTI CAKE)

2 sq. chocolate, melted	2 tsp. butter

Melt chocolate and butter over hot water, in top of double boiler. Cool slightly and pour over a frosted cake, after frosting is "set." Chocolate will trickle down sides. Cake usually called a Raffetti Cake.

CANDIED GRAPEFRUIT PEEL

This is often used as a cake ingredient or cake garnish.

1 grapefruit (or 2 oranges)
1 qt. boiling water
¼ tsp. salt

1 cup sugar
⅔ cup water

{ Boil together 5 minutes to make - a syrup

½ cup sugar

Wash grapefruit or orange peel and cut in long, thin strips. Cook peel in boiling, salted water until tender (1½ hours). Mix 1 cup sugar and ⅔ cup water together and cook slowly over low flame until sugar has dissolved. Simmer for 15 minutes. Drain cooked peel, add to syrup, and cook until most of the liquid has evaporated (10 minutes). Now roll peel, a few pieces at a time, in sugar spread out on sheet of waxed paper. Cool for several hours and store in covered container.

Frosted cakes can be dressed up still more with ready-to-use fruits.

19.

PIES

HOMEMADE pie! The great American dessert. Our own flaky-crusted pies —with delicately browned crust top, or lattice top, or high meringue—are desserts that a bride can make with ease. There are modern oven thermometers and pastry blenders, also glass rolling pins which may be filled with ice water and are a wonderful asset for rolling out pastry. There are also packaged pie crusts easy to use, good to eat.

PLAIN PASTRY

(Standard Method)

For single 8-inch or 9-inch shell	½ tsp. salt
1½ cups all-purpose flour	½ cup shortening
	3 Tbsp. cold water (about)

Sift; measure flour. Add salt and sift again. Cut shortening into flour with pastry blender or two knives until mixture resembles coarse cornmeal. Sprinkle cold water over mixture, a few drops at a time. Press mixture together with a fork, do not stir. Gather together into a ball on end of fork. Use only enough water to hold pastry together to form a ball. Wrap pastry in wax paper. Chill in refrigerator ½ hour. It is easier to handle when chilled. For two-crust pie double this recipe.

PLAIN PASTRY

(New Method Pastry)

Sift flour and salt as above. Measure ⅓ cup of mixture and pour into bowl. Add 3 Tbsp. ice water to form paste. Set aside. Cut shortening into remaining flour-salt mixture as directed above. Stir the flour paste into the flour-shortening mixture to form dough. Gather into ball on end of fork; proceed as in standard pastry.

PASTRY

Things to Do for Light Pastry

1. Sift flour before measuring.
2. Measure all ingredients accurately.
3. For flaky pastry, have liquid ice cold. For more mealy pastry, do not chill water or pastry.
4. Use just enough water to hold the pastry together. Too much water makes the pastry tough.
5. Roll pastry with rolling pin. Use light quick strokes away from body.
6. Flour pastry-board lightly, just enough to prevent dough from sticking to board.
7. Brush lower crust of juicy fruit pies with unbeaten egg white before putting in filling and let chill 5 minutes in refrigerator. This prevents a soggy under-crust.
8. Brush upper crust, before baking, with milk or with 1 egg beaten with 1 Tbsp. of cold water. This gives a highly-glazed surface.
9. Pastry may be wrapped in waxed paper, placed in refrigerator and used within 2 weeks.
10. Fill pie to brim to make a good thick filling.

ROLLING PIE CRUST

Prepare plain pastry. Lightly dust both rolling pin and pie-board with flour. Place dough in center of pie-board; roll quickly and lightly, working out from center in all directions; keep rolling pin from going all the way to edge of dough, so it will not stick to board. To prevent pastry from sticking, slip spatula underneath dough, and sprinkle with flour if needed. Roll until circle is 1/8 inch thick, and about 2 inches larger in diameter than top of pie plate. Dough should be lifted frequently during rolling, but never turned over.

When pastry has reached desired shape and size to fit the pan in which it is to be baked, fold it gently in half and lay it carefully into the ungreased pie pan. Unfold pastry and fit it loosely into pan, being careful not to stretch pastry. Pat it down properly and trim with knife or shears, leaving about 1/2 inch border. Fold this underneath, bringing the double fold to an upright position. Next "flute" crust, by placing top of forefinger of one hand against inside of pastry rim. Then pinch outside fold of pastry at this point, with the tips of the other thumb and index finger. Repeat this at intervals of every 1/2 inch all around pie shell and it is ready for the filling.

LATTICED PIE

STEP 1   STEP 2

ONE CRUST PIE

TWO CRUST PIE

STEP 1   STEP 2

Any of these three types of pie represents good eating. Take your choice and provide a delicious filling that will set off the light flakiness of your pie crust. Photograph in the left center shows step in making graham cracker crust.

UNBAKED PASTRY SHELL

If a filling is to be baked in the pastry shell, it is advisable to chill shell before adding filling.

BAKED PASTRY SHELL

If pie shell is to be baked before it is used, prick entire surface with a fork to remove any air bubbles and bake in a hot oven (450° F.) 15 to 18 minutes. Then chill and fill. Some cooks cover bottom of shell with dried beans to weight bottom crust. Beans may be used repeatedly.

GRAHAM CRACKER PASTRY

1¼ cups crushed graham crackers
2 Tbsp. brown sugar
½ tsp. nutmeg
¼ tsp. cinnamon
⅛ tsp. salt
⅓ cup shortening, melted

Combine crushed wafers and melted shortening. Spread evenly in a 9-inch Spread evenly in a 9-inch pie pan, covering bottom and sides completely; pat mixture down firmly. Chill thoroughly before filling.

VANILLA WAFER PIE CRUST

1¼ cups crushed vanilla or chocolate wafers
5 Tbsp. shortening, melted

Combine crushed wafers and melted shortening. Spread evenly in a 9-inch pie pan, covering bottom and sides completely; pat mixture down firmly. Chill thoroughly before filling.

ONE-CRUST PIE FILLINGS—UNBAKED SHELLS

CUSTARD PIE

1 unbaked 9-inch pie crust
4 eggs
½ cup sugar
½ tsp. salt
3 cups milk, scalded
1 tsp. vanilla
¼ tsp. nutmeg

Prepare one 9-inch pastry shell. Make a fluted edge. Chill thoroughly. Combine eggs, sugar and salt. Pour scalded milk slowly over egg mixture. Add vanilla and nutmeg, and pour into pastry-lined pie shell. Sprinkle with nutmeg. Bake in hot oven (450° F.) 10 minutes; then in moderate oven (350°

F.) 30 minutes, or until a silver knife inserted in center of custard comes out clean.

Variations

Coconut Custard Pie: Prepare custard pie, and over the top sprinkle ½ cup moist shredded coconut, and bake as usual.

Blue Ridge Blueberry Pie: Prepare custard pie, and over the top sprinkle ½ cup blueberries and bake as usual.

PUMPKIN PIE

1 unbaked 9-inch pie shell	¾ cup sugar
2 eggs	¼ tsp. ginger
1½ cups canned, strained pump-kin	1 tsp. cinnamon
	¼ tsp. nutmeg
½ tsp. salt	⅛ tsp. cloves
	1½ cups milk

Line a 9-inch pie pan with plain pastry. Beat eggs, add pumpkin and other ingredients. Beat for 1 minute and pour into unbaked pie shell. Bake in hot oven (450° F.) 10 minutes. Then in a moderate oven (350° F.) 10 minutes, or until a silver knife inserted in center comes out clean.

BAKED PIE SHELLS

LEMON MERINGUE PIE

1 baked 9-inch pie shell	1½ cups boiling water
1 cup sugar	⅓ cup lemon juice
⅛ tsp. salt	2 tsp. grated lemon rind
¼ cup cornstarch	3 egg yolks
	2 Tbsp. butter

Mix sugar, salt and cornstarch. Add water and lemon juice. Cook in top of double boiler over hot water until clear and thick. Pour the hot mixture slowly over the egg yolks and return to double boiler. Cook 1 minute longer. Add butter and cool. Pour into baked pie shell.

Meringue

2 to 3 egg whites	4 to 6 Tbsp. sugar
	½ tsp. vanilla

Beat egg whites until they stand up in peaks, but not dry. Fold in sugar. Add vanilla. (*Note:* Use 2 Tbsp. sugar for each egg white.) Spread meringue on

Strawberry Alaska pie makes a wonderful dessert for company dinners. Fresh or frozen California strawberries and vanilla ice cream make the filling . . . a meringue mix makes the topping.

top of pie, being sure meringue comes to edges of pie with no spaces between, as it is less likely to "weep" or shrink. Bake in slow oven (300° F.) 30 minutes. Cool away from drafts.

QUICK CREAM PIES

QUICK LEMON CREAM PIE

1 baked 9-inch pie shell
2⅔ cups condensed milk

¾ cup lemon juice
2 Tbsp. grated lemon rind
2 eggs, separated

Blend together milk, lemon juice, lemon rind and egg yolks. Pour into baked pie shell. Chill thoroughly. Cover with meringue or cover with whipped cream.

QUICK CHOCOLATE CREAM PIE

1 baked 9-inch pie shell
4 sq. chocolate, melted
2⅔ cups condensed milk

½ cup water
¼ tsp. salt
½ tsp. vanilla
½ cup heavy cream, whipped

Melt chocolate, in top of double boiler over hot water. Add milk and cook for 6 minutes. Remove from heat and add water, salt and vanilla. Pour into baked pie shell. Chill thoroughly. Cover with whipped cream.

CREAM PIE

1 baked 9-inch pie shell	½ tsp. salt
1 cup sugar	2 cups milk
6 Tbsp. flour	3 egg yolks, beaten
	1 tsp. vanilla

Combine sugar, flour and salt, in top of double boiler over hot water. Add milk slowly, and cook 10 minutes, stirring constantly. Pour a little of hot mixture onto beaten egg yolks; add to remaining mixture in double boiler and cook for 4 minutes more. Stir constantly. Cool, add vanilla. Pour into pie shell. Cover with meringue and bake in slow oven (300° F.) 15 minutes or until slightly browned.

Variations

Banana Cream Pie: Prepare filling for cream pie. Arrange slices of peeled banana in bottom of baked pie shell. Pour cream filling over top. Arrange more slices of banana—which have been sprinkled with lemon juice—over the top, cover with meringue, and bake as above.

Chocolate Cream Pie: Cut 3 sq. of chocolate in small pieces; add to sugar and milk mixture before cooking. Bake as above.

Coconut Cream Pie: Prepare filling for cream pie. Stir ½ cup shredded coconut into the filling before pouring into baked pie shell. Cover with meringue, and sprinkle ½ cup shredded coconut over the top. Bake as above.

CHIFFON PIES

VANILLA CHIFFON PIE

1 baked 9-inch pie shell	3 eggs, separated
or	1½ cups milk
1 vanilla wafer 9-inch pie shell	¼ tsp. salt
1 Tbsp. gelatin	½ cup sugar
¼ cup cold water	1 tsp. vanilla

Soften gelatin in water. Combine beaten egg yolks, milk, salt and ¼ cup sugar, in top of double boiler over hot water. Cook until mixture thickens, stirring constantly. Remove from heat. Add softened gelatin and stir until dissolved. Chill until mixture begins to thicken. Beat egg whites until stiff but not dry; gradually add remaining sugar. Add vanilla, fold into gelatin mixture. Pour into pie shell and chill thoroughly.

Variations

Butterscotch Chiffon Pie: Substitute ½ cup brown sugar for ¼ cup white sugar, for mixture in top of double boiler. Add ¼ cup white sugar to be beaten with egg whites.

Chocolate Chiffon Pie: Add 2 sq. of chocolate and ¼ cup more sugar to mixture to be cooked in top of double boiler.

Coffee Chiffon Pie: Substitute strong black coffee for milk.

LEMON CHIFFON PIE

1 baked 9-inch pie shell	4 eggs, separated
or	¾ cup sugar
1 graham cracker 9-inch pie shell	½ tsp. salt
1 Tbsp. gelatin	½ cup lemon juice
¼ cup cold water	1 Tbsp. grated lemon rind

Soften gelatin in water. Combine beaten egg yolks, ½ cup sugar, salt and lemon juice, in top of double boiler over hot water. Cook until mixture thickens, stirring constantly. Remove from hot water. Add softened gelatin and grated lemon rind; stir until dissolved. Chill until mixture begins to thicken. Beat egg whites until stiff but not dry; gradually add remaining sugar. Fold into gelatin mixture. Pour into pie shell and chill thoroughly.

Variations

Lime Chiffon Pie: Substitute lime juice for lemon juice, and grated lime rind for lemon rind.

Cherry Chiffon Pie: Substitute cherry juice for lemon juice, and add to the egg whites 1 cup cooked sour red cherries (finely chopped).

Orange Chiffon Pie: Substitute orange juice for lemon juice, and grated orange rind for lemon rind. Add 1 Tbsp. lemon juice.

NESSELRODE PIE

1 baked 8-inch pie shell	Pinch of salt
1 Tbsp. gelatin	¼ cup Jamaica rum
2 Tbsp. cold water	1 tsp. vanilla extract
1 cup milk	½ cup cream, whipped
½ cup sugar	4 Tbsp. bittersweet chocolate,
3 eggs, separated	shaved thin

Dissolve gelatin in cold water. Scald milk and sugar in upper part of double boiler. Beat egg yolks until thick and lemon-colored, add salt. Add small amount of milk mixture to egg yolks, stir well. Return to pan, stir constantly and cook until mixture coats spoon. Add dissolved gelatin, rum, and vanilla extract. Beat well, remove from fire and cool, stirring frequently. Fill a bowl with cracked ice, place smaller bowl in ice. Pour mixture into inner bowl, beat again and quickly fold in stiffly-beaten egg whites. Beat rapidly until mixture is a smooth frothy mass. Pour filling into baked pie shell, sprinkle top with chocolate slivers. Cool in refrigerator until ready to serve.

TWO-CRUST PIES

Prepare Plain Pastry. Divide pastry in half, roll one portion on a lightly-floured board, into a circle about ⅛ inch thick and 1 inch larger in diameter than top of pan. Fold in half, and cut several slits with a knife in center of folded side, to permit steam to escape from pie. Moisten edge of under crust with cold water. Unfold upper crust, and lay it on top of filling with folded edge of pastry at center point of pie plate. Trim edge of upper crust with a knife or scissors, leaving ½ inch overhanging border all around. Fold edge of upper crust under edge of lower crust and press together with finger tips. Bring this to an upright position. Then flute by placing tip of forefinger of one hand against inside of pastry rim. Pinch outside fold of pastry at this point with tips of other thumb and index finger. Repeat this at even intervals all around pie shell. This high edge forms a wall to prevent juice from bubbling over into the oven. For a high glaze, brush top of pie with milk or egg yolk diluted with 1 Tbsp. water. Bake in hot oven (450° F.) 30 to 40 minutes.

LATTICED PIE TOP

Prepare Plain Pastry. Prepare under crust as directed for two-crust pie, but leave edge extending 1 inch over rim of pan until criss-crosses are in place. Fill

Latticed pie tops are at their best with fruit pies and show off the filling to great advantage.

with desired filling. Roll remaining dough ⅛ inch thick and cut into narrow strips with knife or pastry fluter. Lay strips parallel to each other, and about 1 inch apart, across the top of the pie, extending the strips to the edge of the pie. Press ends of strips down. Lay a second row of strips at right angles to first strips, so that you have a latticed effect. Press down, and trim edges of pie. Or, weave second layer of strips under and over first layer. Turn edges up, and flute with fingers to make a standing rim. Bake as directed for two-crust pie.

TWO-CRUST PIES

APPLE PIE

Pastry for two-crust 9-inch pie
5 cups tart apples, peeled and
   sliced
1 cup sugar
½ tsp. salt

1 Tbsp. flour
¼ tsp. nutmeg
1 tsp. cinnamon
1 Tbsp. lemon juice
2 Tbsp. butter

Prepare pastry and line a 9-inch pie pan. Combine sugar, salt, flour, nutmeg and cinnamon. Mix with apples. Pour into unbaked pie shell. Sprinkle lemon juice over apples, dot with butter. Cover with top crust, or latticed top, following directions for two-crust pie. Bake in hot oven (425° F.) 45 minutes, or until apples are tender.

CANNED CHERRY PIE

Pastry for two-crust 9-inch pie
3 cups drained pitted sour cherries
1 cup sugar
2 Tbsp. flour

¼ tsp. salt
⅔ cup juice drained from canned
   cherries
2 Tbsp. butter

Prepare pastry and line one 9-inch pie pan. Combine sugar, flour, salt, and add cherry juice. Cook about 5 minutes, or until clear. Place cherries in lined pie tin, dot with butter, and pour cherry juice mixture over them. Cover top as for two-crust pie or lattice-top pie, and follow directions for two-crust pie. Bake in hot oven (425° F.) 40 minutes.

DEEP-DISH PIES

A deep-dish pie is an old-fashioned dessert which is as popular today as it was fifty years ago. The same fruit fillings are used as for two-crust pies, but the mixture is poured into a greased baking dish (10x6x2 inches). A single crust is rolled out, and 3 slits cut in center to permit steam to escape. The crust is placed over top of dish, and cut about 1 inch larger than size of dish. Tuck extra inch under to make a firm double edge. Press down all the way around. Bake in hot oven (450° F.) 30 minutes, or until filling is tender. Apples, apricots, peaches, pears or plums are most often selected for deep-dish pies.

Deep-dish apple pie will bring ecstatic response from all who are fortunate enough to receive a serving of this wonderfully rich fruit and pastry duo.

FRESH BERRY PIES
(Basic Recipe)

Pastry for two-crust 9-inch pie	4 Tbsp. flour
4 cups fresh berries	¼ tsp. nutmeg
1 cup sugar	1 Tbsp. lemon juice
½ tsp. salt	2 Tbsp. butter

Prepare pastry and line a 9-inch pan. Combine sugar, salt, flour, nutmeg. Mix with berries and pour into unbaked pie shell. Sprinkle lemon juice over berries, dot with butter. Cover with top crust or latticed top, following directions for two-crust pie. Bake in hot oven (425° F.) 45 minutes.

Variations

Blueberry, cherry, cranberry may all be made according to basic recipe. Sugar may be increased to 1½ cups for tart cranberries.

MINCE PIE

Pastry for two-crust 9-inch pie
3 level cupfuls mince meat

Prepare pastry and line a 9-inch pie pan. Place mince meat on pastry. Cover top with pastry. Flute edge. Bake in hot oven (425° F.) 40 minutes.

Mince Meat

1¼ lbs. round of beef	3 cups sweet cider
1 qt. apples, chopped	1 Tbsp. salt
1 cup suet, chopped	2 Tbsp. cinnamon
1½ cups raisins	1½ tsp. allspice
1 cup currants	½ tsp. cloves
⅛ lb. citron, cut fine	1½ tsp. mace
2 cups sugar	2 tsp. nutmeg
1 cup molasses	Juice of 2 lemons
	1 cup brandy

Cook beef in boiling water to cover. When tender, cool, strain, remove fat. Chop very fine. Add all ingredients and mix thoroughly. Let stand overnight in refrigerator. Heat slowly to boiling point, simmer gently for 1 hour. Pour into hot sterilized jars. Seal at once.

TARTS

TART SHELLS

Prepare Plain Pastry to make ten 4-inch tart shells. Roll out as for pastry shell.

Fruit tarts can be filled with canned cherries, or any of the berries, and topped with whipped cream.

UNBAKED TART SHELLS

Cut and fit into tart pans, or cup cake pans, or muffin pans, as directed for one-crust unbaked pastry shell.

Suggested fillings: Pumpkin Pie. Coconut Custard Pie.

BAKED TART SHELLS

Invert tart pan, or muffin pan, or cup cake pan. Roll pastry ⅛ inch thick and cut in rounds large enough to cover inverted pan. Fit over inverted pan and trim edges. Prick all over with a fork; chill. Bake in hot oven (450° F.) 10 to 15 minutes, or until lightly-browned. Cool before filling. Pastry can be fitted over inverted custard cups, pinched at 4 corners, and pricked and baked as directed above.

FRUIT TARTS

10 baked tart shells	1 Tbsp. cornstarch
3 cups canned or stewed fruit (drained)	1 tsp. lemon juice
	Sugar to taste
⅔ cup fruit juice	½ cup heavy cream

Prepare 10 baked tart shells. Mix 1 Tbsp. fruit juice with cornstarch until smooth. Add remaining fruit juice. Place over low heat, bring to boil. Stir constantly. Boil until clear. Add sugar if fruit juice is not sweet enough. Mix fruit with thickened fruit juice. Add lemon juice. Cool and pour into tart shells. Top with whipped cream.

Suggested fruit fillings: Canned raspberries, blackberries, cherries, blueberries, huckleberries.

FRESH FRUIT TARTS

Bake tart shells and fill with sweetened fresh whole strawberries, raspberries, or sliced peaches. Quick-frozen fruit can also be used. Top with whipped cream and serve.

CREAM TARTS

Bake tart shells and fill with prepared vanilla, chocolate or butterscotch pudding. Or use the same fillings as suggested for any of the cream pies. Top with whipped cream or meringue.

CREAM PUFF SHELLS

1 cup flour	¼ cup butter
¼ tsp. salt	1 cup boiling water
	4 eggs, unbeaten

Sift; measure flour. Add salt and sift again. Melt butter in boiling water. Add dry ingredients all at one time, stir over low heat until mixture forms a ball and leaves sides of pan. Remove from heat. Let cool. This is important. Stir occasionally, then add unbeaten eggs, one at a time, and beat thoroughly after each addition. Drop by tablespoonfuls onto a greased baking sheet about 2 inches apart. Bake in hot oven (450° F.) 20 minutes. Reduce heat to 350° F., and bake 20 minutes. When cool, cut a slit in the side of each and fill with cream filling or sweetened whipped cream.

Greek lamb tarts are traditionally used in that country for a buffet following a tree-trimming party, or to usher in the New Year.

Cream puffs, traditionally light and frivolous, will satisfy a sweet tooth.

20.

DESSERTS

THE DESSERTS in this chapter offer many variations of basic recipes, so that a dessert may always be "something different."

APPLE BROWN BETTY

This is an old, old recipe which has been used for years by thrifty housewives who had extra bread crumbs on hand. Made properly, it is a satisfactory and delicious family dessert.

4 tart apples
1 cup stale bread crumbs
2 to 4 Tbsp. butter, melted
¼ cup soft brown sugar
1 tsp. cinnamon
1 tsp. grated lemon rind
1 Tbsp. lemon juice
¼ cup boiling water

Apple brown Betty can be given a new twist by using graham cracker crumbs instead of bread crumbs.

Core, pare, slice apples. Mix bread crumbs, butter, sugar and spice. Grease a casserole and place layer of sliced apples on bottom. Sprinkle with crumb mixture, then another layer of apples, and so on until ingredients are used up. Cover top with crumb mixture. Mix lemon rind, lemon juice, and boiling water. Pour over apple mixture. Cover casserole and bake in moderate oven

(350°-375° F.) 30 minutes, or until apples are tender. Remove cover for last 5 minutes of baking. Serve with cream, or hard sauce.

Variations

1. *Peach:* Use 4 fresh or canned peaches in place of apples.
2. *Pear:* Use 4 fresh pears in place of apples.
3. Any of the Brown Betty desserts may be made richer by the addition of 1 cup nut meats.

Baked apples are an old stand-by which can be transformed into dressy desserts by topping them with swirls of ginger meringue made with 1/16 tsp. salt, 2 egg whites, unbeaten, ¼ cup sugar, and ¼ tsp. ground ginger. Add salt to unbeaten egg whites; beat until they stand in soft peaks. Beat in sugar, 1 tbsp. at a time. Beat in ginger. Pile on meringue on tops of baked apples. Bake 15 to 20 minutes, in a preheated slow oven.

BAKED APPLES—MODERN STYLE

The individual casserole is a delightful container for a baked apple prepared this way. Select Greenings or Rome Beauty apples.

4 large unblemished apples	4 Tbsp. raisins
Syrup	4 Tbsp. honey
1 cup water	½ tsp. nutmeg
1 cup sugar	

Core the apples and pare about one third of the way down from the stem end. Select a saucepan with deep sides. Make a syrup of sugar and water, boil 5 minutes, add 1 or 2 apples, cover and simmer gently until apples are tender but unbroken. Pierce lightly with steel needle or silver fork. Lift apples out with perforated spoon; place in casseroles or shallow baking dish. Cook remaining apples. Fill center of each apple with raisins and honey, sprinkle with nutmeg. Place casseroles or baking dish under broiler flame, baste with extra sugar syrup left in saucepan. As soon as apple takes on delicate brown color, remove from oven, serve cold.

Variations

1. If apple skin is a bright red, the peeling may be cooked with syrup.
2. Cinnamon drop candies may be cooked in syrup.
3. Red vegetable coloring may be added to syrup.
4. Small apples may be completely pared, cooked in syrup with red coloring and served with cold meat.

CUSTARDS

Sometimes even an old-timer stubs her toe when it comes to making a smooth, velvety-baked custard. In this method of cookery, the oven temperature is the key to success—too high a temperature means a watery custard. Water in outer pan must be as high as custard in cups.

BAKED CUSTARD

1 pt. milk, cold or scalded	2 to 4 Tbsp. sugar
2 to 3 eggs	¼ tsp. salt
	1 tsp. vanilla extract

Beat eggs slightly, add salt, sugar and vanilla. Pour scalded milk on gradually, stirring constantly. Grease custard cups well, stand in a pan of hot water. Pour custard into cups, or use one large glass pudding dish. Bake in moderate oven (350° F.), until silver knife gently thrust into center of custard comes out clean (30 to 45 minutes). Chill, loosen at sides, and turn out on pretty plate.

Variations

1. 1 Tbsp. jam or jelly may be placed in bottom of each cup.
2. 1 sq. melted chocolate may be mixed with custard mixture.
3. 1 Tbsp. maple syrup may be poured in bottom of each cup.

SOFT CUSTARD

3 eggs	Pinch of salt
½ cup sugar	1 pt. milk
	1 tsp. vanilla

Beat eggs slightly; stir in sugar, salt. Pour milk on slowly, stirring constantly. Place in upper part of double boiler, over hot water. Stir constantly to prevent curdling. Cook until mixture forms a smooth coating on silver spoon. Keep water below boiling point. Remove custard from heat, add vanilla. If custard does curdle, it may be made smooth by standing pan in which it was cooked in cold water, and beating vigorously with egg beater.

Many cooks prefer to scald milk first, before pouring it over egg and sugar mixture. It is then returned to double boiler and same procedure followed. This method lessens time of cooking.

ORANGE CUSTARD PUDDING

¾ cup sugar
¼ tsp. salt
3 Tbsp. cornstarch
1 pt. milk, scalded
1 egg, well-beaten
4 navel oranges, peeled and cut in slices
1 tsp. almond extract
¼ cup sugar (for sprinkling)

Custard's delicate flavor can be accented by serving with fresh fruit and a little whipped cream.

Mix dry ingredients together. Pour milk over mixture to make smooth paste. Cook over hot water, stirring frequently until thickened. Pour over egg, cook 1 minute longer. Add flavoring, chill well. Arrange oranges in bottom of dish. Sprinkle with sugar. Pour custard over top. Serve cold.

APPLE SNOW

1 egg white
2 Tbsp. sugar
1 cup apple sauce

1 tsp. grated lemon rind
1 Tbsp. lemon juice
Pinch of salt

Beat egg white until stiff, fold in sugar. Combine sauce, juice and grated rind. Fold into egg white mixture. Heap high in sherbet glasses. Chill, and serve with custard sauce.

PRUNE WHIP

1 egg white	1 tsp. grated lemon rind
2 Tbsp. sugar	2 tsp. lemon juice
1 cup prune pulp	Pinch of salt

Beat egg white until stiff, fold in sugar. Combine prune pulp, juice and grated rind. Fold into egg white mixture. Heap high in sherbet glasses. Chill, and serve with soft custard sauce.

Variation

Apricot Whip: Use 1 cup apricot pulp instead of prune pulp.

DATE TORTE PUDDING

¼ cup flour	1 egg, well-beaten
1 tsp. baking powder	1 cup dates, cut in pieces
¼ tsp. salt	1 cup nut meats, broken
½ cup sugar	1 tsp. vanilla extract
	1 tsp. almond extract

Mix and sift dry ingredients. Add egg, beat well. Add dates, nuts and flavorings. Pour into well-greased shallow square baking pan. Bake in slow oven (325° F.), 1 hour. Leave in pan until cold. Cut into squares, remove to serving plates. Top with sweetened whipped cream. (Graham cracker crumbs or zwieback crumbs may be used in place of flour.)

FRENCH DESSERT

2 doz. lady fingers	¼ cup sugar
¼ cup brandy	¼ lb. butter, creamed
3 eggs, separated	7-oz. pkg. semi-sweet chocolate, melted

Beat egg yolks with sugar until thick. Beat into butter. Melt chocolate and add to mixture. Beat egg whites until stiff. Fold into mixture. Dip lady fingers into brandy and line sherbet glasses with them. Fill center with chocolate mixture. Serve very cold.

HOT PUDDINGS

BAKED INDIAN PUDDING

1½ qts. milk	½ cup molasses
½ cup cornmeal	1 Tbsp. butter
	⅓ tsp. salt

Scald 1 pt. of milk and pour gradually upon cornmeal, stirring all the time. Turn mixture into double boiler and cook for half an hour, stirring frequently. Remove from fire and add molasses, butter, salt, and 1 qt. of cold milk. Add milk gradually, beating well. Pour mixture into a pudding dish, and bake in slow oven (275° F.) 2 to 3 hours. Stir several times during baking.

LEMON PUDDING

1 cup sugar	3 Tbsp. lemon juice
1 Tbsp. flour	1 tsp. grated rind
1 cup milk	¼ tsp. salt
2 egg yolks, slightly-beaten	2 egg whites, stiffly-beaten

Sift together sugar, flour and salt. Add milk, egg yolks, lemon juice and rind, and beat until smooth. Fold in stiffly-beaten egg whites, and pour into a well-greased casserole. Set in pan of hot water to depth of batter. Bake in slow oven (300° F.) 1 hour.

FRUIT ROLY POLY

1 cup water	2 cups flour, sifted
1½ cups cranberries	4 tsp. baking powder
½ cup raisins	1 tsp. salt
1 apple, cut up	2 Tbsp. butter
	¾ cup milk

Make a sauce with water, cranberries, raisins and apple. Drain off the juice and save it for the pudding sauce. Sift flour, baking powder and salt. Cut in butter; add milk. Roll out lightly on floured board. Spread with well-drained fruit. Roll up like jelly roll, and place on pan on a rack over boiling water in a large kettle. Cover tightly and steam without lifting cover for ½ hour. Do not let water touch pudding. Serve hot with Fruit Sauce.

GINGER APPLE PUDDING

¼ cup sugar	½ tsp. nutmeg
¼ cup water	½ tsp. cloves
3 apples, sliced	½ tsp. cinnamon
⅓ cup sugar	½ tsp. salt
1½ cups flour, sifted	1 egg
1 tsp. soda	½ cup molasses
½ tsp. ginger	½ cup hot water
	¼ cup shortening, melted

Combine ¼ cup sugar and water to make syrup. Cook apples in syrup till half done. Drain off extra syrup and spread apples over bottom of well-greased square cake pan. Sift together dry ingredients. Add egg, molasses and hot water. Beat well. Add melted shortening, beat well, and pour batter over apples. Bake in a moderate oven (350° F.) 40 minutes. Pour extra syrup over top.

FRUIT COBBLERS

We may thank the old-fashioned simplicity of our grandmothers for these hearty and filling cobblers.

MIXTURE FOR TOP CRUST

Part I

1 cup all-purpose flour	¼ cup sugar
1½ tsp. baking powder	¼ cup shortening
½ tsp. salt	2 to 4 Tbsp. milk

Sift; measure flour. Add baking powder, salt and sugar, sift again. Cut in shortening with pastry blender. Add milk, stirring quickly to make a soft dough.

MIXTURE FOR FRUIT FILLING

Part II

½ cup sugar	½ tsp. salt
1 Tbsp. flour	2 cups berries or fruit
	1 tsp. nutmeg

Combine sugar, flour, salt. Add fruit and sprinkle with nutmeg. Mix well. Pour into deep, greased baking dish. Roll out soft dough (*Part I*) to ½ inch thickness. Cut 3 slits in dough to permit steam to escape. Cover fruit with dough and press down edges. Bake in hot oven (450° F.) 15 minutes. Reduce heat to moderate (350° F.), and bake 30 minutes longer.

CALIFORNIA PUDDING

1 cup persimmon pulp (soft and ripe)	½ tsp. nutmeg
	¼ tsp. cinnamon
1 cup flour	1 Tbsp. butter
2 tsp. soda	1 cup sugar
¼ tsp. salt	½ cup milk

Sift; measure flour. Add dry ingredients, sift again. Cream butter, add sugar gradually. Add dry mixture, alternately with milk. Turn into greased baking dish and bake in moderate oven (350° F.) 1 hour.

SASKATCHEWAN PUDDING

Batter

1 cup flour	⅓ cup brown sugar
3 tsp. baking powder	1 cup raisins
¼ tsp. salt	½ cup sweet milk

Sift; measure flour. Add baking powder and salt, sift again. Add sugar and milk. Mix well, add raisins. Pour into greased baking dish.

Sauce

2 cups boiling water	1 Tbsp. butter
1 cup brown sugar	¼ tsp. nutmeg

Mix all ingredients together until sugar is melted. Pour over batter in pudding dish. Bake in moderate oven (350° F.) 30 minutes. This is a pudding where the batter rises to the top, and the sauce sinks down to the bottom. It makes a light moist pudding, with its own delectable sauce.

BRIDE'S PUDDING

1 cup flour, sifted	2 Tbsp. butter
2 Tbsp. sugar	½ cup milk
2 tsp. baking powder	1 tsp. vanilla extract
¼ tsp. salt	1 cup stewed fruit pulp, sweetened

Sift dry ingredients together. Cut in butter with pastry blender or two knives. Add milk, beat well to make smooth batter. Add vanilla extract. Grease individual custard cups, and place spoonful of batter in bottom of each cup. Press down in center with spoon to make hollow. Divide fruit evenly among six cups, placing on top of batter. Cover fruit with spoonful of batter, dividing evenly. Bake in moderate oven (350° F.) 30 minutes. Serve hot with Fruit Sauce.

PLUM PUDDING

2 cups fine bread crumbs	¾ cup milk
1 tsp. cinnamon	¾ cup butter, melted
¼ tsp. powdered cloves	1 cup nut meats, chopped
¼ tsp. nutmeg	½ cup citron, cut in fine pieces
2 tsp. baking powder	1 cup seedless raisins, chopped
½ cup molasses	½ cup currants

Sift dry ingredients together. Mix with crumbs. Mix molasses, milk, and melted butter together. Add to dry mixture. Mix fruits together thoroughly and add to mixture by degrees, beating well after each addition. Pour into well-greased mold, cover with waxed paper, tie securely, and steam for 4 hours. (See Fruit Roly Poly.) Serve with Hard Sauce.

OLD-FASHIONED RICE PUDDING

½ cup uncooked rice
1 qt. milk
½ cup seedless raisins
½ tsp. salt
¼ cup sugar
1 tsp. nutmeg or cinnamon

Rice pudding is always popular, always a satisfying dessert. Dates add a touch appealing to eye and taste.

Wash rice in cold water. Grease a casserole and pour all ingredients in dish, setting aside 1 cup of milk. Bake in slow oven (325° F.) 1 hour. Add remaining cup of milk, stirring well. Stir pudding several times during baking process. A golden film will form on the top, and should be stirred right into pudding. Serve cold. (May be baked without raisins.)

BOILED RICE PUDDING

½ cup uncooked rice   ½ tsp. salt
1 pt. milk   1 tsp. vanilla extract

Wash rice in cold water. Sprinkle into pan of boiling water and cook uncovered for 10 minutes. Drain and add milk, salt, and vanilla extract. Cook over hot water until rice is tender. Do not stir while cooking. A cup of raisins may be added. Serve hot.

BLACKBERRY PUDDING

1 cup flour, sifted   ½ cup sugar
2 tsp. baking powder   1 egg, well-beaten
2 Tbsp. butter   ½ cup milk
                             1½ cups fresh blackberries

Sift flour and baking powder together. Cream butter, add sugar and cream, beat until light and fluffy. Add egg, beat well. Add flour and milk alternately, beating well after each addition. Fold berries in lightly. Add vanilla extract. Pour into well-greased baking dish. Bake in moderate oven (350° F.) 45 minutes. Serve with a pitcher of cream or clotted cream. Or serve with custard sauce or even vanilla ice cream.

CARROT PUDDING

1 cup raw carrots, grated fine	¼ cup flour, sifted before measuring
1 tsp. grated lemon rind	3 Tbsp. butter, melted
1 Tbsp. lemon juice	4 eggs, separated
½ cup sugar	1 tsp. vanilla extract
⅛ tsp. salt	

Mix together carrots, lemon rind and juice. Let stand 15 minutes. Sift together sugar, flour and salt; add melted butter and beat well. Add well-beaten egg yolks and fold into mixture. Add carrot mixture, vanilla extract, and blend well. Fold in stiffly-beaten egg whites. Turn into well-greased casserole. Bake in moderate oven (350° F.) 1 hour.

COTTAGE PUDDING

1 cup cake flour, sifted before measuring	2 Tbsp. butter
2 tsp. baking powder	¼ cup sugar
¼ tsp. salt	1 egg, well-beaten
	½ cup milk
	1 tsp. lemon extract

Mix and sift dry ingredients. Cream butter, add sugar slowly, beat until light and fluffy. Add egg, beat well. Add milk and flour alternately. Add lemon extract. Bake in a well-greased 8-inch square pan, in moderate oven (350° F.) 40 minutes. This is a good dessert pennywise, and a perfect basis for your favorite dessert sauce or topping.

ORANGE PUDDING

3 egg whites	3 Tbsp. orange marmalade
3 Tbsp. sugar	½ pt. cream, whipped

Beat egg whites until stiff. Fold in sugar, add marmalade. Put in well-greased upper part of double boiler. Cook covered for ¾ hour over simmering water. Turn out on hot serving dish. Serve with whipped cream. The marmalade flavor gives a different and piquant taste.

LEMON SPONGE CUPS

2 Tbsp. butter	5 Tbsp. lemon juice
1 cup sugar	Rind of 1 lemon, grated
4 Tbsp. flour	3 eggs, separated
¼ tsp. salt	1½ cups milk

Cream butter; add sugar, flour, salt, lemon juice and rind. Stir in beaten egg yolks and milk. Fold in stiffly-beaten whites and pour in greased custard cups. Place in pan of hot water and bake in moderate oven (350° F.) 45 minutes. When cooked, custard is on bottom and cake on top.

CHOCOLATE PUDDING

1 cup milk	½ cup sugar
2 tsp. plain gelatin	2 Tbsp. cold water
¼ cup cold water	1 egg, separated
3 Tbsp. cocoa	Pinch of salt
	½ tsp. vanilla or almond extract

Scald milk, in upper half of double boiler over hot water. Soak gelatin in cold water and dissolve in milk. Mix cocoa, and half of sugar, with the 2 Tbsp. cold water to make a smooth paste. Pour some of hot milk mixture over cocoa paste, mix well, return to double boiler. Beat yolk of egg with remaining sugar and salt. Add hot mixture and blend thoroughly. Return to double boiler; cook for 1 minute, stirring constantly. Cool, add flavoring and stiffly-beaten egg white. Pour into individual cups. Serve cold with cream. Or make a meringue of the egg white and heap on top of each cup.

Strawberry Bavarian Cream with a heart motif makes a pretty picture and is suitable as a dessert on sentimental occasions—but good to eat on other occasions too.

CHOCOLATE CREAM PUDDING

5 Tbsp. cornstarch	3 cups milk
½ cup sugar	1½ sq. chocolate
¼ tsp. salt	2 egg whites
	1 tsp. vanilla

Mix cornstarch, sugar and salt together. Add cold milk gradually, mix well. Place in upper part of double boiler over hot water. Cook until smooth. Melt chocolate over hot water and add to milk. Cook 10 minutes, stirring occasionally. Beat 3 minutes. Cool slightly. Add stiffly-beaten egg whites and vanilla. Pour in mold, chill, and serve.

BAVARIAN CREAM

1 Tbsp. gelatin	2 egg yolks, beaten
¼ cup cold water	Pinch of salt
1 cup milk, scalded	1 Tbsp. vanilla extract
½ cup sugar	2 egg whites, stiffly-beaten
	1 cup cream, whipped

Soak gelatin in cold water. Mix egg yolks, sugar and salt, add milk and cook over hot water. Add gelatin, and cook until mixture coats spoon. Chill thoroughly, add vanilla extract. Fold in egg whites and cream. Turn into molds.

Variations

Without cream: Cream may be omitted and 1 more cup of scalded milk substituted.

Chocolate: Add 2 sq. unsweetened chocolate to milk. Stir well until melted.

Coffee: Add ¼ cup finely-pulverized coffee grounds to milk. Strain through cheesecloth.

Peach: Add 1 cup sliced peaches to mixture just before turning into mold.

SOUFFLÉS

VANILLA SOUFFLÉ

⅓ cup sugar	Pinch of salt
⅓ cup flour	4 eggs, separated
1 cup milk	¼ tsp. cream of tartar
	1 tsp. vanilla

Combine sugar, flour and salt. Add milk gradually. Cook in upper part of double boiler over hot water, stirring constantly until mixture is smooth and thick. Beat egg yolks until thick, add a little of milk mixture. Return to pan.

Cook 15 minutes, cool. Beat egg whites until foamy, add cream of tartar and continue to beat until stiff. Fold into first mixture. Pour into a greased casserole. Bake in slow oven (325° F.) 45 minutes.

Variations

1. *Chocolate:* Add 1 sq. of melted chocolate to thickened milk mixture before pouring onto egg yolks.
2. *Apricot:* Add 1 cup apricot pulp before folding in egg whites.
3. *Peach:* Add 1 cup peach pulp before folding in egg whites.

LEMON SOUFFLÉ

4 Tbsp. butter	2 egg yolks
4 Tbsp. flour	½ cup sugar
1 cup boiling water	1 Tbsp. grated lemon rind
3 Tbsp. lemon juice	3 egg whites, stiffly-beaten

Melt butter in top part of double boiler over hot water. Add flour and stir until well-blended. Add boiling water slowly. Remove to direct heat and cook until smooth and thickened. Remove from heat. Beat egg yolks until thick and lemon-colored, stir in sugar. Add to first mixture, add lemon rind. Fold in egg whites. Pour into casserole, greased on bottom only. Bake in moderate oven (375° F.) 30 minutes or until a silver knife inserted in center comes out clean.

DESSERT SAUCES AND FILLINGS

Popular flavors for desserts may be utilized in many ways. Plain butter cakes or sponge cakes, hot gingerbreads, cottage puddings, all have appeal, if the sauce or filling satisfies the natural craving for sweets. The family-tested recipes which follow have been acclaimed in the average American home, from coast to coast.

BUTTERSCOTCH SAUCE

1½ cups dark brown sugar	1 cup boiling water
4 Tbsp. flour	2 Tbsp. butter
Dash of salt	¼ cup cream
	½ tsp. vanilla

Mix sugar, flour and salt. Slowly add boiling water to dry ingredients. Cook slowly 6 to 8 minutes. Stir while cooking. Add butter, cream, and vanilla. Keep warm in upper part of double boiler until ready to serve.

CUSTARD SAUCE

1 cup milk
2 egg yolks

2 Tbsp. sugar
1/8 tsp. salt
1 tsp. vanilla

Scald milk in top of double boiler. Beat yolks, sugar, and salt together until light, and pour scalded milk over them. Return to boiler and cook until mixture coats spoon, stirring constantly. Chill, add vanilla.

CHOCOLATE SAUCE

1 to 2 sq. chocolate, melted
1 Tbsp. butter
1/3 cup boiling water

1 cup sugar
2 Tbsp. corn syrup
1 tsp. vanilla

Melt chocolate in upper part of double boiler. Add butter and water gradually, bring to boiling point. Add sugar and corn syrup, boil for 5 minutes. Add vanilla.

ROYAL CHOCOLATE SAUCE

2 sq. chocolate
6 Tbsp. water

1/2 cup sugar
3 Tbsp. butter
1 tsp. vanilla

Add chocolate to water, and place over low flame, stirring until blended. Add sugar and salt. Cook until sugar is dissolved and mixture very slightly thickened, stirring constantly. Add butter and vanilla. (This is excellent poured over ice cream or sponge cake.)

HARD SAUCE

1/3 cup butter

1 cup confectioner's sugar
1 tsp. vanilla

Beat butter until soft. Add sugar gradually. Continue until smooth and fluffy. Add flavoring slowly. This is perfect with hot gingerbread or plum pudding.

Variations

Wine Sauce: Prepare Hard Sauce, substituting 1 to 3 Tbsp. Wine for vanilla.
Mocha Sauce: Prepare Hard Sauce, omit vanilla, add 2 tsp. dry cocoa to sugar.
   Flavor with strong coffee, 1 to 3 Tbsp.

LEMON SAUCE

½ cup sugar
1 Tbsp. cornstarch
⅛ tsp. salt

1 cup boiling water
2 Tbsp. butter
2 Tbsp. lemon juice
1 egg yolk, beaten

Mix sugar, cornstarch and salt. Pour boiling water over dry ingredients slowly, stirring constantly, and place in upper part of double boiler. Cook for 5 minutes. Remove from fire, add butter, lemon juice. Pour over beaten egg yolk and cook 1 minute. Cool and serve over cottage pudding, plain cake or gingerbread.

Variation

Orange Sauce: Use same recipe as for Lemon Sauce, substituting 1 cup orange juice for the water.

CRUSHED RASPBERRY SAUCE

1 box quick-frozen red raspberries
¼ cup sugar

1 Tbsp. cornstarch dissolved in 2 Tbsp. cold water
1 tsp. lemon juice

Press raspberries through a sieve. Add sugar and cook slowly for 3 to 5 minutes. Add slowly to cornstarch paste. Cook 1 minute longer. Add lemon juice. Chill before serving.

FRUIT SAUCE

1 cup boiling liquid, fruit juice or water, or combination of two
½ cup sugar
1 Tbsp. cornstarch

¼ tsp. salt
1 tsp. grated lemon rind
2 to 3 Tbsp. lemon juice
2 to 3 Tbsp. butter

Bring liquid to boil. Measure 1 cup, and add to well-mixed dry ingredients. Place over hot water and cook until mixture is thick and clear. Stir in lemon rind and butter. Serve over any hot pudding or gingerbread.

BUTTERSCOTCH FILLING

½ cup brown sugar
5 Tbsp. flour
½ tsp. salt

2 cups milk
2 eggs, beaten
4 Tbsp. butter
½ tsp. vanilla

Mix sugar, flour and salt. Scald milk in upper part of double boiler over hot water. Slowly pour milk over dry ingredients to make a smooth paste. Return to double boiler, continue cooking until it thickens. Pour a small amount of mixture onto eggs. Stir well and return to double boiler to cook 1 minute; add butter when ready to remove from heat. Stir well, cool, add vanilla.

Note: All cooked fillings should be cool before spreading on layer cake.

CREAM FILLING

½ cup sugar	2 cups milk
5 Tbsp. flour	2 eggs, beaten
½ tsp. salt	1 tsp. vanilla

Mix sugar, flour and salt. Scald milk, in upper part of double boiler over hot water. Slowly pour milk over dry ingredients to make a smooth paste. Return to double boiler, continue cooking until it thickens. Pour a small amount of mixture onto eggs. Stir well and return to double boiler to cook 1 minute. Cool, add vanilla.

BANANA CREAM FILLING

Bananas may be sliced and placed over filling. Top layer of cake should be carefully pressed down on lower layer. Toothpicks may be used to skewer two layers together. Keep in cool place until served.

CHOCOLATE CREAM FILLING

¾ cup sugar	2 cups milk
5 Tbsp. flour	1½ sq. chocolate
½ tsp. salt	2 eggs, beaten
	1 tsp. vanilla

Mix sugar, flour and salt. Place milk and chocolate in upper part of double boiler over hot water; cook until chocolate is melted. Slowly pour milk over dry ingredients to make a smooth paste. Return to double boiler, continue cooking until it thickens. Pour a small amount of mixture onto eggs. Stir well, and return to double boiler to cook 1 minute. Cool, add vanilla.

RAISIN FILLING

⅓ cup sugar	¾ cup water
3 Tbsp. flour	½ cup orange juice
½ tsp. salt	2 cups raisins, chopped
	1 Tbsp. grated orange rind

Mix sugar, flour and salt. Heat water and orange juice, in upper part of double boiler over hot water. Slowly pour over dry ingredients, stir to make a smooth paste, return to double boiler. Add raisins, cook 15 minutes. Add rind.

LEMON FILLING

⅔ cup sugar

4 Tbsp. flour

¼ tsp. salt

½ cup boiling water

¼ cup lemon juice

1 egg, well-beaten

2 Tbsp. butter

1 tsp. grated lemon rind

Mix sugar, flour and salt. Slowly add boiling water and juice to make smooth paste. Place in upper part of double boiler over hot water. Cook until thickened. Pour a small amount over egg, return to double boiler. Cook 1 minute, add butter and lemon rind, cool. Spread between layers of sponge or plain cake.

ORANGE FILLING

⅔ cup sugar

4 Tbsp. flour

¼ tsp. salt

½ cup boiling water

⅓ cup orange juice

1 Tbsp. lemon juice

1 egg, well-beaten

2 Tbsp. butter

1 tsp. grated orange rind

Mix sugar, flour and salt. Slowly add boiling water and juices to make smooth paste. Place in upper part of double boiler over hot water. Cook until thickened. Pour small amount over egg, return to double boiler. Cook 1 minute, add butter and lemon rind. Cool. Spread between layers of sponge or plain cake.

WHIPPED CREAM FILLING

½ tsp. gelatin

1 Tbsp. cold water

½ cup heavy cream

3 Tbsp. confectioner's sugar

¼ tsp. vanilla

Soften gelatin in cold water; place over boiling water until dissolved, then cool. Combine with cream and beat until stiff. Fold in sugar, add vanilla. Spread lightly on cake.

CHOCOLATE WHIPPED CREAM FILLING

½ tsp. gelatin

1 Tbsp. cold water

½ cup heavy cream

2 Tbsp. cocoa

¼ cup confectioner's sugar

½ tsp. vanilla

Soften gelatin in cold water; place over boiling water until dissolved, then cool. Combine with cream and cocoa. Beat until stiff. Fold in sugar, add vanilla.

COFFEE WHIPPED CREAM FILLING

Substitute cold black coffee for water in previous recipe.

APRICOT WHIPPED CREAM FILLING

½ tsp. gelatin	½ cup sieved apricot pulp
1 Tbsp. cold water	3 Tbsp. confectioner's sugar
⅓ cup heavy cream	1 tsp. lemon juice

Soften gelatin in cold water, place over boiling water until dissolved. Cool, combine with cream, and beat until stiff. Fold in pulp, add sugar and lemon juice.

QUICK FRUIT FILLING

⅔ cup condensed milk	Sliced fresh strawberries
2 Tbsp. lemon juice	Crushed peaches, drained
½ cup fruit:	Crushed pineapple, drained
Fresh raspberries	Apricot pulp
	Confectioner's sugar

Blend condensed milk and lemon juice. Stir until mixture thickens and fold in one of these fruits. (This is a fine quick filling for plain cake.) Dust confectioner's sugar over top layer.

Bavarian cream mold impresses company. Use any shape mold. Decorate with fruit and cookies. Result is a rich but light dessert.

21.

FROZEN DESSERTS

ICE CREAMS, sherbets, mousses, parfaits, sundaes—the very name of these frozen delicacies intrigues young and old alike. It seems impossible to get too much ice cream for dessert. Even when the making of homemade ice cream was a tedious task, small boys willingly turned the crank of the old-fashioned freezer for the sake of "licking the dasher."

Modern electric refrigerators, electric freezers, and prepared ice cream mixes, have now brought homemade ice cream within the reach of everyone. At the same time, commercial ice cream making has become an industry of enormous proportions, and many flavors have been developed which were unknown 25 years ago. And, of course, when it comes to food value, ice cream provides quick energy and promotes growth by supplying proteins, vitamins, and minerals in liberal amounts.

Today's homemaker may choose a basic recipe for ice cream, mousse or sherbet, and from such a recipe vary the flavor according to her fancy. The varieties of fresh, canned and quick-frozen fruits available offer endless flavors.

VANILLA ICE CREAM

(Gelatin Base)

1 tsp. gelatin	¾ cup sugar
2 Tbsp. cold water	¼ tsp. salt
1 pt. milk	1½ tsp. vanilla
2 eggs, separated	1 pt. light cream

Soften gelatin in cold water. Combine milk, egg yolks, ½ cup sugar, and salt in top of double boiler; beat until ingredients are well-blended. Place over hot water and cook, stirring constantly until mixture coats spoon. Remove from hot water, add softened gelatin; stir until dissolved. Cool. Add vanilla and cream. Turn mixture into freezing tray of refrigerator and freeze until firm. Remove mixture to chilled bowl, beat until smooth, and fold in egg whites, beaten stiff with remaining sugar. Return to tray; freeze firm.

VANILLA ICE CREAM

(Condensed Milk Base)

⅔ cup condensed milk
½ cup cold water

⅛ tsp. salt
1 cup cream, whipped
1 Tbsp. vanilla extract

Mix milk, water, salt; chill, and fold in whipped cream, vanilla. Turn into freezing tray. Freeze until firm.

Variations

Chocolate: Add 2 sq. cooled, melted chocolate before folding in cream.
Coffee: Substitute strong coffee for water.
Strawberry: Add 1 cup crushed fresh, or quick-frozen, berries before folding in cream. 1 cup crushed raspberries, peaches, or sliced bananas may be substituted for strawberries.

OLD-FASHIONED VANILLA ICE CREAM

(Custard Base)

1½ cups milk
1 Tbsp. flour
⅛ tsp. salt

1 cup sugar
1 egg
1 pt. cream
1 Tbsp. vanilla

Scald milk in upper part of double boiler over hot water. Mix flour, salt, ½

Ice cream, that beloved refresher of young and old, takes little time and energy to make.

cup sugar together. Beat egg until light, add to dry mixture, stir well. Pour hot milk slowly over mixture. Return to pan and cook until custard is smooth and thickened. Add remaining ½ cup sugar, and cream. Cool, add vanilla. Freeze in electrically- or hand-turned freezer. (Not in freezing tray.)

Variations

Coffee: Substitute ¾ cup strong coffee for ¾ cup of milk.

Chocolate: Add 2 sq. melted chocolate to cooked custard mixture. Stir well. Proceed as directed above.

Lemon: Substitute ¼ cup lemon juice for ¼ cup milk. Add juice slowly to cooked custard mixture. Proceed as directed above.

NESSELRODE PUDDING OR ICE CREAM

1 cup milk	2 Tbsp. candied pineapple
½ cup sugar	¼ cup marrons
2 egg yolks, slightly-beaten	2 Tbsp. marron syrup or rum
Pinch of salt	1 tsp. almond extract
2 Tbsp. candied cherries	1 cup cream, whipped
	2 Tbsp. raisins

Scald milk over hot water. Beat sugar, salt, and egg yolks together. Slowly pour on milk, return to heat and cook until mixture coats spoon. Cool thoroughly. Press marrons through sieve. Add syrup, candied fruits, and raisins cut fine, and mix well. Add rum, fold in cream, and turn into freezing tray of automatic refrigerator or into individual molds. Freeze in refrigerator freezing unit until firm.

BISCUIT TORTONI

1 pt. heavy cream	1 tsp. almond extract
½ cup powdered sugar	½ cup stale macaroon crumbs
2 tsp. vanilla extract	¼ cup slivered, toasted almonds

Whip cream just enough to hold its shape. Rub sugar through sieve to remove any fine lumps. Fold sugar in lightly. Add crumbs and flavorings. Pour into tiny fluted paper cups. Garnish with almonds. Place cups in freezing tray. Set control for fast-freezing. Freeze until set.

EVAPORATED MILK

Evaporated milk is a food which blends perfectly with other ingredients to make homemade ice cream.

Mix center. Standing or sitting, the homemaker easily reaches supplies and utensils.

HINTS ON WHIPPING EVAPORATED MILK

1. Have the beater and bowl thoroughly chilled; whip vigorously with a rotary egg beater or with an electric beater at high speed.
2. If the weather is warm, or kitchen overheated from baking, surround the bowl with cracked ice.
3. If you use a cooking thermometer, you will find that the temperature of the evaporated milk is about 150° F. when sufficiently heated, and about 45° F. when thoroughly chilled.
4. The best sized bowl to use is one of china or enamel which measures about 4 inches across the base.

VANILLA ICE CREAM

(Evaporated Milk Base)

2 cups evaporated milk	2 eggs, well-beaten
2 cups water	Pinch of salt
1 cup sugar	1 Tbsp. vanilla

Scald milk and water in upper part of double boiler over hot water. Add sugar, stir until dissolved. Slowly stir into eggs, return to heat, cook until mixture coats spoon. Add salt and vanilla. Cool and freeze in electrically- or hand-turned freezer. (Not in freezing tray.)

Variations

Banana: Add 1 cup mashed banana pulp, substitute lemon juice for vanilla.
Coffee: Substitute strong coffee for water.
Chocolate: Add 2 sq. of melted chocolate to custard mixture.

VANILLA ICE CREAM

(Philadelphia Style)

1 qt. light cream	2 Tbsp. vanilla extract
1 cup sugar	⅛ tsp. salt

Combine all ingredients and stir until sugar is dissolved. Freeze according to directions for crank-turned freezer.

Party clowns are the result of a little ingenuity with a ball of ice cream, cookies, chocolate chips, orange rinds, maraschino cherries, and ice cream cones.

PLAIN MOUSSE

A mousse is a rich mixture which depends upon heavy cream as the base, diluted to be palatable. A mousse is frozen without stirring, and quick-freezing is essential for best results. The mousse does not have the same texture as an ice cream, but is flaky, sweet, and a most pleasing dessert. Mousses may be used as a foundation for sundaes and parfaits. They may be decorated with extra whipped cream, fruits, nuts, candy, etc.

VANILLA MOUSSE

1 tsp. gelatin	1 cup cream, whipped
1 cup milk	2 egg whites, well-beaten
6 Tbsp. sugar	Pinch of salt
	1 Tbsp. vanilla

Soak the gelatin until soft in a little of the milk. Heat remainder of milk and pour over gelatin. Add sugar, stir until dissolved, and set mixture aside to chill. When mixture containing gelatin has thickened slightly, beat it to incorporate air. Fold in cream, egg whites, salt, and vanilla. Turn into freezing tray. Freeze until firm.

Variations

Coffee: Substitute ½ cup strong coffee for ½ cup of milk.
Peppermint: Substitute ¼ lb. of peppermint stick candy for sugar.

A mousse is an incredibly rich, wonderful mixture which can stand on its own merits, but if you feel the need of decorating the service platter, add touches of whipped cream, fruit, and nuts.

CHOCOLATE MOUSSE

1 cup milk	1 cup cream, whipped
2 sq. chocolate	2 egg whites, well-beaten
½ cup sugar	Pinch of salt
	1 Tbsp. vanilla

Place milk and chocolate in upper part of double boiler over hot water. Heat until chocolate melts, add sugar and salt, stir until sugar is dissolved. Cool, fold in cream and eggs, add vanilla. Turn into freezing tray. Freeze until firm.

STRAWBERRY MOUSSE

2 egg whites, well-beaten	½ cup sugar
Pinch of salt	1 cup crushed strawberries
	1 cup cream, whipped

Place egg whites in bowl, add pinch of salt. Beat until stiff enough to stand up in peaks. Combine sugar and fruit. Stir until sugar is dissolved, and fold into cream. Fold egg whites in last. Turn into freezing tray. Freeze until firm.

Variations

Any other crushed fruit may be used in same proportion as strawberries.

VANILLA MOUSSE

(Evaporated Milk Base)

1½ cups evaporated milk	½ cup water
½ cup marshmallows	⅛ tsp. salt
	1 Tbsp. vanilla

Chill 1 cup milk and whip until stiff. Heat ½ cup milk, water, and marshmallows over hot water until candy is melted. Chill, fold whipped milk into marshmallow mixture. Add salt and vanilla. Turn into freezing tray. Freeze until firm.

ICE CREAM SANDWICH

Bake sponge cake in a pan twice the size of ice cream tray, if ice cream is frozen in refrigerator trays. After removing cake from pan, cut it into 2 pieces just the size of tray. Place one section of cake in a platter, lay the mold of ice cream on cake, and place second portion of cake on top. Serve ice cream sandwich plain, or with chocolate sauce, or with fresh fruit.

FROZEN VANILLA CUSTARD

2 eggs	1 tsp. vanilla extract
½ cup sugar	1⅓ cups evaporated milk, chilled
Pinch of salt	icy-cold

Beat eggs; add sugar, salt, vanilla, and beat until sugar is dissolved. Whip milk very stiff. Fold in egg mixture lightly. Turn into freezing tray. Freeze until firm.

FROZEN LEMON CUSTARD

2 eggs	1⅓ cups evaporated milk, chilled
Pinch of salt	icy-cold
½ cup sugar	3 Tbsp. lemon juice
	½ tsp. grated lemon rind

Beat eggs; add sugar, salt, and beat until sugar is dissolved. Whip milk very stiff. Fold in lemon juice and rind, then fold in egg mixture lightly. Turn into freezing tray. Freeze until firm.

FROZEN LEMON PIE

3 egg yolks	1 tsp. grated lemon rind
½ cup sugar	1 cup cream, whipped
Juice 2 lemons	3 egg whites, stiffly-beaten
	1 cup vanilla wafers, crushed

Beat egg yolks until thick and lemon-colored. Add sugar, lemon juice and rind. Fold in cream and egg whites. Grease refrigerator tray and line with ½ cup of crumbs. Pour in lemon mixture, cover with remaining ½ cup crumbs. Freeze in electric refrigerator.

PARFAITS

Some people call a frozen mousse and a parfait the same thing. Chefs are apt to serve ice cream in a tall, slender glass, ornament it with whipped cream, and name it "parfait." Others describe such a dessert as follows:

BASIC PARFAIT—YELLOW

½ cup sugar	1½ tsp. gelatin
½ cup water	1 Tbsp. cold water
¼ tsp. salt	1 cup cream, whipped
2 egg yolks, well-beaten	1 Tbsp. extract

Boil sugar, salt and water to soft ball stage (238° F.). Pour slowly over egg yolks, cook over hot water until thick. Pour over gelatin dissolved in cold water. Cool, fold in whipped cream. Flavor with 1 Tbsp. vanilla, lemon, almond, or pistachio extract. Turn into freezing tray. Freeze until firm.

BASIC PARFAIT—WHITE

Substitute 2 egg whites for egg yolks. Pour sugar syrup slowly over stiffly-beaten egg whites. Add dissolved gelatin, cool, fold in cream and extract. Proceed as directed above.

A parfait is another dessert which practically makes itself in your refrigerator freezing tray. Keep it in mind for summer occasions.

SHERBETS

LEMON CREAM SHERBET

1 cup sugar	Grated rind 1 lemon
1 cup water	Pinch of salt
Juice 3 lemons	1 cup cream, whipped

Cook sugar and water together for 5 minutes. Cool, add lemon juice, rind and salt. Let stand 1 hour to chill and ripen. Fold in whipped cream. Pour into freezing tray of refrigerator. At least twice during freezing process, remove to chilled bowl and beat thoroughly. Return to refrigerator tray to finish freezing. Freeze until firm.

Variation

Grape-Lemon: Substitute 1 cup grape juice for water. Proceed as above.

PINEAPPLE-BUTTERMILK SHERBET

1 cup crushed pineapple	¾ cup sugar
	2 cups buttermilk

Mix ingredients together. Freeze in refrigerator. When partially frozen remove to chilled bowl. Beat thoroughly and proceed as above.

OLD-FASHIONED LEMON SHERBET

1½ cups sugar	Juice of 3 lemons
3 cups water	Grated rind 1 lemon

Mix all ingredients together. Chill in refrigerator for 1 hour. Freeze in electrically- or hand-turned freezer. (Not in feezing tray.)

ORANGE SHERBET

6 oranges	1 pt. water
1 lemon	1 cup sugar

Grate rind of 2 oranges, add juice of 3 oranges. Let stand for 1 hour. Make syrup of sugar and water. Simmer gently for 20 minutes. Cool, add juice of 4 oranges and lemons. Strain juice in which grated rind stood. Add strained juice. Freeze in crank-turned freezer.

22.

FRUITS

FAST transportation in refrigerator cars and trucks, modern methods of canning, the development of quick-frozen foods, and cargo airplane flights, have all helped to bring the once luxury fruits into year-round use. The daily diet has been immeasurably improved by citrus fruits and juices; salads, desserts, and frozen desserts all include out-of-season berries and fruits as a matter of course.

QUICK-FROZEN FRUITS

The packers of these delightful products print precise directions on every package. These should be followed accurately, for best results in thawing and caring for the fruit or berries. A general statement can be made to the effect that the fruit should be thawed and unwrapped at room temperature, but for more specific directions and recipes, see Chapter 24.

APPLE SAUCE

4 greenings or other tart apples	4 Tbsp. sugar
Water to cover	¼ tsp. nutmeg

Wash, core, and peel apples. Cut in thin slices, place in enamel or glass saucepan with just enough water to cover. Cook over low heat until apples are soft. Apples may be well-beaten, but the preferable method is to press through a coarse sieve. Add sugar, cool, and sprinkle nutmeg over top.

BAKED APPLES

(See Desserts, Chapter 20)

APPLES GLACÉ

4 tart apples	½ cup water
1 Tbsp. lemon juice	1 slice unpeeled lemon
½ cup sugar	2 cloves

Prepare apples as above. Cut each apple into eighths. Drop into cold water with lemon juice. Cook sugar, water and lemon slice together, stirring constantly until sugar is dissolved. Boil 2 minutes. Add cloves. Lift apples out of water with perforated spoon, drain well. Cook a few pieces at a time in syrup until clear and transparent. Remove to pretty dish, laying apples in without breaking. Pour remaining syrup over top. Serve cold.

APRICOTS

Select ripe, firm fruit. Wash well, dry. Serve chilled.

BANANAS

This fruit is one which behaves better at room temperature. Do not place bananas in the refrigerator. Ripe bananas should be yellow, flecked with brown, and the top should be dark with no trace of green. If bananas must stand after they are sliced, sprinkle with lemon juice. Good with sugar and cream. Bananas may be peeled and fried in butter, or baked in the oven, with skin on, if a lengthwise slit is made in skin. Boiled (see Chapter 31).

BERRIES

Berries, always regarded as a delicacy when purchased at a market, should be selected early in the day. Examine the box carefully to see if mold has formed, because moldy, soft berries are worthless. As soon as you have berries at home, turn them out on a flat plate and place in the refrigerator. When ready to use, wash and drain berries, then stem or hull them.

CRANBERRY SAUCE

2 cups cranberries	½ cup cold water
	1 cup sugar

Wash berries, remove bits of stem, discard soft berries. Add water, cover, and cook until skins burst. Stir well, add sugar and boil 3 to 5 minutes.

MOLDED CRANBERRIES

2 cups cranberries   1 cup water
                           1 cup sugar

Prepare berries as above. Cook until skins burst, then press through a fine sieve. Add sugar and boil for 10 minutes. Pour into fancy mold, rinsed out in cold water. Chill until firm. Turn out on plate.

GRAPEFRUIT

For breakfast service: Select firm, heavy fruit. Wash and dry. Place in refrigerator to chill. Cut in halves crosswise. Use a special grapefruit knife, and run knife around edge, loosening fruit entirely. With a sharp paring knife, discard seeds, making incision on each side of every segment. Add sugar, honey, or maple syrup, if desired.

For salad service: Wash and dry heavy fruit. Select a sharp knife and remove entire skin from fruit. Then go over peeled fruit once more and remove all traces of the thick white membrane. Remove each segment of the fruit by cutting down to center core, on each side of dividing tough membrane. Each segment lifts away free from the core. Navel oranges may be cut into segments for salads by same method.

BROILED GRAPEFRUIT

Prepare fruit as for breakfast. Sprinkle each half with 1 Tbsp. of sugar and 1 Tbsp. of melted butter. Place on shallow pan, broil under low heat until heated through (about 15 minutes).

BAKED PEARS

Do not place raw pears in refrigerator. Choose firm, ripe pears. Wash, peel, core, cut in half lengthwise.

4 pears   8 whole cloves
½ cup sugar   or
½ cup water   1 cinnamon stick, 2 inches

Cook syrup as for peaches. Stud each pear half with whole clove, or add cinnamon to syrup. Place pears in baking dish. Cover with syrup and bake in moderate oven (375° F.) 30 to 45 minutes.

PINEAPPLE

A pineapple is ripe when the prickly spines are easily pulled out. To cut:

A jellied cranberry ring (top) molded with vegetables is an all-time luncheon favorite.

Strawberries (bottom), fresh or frozen, make a regal appearance on strawberry shortcake.

Banana mixed grill (right), a brilliant thought for a picnic. Broil meat 6 or 8 minutes before adding bananas in peel. Coconut topped rolls and cocoa or coffee complete the meal.

Lay flat on cutting board, grasp crown or top of fruit with hand. Cut off top with sharp knife. Cut fruit in round thick slices, discard bottom slice. Peel and remove brown "eyes" with sharp point of knife. Cut each slice in segments as far as hard center core. Discard core. Sprinkle fruit with sugar.

Fancy dessert: Cut pineapple lengthwise, do not remove spiny top. Lay fruit on large platter, alternate top and bottom. Loosen sections of fruit with sharp knife, mix with moist coconut and replace. Or serve sherbet in shell along with portions of fruit.

MELONS

Melons are served chilled. Choose a ripe melon. It will be slightly soft to the touch when lightly pressed at the stem end, and will have a fragrant odor of ripeness. Chill thoroughly before cutting. Remove seeds and scrape out stringy portions. Accepted accompaniments are salt, or limes or lemons cut in wedges.

MELON RINGS

Cantaloupe presents an appealing appearance when cut in slices 1 inch thick. The round slice is usually served on a glass plate, with a decorative leaf. The ring is often filled with fresh berries, sherbet or ice cream.

ORANGES

Choose firm, thin-skinned fruit for juice extraction. The seedless navel orange is ideally adapted for salad and dessert service.

PEACHES

Choose peaches that are firm, but ripe and free from blemishes. Wash, dry, and peel fruit, or dip in boiling water briefly. The skin then slips off like a glove. Peaches may be sliced directly into serving bowl and sprinkled with sugar, or dropped into cold water to which lemon juice has been added (1 Tbsp. to 1 qt. water). Just before serving, place in refrigerator to chill.

POACHED PEACHES

6 to 8 peaches   ½ cup sugar
                                   ½ cup water

Cook sugar and water together, stirring constantly until sugar is dissolved. Boil 2 minutes. Peel, cut peaches in half. Drop into syrup. Cook gently until tender. Cool.

Pear hollows (top) filled with cranberries, spices, and lemon make a refreshing dessert.

American blue cheese banana split salad (right) garnished with prunes.

STEWED PLUMS

Select firm ripe fruit. Wash and dry. Cut in half, or leave whole. Place in saucepan with just enough water to cover fruit. Cook, in covered saucepan, over low heat until skins burst. Add ½ cup sugar to 2 cups of fruit. Cook, uncovered, for 5 minutes longer. Stir several times.

STEWED RHUBARB

1 bunch fresh rhubarb   Sugar
                               Water

Wash stalks, discard leaves and stem ends. Cut stalks in 1 inch lengths. Measure cut rhubarb. To 1 pt. of fruit, add ¼ cup sugar and ¼ cup water. Stew gently until soft. More sugar may be added if desired.

Variation

Fruit, sugar and water may be mixed together and baked in covered dish, in moderate oven (350° F.) 45 minutes to 1 hour.

STEWED DRIED FRUITS

Cooking dried fruit by the quick method—no soaking required—yields stewed fruit superior in flavor, texture and appearance. Modern methods of processing dried fruits make overnight soaking and long, slow simmering unnecessary. For best results with each fruit, use the directions given below. Count cooking time after water boils and keep at a brisk boil, adding more water if needed. Unless otherwise specified, add sugar only for last 5 minutes of cooking.

1. *Prunes:* Rinse, cover with water and cook 45 minutes to 1 hour. No sugar is needed, but 2 Tbsp. for each cup of prunes may be added if desired.
2. *Apricots:* Rinse, cover with water and boil 30 to 40 minutes. Allow ¼ to ½ cup sugar for each cup of apricots, depending on taste for sweetness.
3. *Peaches:* Rinse, cover with water, boil 5 minutes, drain and remove skins. Cover with fresh water and boil 35 to 45 minutes. Add sugar. Allow ¼ cup sugar for each cup of peaches.
4. *Figs:* Rinse, cover with water, and boil 20 to 30 minutes. Allow 1 Tbsp. sugar for each cup of figs. Add sugar before last 15 minutes of cooking.
5. *Pears:* Rinse, remove cores, cover with water, and boil 25 to 35 minutes. Allow ¼ cup sugar for each cup of pears.
6. *Apples:* Remove particles of core, if any, from apple rings or quarters. Rinse, cover with water, and boil 40 minutes. Sugar may be omitted entirely, giving a fresh apple flavor, or ¼ cup sugar allowed for each cup of fruit. The addition of a few grains of salt rounds out the flavor. The preparation of whole apples differs slightly in that the whole fruit should be covered with cold water, brought slowly to a boil in a covered utensil, and simmered about 1 hour until tender.

FRUIT PURÉES

Cook fruit slightly longer than when it is to be served whole. Force through a colander, sieve or ricer (pits should be removed from prunes if ricer is used). One cup of uncooked dried fruit will yield about 1 cup of purée. For some recipes, such as whips and sauces, the cooked fruit may be beaten to a pulp rather than made into purée.

23.

NEW METHODS

OF COOKERY

PRESSURE COOKERY AND ELECTRONIC COOKERY

WHEN historians trace the history of civilization, they speak of man's first efforts to harness fire for warmth and food, and usually of the casserole as the first cooking utensil. From the crude earthenware used by early mankind, heated by hot stones, cookery methods have developed slowly and tediously—from braziers with their lumps of charcoal, to oil and wood, coal, gas and electricity. The use of steam under pressure is a rather new development in the centuries of progress.

Even newer than pressure cookery is electromagnetic cookery, which has already been put to use in hotels and restaurants in a few of our larger cities and holds tremendous promise for the future household.

Pressure cookers are available now, for family use, in many styles and types, and this amazing kitchen utensil has excited more controversy for its size than any other single kitchen appliance. However, the millions of housewives who have learned how to use it, regard this new method of cookery as an extremely valuable addition to their household equipment.

The first requirement, and this is important, is intelligent use of the appliance. When food is to be cooked by live steam, at a temperature many degrees higher than boiling, with pressure inside the cooker averaging 15 pounds, it is easily understood that the operator must be fully aware of the proper steps to be followed. The housewife must familiarize herself with the exact operation of the pressure cooker she owns, by studying the manufacturer's directions for cooking, and also for cooling or reducing pressure after cooking.

Pressure cookers have become popular for a number of reasons, in addition to time-saving. The green and yellow vegetables have an attractive appearance, due to the speed with which they are cooked. Meats and poultry shrink less, which adds to appearance and reduces waste. The short cooking time, together with the small quantity of water required for this method, means that the natural flavors of raw foods are retained to an amazing degree. This means that the natural vitamins and minerals of the foods are also retained.

To the housewife who watches costs of fuel, one value of the pressure cooker is immediately apparent—minutes instead of hours for some types of cookery. Coolness of the kitchen is another decided advantage in torrid summer months.

SHOP CAREFULLY

The housewares departments, specialty stores, and hardware stores, carry in stock many varieties of pressure saucepans or cookers, and each type has its own special claims for your attention. These include elliptical tops, spring tops, handles that slide together and close, collar closing, flexible tops; there are pet-cocks or valves for instant release of the live steam. Every reliable cooker manufactured has a special device which is a safety precaution to take care of over-pressure in cooking.

The original conception of *a* pressure cooker as one of the kitchen utensils has been rapidly revised to include the purchase of a specially designed pressure saucepan (in addition to the cooker) for meat cookery. Many families now use two or three pressure cookers to prepare a variety of foods for an entire meal.

WHEN COOKING PRESSURE IS REACHED

As soon as the steam issues in a steady stream, the heat is reduced from high to low or simmer, depending upon type of heat used. It is then time to start counting the minutes, *but not before then.* Just enough heat is required to keep the food cooking. The heat must not be so low that the food does not cook at all, but neither must it be turned up so that the food cooks too rapidly. Scorching occurs very easily when food is cooked under pressure.

LENGTH OF TIME FOR COOKING

In practically every instance, it is impossible to give the exact number of minutes for cooking each specific food. The tenderness of vegetables, the size of the pieces, the thickness and juiciness of the roast, the quality of the poultry must all be considered. A time table will be found further on in this chapter which shows the *approximate* time necessary.

REDUCING PRESSURE

When the food is cooked, the pressure has to be reduced before the cover

Caesar Salad is the traditional western appetizer. Chef Caesar is credited with originating the salad during the heyday of the famous resort, Aqua Caliente.

Pressure cookers are great time-savers but must be carefully cared for if they are to give maximum efficiency.

can be removed. This may be done in one of two ways: (1) the pressure may be allowed to return to normal by gradual degrees, by removing the cooker from heat and letting it stand at room temperature; or (2), it may be reduced instantly either by permitting cool water to flow over the sides of the cooker or by placing it in a pan of cool water. The foods which may be reduced by this quick method are marked * in the time table.

THINGS TO AVOID IN PRESSURE COOKERY

1. Never let the cover soak in a dishpan. Wipe it clean as soon as it is cool.
2. Never let the cover become dented or warped. It must fit perfectly to make a steamtight seal.
3. Never strike the rim of the cooker nor force the cover off.
4. Never store the cooker with the cover locked on. Put the cover on as usual, or upside down.
5. Don't add soda to food or water in cooker.
6. Never fill cooker more than ⅔ full for solid foods; not more than ½ full for soups.
7. Never lay the cover on a hot stove.
8. Never pour cold water into a dry overheated cooker.

Pressure cookers can quickly prepare many different kinds of soups.

FOLLOW DIRECTIONS OF MANUFACTURER FOR BEST RESULTS!

HOW TO USE REGULAR RECIPES IN PRESSURE COOKERY

Any tested recipe for the usual type of cookery may be adapted to pressure cookery if the following precautions are observed:

In the case of soup, cereal, meat, or poultry it is necessary to reduce the amount of liquid called for in the usual type of cookery. Simply use the amount of water called for in the pressure cooker book of instructions which is issued by each manufacturer, and which you get when you purchase your pressure cooker. As the amount of liquid is less, naturally seasonings quantities are also reduced.

A smaller amount of fat is used in pressure cookery—approximately one-quarter less than in recipes for the usual types of cooking.

The time table given in this book will serve as a guide for the pressure cooker recipes in other chapters.

COOKING VEGETABLES IN PRESSURE COOKER

1. Select fresh or quick-frozen vegetables.
2. Place in cooker with required amount of hot water. Break quick-frozen style into 6 or 8 pieces.
3. When vegetables are cooked, reduce pressure instantly if * so indicates. Reduce pressure gradually for all others.
4. For potatoes pressure must be reduced gradually.
5. Vegetables may be seasoned before or after cooking.
6. One or more vegetables may be cooked at same time when length of time required is identical. (Beets are the only exception.)
7. Save the precious liquid remaining in the cooker after vegetables are cooked. The vitamins and mineral salts are found here.
8. The liquid may be used as a base for a cream sauce, or added to butter and poured over vegetables, or saved for soup stock.

TIME TABLE FOR FRESH VEGETABLES

VEGETABLE AND PREPARATION	COOKING TIME IN MINUTES AFTER COOKING PRESSURE IS REACHED	WATER
* Artichokes—trimmed and washed.............	10	½ cup of
* Asparagus—scrubbed, scraped, tied in bundles	1 to 2	water is
* Beans, green, wax—cleaned, cut	2 to 4	used, no
* Beets, whole—with 1 inch stem	10 to 18	matter
* Broccoli—leaves and stalks trimmed	2 to 3	what
* Cabbage—sliced thin in shreds	1 to 2	amount of
* Carrots—scrubbed, scraped	2 to 3	vegetable
* Cauliflower—separate into flowerets	2 to 3	is cooked.
* Onions—peeled.............................	5 to 6	
* Peas—shelled, leave few pods in................	1 to 2	
Potatoes—scrubbed, peeled	10 to 15	
* Spinach—picked over, trimmed.................	1	
* All other greens.............................	1	
* Tomatoes—cored, peeled	1	
* Turnips—scrubbed, pared, cut in cubes	3 to 5	

Note: The preparation of the raw vegetable is the same for pressure cookery as for any other saucepan. It is only the cooking time that is different.

* Indicates pressure should be reduced instantly.

RECIPES FOR FRESH VEGETABLES

HARVARD BEETS

6 to 8 beets, peeled and sliced   ½ cup water

Place beets in pressure cooker, add ½ cup water and cook at 15 lbs. pressure for 4 minutes. Cool, add sauce and reheat.

Sauce

¼ cup sugar   ½ cup vinegar
2 Tbsp. flour   ¼ tsp. salt
¼ cup water   2 Tbsp. butter
                     1 tsp. grated orange rind

Mix dry ingredients. Boil liquids, pour over dry mixture. Bring to boil, stirring constantly. Add rind.

MASHED POTATOES

4 to 6 potatoes   ¼ tsp. salt
½ cup water   4 Tbsp. butter
                     ½ cup milk, scalded

Place potatoes in pressure cooker, add ½ cup of water and cook at 15 lbs. pressure for 12 minutes. Cool, drain, mash. Add butter and milk gradually, beating well after each addition. Keep hot over a pan of hot water.

COMBINATION VEGETABLE DINNER

3 to 4 onions	4 potatoes, diced
4 tomatoes	¼ cup olive oil or melted butter
	1 cup quick-frozen cooked string beans

Place onions, tomatoes, potatoes and beans in cooker. Cook at 15 lbs. pressure for 3 minutes. Cool instantly. Add olive oil or butter, and heat for 2 minutes.

CAULIFLOWER AU GRATIN

1 head cauliflower	1 cup medium white sauce
¼ cup water	½ cup buttered bread crumbs
¼ tsp. salt	¼ cup grated cheese

Soak cauliflower in salted water. Separate into large flowerets. Drain and place in pressure cooker. Add water and cook at 15 lbs. pressure for 1½ minutes. Cool, drain and place in buttered casserole. Cover with sauce. Sprinkle with crumbs and cheese. Brown under broiler for 1 or 2 minutes.

RED CABBAGE WITH SPICES

2 Tbsp. butter	2 Tbsp. cider vinegar
1 cup seedless raisins	1 tsp. pickling spice, tied in
1 cup chopped tart apples	cheesecloth
¼ cup sliced onions	2 Tbsp. water
3 cups shredded red cabbage	¼ tsp. salt
	1 Tbsp. sugar

Soak raisins for 5 minutes in boiling water. Drain. Melt butter in pan. Add cabbage and other ingredients. Cook 5 minutes at 15 lbs. pressure. Cool, uncover, and simmer 5 minutes until liquid evaporates.

SWEET POTATOES OR YAMS

4 to 6 sweet potatoes or yams	½ cup boiling water
	¼ tsp. salt

Scrub potatoes well. Dry and place in pressure cooker. Add water and salt. Cover and bring pressure up to 15 lbs. Cook 8 to 10 minutes. Allow pressure to drop gradually.

TURNIPS, WHITE OR YELLOW

4 to 6 turnips   ⅓ cup boiling water

Scrub turnips well. Peel and cut into 1-inch cubes. Add water. Cover and bring pressure up to 15 lbs. Cook 5 minutes. Cool, and remove cover. Add salt, pepper and butter. Press through a sieve or ricer, or beat well with spoon.

PRESSURE COOKER SOUPS

BEEF STOCK FOR VEGETABLE SOUPS

4 to 5 lbs. soup meat and soup
   bones, cracked
1 tsp. salt
2 qts. cold water
1 cup diced turnips
1 cup diced carrots

Few stalks celery
1 to 2 onions, sliced
1 bay leaf
3 to 4 peppercorns
1 cup canned tomatoes or 1 tin
   tomato purée
1 clove garlic

Cover meat with cold water, add salt and peppercorns. Bring pressure up to 15 lbs. Cook 30 to 40 minutes. Reduce pressure gradually and add vegetables. Bring pressure up and cook 10 more minutes. Cool in large bowl. Strain off fat, set aside and use for soup stock. Add any combination of vegetables, or noodles or rice when desired.

CHICKEN SOUP

1 fowl, disjointed
2 qts. cold water
1 tsp. salt

1 bay leaf
1 cup mixed vegetables, celery,
   carrots, onions

Cover meat with water, add salt and seasonings. Bring pressure up to 15 lbs. Cook 30 to 40 minutes. Reduce pressure gradually and add vegetables. Bring pressure up and cook 10 more minutes. More water may be added to dilute if necessary.

OLD-FASHIONED BEEF SOUP

2 lbs. beef, cut from round
2 qts. cold water
2 onions
1 carrot
Several stalks celery

2 raw potatoes, diced
½ cup rice
2 Tbsp. butter
2 Tbsp. flour
1 tsp. salt
½ tsp. pepper

Cut meat in cubes, and place in pressure cooker with cold water. Add vegetables and rice. Cover. Bring pressure up to 15 lbs. Cook 25 minutes, reduce pressure gradually. Melt butter in saucepan. Add flour and cook until smooth and bubbly. Stir constantly until well-browned. Pour soup over mixture, stir until smooth, return to pan and serve hot. Sprinkle each portion with minced celery.

OXTAIL SOUP

1 oxtail, cut in small pieces at joint	1 Tbsp. onion, minced fine
1 qt. water	1 Tbsp. carrot, minced fine
1 pt. old-fashioned beef soup, strained	Bay leaf
	Clove
1 Tbsp. celery, minced fine	Peppercorns

Wash oxtail thoroughly. Place in pressure cooker with cold water. Cover. Bring pressure up to 15 lbs. Cook 25 minutes, reduce pressure gradually. Turn out into bowl, and cool quickly. Place in refrigerator. When fat has hardened, skim off. Heat soup to taste with sherry wine.

WINTER POTATO SOUP

1 qt. raw potatoes, peeled, cut in cubes	1 onion, sliced
	1 tsp. salt
1 bunch celery, diced	¼ tsp. pepper
1 bay leaf	2 Tbsp. butter
	2 qts. water

Melt butter in pressure cooker. Add onion, celery, seasonings, water and potatoes. Cover and place over high heat. Bring pressure up to 15 lbs. Reduce to low and cook 5 minutes. Allow pressure to reduce gradually. Sprinkle with minced parsley. Thicken with flour if necessary.

TOMATO SOUP

1 qt. tomatoes	2 Tbsp. onion, minced fine
1 cup cold water	2 cloves
1 tsp. salt	Thickening
½ tsp. pepper	
1 tsp. sugar	2 Tbsp. flour
1 Tbsp. carrot, minced fine	2 Tbsp. butter

Place all ingredients in pressure cooker (except flour and butter). Cover. Bring pressure up to 15 lbs. Cook 5 minutes. Reduce pressure gradually. Rub through a fine sieve. Rub butter and flour together. Pour over soup. Stir until smooth, return to heat until thoroughly heated. Serve with croutons.

LENTIL SOUP

1 pt. lentils	1 bay leaf
1 qt. water	1 tsp. salt
1 cup soup stock	1 Tbsp. butter
1 onion, sliced	1 Tbsp. flour
3 stalks celery	2 Tbsp. vinegar

Soak lentils overnight. Drain and place in pressure cooker. Add water, stock, vegetables and seasonings. Cover. Bring pressure up to 15 lbs. Cook 30 minutes. Reduce pressure gradually. Rub butter and flour together, add small amount of soup (after straining through sieve). Return to cooker and stir until heated. Season with vinegar.

CEREALS

The quick-cooking cereals so popular today do not require pressure cooking, but the slow-cooking cereals, and the whole grain coarse cereals, are ideal for this new method.

The proportion of water varies with the type of cereal to be cooked. Cereals of a flaky nature, such as rolled cereals, absorb two to three times as much water as the original bulk of the cereal. Whole-grain cereals absorb three to four times as much water; and granular cereals four to six times as much. It will be necessary to experiment to find the exact consistency which pleases the individual family.

METHOD OF COOKING

Measure correct amount of boiling water. Salt to taste. Slowly add dry cereal, keeping water at a boil. Reduce heat, cover, let steam escape in steady stream. Seal and bring pressure up to 15 lbs. Cook 5 to 20 minutes, depending upon coarseness of cereal.

OATMEAL

1 cup rolled oats	3 cups water
	1 tsp. salt

Bring water and salt to full rolling boil in pressure cooker. Slowly add the cereal, stirring constantly to prevent lumpiness. Boil 1 minute. Cover, and bring pressure up to 15 lbs. Steam 5 minutes. Allow pressure to reduce gradually.

SPAGHETTI, MACARONI, NOODLES

1 8-oz. pkg. spaghetti, macaroni or noodles	6 cups water 2 tsp. salt

Same directions as Oatmeal. Cook as follows:
Spaghetti—8 minutes
Macaroni—5 minutes
Noodles—5 minutes

RICE

1 cup rice	3 cups water 1 tsp. salt

Same directions as for Oatmeal. Cook 5 minutes only.

BROWN RICE

1 cup brown rice	4 cups water

Same directions as for Oatmeal. Cook 15 minutes.

DRIED BEANS AND PEAS

General pointers for dried legumes:
1. All dried beans should be soaked overnight.
2. A new method of processing for dried split peas permits them to be cooked without previous soaking.
3. Add the required amount of hot water to dried foods, according to manu- facturer's recipe booklet.
4. Cover, and cook over low heat.
5. Cook only the time specified in recipe booklet.
6. When cooking time has been completed, allow pressure to drop gradually.

KIDNEY, LIMA AND NAVY BEANS

1. Wash, remove any bits of foreign matter.
2. Soak overnight. Place in cooker and add boiling water just enough to cover.
3. Allow 1 tsp. salt to every cup of beans.
4. Cover pressure cooker and place over low heat.
5. Follow manufacturer's instructions for bringing pressure up to 5, 10 and 15 lbs.
6. Reduce heat to low.

Cook kidney beans—15 minutes.
Cook lima beans—20 minutes.
Cook navy beans—30 minutes.

CHILI CON CARNE

1 lb. beef, ground	1 cup condensed tomato soup
¼ cup onion, finely minced	2 Tbsp. boiling water
2 Tbsp. fat	1 tsp. salt
1 lb. dried kidney beans	1 clove garlic
	½ tsp. chili powder

Soak beans overnight. Melt fat in pressure cooker, add meat and onions. Stir constantly until well-browned. Drain beans, and add to meat. Add other ingredients. Stir mixture together. Cover and bring pressure up to 15 lbs. Cook 15 minutes. Allow pressure to reduce gradually. (Chili seasoning may be added according to personal taste.)

BOSTON BAKED BEANS

1 pt. navy beans	½ tsp. dry mustard
¼ lb. salt pork	1 onion
2 Tbsp. brown sugar	1 tsp. salt
2 Tbsp. molasses	¼ tsp. pepper

Wash beans, soak overnight. Drain. Dice salt pork and brown on all sides in pressure cooker. Add onion, cook 1 minute. Add all ingredients, just cover with water, and cook until steam escapes. Cover and bring pressure up to 15 lbs. Cook 45 minutes. Allow pressure to reduce gradually. Pour into baking dish and brown in slow oven (325° F.).

MEAT COOKERY

The cost of meat, its importance in the diet, the amount of skill required in its preparation, the length of time it takes to cook a pot roast, a roast, a stew, or a casserole dish make the use of a pressure cooker an appliance to be considered favorably.

The less tender cuts of meat have long been admired for their flavor and lower cost, but the time required for their preparation has been regarded as a handicap.

No hard-and-fast rule can be laid down for meat cookery. Too many things enter into the picture: the amount and distribution of fat, the size and weight of the bone, the thickness of the cut, the variety of the cut. Chunky, thick roasts take a longer time than flat roasts. Rolled roasts take longer than roasts with bone left in. Cured, smoked meats such as ham, tongue, corned beef, require a greater amount of water than do fresh meats.

POINTERS ON MEAT PREPARATION

1. The cooker must be heated over a low heat, and then about 1 Tbsp. of fat (any kind will do) should be added. As soon as the fat is melted, add meat and brown on all sides. If recipe says to use rack, lift out browned meat and place on rack.
2. Add amount of water called for in recipe. Seal cooker and proceed according to directions.
3. Cured and salt meats require more water than fresh cuts of meat. Allow about 2 cups of water. Cook lean side down, fat side up.
4. If cover does not seem to fit on easily, let it remain in place for a minute or two to permit expansion.
5. Meat and vegetables may be cooked together. Add latter when meat is nearly done.

MEAT RECIPES

BEEF STEW

2 Tbsp. fat
2 to 3 lbs. chuck or flank,
  cut in cubes
4 small onions
4 potatoes, cubed
4 carrots, sliced
1 cup green peas, shelled
1 tsp. salt
¼ tsp. pepper
1 bay leaf
½ cup water
1 pt. canned tomatoes
2 Tbsp. flour

Filling, meaty stews take well under half an hour to prepare in a pressure cooker. Season with Angostura bitters for a gourmet touch.

Melt fat in frying pan. Brown meat on all sides in fat. Place on rack in cooker. Add water. Bring up pressure to 15 lbs. Steam 10 minutes. Reduce pressure with cool water. Add seasonings, vegetables, and steam 5 minutes more. Reduce pressure. Remove stew and rack. Thicken liquid with flour to make gravy. Stir until smooth and thickened.

CORNED BEEF

4 to 5 lbs. corned beef, brisket	1 bay leaf
2 cups boiling water	2 or 3 cloves
	1 clove garlic

Cover corned beef with cold water and let soak 1 hour with seasonings. Drain. Place meat on rack in cooker. Insert clove of garlic in fat. Add boiling water. Place cover on cooker. When steam flows, bring pressure up to 15 lbs. Process 12 minutes per lb.

MEAT BALLS

2 lbs. beef, ground	¼ tsp. pepper
1 onion, minced	1 Tbsp. fat
½ tsp. salt	1 Tbsp. water

Mix meat with onion and seasonings. Form into small balls. Preheat cooker, melt fat. Brown meat balls on all sides. Put rack in cooker, add water. Place meat balls on rack. Bring pressure up to 15 lbs. Steam 5 minutes.

POT ROAST OF BEEF

1 Tbsp. fat	1 bay leaf
4 to 5 lbs. beef, tied for pot roast	½ tsp. salt
	¼ tsp. pepper
1 onion, sliced	1 cup water

Preheat cooker, melt fat. Brown meat on all sides. Place rack in cooker. Add seasonings and meat. Add water. Bring pressure up to 15 lbs. Process 11 minutes per lb. Serve with gravy made from liquid in pan.

SHORT RIBS OF BEEF

3 to 4 lbs. short ribs	1 tsp. salt
2 Tbsp. fat	½ tsp. pepper
	1 cup boiling water

Melt fat in cooker. When thoroughly heated, add meat, and brown well on all sides. Place rack in cooker. Season and add water. Put meat on rack. Cover and place over high heat. Bring pressure up to 15 lbs. Steam 20 minutes. Allow pressure to drop gradually. Make gravy from liquid.

SWISS STEAK

2 to 3 lbs. round of beef, cut 1 inch thick	1 cup onions, sliced
1 tsp. salt	¼ cup boiling water
¼ tsp. pepper	Flour Mixture
¼ cup flour	2 Tbsp. flour
2 Tbsp. fat	¼ cup water

Mix flour, salt and pepper. With side of heavy saucer, pound mixture into steak until well-absorbed. Heat fat in pressure cooker. Add meat, and brown on both sides. Add onions and water. Cover and place over high heat. Bring pressure up to 15 lbs. Steam 15 minutes. Remove meat. Thicken liquid with flour mixture, by pouring a little of hot liquid over mixture and stirring until smooth. Return to pan and let come to boil. Stir until smooth and thickened.

THRIFTY STEW OF SHINBONE OF BEEF

2 to 3 lbs. shinbone of beef	1 sprig parsley
1 onion	1 tsp. salt
1 bay leaf	½ tsp. pepper
1 whole clove	2 Tbsp. butter
1 slice carrot	2 Tbsp. flour
	1½ qts. boiling water

Have shinbone cut into 6 parts. Wipe with damp cloth. Place in pressure cooker with other ingredients (except butter and flour). Add boiling water. Cover and place over high heat. Bring pressure up to 15 lbs. Steam 10 minutes. Reduce pressure gradually. Place butter in saucepan. When melted, add flour and stir until smooth and bubbly. When it begins to brown, add liquid in cooker and stir until smooth. Return to cooker and allow to heat thoroughly. Serve with steamed potatoes.

FRICASSEE OF VEAL

2 to 3 lbs. rump of veal, cut in cubes	1 sprig parsley
1 onion	1 tsp. salt
1 carrot	½ tsp. pepper
3 celery stalks	¼ cup boiling water
1 bay leaf	2 Tbsp. butter
	2 Tbsp. flour

Energy-saving kitchen arrangement is the complement to time-saving cooking methods. Sit and do other chores while your pressure cooker works.

Place veal in pressure cooker with seasonings and vegetables. Add water. Cover and place over heat. Bring pressure up to 15 lbs. Steam 5 minutes. Reduce pressure gradually. Place butter in saucepan and proceed as for Shinbone of Beef.

GNOCCHI

1 cup cornmeal	1 lb. beef liver, chopped fine
5 cups milk	1 bay leaf
1 tsp. salt	¼ tsp. sage
2 egg yolks	1 garlic clove
2 Tbsp. butter	1 can tomato sauce
2 Tbsp. salad oil	2 Tbsp. grated Parmesan cheese

Bring milk to boil in pressure cooker. Add salt and slowly sift in cornmeal, stirring constantly to prevent lumpiness. Cover, bring pressure up to 15 lbs.

Steam 10 minutes. Allow pressure to reduce gradually. Cool, add egg yolks and butter. Beat well and spread in oblong pans to thickness of 1 inch. When firm, cut into rounds with biscuit cutter. Heat oil in skillet, add liver and seasonings. Brown well, add tomato sauce, and simmer 20 minutes. Place rounds of cornmeal mixture in well-greased casserole, cover with meat, sprinkle with cheese, and brown in oven.

HAM BUTT

3 to 5 lb. boneless ham butt	¼ box whole cloves
1 cup cold water	½ cup brown sugar

Soak ham in cold water for 2 or more hours. Drain and place on rack in cooker. Add the cold water. Bring pressure up to 15 lbs. Steam 35 to 45 minutes. Reduce pressure gradually. Remove skin of ham by winding it around the tines of a long-handled fork. (It will come off the meat like a glove.) Stud the ham with cloves in a pattern of diamonds or rows. Cover ham with sugar, pressing it in lightly. Place in hot oven to brown.

HAM SLICE

1 tsp. fat	4 to 6 cloves
1½ lb. ham (regular) slice	4 peach halves
1 Tbsp. brown sugar	½ cup water

Preheat cooker, melt fat. Sear ham on both sides. Remove to flat board and mark with sharp knife in diamond design. Prick with cloves, sprinkle with brown sugar. Place ham on rack, add water and bring pressure up to 15 lbs. Steam 15 minutes. Reduce pressure gradually. Cook peach syrup in open cooker, pour over ham on platter. Garnish with peach halves.

LEG OF LAMB

3 to 5 lb. leg of lamb	½ tsp. salt
1 Tbsp. fat	¼ tsp. pepper
	2 Tbsp. water

Trim meat to fit into cooker. Preheat cooker. Melt fat, and brown lamb on all sides. Season with salt and pepper. Place rack in cooker. Add water. Put in meat. Cover. Bring pressure up to 15 lbs. Allow 12 minutes per lb. Reduce pressure gradually. To give the roast the familiar crackly brown finish, place under broiler for a few minutes before serving.

LAMB STEW

2 to 3 lbs. shoulder of lamb, boned and cubed	1 bay leaf
1/4 cup flour	4 small onions
1 tsp. salt	4 small carrots, quartered
1/4 tsp. pepper	4 small potatoes, quartered
1/4 cup fat	1 cup boiling water
	Few stalks celery, cut coarse

Wipe pieces of lamb with damp cloth. Roll in flour and salt. Shake off loose flour. Preheat cooker, melt fat, and brown meat on all sides. Place meat on rack and add water. Cover and bring pressure up to 15 lbs. Cook 7 minutes. Reduce pressure with cool water. Add vegetables, cover and cook 5 minutes more after pressure is again 15 lbs. Gravy may be made by mixing flour with liquid.

PORK CHOPS

4 loin pork chops, cut 1 1/2 inches thick	1/2 tsp. pepper
1 tsp. salt	1 cup tomato pulp
	1 Tbsp. boiling water

Season chops with salt and pepper. Place in pressure cooker and brown on both sides. Place rack in cooker. Add liquids and bring pressure up to 15 lbs. Cook 12 minutes.

ROAST LOIN OF PORK OR SHOULDER OF PORK

4 to 5 lbs. loin of pork	3 celery stalks
1 Tbsp. fat	2 Tbsp. boiling water
1 onion	1 tsp. salt
1 carrot	1/2 tsp. pepper

Melt fat in bottom of pressure cooker. When thoroughly heated, add meat, and brown on all sides. Season with salt and pepper. Place rack in cooker. Add vegetables and water. Cover and bring pressure up to 15 lbs. Cook 12 minutes per lb. of trimmed weight. Allow pressure to reduce gradually.

BARBECUED SPARERIBS

2 to 3 lbs. spareribs, cut in 2 inch lengths	1/2 cup chili sauce
1/4 cup flour	1/2 cup boiling water
2 Tbsp. fat	Pinch of chili powder
	1/8 tsp. curry powder
	1 Tbsp. onion, minced fine

Toss spareribs in flour until each piece is covered. Shake off excess flour. Melt fat in pressure cooker. Add floured meat, and brown well on both sides. Put rack in cooker, add meat. Add onion and cook 1 minute longer. Combine other ingredients and pour over meat. Cover and bring pressure up to 15 lbs. Cook 15 minutes. Allow pressure to reduce gradually. Make gravy from liquid in cooker.

POTPOURRI OF PORK

1 lb. fresh pork	1 cup cabbage, sliced
½ lb. round of beef	2 Tbsp. soya sauce
1 Tbsp. fat	1 tsp. molasses
1 qt. canned tomatoes	Garnish
1 cup celery, diced	
1 cup onions, sliced	4 slices pineapple
1 cup carrots, sliced	2 cups cooked rice

Slice meat in thin strips. Brown in hot fat. Add seasonings and vegetables. Cover and bring pressure up to 15 lbs. Cook 8 minutes. Allow pressure to reduce gradually. Serve on platter with garnish.

POULTRY

ROAST CHICKEN

3 to 4 lb. roasting chicken	¼ cup boiling water
4 Tbsp. fat	¼ tsp. salt
	⅛ tsp. pepper

Clean and stuff chicken in usual manner. Brown in hot fat. Pour water in cooker. Place chicken on rack. Add salt and pepper. Cover, place over heat. Bring pressure up to 15 lbs. Allow 7 minutes per lb. Allow pressure to reduce

Roast chicken in the pressure-cooker manner will save you much time and fuel. When chicken is ready to be taken from cooker, only a brief interval is required for browning in the oven. The liquid left in your cooker will make a marvelous gravy.

gradually. Remove chicken, place in uncovered roasting pan in hot oven. Baste with melted shortening and remove when surface is well browned. Make gravy from liquid in cooker.

FRIED CHICKEN

1 frying chicken	¼ tsp. pepper
½ cup flour	3 Tbsp. fat
1 tsp. salt	3 Tbsp. boiling water

Cut chicken into serving-piece sizes. Mix flour, salt and pepper in platter. Cover each piece of chicken with seasoned flour. Place in paper bag and shake to remove excess flour. Melt fat in bottom of heavy skillet. Brown pieces of chicken. Place rack in cooker. Pour in boiling water. Add chicken. Cover, and bring pressure up to 15 lbs. Steam 15 minutes. Reduce pressure gradually. Lift out pieces of chicken. Make gravy from liquid in cooker. Add extra cream for cream gravy.

CHICKEN FRICASSEE

1 chicken, disjointed	¼ cup water
2 Tbsp. fat	1 cup milk
½ tsp. salt	1 or 2 egg yolks
¼ tsp. pepper	1 or 2 Tbsp. flour
⅛ lb. salt pork, diced	½ cup water, if needed

Wipe pieces of chicken with damp cloth. Preheat cooker, melt fat, and brown chicken lightly on all sides. Add seasonings, salt pork and water. Place rack in cooker. Add meat. Cover and bring pressure up to 15 lbs. Steam 15 minutes. Reduce pressure gradually. Remove cover. Beat egg yolk with milk, pour a little of hot liquid over mixture. Return to cooker and stir until thickened. (For a thicker fricassee sauce, 2 Tbsp. flour may be mixed with ¼ cup cold water, and added to gravy.)

CURRIED CHICKEN

1 large chicken, disjointed	½ cup sliced onions
½ cup flour	3 Tbsp. flour
1 tsp. salt	1 pt. chicken broth
½ tsp. pepper	1 tsp. curry powder
3 Tbsp. fat	2 cups carrots, julienne style
	2 cups cooked rice

Cook chicken fricassee style. Remove from cooker, and skim off fat. Melt fat in skillet, add onions and cook until yellow. Add flour and stir until smooth and bubbly. Measure broth and add slowly. When thickened, add curry powder. Turn out on platter, surround with mounds of carrots and rice. Pour gravy over dish.

CHICKEN GUMBO

1 large chicken, disjointed	1 to 3 tsp. filé powder
1 qt. peeled fresh tomatoes	Salt
1 onion, sliced	Cayenne pepper
½ lb. smoked ham, raw	2 cups cooked rice

Cook chicken fricassee style. About 5 minutes before cooking time is up, reduce pressure. Gradually open cover and add tomatoes and onions. Fry ham in its own fat and add to cooker. Cook slowly uncovered. Season to taste. Just before serving, add filé powder, stir in thoroughly. Serve over flaky cooked rice. *Note:* Cut ham in strips before cooking.

TIME TABLE FOR MEATS AND POULTRY

MEATS	COOKING TIME AFTER SEARING, COVER SEALED, AND PRESSURE REACHED	AMOUNT OF WATER TO BE ADDED AFTER SEARING
Corned Beef................	10-12 min. per lb.	2 cups
Beef Stew	15 min. complete	½ cup
Meat Balls	10-12 min. complete	1 Tbsp.
Pot Roast	8-10 min. per lb.	2 Tbsp.
Swiss Steak—¾ inch thick.....	15-20 min. complete	¼ cup
Ham Butt (smoked, boneless) ..	12-15 min. per lb.	1 cup—cook on rack
Ham Slice—1½ lb.	15 min. complete	½ cup
Leg of Lamb	12 min. per lb.	2 Tbsp.
Lamb Stew (2 lbs.)	12-15 min. complete	1 cup
Chicken Fricassee	20-30 min. complete	1 cup

MISCELLANEOUS RECIPES FOR PRESSURE COOKER

A busy housewife finds the problem of hot weather meals a trial unless she has a handful of trusted recipes for dishes which are exceptionally attractive. The use of fresh fish for mousse, soufflé, or salad, or in aspic, offers some interesting ideas, and if a pressure cooker is used for the initial steaming, it does away with all the objectionable features of cooking fish at home.

STEAMED FISH
(Basic Recipe)

Cod, haddock, salmon, white fish, halibut steak, shrimp, are all good choices for this type of cookery. Either fresh fish or quick-frozen may be used. Sprinkle fish with salt and a little lemon juice, wrap loosely in cheesecloth. Place on rack. Add:

¾ cup water

1 tsp. salt
1 Tbsp. lemon juice or vinegar

Bring up pressure. Cover, and when steam is flowing, reduce heat to low and count 6 to 8 minutes per lb., depending on size of fish.

Variations

1. Serve with Egg Sauce.
2. Combine 1 cup steamed fish and 2 cups celery for fish salad. Add mayonnaise, thinned with lemon juice.
3. Toss 1 cup steamed fish lightly with cooked, chilled vegetables and French dressing seasoned with lemon juice. Serve on crisp lettuce.

FISH MOUSSE

1 lb. halibut steak, steamed
   and flaked
3 eggs
1 cup heavy cream
¼ tsp. salt
⅛ tsp. paprika
1 tsp. grated lemon rind

Fish mousse is a showy dish but requires little effort to concoct, especially when the fish has been steamed in a pressure cooker.

Separate egg yolks and whites. Flake fish into fine pieces. Add egg yolks, cream and seasonings. Beat egg whites until they stand in peaks but are not dry, and add to mixture. Butter a ring mold and pour contents into mold. Stand in pan of hot water, and bake in moderate oven (350° F.) until set. Turn out on warm platter and surround with any sauce. Garnish with parsley minced fine.

FISH IN ASPIC WITH CUCUMBER

1 cup cold steamed fish (halibut
    or salmon or shrimp)
¼ tsp. salt
1 tsp. lemon juice

1 tsp. gelatin
1 Tbsp. cold water
1 cup cream, whipped
Mayonnaise
1 cup cucumber, minced fine

Flake fish into fine pieces, and sprinkle with salt and lemon juice. Dissolve gelatin in water and melt over hot water. Whip cream, add cooled gelatin, and fold in seasoned fish. Turn into mold and place in refrigerator until set. Serve with mayonnaise to which cucumber has been added.

PUDDING AND DESSERT RECIPES

Among the groups of food most popular with the American public are steamed puddings and breads. Any recipe the housewife prefers may be used for steaming in the pressure cooker. All that is necessary is to choose a mold which will fit into the cooker. A mold must be used without a cover for pressure cooking.

Fill the mold ⅔ full to allow room for the food to expand during the steaming process. Cover the top of the mold with heavy waxed paper or with parchment paper, and tie it securely. Individual molds or heat-proof glass cups may be used.

STEAMED FIG OR DATE PUDDING

¾ cup dried fruit
½ cup butter
½ cup sugar
1 egg, well-beaten

1¼ cup flour
½ tsp. salt
¾ tsp. baking soda
½ cup milk
1 Tbsp. vanilla extract

A well-set table is the mark of a good homemaker. Creating different settings is fun; mealtimes are looked forward to.

Cut fruit into small pieces. Cream butter and sugar together until light and fluffy. Add egg and fruit. Sift flour, salt and soda together. Add alternately with milk. Add vanilla extract. Pour into mold (about 1 pt. in size). Cover with paper. Pour 2 cups boiling water in cooker. Place mold on rack, cover and steam 15 minutes. At end of 15 minutes, bring pressure up to 15 lbs. Steam 30 minutes. Reduce pressure gradually at first, then under cool water. Serve with hard sauce.

STEAMED FRUIT PUDDINGS

2 cups flour, sifted
1 Tbsp. baking powder
1 cup sugar
¼ cup butter
3 eggs, slightly-beaten

½ cup milk
2 cups berries or cherries (fresh, canned or quick-frozen)
1 Tbsp. vanilla extract or lemon extract

Sift dry ingredients together. Set aside. Cream butter; add sugar, and cream together until light and fluffy. Add eggs and beat well. Add flour and baking powder mixture alternately with milk. Add extract and drained fruit. Fold in lightly. Pour into well-greased tin mold. Fill ⅔ full. Cover with waxed paper and tie securely. Place on rack, add ½ cup water, and steam 15 minutes without pressure. Raise pressure to 15 lbs. and steam 30 minutes.

PREPARATION OF FRUIT

Fresh fruits should be washed, berries stoned, cherries stoned.
Larger fruit should be cut into small pieces after peeling.
Canned fruit should be drained well.
Quick-frozen fruit should be thawed and drained.

STEAMED APPLE PUDDING

2 cups cake flour, sifted
1 cup milk
3 tsp. baking powder
½ tsp. salt

½ cup sugar
1 Tbsp. butter
6 cups tart apples, peeled and sliced

Mix and sift dry ingredients. Melt butter, add milk and stir into sifted mixture. Turn out on floured board and roll very thin. Grease a melon-shaped mold and line with dough, allowing extra dough to hang over edge. Fill with apples. Sprinkle with sugar, turn edges of dough over apples. Cover mold with waxed paper and tie securely. Follow directions for Steamed Fruit Pudding. Steam 40 minutes. Serve with hot vanilla or lemon sauce.

TWENTY-FOUR HOUR PLUM PUDDING

1 cup seedless raisins	1 cup brown sugar
1 cup currants	½ cup milk
½ cup citron, sliced thin	2 eggs, well-beaten
½ cup candied cherries	1 cup cake flour, sifted
½ cup candied pineapple	1 tsp. baking soda
2 Tbsp. flour (for sifting over cut fruit)	½ tsp. nutmeg
	½ tsp. cinnamon
1 cup suet, ground fine	¼ tsp. allspice
	1 cup fine bread crumbs

Wash raisins and currants, dry thoroughly. Add citron, cherries and pineapple. Sift the 2 Tbsp. flour over fruit and blend lightly with finger tips. Shake in towel to remove excess flour. Let stand 24 hours. On the following day, mix suet, sugar and milk together. Add eggs, beat well. Sift all dry ingredients together. Add to egg mixture, beat well. Add floured fruit gradually. Beat well after each addition. Pour pudding into well-greased bowl. Follow directions for Steamed Fruit Pudding. Steam 40 minutes.

STEAMED INDIAN BREAD

2 cups flour	1 pt. sour milk
1 cup yellow cornmeal	½ tsp. baking soda
½ tsp. salt	¼ cup cold water
¼ cup molasses	1 Tbsp. butter, melted

Sift dry ingredients together. Mix molasses and milk together, and add baking soda dissolved in water. Add to flour and cornmeal mixture. Beat well until thoroughly blended. Add butter and beat again. Turn into well-greased tins, cover with waxed paper. Tie securely and follow directions for Steamed Fruit Pudding. Steam 30 minutes. Remove from pressure cooker and bake in slow oven (325° F.) 30 minutes more.

STEAMED ENGLISH PUDDING

2 eggs	½ tsp. nutmeg
1 Tbsp. sugar	8 slices bread
¼ tsp. salt	½ cup seedless raisins
	1½ cups milk

Beat eggs, sugar, salt and nutmeg together until light and fluffy. Cut crusts off bread, and place slice or two in bottom of well-greased bowl. Sprinkle with raisins. Add another slice of bread and continue until all are used. Add milk to beaten egg and sugar mixture. Pour carefully over bread, stand in cool place for 2 hours. Cover with waxed paper, tie securely, and follow directions for Steamed Fruit Pudding. Steam 15 minutes.

NEW ORLEANS PUDDING

½ cup molasses	¼ tsp. allspice
½ cup milk	¼ tsp. salt
½ cup vegetable shortening	1½ cups cake flour, sifted
¼ cup lemon juice	1 Tbsp. lemon rind, grated
½ cup raisins	½ tsp. baking soda
1 tsp. cinnamon	1 Tbsp. cold water

Mix molasses, milk, shortening, lemon juice, raisins and spices together until well-blended. Add soda dissolved in water, and beat well. Add flour, and beat thoroughly. Add lemon rind. Turn into well-greased bowl, cover with waxed paper, tie securely and follow directions for Steamed Fruit Pudding. Steam 30 minutes. Serve with hard sauce.

JAM PUDDING

2 Tbsp. butter	1 Tbsp. sour cream
½ cup sugar	1 tsp. cold water
1 egg, well-beaten	½ cup jam
½ tsp. baking soda	1 cup cake flour, sifted
	½ tsp. nutmeg

Beat butter until light and lemon-colored. Add sugar and beat until fluffy. Add egg. Add soda, dissolved in water, and cream. Beat well. Add jam, flour, and nutmeg. Turn into well-greased bowl, tie securely and follow directions for Steamed Fruit Pudding. Steam 30 minutes.

GRAHAM CRACKER STEAMED PUDDING

¼ cup butter	½ cup milk
½ cup sugar	¼ tsp. salt
2 eggs, well-beaten	3 cups graham cracker crumbs
1 tsp. baking powder	1 tsp. vanilla extract
	3 cups hot water

Cream butter and sugar together until light and fluffy. Add eggs. Beat well, and add dry ingredients alternately with milk. Add vanilla extract. Pour mixture into well-greased mold. Cover with waxed paper and tie securely. Place on rack, and add hot water. Steam without pressure for 30 minutes. Bring pressure up to 15 lbs. Steam 30 minutes. Reduce pressure instantly. Serve with any sauce.

STEAMED CHOCOLATE PUDDING

¼ cup butter	2 cups flour, sifted
½ cup sugar	1 Tbsp. baking powder
2 eggs, well-beaten	2 sq. chocolate, melted
½ cup milk	3 cups hot water

Cream butter and sugar together until light and fluffy. Add eggs. Beat well. Add dry ingredients alternately with milk. Add melted chocolate, beat well. Pour mixture into well-greased mold. Cover with waxed paper and tie securely. Place on rack, add hot water. Steam without pressure for 30 minutes. Bring pressure up to 15 lbs. Steam 30 minutes. Reduce pressure instantly.

RHUBARB PUDDING

6 slices bread	1 cup raw rhubarb, cut into
Butter for spreading	thin slices
	¾ cup sugar

Spread bread with butter. Place a slice in bottom of well-greased bowl. Cover with rhubarb, sprinkle with sugar. Continue process until bread, rhubarb and sugar are used. Finish with a slice of bread. Cover with waxed paper, tie securely and follow directions for Steamed Fruit Pudding. Steam 5 minutes.

APPLE SAUCE

One of the most satisfactory uses for a pressure cooker is for making home-made apple sauce. It is especially useful if there is a great quantity on hand, ready to be "put up" for the winter.

6 lbs. greenings	1½ cups water
	¾ cup sugar

Wash, quarter and core apples, but do not peel. Place in cooker with water and sugar. Place cover on cooker. Bring pressure up to 15 lbs. Steam for 1 minute. Reduce pressure gradually.

APPLES GLACÉ

4 or more Rome Beauties	½ cup water
	½ cup sugar

Wash and core apples. Peel top of apple to about center. Place on rack in cooker with water. Fill centers with sugar. Bring up to 15 lbs. pressure. Steam apples 3 to 5 minutes. Cool instantly. Remove apples, and cook syrup until thick and clear. Pour over apples. Serve cold with cream, if desired.

CRANBERRY JELLY

1 qt. cranberries   ¼ cup boiling water

2 cups sugar

Wash, pick over berries, remove any soft ones. Place berries and water in pressure cooker. Cover, place over high heat. When pressure is up to 15 lbs., reduce heat to low instantly. Steam 2 minutes. Cool at once. Rub berries through a sieve. Add sugar, bring to full rolling boil. Reduce heat and simmer 3 to 5 minutes.

ELECTRONIC COOKERY

The principles of electronic cookery are still so new that they seem revolutionary to everyone but research scientists. There are many descriptions of this entirely new development in cookery, but perhaps the simplest explanation is to compare cooking by radio frequency energy to the familiar radiant heat-cooking process as performed over a bed of glowing charcoal.

The scientists tell us that the world around us is composed of electromagnetic energies. The combination of these energies is called the spectrum. And the most commonly understood example of this is light. Above the light, as we know it, are the ultraviolet ray and the X-ray. Below the light are radar, radio waves, and the infrared light whose beneficial rays are felt when one indulges in a sun bath.

Science has learned how to harness this form of electromagnetic energy, and confine it in a given space in such a way that the energy is absorbed into the food and heat is created.

The energy is used or generated by means of a high frequency magnetrone tube. This has a longer wave length than infrared rays and is capable of deeper penetration. And it is this penetration which makes it possible for cooking to be accomplished.

These infrared radiations heat the surface of the food with extreme rapidity, but the penetration only goes to a depth of approximately 2½ inches. The rest of the cooking is done by the slow process of conduction until the heat reaches the center of the food.

At the present stage of development the electronic cookers are capable of baking a single layer of cake or small cup cakes, grilled sandwiches, frankfurters in rolls, hamburgers in buns, small lobsters, small fryers. Steaks and chops may be seared in a special oven and broiled in one minute to a succulence heretofore undreamed of.

The roadside stands of tomorrow will use radar for cooking, for the new stoves operate on the energy-absorption principle of this newest dream of science.

24.

CANNING,

PRESERVING,

QUICK-FREEZING

WHEN gardens and orchards are heavy with vegetables and fruits, then the urge to store these good foods against a long winter comes over the thrifty housewife. Her instincts are strong to save the harvest when it is plentiful. Fortunately for today's young homemaker, commercial methods have taken weeks of tedious yearly canning out of the home kitchen. However, when there is a home garden or a nearby orchard, and the produce is fresh and prices low, then the home kitchen may still be put to good use.

No longer does a homemaker speak only of the quarts of canned fruit and vegetables she has "put up." Science has brought a new method into the home kitchen, which is called "quick-freezing." The food is prepared according to directions given further on in this chapter, and then stored in deep-freeze lockers until ready to use.

EQUIPMENT FOR HOME CANNING AND PRESERVING

A special set of kitchen utensils should be purchased with the definite idea that they will be used year after year:

Water-bath canner (any deep kettle, 12 or more inches deep, may be used)
Rack to fit in bottom of canner
Funnel for pouring syrups
Pair of tongs to lift hot jars
Wire basket to hold jars while they are in canner
Wooden spoon to stir apple or other fruit butter, chili sauce, ketchups
Steam pressure cooker or canner

Large kettle of aluminum, enamelware, or stainless steel
Colander
Coarse strainer
Jelly bag
Jelly glasses
Glass jars
Paraffin
New rubber rings

WHY CANNED FOODS SPOIL

Bacteriologists have carried on a campaign for many years to explain to the public the reasons for food spoilage. As the authorities say, "Plant organisms, too small to be seen without a microscope, exist everywhere—in the air, water, and soil. These organisms are called molds, yeasts, and bacteria; they need food for growth and reproduction. But it is just this growth which spoils food." Lack of cleanliness is one of the major causes of food spoilage. All equipment, all food, must be as clean as possible. Packing jars too tightly, or with insufficient liquid, also causes spoilage.

HOW TO STERILIZE GLASS JARS AND GLASSES

Examine jars and glasses. Be sure the sealing surface is free from nicks, and that the edge of the jar is smooth to the touch. The sealing surface of a glass jar is the ledge or shoulder about ¾ inch below the top of the jar. Place two large pans side by side. Fill one pan with hot, soapy water. Fill other pan with clear hot water. Wash and rinse jars. Place in rack in large kettle, cover with hot water, and bring to boil. Keep hot until ready to use. Do not boil rubbers, simply dip in boiling water before placing on jars.

METHODS OF CANNING

No. 1—Open-Kettle Method

All fruits, tomatoes, preserves and pickles are adaptable to this method.

Food which is fresh, sound, and free from spots or blemishes, is prepared according to recipes in following pages. The food is cooked in an open kettle, as a means of killing the bacteria. It is then packed, while still boiling hot, into a sterilized glass jar, with a rubber ring, or sealing composition lid. The lid is closed and sealed immediately.

1. Fill one jar at a time. Fill to within ½ inch of the top with the food product, and the boiling hot liquid.
2. Wipe the jar top clean of syrup, seeds or pulp.

3. Set the jar on a clean thick cloth, away from a draft, right side up. Store in a cool, dark place.

TO FIGURE YIELD OF CANNED FRUIT FROM FRESH

Legal weight of a bushel of fruit varies in different States. These are average weights:

Food	Fresh	Canned
Apples	1 bu. (48 lb.)	16 to 20 qt.
	2½ to 3 lb.	1 qt.
Berries, except strawberries	24-qt. crate	12 to 18 qt.
	5 to 8 cups	1 qt.
Cherries, as picked	1 bu. (56 lb.)	22 to 32 qt.
	6 to 8 cups	1 qt.
Peaches	1 bu. (48 lb.)	18 to 24 qt.
	2 to 2½ lb.	1 qt.
Pears	1 bu. (50 lb.)	20 to 25 qt.
	2 to 2½ lb.	1 qt.
Plums	1 bu. (56 lb.)	24 to 30 qt.
	2 to 2½ lb.	1 qt.
Strawberries	24-qt. crate	12 to 16 qt.
	6 to 8 cups	1 qt.
Tomatoes	1 bu. (53 lb.)	15 to 20 qt.
	2½ to 3 lb.	1 qt.

No. 2—Boiling-Water-Bath Method

Fruits, rhubarb, and tomatoes are excellent choices for this method.

Boiling-water-bath processing of canned fruits consists of plunging the filled and closed glass jars into a kettle of boiling water, which is quickly brought to a boil again and kept actively boiling during required length of time. Kettle must be tightly covered, and water must be at least 1 inch above tops of jars throughout entire heating process.

Processing time is counted from the time the water begins to boil again, after the glass containers are placed in it.

STEPS TO FOLLOW IN BOILING-WATER BATH

1. Select a few sterilized glass jars, enough to fit into container.

2. Prepare from ⅔ to 1 cup of syrup for each quart jar of fruit.
3. Select only as much fruit as can be handled quickly at one time.
4. Wash fruit in wire rack lowered into kettle of boiling water. Lift rack out. Plunge into cold water.
5. Peel fruit quickly, and prepare according to hot-pack or cold-pack method.
6. Place a sterilized, wet, new rubber ring on each jar, or use the new sealing composition lid.
7. Pack the prepared fruit as directed, and be careful not to crush it. Do not pack too tightly.
8. Fill each jar to within ¼ inch from the top with the boiling sugar syrup. Use a spatula to run down the side of jar to work out any air bubbles.
9. Wipe tops of jars, and rubber rings on jars, with a clean, damp cloth. Fit lids carefully into place.
10. Seal jars completely. Lower hot containers in rack into boiling-water bath. Do not allow them to touch each other.

PACKING THE FOOD

There are two different methods used for packing foods into jars before food is cooked, or, as it is more commonly expressed, "processed." The food is either packed raw, called "cold-pack," or partially cooked and packed into the jars while hot, called "hot-pack."

Fruit, rhubarb, and tomatoes may be packed according to either method. Vegetables must always be packed hot, and processed by means of a steam pressure cooker. This is a highly technical process, and the home-canner is advised to use the complete leaflets on Home Canning put out by the different State Agricultural Colleges, or the Farmer's Bulletin on Home Canning printed by the U. S. Department of Agriculture.

COLD-PACK

The food is washed and peeled; left whole, or cut in half or in pieces. The sterilized jars are at hand, and the food is packed into jars, then covered with boiling liquid or syrup. Jars are completely sealed, then processed immediately.

HOT-PACK

The food is washed and peeled; left whole, or cut in half or in pieces, and pre-cooked a few minutes in water or sugar syrup. The sterilized jars are at hand, the food is packed into jars quickly, then covered with boiling liquid or syrup. Jars are completely sealed, then processed immediately.

No. 3—Pressure-Canner Method

If such foods as meat, poultry, and fish—as well as non-acid vegetables—are to be canned at home, a steam pressure cooker is an essential piece of equipment. There are a number of pressure cookers on the market especially designed for large quantity canning, and a booklet of detailed instructions is issued with each canner. The housewife is urged to follow directions of manufacturer with the utmost care.

1. The produce selected for pressure cooking must be of the best quality. Sort over the vegetables, wash thoroughly, and prepare according to the recipe.
2. Pour boiling water into the pressure cooker to a level of about 2 inches.
3. Set another kettle of water on the stove for heating the glass jars.
4. Vegetables are scalded (blanched), or partially cooked, before being placed in jars. In every recipe where food is pre-cooked, save liquid to add to contents of jar.
5. Pack vegetables lightly in sterilized hot jars. Leave ½ to 1 inch of space at top of jar. Add enough liquid to cover food, shake jar lightly, and add extra vegetables if needed.
6. Seal, or partially seal, covers in place.
7. Place filled jars on rack. It is of utmost importance in using this method that jars are not permitted to touch one another.
8. Adjust cover of canner and fasten top securely. Always fasten top of cooker by tightening clamps alternately.
9. Let water come to boil until steam escapes from petcock on cover. Count 7 minutes from time steam escapes before closing petcock. Fasten securely, and watch pressure gauge until it registers desired number of pounds. This is the essential step.
10. As soon as the correct pressure is reached, start to count the number of minutes. The heat must be regulated so that the pressure is constant during this processing time. *Some of the faults with home canning occur because this pressure and time element is not understood.* (See time table, which follows after Item 14.)
11. Turn off heat, and leave pressure cooker alone until the dial on the pressure gauge returns to zero. Then open the petcock gradually to permit steam to escape. Open clamps alternately, lift lid carefully away from face.
12. Lift rack of jars from canner. Seal jars.
13. Cover table with several thicknesses of cloth, and do not permit jars to stand in draft. Wipe off all moisture. Store in cool, dry place.
14. Do not permit cover of pressure cooker to be immersed in water. Keep cooker scrupulously clean.

When berries and fruits are in season make the most of the harvest by canning, preserving, or quick-freezing. Let the young people participate by giving them tasks appropriate to their age and skill.

TIME TABLE FOR PROCESSING NON-ACID VEGETABLES IN PRESSURE COOKER

This time table is designed for use in localities where the altitude is 2000 feet or less. At altitudes over 2000 feet, add 1 lb. pressure for each additional 2000 feet.

	PINT GLASS JARS		QUART GLASS JARS	
PRODUCT	240° F. 10 lbs. pressure	250° F. 15 lbs. pressure	240° F. 10 lbs. pressure	250° F. 15 lbs. pressure
Asparagus..............	30 min.		35 min.	
Beets..................	30 min.		35 min.	
Carrots................	30 min.		35 min.	
Corn, whole grain........	60 min	75 min.	70 min.	
Green Lima Beans.......	50 min.		55 min.	
Green String Beans.......	30 min.		35 min.	
Peas..................	45 min.		55 min.	
Squash................		60 min.		75 min.

Young vegetables, fresh from the garden, tender, firm, and crisp, should be selected for pressure cooking. Wash thoroughly, lifting vegetables out of water each time so that dirt will not be drained back over them.

Trim and cut beans. Prepare only enough for one canner load at a time.

Remove air bubbles by working the blade of a table knife down the sides of the jar. Add more liquid if needed to fill jar to ½ inch of top.

Wipe jar rim clean, so no speck of food will keep the lid from making an airtight seal with the jar.

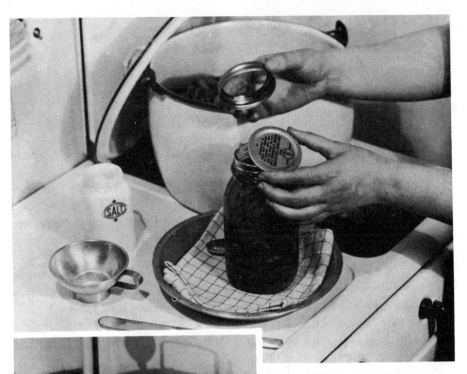

Place clean, hot metal lid on jar so that sealing compound is next to the glass. Screw metal band on firmly.

When pressure falls to zero wait a minute or two, no longer. Then slowly open petcock, or take off weighted gage. Unfasten cover. Tilt far side up, away from your face.

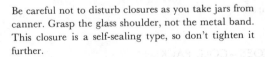

Be careful not to disturb closures as you take jars from canner. Grasp the glass shoulder, not the metal band. This closure is a self-sealing type, so don't tighten it further.

RECIPES FOR NON-ACID VEGETABLES

IN PRESSURE COOKER

Asparagus: Select tender young stalks; sort according to size. Wash thoroughly, scrape skin and cut off ½ inch at bottom. Tie in small bundles, stand upright in boiling water and cook covered for 3 minutes. Pack boiling hot, in wide-mouthed jars. Add 1 tsp. salt to every quart, and cover with boiling water in which cooked. Process as directed in preceding time table.

Beets: Select tender young beets. Wash thoroughly, but leave on all roots and 1 inch of stem. Scald in boiling water until skins slip off easily. Pack into glass jars. Add 1 tsp. salt to each quart. Process as directed in preceding time table.

Carrots: Same as beets.

Corn, whole grain: Cut corn from cob, but do not scrape. Weigh corn on scales and allow half as much boiling water by weight, and 1 tsp. salt to every quart. Bring to boil and process as directed in preceding time table.

Green lima beans: Shell young tender beans. Wash and cover with boiling water. Bring to boil. Pack boiling hot. Add 1 tsp. salt to each quart. Process as directed in preceding time table.

Green string beans: Wash thoroughly and cut in pieces—or in lengthwise slices, French style. Cover with boiling water. Simmer for 5 minutes. Pack boiling hot. Add 1 tsp. salt to each quart. Cover with boiling water in which cooked. Process as directed in preceding time table.

Peas: Same as beans. Pint jars are preferable for size.

Squash: Wash, peel and cut into neat cubes. Simmer in small amount of boiling water until heated through, stir frequently. Pack boiling hot. Add 1 tsp. salt to each quart. Cover with water in which heated. Process as directed in preceding time table.

TOMATOES

Tomatoes are commonly classified as a vegetable; actually they are a fruit. The tomato is one of the easiest products to can at home, but the fruit must be fresh, firm and free from blemish.

Wash the tomatoes carefully before scalding (blanching). Dip only small quantities in the boiling water at one time, then dip in cold water, and drain. Always cut out the hard green core.

TOMATOES—COLD-PACK

Wash firm, fresh, sound, ripe tomatoes. Scald (a few at a time) and drain. Cut out core, then skin tomatoes. Pack solidly into hot jars. Add 1 tsp. salt to

The cold-pack method—with tomatoes. Wash tomatoes and place in a wire basket or thin cloth. Dip into boiling water for about ½ minute, covering pan. Then dip tomatoes quickly into cold water.

Pack tomatoes into jars, pressing down enough to fill any spaces. Fill jars to within ¼ inch of top. Add salt—½ tsp. to a pint jar; 1 tsp. to a quart jar.

Wipe jar rim and rubber ring with a clean, damp cloth, after removing air bubbles by working the blade of a knife down the sides of jar. Screw cap on tight, then turn back ¼ inch. Process jars in hot-water bath. Be careful in adding water to cover jar tops that you do not pour water directly on jars.

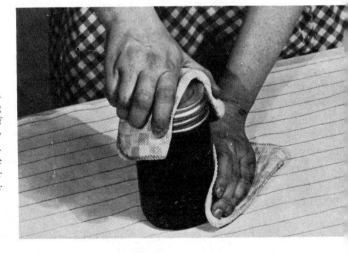

each quart. (Add no liquid.) Process 45 minutes in hot-water-bath. Tomatoes may be cut in half or in quarters.

Or boil prepared tomatoes 5 minutes. Pour into hot jars and process 20 minutes in hot-water bath.

TOMATOES—SOLID-PACK

Wash small, smooth, firm, fresh, ripe tomatoes. Scald (a few at a time), cold-dip, and drain. Remove core. Pack into hot jars as closely as possible without crushing. Add 1 tsp. salt to each quart. Cover tomatoes with hot tomato juice. Process 30 minutes in hot-water bath.

TOMATO PASTE

Wash, core, and chop 12 lbs. of firm ripe tomatoes, and 2 red sweet peppers. Add 6 bay leaves and 3 tsp. salt. Cook about 1 hour. Rub through sieve. Add 1 clove garlic. Cook very slowly, until thick enough to round up on spoon. Remove garlic, add spices if desired. Pour into clean hot jars. Process 1 hour in hot-water bath.

TOMATO CATSUP

(Old English Recipe)

4 qts. tomatoes	1 Tbsp. cloves
2 qts. vinegar	1 tsp. salt
2 Tbsp. red pepper	1 ground nutmeg
4 Tbsp. black pepper	½ lb. sugar

Boil ingredients (except sugar) together until thick. Strain, add sugar. Pour catsup into sterilized bottles. Seal at once.

QUICK CATSUP

1 qt. cooked strained tomatoes	1 tsp. cloves
1 tsp. allspice	1 Tbsp. salt
	1 qt. white wine vinegar

Boil ingredients together for 1 hour. Pour into sterilized bottles. Seal at once.

APPLES

APPLES—HOT-PACK

Wash, pare, core, and cut apples. Drop into vinegar and salt water (1 Tbsp. each to 1 gal. water). Boil equal parts sugar and water together 2 minutes. Rinse apples. Add to hot syrup. Cook gently 5 to 10 minutes. Pack in overlapping layers into hot jars. Process 20 minutes in hot-water bath.

APPLES—FOR PIES

Slice apples, and cook in syrup made of 2 parts water to 1 part sugar.

APPLE SAUCE

Wash, pare, core, and slice apples. Add a little water to start cooking. Cook until soft. Press through strainer. Sweeten to taste. Reheat to boiling. Pour into hot jars. Process 15 minutes in hot-water bath.

APRICOTS—HOT-PACK

Wash, scald, and drop fruit in cold salted water (4 Tbsp. salt to 1 gal. water). Peel, leave whole or cut in halves, and remove pits. Rinse well. Simmer 3 to 6 minutes in syrup made of equal parts sugar and water. Pack into hot jars. Process 15 minutes in hot-water bath.

PEACHES—COLD-PACK

Pack peaches into hot jars, layers overlapping, cavity side down. Cover with boiling syrup made with 1 or 2 parts sugar to 1 of water. Process from 20 to 35 minutes in hot-water bath. Use the longer period for extra-large fruit.

PEACHES—HOT-PACK

Make a syrup of 1 or 2 parts sugar to 1 of water. Add peaches, a few at a time, and simmer until hot through (10 minutes). Pack into hot jars, cavity side down. Cover with syrup in which peaches were cooked. Process 10 to 20 minutes in hot-water bath.

PEARS

The Bartlett pear is best for canning. Unlike other fruits, pears should be removed from the tree before ripe, and stored in a cool place (60–65° F.) until ripe—but not soft.

Wash, pare, halve or quarter, and core pears (except when the fruit is canned whole). Drop the pared fruit into water containing salt and vinegar (1 Tbsp. of each to 1 gal. water). Rinse. Boil gently from 4 to 8 minutes in syrup made of 1 part sugar to 2 or 3 parts water. Pack into hot jars, cavity side down. Cover with syrup in which cooked. Process 20 to 25 minutes in hot-water bath. Use the longer period for large fruit.

Pears are well adapted to combination with other flavors.

CINNAMON PEARS

Use 2 or 3 Tbsp. of cinnamon drop candy to each qt. of syrup, or use stick cinnamon and a few drops of red coloring.

PLUMS

Green gage plums are better for canning than the more juicy varieties. Plums may be scalded and skinned, but the skins are usually left on. Prick with a needle to prevent bursting of the fruit.

Drop plums into boiling syrup made of 1 part sugar to 1 of water. The plums should not be more than 2 deep in the pan. Remove pan from stove 2 minutes after adding fruit. Let stand covered from 20 to 30 minutes. Pack plums into hot jars. Cover with the syrup. Process 10 minutes in hot-water bath. The extra syrup may be canned to use in beverages.

PLUMS—OPEN KETTLE

Wash, prick, and measure plums. To each quart plums, add from ½ to ¾ cup sugar and ½ cup water. Heat slowly to boiling. Boil until thoroughly cooked (10 to 20 minutes). Pour hot into hot jars; seal at once.

SPICED PLUMS—OPEN KETTLE

3 lbs. sugar	½ tsp. cinnamon
3 lbs. plums	½ tsp. allspice
1 pt. vinegar	½ tsp. clove
	½ tsp. mace

Make a syrup of sugar and vinegar. Prick the plums, place in a large bowl. Bring syrup to a boil again and pour over plums. Let stand in cool place for 3 days. Fill hot sterilized jars with drained plums. Add spices to syrup and boil down until thick. Pour over plums. Seal immediately.

CRANBERRY SAUCE

Wash and stem cranberries. Boil 4 cups sugar with 4 cups water, 5 minutes. Add 2 qts. berries; boil without stirring until skins burst. Pour into hot jars. Seal immediately.

CRAB APPLES WITH STEMS

(A relish for cold meat)

Make a syrup of 3 lbs. sugar to 3 cups water. Allow about ½ lb. of sugar to every lb. of fruit. Rub the blossom end off the crab apples. Wash well and drain. Prick each apple with needle, and drop into boiling syrup. Cook until tender when pierced with silver fork. Fill hot, sterilized jars with fruit. Add boiling syrup to within ½ inch from top. Seal immediately.

QUINCES

Use firm, ripe fruit. Wash, peel, core and cut into quarters. Steam in small amount of water until tender. Pack into hot jars. Cover with syrup made with equal parts sugar and water. Process 30 minutes in hot-water bath.

RHUBARB

Select firm, ripe stalks. Wash thoroughly and cut in neat ½ inch pieces.

RHUBARB—COLD-PACK

Pack fruit tightly in hot jars and pour boiling syrup to within ½ inch of top of jar. Process 20 minutes in hot-water bath.

RHUBARB—HOT-PACK

Cook rhubarb in syrup until tender, but not soft and shapeless. Pack immediately in hot jars. Process 5 minutes in hot-water bath.

BERRIES

ALL BERRIES—COLD-PACK

Use any variety of edible berry, *except strawberries and red raspberries.* Wash firm, ripe berries. Drain. Pack into hot jars as tightly as possible without crushing. Cover with hot syrup made of 1 part sugar and 1 part berry juice or water. Process 20 minutes in hot-water bath.

ALL BERRIES—HOT-PACK

Use any variety of edible berry, *except strawberries and red raspberries.* Wash and measure firm, ripe berries. Drain. Use from ¼ to ½ cup sugar to 1 qt. berries. Place layers of sugar and berries in a broad, shallow pan. Let stand 2 hours, then cook by simmering until the sugar is dissolved and berries heated through. Pack into hot jars. Process 5 minutes. Pour boiling hot into hot jars, seal at once.

ALL BERRIES—OPEN KETTLE

Use any variety of edible berries, *except strawberries and red raspberries.* Wash berries. Add from ¼ to ½ cup sugar for each quart berries. Boil 10 minutes. Pour boiling hot into hot jars, seal at once.

STRAWBERRIES

Wash, cap, drain and measure berries. Work with 2 or 3 qts. at a time. Use from 1 to 2 cups sugar to each quart of berries. Place sugar and berries in alternate layers in a broad bottom pan. Let stand 2 hours. Simmer 5 minutes without stirring. Cover and let stand overnight. Pack cold berries into hot jars. Process 15 minutes in hot-water bath.

RED RASPBERRIES

Red raspberries may be canned by any berry recipe; but they keep color, shape and flavor better if instructions for canning strawberries are followed.

HUCKLEBERRIES

For Muffins and Pies

Wash 3 to 4 qts. huckleberries, pick over to remove stems. Drain and pour (a qt. at a time) into a square of cheesecloth. Tie securely and dip into boiling water until thoroughly wet. Dip quickly into cold water. Pour tightly into hot sterilized jars. Do not add either sugar or liquid. Process 20 minutes in hot-water bath.

TWO OLD-FASHIONED RECIPES

(1) Sun-Cooked Strawberries

Prepare strawberries for cooking. Weigh accurately. Add an equal amount of sugar, or as the old saying reads, "pound for pound." Use a small amount at a time. Do not have the fruit and sugar more than 3 inches deep in the preserving kettle.

Place over low heat and slowly bring to boiling point. Let the preserves cook for 10 minutes from the time boiling begins, skim off foam as it rises to top. Pour preserves into large, shallow platters, about 1½ inch in depth. Cover platters with coarse netting and let stand in sunny window for a full 24 hours of sunshine. Fill jelly glasses when preserve has become thick. Cover with paraffin. Gourmets and epicures regard this preserve as the finest made.

(2) Stone-Crock Preserves (Tutti Frutti)

This time-honored rich preserve requires a large, stone crock with a cover, and calls for a full pint of fine brandy or grain alcohol. The crock is scalded and dried, and the first fresh fruit or berry of the season is prepared for its bath.

How to hot-pack fruits for the boiling water bath:
(1) Put food in boiling water or boiling sugar syrup. Heat fruit through but not until soft.
(2) Meantime, heat clean jars and lids in water. Remove from water and put hot, wet rubber ring on jar. Pack food loosely. Leave ½ inch space at top of jar.
(3) Wipe top of jar and rubber ring with a clean, damp cloth. Fit on glass lid.
(4) Seal jars completely. Lower jars into canner as soon as they are filled. Do not allow jars to touch each other.

Pour 1 qt. of sugar into the bottom of the crock and add an equal quantity of prepared fruit. Pour brandy or alcohol on top, and stir the mixture thoroughly. Cover crock tightly, then store in a cool, dark, dry place. Stir mixture about once a week. As the spring and summer seasons advance, add each fresh fruit or berry, plus an equal amount of sugar, to the crock. The amount depends on your own decision. Cherries should be pitted and stemmed, peaches peeled and sliced. If grapes are included, they should be of the seedless variety. Strawberries should be hulled, and fresh pineapple finely shredded. This delightful sauce lasts all through the winter, and is a sophisticated topping for ice cream.

CHERRIES

CHERRIES—COLD-PACK

Wash, stem and pit cherries, or leave whole. (Prick each unpitted cherry with needle.) Pack into hot jars. Cover sour cherries with boiling syrup made of 1 part sugar and 1 of water or cherry juice, and sweet cherries with syrup made of ½ to 1 part sugar and liquid. Process 20 minutes in hot-water bath.

CHERRIES—HOT-PACK

Wash, pit, and measure cherries. Mix with ½ to 1 cup sugar to each quart pitted cherries. Let stand 1 to 2 hours; simmer 10 minutes. Pack into hot jars. Process 10 minutes in hot-water bath.

CHERRIES—OPEN KETTLE

Wash, drain, stem, pit, and measure cherries. Add from ½ to 1 cup sugar for each quart pitted fruit. Heat slowly to boiling, then boil rapidly 15 minutes. Pour into hot jars; seal at once.

JUICES

GRAPE JUICE

Wash, stem, and crush fresh grapes. Add 1 cup water to each gallon crushed grapes. Heat 10 minutes at simmering temperature. Strain through several layers of cheesecloth. Let stand in a cool place, preferably in refrigerator, 24 hours. Strain again. Reheat to simmering. Pour into hot jars. Process 30 minutes in hot-water bath at 175° to 185° F.

CRANBERRY FRUIT JUICE

(Pasteurized)

2 lbs. fresh cranberries	1 qt. water
	2 Tbsp. sugar

Put cranberries through food chopper. Add water and heat to simmering point. Strain through cheesecloth or fine sieve, pressing pulp through. Add sugar. Pasteurize by heating in top of double boiler to simmering point (170° F.). Fill sterilized jars to overflowing; seal. Place jars in hot water to cover, at 170° F., for 5 minutes to sterilize tops. Cool and store until ready to use. Before serving, chill well and dilute up to one-half with water.

Closet filled with home-canned produce is a satisfying sight.

TOMATO JUICE I

No tomato juice is finer than that made by pressing home-canned tomatoes through a fine sieve whenever juice is required.

TOMATO JUICE II

Use firm, red-ripe tomatoes. Discard any that are bruised or specked. Wash carefully. Cut into small pieces and cook until soft. Press the hot tomatoes through a fine sieve. Reheat to simmering (195° to 205° F.). Pour into hot jars. Process 20 minutes in hot-water bath at simmering, or 10 minutes at boiling.

JELLIES

When the jars of clear, sparkling, tender jelly stand in shining rows on the kitchen table, then the artist in the woman is satisfied.

Of all delicacies, the care and attention which must be lavished upon fruit when making jelly, is probably greater than that required by any other single food. Some fruits contain enough of the natural substance, pectin, and enough acid, to make a perfect glass of jelly when combined with exactly the right amount of sugar. Practically all small fruits and berries have this quality; but strawberries, red and black raspberries, cherries, and peaches need the addition of commercial pectin to insure the best results.

This rather new product is frequently used with all fruits, because the method is simpler and a great deal quicker. The directions included in the packages of fruit pectin must be followed exactly.

SEVEN STEPS TO JELLY MAKING

1. *Selecting the fruit:* Slightly under-ripe fruits are richer in both acid and pectin than those which are fully ripe, and they give a lighter-colored, clearer jelly.
2. *Preparing fruit:* Wash and drain fruits before cutting or hulling. Remove stems and hulls, and cut out any bruises, or fresh cracks. Retain peelings. Cut large fruits into small pieces, or slice them.
3. *Extracting juice:* Put fruit on to boil. Do not add too much water; use just enough to prevent scorching. Heat gradually and simmer gently. For a clear, bright jelly, shake pan rather than stir fruit, and do not mash.
4. *Getting jars ready:* While fruit is draining, get pint jars ready by washing thoroughly in hot soapy water, rinsing carefully, and boiling in clear water 15 minutes. Keep them hot in the water.
5. *Cooking jelly; the jelly test:* Bring juice to a boil in a shallow pan, add sugar (see recipes for amounts), and boil briskly, skimming off foam. Test with a metal spoon, dipping up boiling hot syrup and allowing it to run off the edge. When two drops form, and then flow together to form a sheet, the jelly is done and should be removed immediately from heat. Continued boiling will give a stiff, tough product.
6. *Filling jars:* Have the sterile jars ready when jelly is done. Place a clean metal spoon in the jar being filled, and pour hot jelly in, to within ½ inch of top. Cool until jelly is set. Seal with hot melted paraffin.

7. *Labeling and storing:* Put on labels with name of jelly and date of making. Several of the red jellies look somewhat alike, so name labels are important. Store cooled jellies in a dark, dry, cool place.

JELLY-MAKING GUIDE

FRUIT	CHOOSE	PREPARATION OF FRUIT	AMOUNT OF WATER TO ADD PER QT.	COOKING	AMOUNT OF SUGAR FOR EACH QT. OF JUICE
Apple	Slightly under-ripe	Wash, quarter, remove seeds, slice thin	Barely to cover	Boil gently until soft, not mushy	3 cups
Crab apples	Slightly under-ripe juicy	Wash, remove blossom and quarter, remove seeds	Barely to cover	Boil gently until soft, not mushy	4 cups
Cranberry	Firm, bright red	Wash and stem	Barely to cover	Boil gently until berries begin to burst	3 cups
Currant	Fully ripe	Wash and stem	¼ cup	Boil gently until currants have a whitish color	4 cups
Grape (Concord)	Barely ripe	Wash and remove from stem	¼ cup	Boil gently until grapes swim in their own juice	3 cups
Loganberry	Barely ripe	Pick over, wash and stem	2 to 4 Tbsp.	Boil gently until they swim in their own juice	3 cups
Quince	Ripe	Wash thoroughly, remove stem and blossom ends, cut in quarters, remove core, slice thin	Barely to cover	Boil gently until soft	4 cups

HOW TO TELL WHEN JELLY IS DONE

A candy thermometer may be used for testing when jelly is done. Cook until a temperature of 221° F. is reached. The old-fashioned way to test jelly (prior to the invention of a thermometer) was as follows: Dip a spoon in the boiling mass. Remove, and cool by moving back and forth for a few seconds, then allow jelly to drop from spoon. As long as there is syrup present, it will run or drop from the spoon. When the jellying point is reached, it will break from the spoon in sheets—and must be removed immediately from the heat, and skimmed. Skimming at this point saves waste.

A Word of Warning: Be sure to use a large enough kettle for jelly-making, to prevent juice boiling over.

Amount of Sugar to Use: Usually ¾ cup of sugar to each cup of fruit juice is a good proportion to follow.

APPLE JELLY

Select firm, sour apples. Wash, and cut in slices about ¾ inch thick, without peeling or coring. Add just enough water to cover, and cook rapidly in a covered vessel for about 25 minutes or until soft. Strain through a flannel jelly bag. The average proportion is ¾ cup sugar to 1 cup apple juice. Bring the juice to boiling, add the sugar, and stir until dissolved. Cook rapidly to jelly stage, skim and pour into hot, sterilized glasses. Cover with hot paraffin at once.

MINT JELLY

1 cup fresh mint leaves	¼ cup sugar
¼ cup boiling water	1 qt. apple juice
	2½ cups sugar

Wash mint leaves, snip from stems, add boiling water and sugar, let stand few hours. Bring to boiling point and strain through several layers of cheese-cloth. Cook apples (see Apple Jelly), strain through a flannel bag, and measure to 1 qt. Heat in enamelware saucepan, add 2½ cups sugar. Stir until sugar is fully dissolved, add liquid mint, and cook until it reacts to jelly test. Skim, and pour into hot sterilized jelly glasses. Seal with paraffin. If the color is too pale, pure vegetable coloring may be added to tint the jelly a deeper green.

JELLIES FROM CANNED JUICES

During the canning season, the fresh fruits and vegetables come on so rapidly that many homemakers find it an advantage to can fruit juices unsweetened, and make the jelly at a later date. It is often possible to use small amounts of fruit in this way, canning only 1 or 2 jars of juice at a time. In addition, this practice saves storage space, since the juice can be packed in quart or half-gallon jars; also, the freshly-made jelly will be superior in flavor to jelly which has been stored for several weeks or months.

PRESERVES—JAM MAKING

The instinctive urge to "put up" homemade preserves is often dissipated by the thought of the labor involved. But again, as in so many other food categories, commercial aids are available to ease the task. In this instance, bottled pectin is available, and the homemaker will find that these preserving aids are sold with accurate directions for their use. However, the procedure is completely different when the time-honored method of making preserves is followed.

In this process, the large quantity of sugar used in jams and preserves is the principal factor in the "keeping" quality of the finished product. Beginners are advised to preserve small amounts at one time; not more than six pints of berries.

If kitchen scales are part of the home's equipment, results are bound to be more uniform when the fruit and sugar are weighed, instead of measured. *The usual proportion is ¾ lb. of sugar to 1 lb. of fruit.* However, if scales are not used, the jam which is made by measure is very good eating, too.

BERRY JAM

4 cups berries   3 cups sugar

Use blackberries, raspberries, loganberries or strawberries. Wash berries (hull strawberries). Drain in colander. Crush with potato masher. Measure sugar and set aside. Place berries in saucepan. Heat slowly, stir constantly. Add sugar slowly, continue to stir until sugar is completely dissolved. Cook rapidly, stir often until syrup gives jelly test. (See Item 5 under Seven Steps To Jelly Making.) Pour preserves into hot sterilized jelly glasses. Seal while hot.

PEACH OR APRICOT JAM

4 cups crushed fruit   2 to 4 Tbsp. vinegar,
3 cups sugar   lime or lemon juice

Place fruit in wire colander, immerse in boiling water for 1 minute. Plunge into cold water. Peel quickly. Cut in halves and remove pits. Crush, and measure. Place fruit, sugar and vinegar, lime or lemon juice in a saucepan. Heat slowly, stir until sugar is dissolved. Boil rapidly until thick. Pour into hot sterilized jelly glasses. Seal while hot.

FRESH ORANGE AND GRAPEFRUIT CONSERVE

3 medium fresh grapefruit	4 cups cold water
6 medium fresh oranges	10 cups sugar
2 medium fresh lemons	1½ cups chopped pecans or walnuts
Water to cover fruit	5 tsp. pure vanilla extract

Wash fruit, remove seeds, slice in ⅛ inch strips. Measure (there should be about 7 cups grapefruit and 5¾ cups oranges). Place fruit in an 8-qt. kettle. Add water to cover, and bring to boiling point. Drain. Repeat twice. Add the 4 cups water and cook, uncovered, 1½ hours or until fruit is tender. Measure (there should be about 10 cups). Add 1 cup sugar for each cup of fruit. Cook over medium heat until thick, about 1½ hours, stirring frequently. Add the chopped nuts and pure vanilla extract. Pour into hot sterilized jars. Seal at once.

PLUM CONSERVE

3 lbs. Damson plums	1 cup golden raisins
1 orange	4 cups sugar
1 lemon	1 cup walnut meats, chopped coarsely

Cut plums into small pieces. Slice unpeeled orange and lemon into thin slices. Cook fruits and sugar over low heat until thick. Add nut meats. Pour into hot sterilized jelly glasses. Seal at once.

APPLE BUTTER

1 qt. sweet cider	¾ cup sugar
2½ lbs. tart apples, cut	⅛ tsp. cinnamon
in quarters, unpeeled	⅛ tsp. allspice
	Pinch of cloves

Cook cider until it is down to 1 pt. Add apple quarters. Cook until soft, stir frequently. Rub through sieve. Add other ingredients. (Lemon juice might be added to improve flavor, if desired.) Cook until thick and glossy. Pour into hot sterilized jars. Seal partially. Process in boiling water for 5 minutes. Complete sealing of jars.

PICKLES AND RELISHES

CORN RELISH

(Open Kettle)

Mixture I

1 large head of cabbage	20 ears of corn, scraped from cob
4 large onions	1½ cups sugar
4 green peppers	½ cup salt
6 sweet red peppers	1 qt. cider vinegar

Mixture II

3 Tbsp. dry mustard	1 Tbsp. celery seed
1 Tbsp. tumeric	3 cups vinegar

Cut cabbage in pieces. Put pieces through food chopper. Peel onions, remove tops and all seeds from peppers. Grind well. Add remaining ingredients of Mixture I. Bring to boil. Add Mixture II. Simmer for 30 minutes. Pour into hot sterilized jars. Seal immediately.

SWEET TOMATO PICKLE

(Open Kettle)

1 peck green tomatoes, sliced	2 Tbsp. clove
6 large onions, sliced	2 Tbsp. allspice
1 cup salt	2 Tbsp. ginger
2 qts. water	2 Tbsp. mustard
1 qt. vinegar	2 Tbsp. cinnamon
2 lbs. sugar	1 tsp. cayenne pepper
	2 qts. vinegar

Sprinkle tomatoes and onions with salt, let stand overnight. Drain next morning, add the water and 1 qt. vinegar. Bring to boil, and cook 15 minutes. Drain, discard vinegar water. Mix remaining ingredients thoroughly. Add mixture and simmer for 15 minutes. Pour into hot sterilized jars. Seal at once.

CRANBERRY APPLE RELISH

1 pt. cranberries	1 orange, unpeeled
1 apple, pared and cored	½ lemon, unpeeled
	1 cup sugar

Put cranberries and apples through food chopper. Cut orange and lemon in pieces, remove seeds and put through chopper. Add sugar and blend thoroughly. Chill in refrigerator for 24 hours. (This sauce will keep well in the refrigerator for several weeks.)

CRANBERRY HONEY CONSERVE

1 qt. cranberries	1 cup seedless raisins
1 cup water	⅓ cup orange juice
1 cup sugar	Grated rind 1 orange
⅔ cup honey	1 cup broken pecan nut meats

Cook cranberries in water until skins pop open. Rub through fine sieve. Add sugar, honey, raisins, orange juice, and rind. Cook together for 15 minutes. Remove from heat. Add nut meats. Pack in sterilized jars and seal with paraffin.

PROCESSING FRUIT AND TOMATOES

TIME TABLE FOR PROCESSING FRUITS

This time table is designed for use in localities where the altitude is 1000 feet or less. Increase the time 20% for each additional 1000 feet. The time specified is for quarts or pints.

PROCESSING TABLE

PRODUCT	SYRUP	PACK	WATER BATH PROCESS AT BOILING
Apples	Medium to Heavy	Hot-Pack	20 minutes
Apricots	Medium to Heavy	Hot-Pack	15 minutes
Berries (All)	Medium to Heavy	Hot-Pack	5 minutes
Cherries	Medium to Heavy	Hot-Pack	10 minutes
		Cold-Pack	20 minutes
Currants	Medium to Heavy	Hot-Pack	5 minutes
		Cold-Pack	20 minutes
Figs	Medium to Heavy	Hot-Pack	30 minutes

PRODUCT	SYRUP	PACK	WATER BATH PROCESS AT BOILING
Grapes	Light to Medium	Hot-Pack	5 minutes
		Cold-Pack	20 minutes
Peaches	Heavy to Extra Heavy	Hot-Pack	10 to 20 minutes
		Cold-Pack	20 to 35 minutes
Pears	Light to Medium	Hot-Pack	20 to 25 minutes
Pineapple	Light to Medium	Hot-Pack	15 minutes
		Cold-Pack	30 to 40 minutes
Plums	Medium to Heavy	Hot-Pack	10 minutes
		Cold-Pack	20 minutes
Rhubarb	Heavy	Hot-Pack	5 minutes
		Cold-Pack	20 minutes
Tomatoes	Tomato Juice	Cold-Pack	45 minutes

SYRUP FOR FRUITS

SYRUP	AMOUNT OF SUGAR TO LIQUID	TO MAKE
Light	1 part sugar to 3 parts water or fruit juice	Mix and boil until sugar dissolves
Medium	1 part sugar to 2 parts water or fruit juice	Keep hot
Heavy	1 part sugar to 1 part water or fruit juice	
Extra Heavy	2 parts sugar to 1 part water or fruit juice	
Corn Syrup	1 pt. corn syrup, 1 pt. sugar, ½ pt. water, ⅛ teaspoon salt	

The type of syrup used may be varied to suit the individual taste. All fruits may be canned with plain water, or with unsweetened fruit juice. The method of preparing and processing is the same as when syrup is used. From ¾ to 1 cup syrup is usually needed for each quart of fruit.

HOME-FREEZING IS THE NEW SCIENCE

Home-freezing has won many home canners to its use. Its methods are simple, but must be handled precisely. There is no mystery about the process, but each step must be followed with the utmost exactness.

VEGETABLES · FOR · FREEZING

VEGETABLE	HOW TO PREPARE	TIME TO SCALD*
Asparagus.....	Wash well and cut into desired lengths. Sort into 3 groups, according to thickness of stalk. Scald, chill, and pack.	2 to 4 minutes in boiling water, according to size of stalk.
Beans, lima....	Shell, wash, and sort according to size. Scald and chill. Then sort out any beans that have turned white; these may be cooked or canned. Pack.	2 to 3 minutes in boiling water, according to size.
Beans, snap....	Wash well, cut off stem and tips. Leave whole, slice, or cut into pieces. Scald, chill, and pack.	2 to 3 minutes in boiling water.
Broccoli.......	Cut off large leaves and tough stalks. Wash well and soak, heads down in salted water (4 teaspoons salt to 1 gallon cold water), for about ½ hour. Split lengthwise so heads are not more than 1½ inches across. Scald, chill, and pack.	5 minutes in steam, or 4 minutes in boiling water.
Cauliflower	Select white, compact heads. Break flowerlets into pieces about 1 inch across. Wash, scald, chill, and pack.	3 minutes in boiling water.

* If you live 5,000 or more feet above sea level, scald the vegetables 1 minute longer. Reprinted from "Home Freezing of Fruits and Vegetables," published by the U. S. Dept. of Agriculture.

---

1. *Careful selection:* The quality which comes out of a quick-frozen product is the same quality which went into it. Quick-freezing does not change the quality of the raw material. Choose the very best quality available for quick-freezing. Fruits and vegetables should be ripe, mature, free from blemish or damage. Certain varieties are best. Read U. S. Department of Agriculture Bulletins on Varieties for Quick-Freezing.
2. *Proper preparation:* Each equipment manufacturer offers precise directions for the best results. The scalding (blanching) of vegetables is a process

VEGETABLE	HOW TO PREPARE	TIME TO SCALD*
Corn, on cob...	Husk, remove silk and trim off bad spots. Wash. Scald, chill, and pack.	7 minutes in boiling water for slender ears; 9 minutes for medium; 11 minutes for large, thick ears.
Corn, whole-grain	Husk, remove silk, and trim off bad spots. Wash and sort according to thickness of ear. Scald, then chill. Cut kernels off cob. Pack.	5 to 7 minutes in boiling water.
Greens........	Wash well, remove imperfect leaves and large, tough stems. Scald, chill, and pack.	1 to 2 minutes in boiling water.
Peas..........	Shell, sort out immature and tough peas, wash, scald, chill, and pack.	1 minute in boiling water.
Peppers, green and pimiento	Wash. Remove seeds and slice or cut as desired. Scald and chill. Pack in brine of 1 teaspoon salt to 1 cup cold water.	2 minutes in boiling water.
Soybeans......	Boil in pods for 5 minutes. Chill. Squeeze beans out of pods. Wash, drain, and pack.	No additional scalding required.

* If you live 5,000 or more feet above sea level, scald the vegetables 1 minute longer. Reprinted from "Home Freezing of Fruits and Vegetables," published by the U. S. Dept. of Agriculture.

---

which differs with each vegetable. Study directions before starting.

3. *Chill foods before freezing:* Fruits may be put into freezer when they reach room temperature. Vegetables which have been scalded must be cooled down with ice water. With meats, poultry, game and fish, all animal heat must be removed from food before it is put into freezer. The family refrigerator may be used to chill small quantities of meat and poultry.

4. *Proper packaging:* Don't economize on packages. The package must be moisture-vaporproof. There are a great number of packaging materials avail-

able for home-freezing. Locker paper, cellophane, cartons with cellophane-lined bags, moisture-vaporproof boxes, self-sealing bags, and aluminum foil.

5. *Prompt freezing essential:* The science is so new that a final word of caution is not amiss. Speed is vital in preparation of the food. Prepare no more of the food to be frozen than the compartment will hold. The quicker the package of food gets into the freezer, the better.

DEFROSTING QUICK-FROZEN FOOD

Probably the least understood step in the entire process of quick-frozen food and its consumption is the final step of thawing or defrosting before cooking and eating.

All frozen foods should be used immediately after thawing. Because freezing tends to soften the cell structure of some foods, such as fruits, the thawed foods should be used quickly.

Quick-frozen vegetables should usually be cooked in their frozen state, without thawing, or only partially thawed. Fruits should always be thawed in the container in which they were frozen. The carton should remain closed until fruit is almost thawed. Between 2 and 3 hours at room temperature is usually sufficient. Roasts may be cooked directly from the frozen state, or they may be allowed to thaw first. Steaks are juicier and better-flavored if broiled direct from frozen state, allowing an extra 20 to 30 minutes cooking time.

Users of quick-frozen foods are urged to read directions on packages of commercially-prepared foods. If home-freezing is done, excellent booklets are published by State Agricultural Colleges and by manufacturers of equipment.

HOW TO PREPARE VEGETABLES FOR FREEZING

Wash vegetables thoroughly. It is important that all loose dirt be completely removed. Scrupulous cleanliness is the secret of successful quick-freezing. Prepare vegetables as if ready to cook for dinner. Plunge into boiling water to blanch, or blanch over steam (5 minutes is the maximum time for blanching—exceptions indicated on chart). Immediately after blanching, plunge into large pan of ice water to quick-cool for 1 minute. Pack vegetables in cartons, and seal as described above.

HOW TO PREPARE FRUITS FOR FREEZING

Wash fruits thoroughly, remove all skins and stems. In the case of berries and cherries, remove caps and stems after washing. Do not blanch fruits. Pack them in glass jars or in cartons. Fruits may be packed with dry sugar or cold syrup. When fruit is stored in cold-freeze lockers, care must be taken to see that the fruit is stored in an upright position.

COLD SYRUP

1 cup sugar   1¼ cups water

Mix sugar and water together. Bring to boil and cook until syrup is thick. Chill thoroughly before pouring over fruit. Pack fruit loosely in glass jars, or in cartons. Add syrup and seal.

DRY SUGAR

If dry sugar is used, sprinkle fruit lightly with sugar. Stir sugar through fruit. Place in cartons and seal.

POINTERS ON PREPARATION OF QUICK-FROZEN FOODS

The actual preparation of quick-frozen foods for the table is somewhat different from the preparation of fresh or canned food. Quick-frozen vegetables such as spinach, corn and peas, may be cooked without defrosting. Other vegetables give more satisfactory results if they are partially thawed. This is especially true of lima beans.

PEAS

1 pkg. quick-frozen peas   ½ cup boiling water
                                    ½ tsp. salt

Drop peas into salted water. (If they are in solid block, separate carefully with silver fork.) Cover and simmer gently 5 to 8 minutes or until tender.

CORN

1 pkg. quick-frozen cut corn   ⅓ cup boiling water or milk

Drop corn into water or milk and simmer 2 minutes. Corn on the cob must be defrosted before cooking. (No salt is used for corn.)

SPINACH

1 pkg. quick-frozen spinach   ¼ cup boiling water
                                    ½ tsp. salt

If the spinach is in a solid block, it may be cut into cubes with a heavy knife before cooking. Drop spinach into salted water, cover. Simmer 5 minutes.

PORK CHOPS

Pork chops may be cooked without defrosting, unless they are frozen together in a solid block. Cook as for fresh pork chops; but if hard-frozen, cook twice as long. Use a low heat to prevent drying out.

FRUIT	HOW TO PREPARE	HOW TO PACK
Apples.......	Peel, core, and cut into sections of uniform thickness (about 12 sections for medium-sized, more for larger apples to insure sufficient scalding). Scald apples in steam or boiling water 1½ to 2 minutes to prevent darkening. Or if syrup is used for packing you can slice apples directly into it.	Pack in 1 part by weight of sugar to 3 or 4 parts by weight of fruit (1 cup sugar to 5 cups fruit); or in syrup to cover (3 to 4 cups sugar to 4 cups water).
Apricots......	Sort for ripeness. Wash, halve, pit, and cut in sections. To keep from darkening, dip for 1 to 2 minutes in a solution of ¼ teaspoon citric acid dissolved in 1 quart water or use ascorbic acid (see How to Pack).	*With citric acid.* Pack in 1 part by weight of sugar to 3 or 4 parts by weight of fruit (1 cup sugar to 4½ to 6 cups fruit); or in syrup to cover (3 or 4 cups sugar to 4 cups water). *With ascorbic acid.* Put apricots directly into sugar syrup to which has been added ¼ teaspoon ascorbic acid to each 1 to 1½ cups syrup.
Berries (except blueberries and strawberries).....	Pick over, wash, drain well. Do not wash raspberries unless necessary.	Pack without sugar; or pack in 1 part by weight of sugar to 4 parts by weight of fruit (1 cup sugar to 6 cups fruit); or in syrup to cover (3 cups sugar to 4 cups water).
Blueberries...	Pick over, wash, drain well.	Pack in 1 part by weight of sugar to 4 parts by weight of fruit (1 cup sugar to 6 cups fruit); or in syrup to cover (3 cups sugar to 4 cups water; or pack without sugar).
Cherries, sour..	Wash, drain, and pit.	Pack in 1 part by weight of sugar to 3 or 4 parts by weight of fruit (1 cup sugar to 4 to 5 cups fruit).
Cherries, sweet	Wash and drain. Pit or not, as desired.	*Pitted cherries.* Pack in 1 part by weight of sugar to 4 parts by weight of fruit (1 cup sugar to 5 cups fruit). *Whole cherries.* Pack in syrup to cover (3 cups sugar to 4 cups water with ¼ teaspoon ascorbic acid added to each 1 to 1½ cups syrup).
Cranberries...	Pick over and wash.	Pack without sugar; or pack in 1 part by weight of sugar to 3 or 4 parts by weight of berries (1 cup sugar to 6 to 8 cups berries; or pack in syrup to cover (4 cups sugar to 4 cups water).
Figs.........	Sort, wash, remove stems. Leave whole, halve, or slice.	Pack without sugar; or pack in 1 part by weight of sugar to 4 parts by weight of fruit (1 cup sugar to 6 cups fruit); or pack in syrup to cover (3 cups sugar to 4 cups water).

FRUIT	HOW TO PREPARE	HOW TO PACK
Peaches (freestone) and nectarines ..	Sort, pit, peel (skins may be loosened by scalding whole peaches 15 to 30 seconds in boiling water). Cut in sections. To keep from darkening, dip sections for 1 to 2 minutes in a solution of ¼ teaspoon citric acid dissolved in 1 quart water or use ascorbic acid (see How to Pack).	*With citric acid.* Pack in 1 part by weight of sugar to 3 or 4 parts by weight of fruit (1 cup sugar to 4½ to 6 cups fruit); or in syrup to cover (3 cups sugar to 4 cups water). *With ascorbic acid.* Put peaches directly into sugar syrup to which has been added ¼ teaspoon ascorbic acid for each 1 to 1½ cups syrup.
Plums and prunes	Sort, wash, halve, and pit.	Pack in 1 part by weight of sugar to 3 to 5 parts by weight of fruit (1 cup sugar to 4½ to 10 cups fruit); or in syrup to cover (3 to 5 cups sugar to 4 cups water, with ¼ teaspoon ascorbic acid added to each 1 to 1½ cups syrup).
Rhubarb	Wash, trim, and cut stalks into 1-inch pieces.	Pack without sugar; or pack in 1 part by weight of sugar to 4 or 5 parts by weight of rhubarb (1 cup sugar to 5 to 6 cups fruit); or in syrup to cover (3 cups sugar to 4 cups water).
Strawberries..	Cap and sort, wash, and drain well. Leave berries whole, or slice.	Pack in 1 part by weight of sugar to 3 or 4 parts by weight of fruit (1 cup sugar to 5 to 8 cups fruit). Pack tightly so juice covers berries.

Head space:

In carton or bag, leave ½ inch head space if packed without liquid. Leave 1 inch head space if packed with syrup, or for purées or crushed fruits. In glass jars or tin cans leave 1½ inches head space.

Packing fruit in dry sugar:

When packing fruits in dry sugar, be sure to mix thoroughly until all sugar is dissolved and sufficient syrup is formed to cover the fruit when packed. If necessary press fruit down in package until syrup covers the fruit.

Reprinted from U. S. D. A. pub. "Home Freezing of Fruits and Vegetables."

Pickled assortment. Real old-fashioned pickled vegetables and fruits are best canned at home.

STUFFED PORK CHOPS

4 quick-frozen pork chops
1½ cups mashed potatoes

1 cup chopped tart apples
½ tsp. salt
¼ tsp. pepper

Partially defrost chops and slit lengthwise through center to make a pocket to hold stuffing. Combine all ingredients and fill pockets of chops. Hold edges of chops together with skewers or toothpicks. Place chops in greased baking pan, add 1 cup milk. Bake covered, in moderate oven (350° F.) 1½ hours.

SMOTHERED CHICKEN

1 quick-frozen fryer
¼ cup flour

1 tsp. salt
½ tsp. pepper
½ pt. sour cream

Partially defrost chicken. Cut in serving pieces. Dredge each piece in seasoned flour. Sauté until golden brown. Add cream, cover tightly, and bake in moderate oven (350° F.) 1½ hours.

SPINACH SOUFFLÉ

1 pkg. quick-frozen spinach
2 Tbsp. minced onion
3 Tbsp. butter
3 Tbsp. flour

¼ tsp. salt
¼ tsp. pepper
1 cup milk
3 eggs

Defrost, cook, and drain spinach. If there is any liquid left, add to milk to measure 1 cup of liquid. Sauté onion in butter. Add flour, cook until smooth and bubbly. Add liquid and stir until thick. Add seasonings and cool slightly. Separate egg yolks and whites. Add egg yolks, beat well, then fold in stiffly-beaten egg whites. Turn into well-greased baking dish, place in pan of hot water, and bake in moderate oven (350° F.) 1 hour, or until firm to touch.

SLICED STRAWBERRIES

If strawberries are to be served plain, defrost. Leave package unopened in refrigerator 4 hours, or at room temperature 2 hours, or under running cold water 45 minutes.

If strawberries are to be used in cooking, they need to be defrosted just sufficiently to handle them. Cut above time in half.

PEACHES

If peaches are to be served raw, defrost. Leave package unopened and let stand in refrigerator 5 to 6 hours, or at room temperature 3 to 4 hours, or under running cold water 45 minutes. If used for cooking, proceed as for strawberries.

STRAWBERRY-PEACH COMPOTE

1 pkg. quick-frozen peaches   1 pkg. quick-frozen strawberries
                                   2 Tbsp. lemon juice

Defrost as directed. Add lemon juice. Serve at once.

PINEAPPLE UPSIDE DOWN CAKE

Substitute 4 slices quick-frozen pineapple for canned pineapple. Defrost, and follow recipe for Upside Down Cake in Chapter 20.

SUGGESTED MENUS FOR QUICK-FROZEN FOODS

DINNER MENU

Smothered Chicken—Gravy
Mashed Sweet Potatoes
Asparagus and Endive Salad with French Dressing
Fruit Compote
Coffee

LUNCHEON MENU

Stuffed Pork Chops—Baked Potatoes
Mixed Green Salad with French Dressing
Pineapple Upside Down Cake

SUPPER MENU

Spinach Soufflé with Broiled Bacon
Carrots and Peas
Prune Whip—Chocolate Cup Cakes with Frosting

25.

CASSEROLE AND
BUDGET COOKERY

ONE-DISH MEALS

WHILE the earthenware cooking dish known as a casserole is used in many lands, its popularity in America is fairly recent. But once a housewife buys a casserole, or two or three, her interest becomes unbounded, and her devotion great. For after one or two initial attempts, she realizes that casserole cookery offers a great variety of those "extras" necessary for interesting and attractive meals.

Casserole cookery enables the thrifty housewife to use appetizing bits of meat, small quantities of vegetables, a meat bone or two, and extra gravy from a roast. Many a good soup is made from these tiny portions of food. Soup, stews, ragouts, entrées which feature dried peas or beans, cheese, eggs, macaroni products—for all these types of economical cookery, the casserole is the dish!

Many people think of a casserole as being only one large round baking dish. But the chinaware shops show a great variety of these dishes, other than the one utility baker. The casseroles are round or oval, covered or uncovered, individual sizes or large family sizes; some are without handles, others have good substantial handles. Deep pots suitable for soups are favorites, but so are shallow ones for fish or egg entrées.

The American nation is developing a lively interest in the nutritive value of the food its eats, and casserole cookery preserves the juices of the cooked food perfectly.

Still another reason for the interest in casserole cookery is the steadily increasing interest in efficient kitchen operations, due in large part to the fact that so many business women (and men, too) like to come home to their own kitchen and have the joy of preparing their own meals. Casserole cookery is a boon to the person who combines a career with home life!

One word of warning must be written at this point—a casserole, whether glass or earthenware, must be handled with care. Every new type of dish introduced for sale generally carries a printed list of special directions for its care and use.

GENERAL POINTERS ON CASSEROLE CARE

1. When using a top-of-the-stove casserole, heat the dish gradually over low heat. Usually an asbestos mat must be placed under the dish.
2. Never heat an empty dish—put a little hot water in it.
3. If the food is cold, place it in a cold casserole.
4. If the food is hot, first scald the casserole with boiling water.
5. Never pick up a hot casserole with a damp cloth.
6. Never place a hot casserole on a wet table or sink top.

CASSEROLE MENUS

NO. 1

Lentil Soup in Casserole
Romaine, endive, avocado pear salad
with French Dressing
Lemon Soufflé
Custard Sauce
Beverage

NO. 2

Tomato Juice Cocktail—lemon wedges
Crab Meat Casserole
Stuffed Baked Potatoes
Asparagus Tip Salad
Honey Dew Melon
Beverage

NO. 3

Broiled Half Grapefruit
Macaroni and Chipped Beef in Casserole
Tossed Green Salad
Garlic French Dressing
Baked Apples
Beverage

NO. 4

Fruit Cup
Casserole of Beef with Vegetables
Wedges of Iceberg Lettuce
Hearts of Celery
Orange Chiffon Pie
Beverage

NO. 5

Jellied Beef Bouillon (canned)
Casserole of Ham and Rice
Buttered Green Peas
(quick frozen)
Compote of Fruit
Chocolate Cup Cakes
Beverage

NO. 6

Brunswick Stew in Casserole
Green Salad
(with diced tomatoes and celery)
French Dressing
Chocolate Ice Cream
Chocolate Sauce

Recipes for other casserole dishes which are excellent stand-bys may be found in the following chapters:

8. Eggplant in casserole
8. Potatoes au gratin
8. Scalloped potatoes
9. Cheese supper dish
9. Baked eggs
9. Eggs Benedict
10. Casserole of beef
10. Braised short ribs of beef
10. Casserole of ham and rice
10. Lamb en casserole
10. Meat pie
10. Braised oxtail
10. Sausage casserole

10. Veal-ham loaf
11. Brunswick stew in casserole
11. Chicken and noodle casserole
11. Casserole fowl with vegetables
12. Crab meat casserole
12. Shrimp and olive casserole
12. Tuna fish supreme
20. Apple brown Betty
20. Lemon pudding
20. Lemon soufflé
20. Old-fashioned rice pudding
20. Vanilla soufflé

Pizzini, little tomato pies adapt themselves with ease to casserole service. Cottage cheese and mozzarella are used in the spicy tomato filling.

Lamb stew acquires St. Patrick's Day glamor when offered with biscuit shapes of shamrocks in individual casserole dishes.

A DIET ON A BUDGET

How often one hears a young homemaker sigh for a larger food budget so that the family can have better meals. This is a popular idea, but not one which holds up in the light of facts. Menus for a day or a week, no matter which, depend more upon a knowledge of food values than upon the amount of money for spending.

The recipes given below illustrate how a family operating on a moderate food budget may enjoy excellent meals.

MAIN COURSE DISHES

BEEF AND KIDNEY PIE

1 lb. kidneys (beef, pork, veal or lamb)	2 Tbsp. drippings or other fat
1 lb. beef	6 potatoes, cut in small pieces
6 onions	1 turnip, sliced
6 carrots	4 cups meat stock
	5 Tbsp. flour
	5 Tbsp. hot drippings

Remove outside membrane and fat from kidneys. Split lengthwise and take out fibrous part with a sharp pointed knife. Soak in cold salted water 1 hour or more. Chop onions and carrots, and brown in drippings or other fat. Add beef. Sear well on both sides. Cover with boiling water, add salt and pepper, and simmer until tender. During last half hour cook kidneys, potatoes and turnip with the beef. Remove beef and kidneys from liquid, and cut in small pieces. Make a gravy by thickening the meat stock with flour blended with hot drippings. Stir until thickened. Season to taste. Place all the meat, vegetables and gravy in a deep baking dish. *4 servings.*

Topping

1 cup flour	2 tsp. baking powder
1½ Tbsp. shortening	½ tsp. salt
	⅓ cup water

Combine ingredients. Roll out crust and place on top of baking dish. Bake 20 minutes in hot oven (450° F.) until browned.

When the heat has everyone feeling down and out and the budget is not too chipper either, perk up with an informal picnic meal of varied cold cuts, olives, scallions, and cottage cheese.

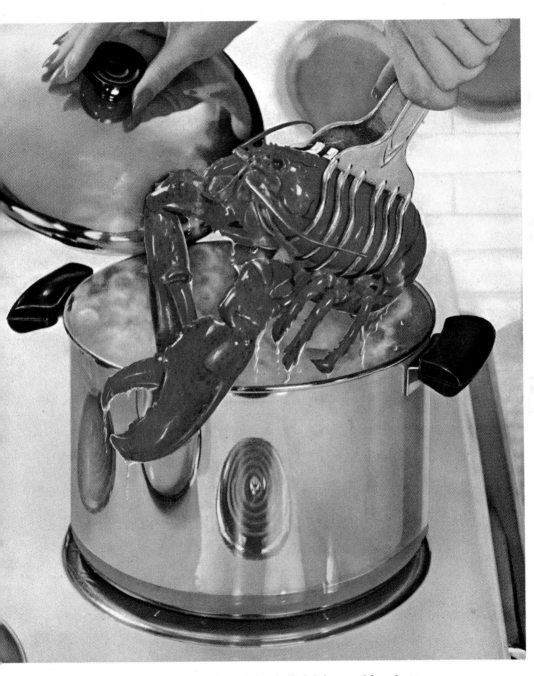

Be it Lobster à la Newburg or just plain, boiled lobster with a butter sauce, you're headed for sumptuous, tasteful eating with freshly cooked Maine lobster.

TASTE TEMPTERS FOR EVERY DAY

Shape corned beef hash into 1-inch thick cakes the same size as hamburger buns. Fry slowly in hot drippings, turning to brown on both sides; or brown under broiler. Serve as open face sandwiches on toasted buttered buns with sliced dill pickles and cole slaw. For garden sandwiches, spread bread slices with soft butter or margarine. Chop desired raw vegetables separately—carrots, green pepper, radishes, cucumber, celery, roasted peanuts, etc. Place on waxed paper. Dip bread into vegetable; cut in triangles. Arrange around cottage cheese in lettuce cups; garnish with sliced peaches.

AMERICAN CHOP SUEY

1 lb. pork butts, cut in small pieces
2 Tbsp. flour
2½ qts. water
2 onions, chopped

4 cups celery, cut in ½ inch pieces
1½ cups uncooked rice
2 Tbsp. sugar
2 Tbsp. salt

Cut a small amount of fat from the pork butts, place in a hot frying pan, and when melted, blend in flour. Add water. Cook pork and onions in this fat. When partially cooked, add celery, rice, sugar and salt. Cover and simmer slowly 50 to 60 minutes. *4 servings.*

BEEF OR PORK HEARTS WITH VEGETABLES

1 lb. heart
6 potatoes, sliced

1½ cups celery, cut in small pieces
2 cups tomato pulp

Remove all gristle from heart. Soak in cold, salted water (1 Tbsp. salt to each qt. water) for 1 hour. Parboil 30 minutes. Slice. Brown in hot fat. Simmer with potatoes, celery and tomato pulp, in water to cover, until meat is tender. *4 to 6 servings.*

CABBAGE AU GRATIN

1½ lbs. cabbage
2 Tbsp. butter
6 Tbsp. flour

2 cups milk
¼ lb. cheese, shaved or grated

Cut up cabbage and cook in salted water till tender. Make a white sauce with the butter, flour and milk. Fill a greased baking dish with alternate layers of cabbage and white sauce. Cover top with cheese, and bake in moderate oven (350° F.) 20 minutes.

MOCK CHICKEN STEW

1½ lbs. veal shoulder or neck
2½ tsp. salt
½ tsp. pepper
3 Tbsp. flour
4 Tbsp. margarine

2 cups water
6 carrots
6 small potatoes
6 small onions
6 cups hot water

Cut veal into serving pieces; sprinkle with half the salt and pepper; roll in flour. Brown in margarine over low heat. Add 2 cups water, cover and cook slowly 1 hour. Add carrots, potatoes and onions; add remaining seasonings and water. Cover and cook slowly another hour. Thicken gravy with flour mixed with water. *4 to 6 servings.*

HEART STEW IN NOODLE RING

2 lbs. heart (beef, veal, pork or lamb)
1 Tbsp. drippings
½ cup chopped onion
4 stalks celery
3 carrots
1 tsp. salt

⅛ tsp. pepper
2 Tbsp. flour
¼ cup water

Noodles

2 8-oz. packages noodles
3 qts. water
2 tsp. salt

Wash heart thoroughly, split and remove veins and arteries. Cut into serving size pieces. Brown onion in drippings, and add to the heart, with celery and carrots which have been cut in pieces. Season with salt and pepper. Cover with boiling water and simmer until heart is tender, adding water as needed. Time required, from 2½ to 3½ hours. Remove meat and thicken stock with flour mixed with water.

Cook noodles in boiling salted water about 10 minutes or until tender. Drain and pack in greased ring-mold. Turn out on a warm plate and fill center with heart stew. *6 to 8 servings.*

BRAISED OX JOINTS WITH VEGETABLES

3 lbs. ox joints
2 Tbsp. flour
2 Tbsp. margarine
2 cups water
1 cup canned or stewed tomatoes
1 tsp. salt
⅛ tsp. pepper
1 tsp. celery salt
4 cloves

1 bay leaf

Vegetables

3 cups diced carrots
½ cup chopped onion
¼ cup diced turnip
½ clove garlic
1 Tbsp. margarine
½ cup canned peas
¼ cup lemon juice

Roll ox joints in flour and brown slowly in margarine. Add water, tomatoes, salt, pepper, celery salt, cloves and bay leaf. Simmer about 2 hours or until tender. Brown carrots, onion, turnips and garlic lightly in margarine. Add to meat and cook ½ hour longer. Add peas and lemon juice during last 3 minutes of cooking. *6 to 8 servings.*

Shrimp à la Newburg with popovers, a filling one-dish main course, can be set off to great advantage by cole slaw and tart relishes.

26.

THE WOMAN
WHO WORKS

A SPECIAL Providence looks out for the modern woman who combines home-making and business or a profession. Not for her the long, leisurely hours of cooking foods which require elaborate advance preparation. This holds true also for the young mother with small children. Today's living, as handled by housewives the country over, takes advantage of modern food processing, packaging, freezing, canning and drying.

Today's shopper turns to the bulging shelves of her supermarkets where many thousands of items demand her attention. The woman who works chooses a collection of canned, quick-frozen, ready-prepared and fresh foods to stock her pantry shelves.

Following is a list of foods that will enable the modern woman to feed her family thriftily, nutritiously and in variety. There is no need for dull meals today.

PANTRY SHELF

Pancake mixes
Cake and cookie mixes
Pie crust mixes
Biscuit and roll mixes
Wafers for crumbs (vanilla and ginger)
Chocolate
Graham crackers for pie crust
Canned fruits: apples, apple slices, apple sauce, apricots (whole, halves, purées), berries, peaches, pears, pineapple, other fruits
Quick-frozen fruits and berries
Quick-frozen meats, chickens (breasts, drumsticks, thighs), turkeys (whole, halves)

Dried fruits: prunes, apricots, apples, pears

Milk: canned, evaporated, condensed, dried skim

Baby foods: vegetables, strained meats, fruit purées, fruits, junior meats (Grocers report that the senior citizens are also purchasing baby foods for their easy digestibility.)

Jams, jellies, preserves (regular sweet, or special ones for dieters)

No-salt foods for salt-free diets

Dietectic fruits and vegetables

MUSHROOMS

Mushrooms are delightful when they are added to gravies, sauces and other dishes; but they are equally delicious when served alone as a vegetable. Simmer them gently in a little butter, add salt and pepper to taste. Stuffed and broiled, they make a delicious luncheon or supper dish; and tossed in lemon French dressing with lettuce, they make a marvelous salad vegetable to serve with hamburgers.

CREAMED MUSHROOMS

1½ lbs. fresh mushrooms, or 2 6-oz. cans whole mushrooms drained	1 cup light cream or 1 cup thin white sauce
4 Tbsp. butter	2 egg yolks
½ cup sherry wine	Salt, paprika
	⅛ tsp. nutmeg

If fresh mushrooms are used, omit stems. (Save the stems for soup.) Lightly brown mushrooms in butter, add wine. Simmer gently over low heat for about 5 minutes. Add cream sauce or cream, stirring constantly. Cook 5 minutes. Add seasonings. Beat egg yolks with a few tablespoons of wine. Pour small amount of hot mixture over egg yolks. Stir vigorously. Return to mixture in saucepan, cook 1 minute. Serve at once on hot buttered toast. *Serves 4.*

ASPARAGUS AND MUSHROOMS WITH POACHED EGGS

1 pkg. quick-frozen asparagus	1 cup canned white sauce
1 cup canned whole mushrooms, drained	4 poached eggs
	4 English muffins
	Butter

Lemon Sauce:

½ cup mayonnaise	2 Tbsp. sour cream
	2 Tbsp. lemon juice

Cook asparagus according to directions on package. Drain, set aside. Poach eggs, cover. Split and toast muffins. Heat white sauce in small saucepan with liquid from canned mushrooms, over low heat. Arrange muffins on plate, divide asparagus into 4 portions. Place each portion on top of one-half of muffin. Cover with white sauce. Place poached egg on each plate on the second half of muffin. Combine ingredients for lemon sauce. Cover egg with sauce. Serve at once. *Serves 4.*

RAGOUT OF VEAL AND MUSHROOMS

2 lbs. veal (cut in thin strips)
½ cup butter
1 medium onion, sliced thinly
½ lb. fresh mushrooms, sliced
1 pt. boiling water

2 chicken bouillon cubes
½ tsp. salt
¼ tsp. pepper
Paprika to taste
¼ cup white wine

Melt half the amount of butter in skillet. Add onion. Cook slowly until onion is soft and yellow. Coat meat strips with flour. Add meat to skillet, stirring constantly until lightly browned. Pour water and seasonings over mixture. Cover tightly. Reduce heat. Simmer gently (about 30 minutes). In the meantime, cook mushrooms 10 minutes in butter. Add to skillet the mushrooms and wine, stir well, cook 1 minute. Serve over bed of fluffy rice or noodles. *Serves 4.*

CHICKEN AND VEGETABLES

4 cooked chicken breasts (fresh or quick-frozen)
½ pkg. each: quick-frozen corn, lima beans and peas
1 cup cooked, drained carrots

⅛ lb. butter
1 cup milk thickened with 1 Tbsp. flour
¼ tsp. each: oregano, basil and rosemary
1 tsp. minced, dried onion flakes

Melt butter in skillet. Add onion. Simmer 1 minute. Add corn, peas, lima beans. Cover tightly, over low heat. Simmer until steam escapes. Add ½ cup rapidly boiling water. Cover tightly. Simmer 6–8 minutes. Arrange carrots over top, cover with chicken, sprinkle with seasonings. Simmer 3–5 minutes. Lift out chicken portions, arrange on plates, add a portion of each vegetable. Pour milk into remaining liquid in skillet, stirring constantly. Let boil up once. Pour over each portion. *Serves 4.*

ROCK CORNISH HEN WITH RICE

4 Rock Cornish hens (quick-frozen)
⅔ cup wild rice or whole grain rice

2 Tbsp. butter for rice
1 pt. boiling water poured on 2 chicken bouillon cubes
¼ cup butter
Salt, pepper, garlic salt

A little foresight can result in a lavish dinner if the busy chef removes the fowl from the freezer before going to work. Once thawed, the hen and trimmings can be ready for the table in little more than an hour.

Thaw birds. Clean inside and out according to directions on package. Sprinkle inside with salt, stuff with crumpled paper toweling to dry cavity. Wipe outside of birds, sprinkle with garlic salt or seasoning salt. Truss as explained on page 133 for poultry. Melt butter in deep skillet. Brown the birds in skillet one at a time, turning carefully. Remove to deep casserole or Dutch oven. Cover tightly, reduce heat and cook until tender (45–60 minutes).

RICE

Wash rice, dry on paper towel. Melt butter in deep saucepan or skillet. Stir rice into butter until each grain is well-coated. Add water seasoned with bouillon cubes. Bring to boil. Cover tightly. Reduce heat. Cook gently until each grain is tender, but not mushy. Rice will be done at the same time the birds are cooked. *Serves 4.*

BEEF LOAF WITH CHEESE FILLING

Meat Layer

1 cup evaporated milk	2 lbs. ground beef
2 eggs	2 Tbsp. minced onion
2 cups soft bread crumbs	2 tsp. salt
	½ tsp. garlic salt

Mix milk and eggs in large bowl. Beat with egg beater until well blended. Add remaining ingredients, mix lightly but thoroughly.

Cheese Layer

4 Tbsp. butter	⅔ cup evaporated milk added
4 Tbsp. flour	to ⅓ cup water
½ tsp. salt	2 cups cooked rice
⅛ tsp. pepper	½ cup grated cheddar cheese

Melt butter, add flour, salt and pepper. Stir to smooth paste. Add milk (with its added water). Stir over low heat until smooth and bubbly. Remove from heat. Add rice, stir lightly. Add cheese.

Spread half of the meat mixture in a 9 x 5 x 3-inch loaf pan. Cover with cheese-and-rice mixture. Smooth evenly, and cover with remaining meat mixture. Bake in moderate oven (350° F.) for 1¼ hours. Cool for 10 minutes. Invert on warm platter. *Serves 8.*

BEEF PATTIES AND BROILED FRUIT

4 whole, peeled bananas
4 ground beef patties
4 slices canned pineapple

4 tsp. butter, melted
4 tsp. brown sugar
4 English muffins, split
Salt and pepper to taste

Line large shallow pan or broiler pan with layer of heavy-duty aluminum foil. Brush fruit with butter. Preheat broiler to 450° F. for 5 minutes. Broil 3 minutes, and season meat. Turn with spatula. Brush other side of fruit with butter and sprinkle brown sugar (or honey or syrup) on top. Broil meat 3 minutes more. *Serves 4.*

LAMB OR VEAL CASSEROLE

(Use left-overs of roast)

2 Tbsp. butter
1 tsp. dried, minced onion
1 tsp. thyme
1 Tbsp. dried parsley flakes
1 cup sliced celery

2 cups cooked, diced lamb or
    veal
1 can beef gravy (or 1 cup left-
    over gravy)
Salt and pepper to taste
2 cups mashed potatoes

Melt butter in skillet, add herbs and celery. Simmer gently 5 minutes. Add meat, stir well. Add gravy, cook 5 minutes. Pour into casserole or 4 individual casseroles. Top with mashed potato. Dot with butter, sprinkle with paprika. Brown in oven. *Serves 4.*

MAKE-AHEAD MEAT AND RICE CASSEROLE

2½ lbs. boneless lean mutton,
    lamb or veal (cut into ½-inch
    pieces)
2 Tbsp. salad oil
1 cup sliced onions
1 tsp. salt (or salt to taste)
¼ tsp. pepper
1¼ cups chicken bouillon

(canned or cubes or meat stock)
1 Tbsp. wine vinegar
4 cups cooked white rice
½ cup golden raisins (soak in
    small amount of boiling water
    30 minutes; drain)
½ cup thin flakes coconut
½ cup light cream or evaporated
    milk

Trim excess fat from meat. Brown meat in oil in hot skillet. Remove meat, add onion, and cook until onion is soft but not brown. Add seasonings, liquid and meat. Cover tightly, simmer until meat is tender (about 40 minutes). Remove cover and simmer until liquid is nearly absorbed. Add cream or milk. Let boil up once. Spread rice on warm platter, cover with meat and liquid. Pass raisins and coconut in small dishes. Salted nuts are also good served with this dish. *Serves 4–6.* (This dish is even better second time it is served.)

Company casserole. This hearty and unusual dish is a complete meal the busy hostess can prepare the day before.

CORNMEAL DUMPLINGS

¾ cup cornmeal	½ tsp. salt
½ cup all-purpose flour	1 egg
1¼ tsp. baking powder	½ cup milk
1 tsp. dry mustard, if desired	1 Tbsp. melted butter

Sift, measure and mix dry ingredients. Mix egg, milk, and beat lightly. Pour onto cornmeal mixture, stir thoroughly. Add melted shortening. Drop by small spoonfuls onto any hot liquid such as tomato sauce, or a bubbling hot stew, or any kettle of soup. The secret is to cover tightly and simmer for 10–12 minutes without lifting lid. Lift out dumplings with slotted spoon. Serve at once. *Serves 4.*

When dumplings are one of the family's favorites, it is a great time-saver for a busy housewife to mix and sift the dry ingredients in quantity. Measure the amount for one batch of dumplings, then multiply by any desired number. Cover tightly in a tin (an airtight one). It is then just a matter of minutes to add egg, milk and butter at dinner time.

Variation:

Dumpling may be seasoned with a small amount of any mild herb to vary the flavor. Add ½ tsp. herbs to 2 cups of dry ingredients.

FISH FILLET WITH CHEESE STUFFING

2 lbs. fish fillets, fresh or frozen
½ cup Roquefort cheese
¼ cup finely minced parsley
1 Tbsp. finely chopped onion
1 tsp. thyme
Salt and pepper to taste
Paprika
¼ cup white wine

Cheese-stuffed fish fillets made with piquant Roquefort cheese appeal to those who usually pass up fish.

Thaw fillets, lay flat, wipe them with cheesecloth. To make the stuffing, mix cheese, parsley and onion together. Add seasonings. Spread cheese mixture on fillets. Roll each fillet and fasten with toothpicks. Preheat oven to moderate (350° F.). Butter the baking dish. Place fillets in dish, add wine. Baste 2–3 times. Bake for 25–30 minutes. Sprinkle with paprika. Fish is done when it flakes easily when broken with fork. *Serves 4–6.*

BROILED HALIBUT, TOMATO SAUCE

2 halibut or other fish steaks (about 1 inch thick)	1 tsp. salt
	½ tsp. paprika
4 Tbsp. butter	1 Tbsp. lemon juice

Preheat broiler, electric skillet or portable rotisserie. Combine butter, lemon juice and seasonings. Spread mixture on one side of each steak. Line broiler pan with heavy-duty metal foil. Broil 5 minutes. Turn with spatula, and spread mixture on other side of steaks. Broil 5 minutes more. (Fish is cooked when a fork will flake the fish easily.) *Serves 4.*

Serve with your favorite tomato sauce.

Cornmeal dumplings are also good with this dish.

SALMON OR TUNA FISH LOAF

2 1-lb. cans salmon or tuna fish	2 Tbsp. lemon juice
1 cup dry bread crumbs	2 Tbsp. butter
4 eggs	2 Tbsp. flour
½ tsp. salt	1 cup liquid: milk, tomato juice,
¼ tsp. pepper	or salted water in which
	peeled potatoes were boiled

Drain oil from fish, remove any skin and bones. Flake fish. Add crumbs, eggs, seasonings. Mix well. Melt butter, stir in flour, cook until bubbly. Pour hot liquid over mixture, stir and cook over low heat until smooth. Cool slightly. Pour over fish mixture, mix well but lightly. Turn into well-greased 9 x 5 x 3-inch loaf pan. Preheat moderate oven to 350° F. Bake the loaf 30–40 minutes, or until firm to touch. *Serves 8.*

Variation:

Loaf may be baked in 2 half-size loaf pans, and one pan cooled and refrigerated for 36 hours. It may then be reheated and served with a cream or tomato or mushroom sauce. It is this kind of "trick" or short cut that saves time and effort for the busy woman.

Creole sauce seasoned with light, mild molasses and swimming with mushrooms, garlic, olives, and green pepper provides the perfect solution for using left-overs.

SALMON OR TUNA FISH CASSEROLE

1-lb. can salmon or tuna fish	¼ cup milk
1 pkg. quick-frozen mixed vege- tables	¼ tsp. salt
	¼ tsp. pepper
1 10-oz. can cream of mushroom soup	¼ tsp. paprika

Drain oil from fish, remove any skin and bones. Flake fish. Combine fish, vegetables, soup and milk. Turn into well-greased casserole. Bake in preheated moderate oven (375° F.) for 20–30 minutes. Buttered bread crumbs or mashed potatoes dotted with pieces of butter may be used to cover top. *Serves 4.*

This may be prepared 24 hours in advance, chilled in refrigerator, and reheated.

AVOCADO RING WITH SALAD CENTER

2 envelopes unflavored gelatin	2½ tsp. salt
½ cup grapefruit juice	3 cups (3–4) sieved avocados
1¼ cups hot water	Pimiento strip for garnish
Juice of 1 lime	3 cups ham, chicken or tuna fish
1½ tsp. grated onion	salad

Soften gelatin in grapefruit juice. Dissolve in hot water. Add lime juice and seasonings. Stir in avocado purée and salad dressing. Cut pimiento into ¼-inch strips and place in bottom of a 1-qt. mold. Carefully spoon 1 cup of avocado mixture over the pimiento strips. Chill until firm, pour in remaining mixture. Chill until ready to serve. Unmold onto serving plate. Fill center with ham or chicken or tuna fish salad. Garnish with curly endive or watercress. Serve with mayonnaise. *Serves 6–8.*

SHRIMP IN CUCUMBER BOATS

4 cucumbers 6–7 inches long	1 Tbsp. lemon juice
½ cup diced cucumber centers	3 Tbsp. mayonnaise
¾ lb. quick-frozen shrimp	¾ tsp. salt
1 cup celery, diced	¼ tsp. pepper
	Salad greens

Wash cucumbers and cut a ½-inch lengthwise strip from each. Scoop out centers with a spoon. Dice ½ cup of the centers and the shrimp (but save 16 whole shrimp for garnishing). Mix with celery, lemon juice, mayonnaise, salt and pepper. Spoon the mixture into the cucumber boats. Place on a bed of salad greens. Garnish each with 4 whole shrimp. *Serves 4.*

SWEET POTATO AND CHEESE CASSEROLE

2 lbs. (4 medium) raw sweet potatoes (or canned, drained)	⅛ tsp. pepper
	2 Tbsp. butter
2 Tbsp. sugar	½ cup milk
½ tsp. salt	½ cup grated cheddar cheese

Cook sweet potatoes in jackets (or heat the canned potatoes). Peel, slice and arrange in a 1-qt. casserole. Combine sugar, salt and pepper; sprinkle over each layer. Dot with butter. Add milk. Bake uncovered, 30 minutes, in a preheated moderate (350° F.) oven. Sprinkle with cheese. Bake 15 minutes. *Serves 4.*

ORANGE AND SWEET POTATO CASSEROLE

3 lbs. (6 medium) raw sweet potatoes (or 6 canned, drained potatoes)	⅓ cup light cream or top milk
	¾ tsp. salt
	¼ cup butter
¼ cup brown sugar, firmly packed	2 large oranges
	⅓ cup white sugar

Cook sweet potatoes in jacket (or heat canned potatoes). Peel, slice, and arrange in a 1½-qt. casserole. Combine sugar, cream or milk and salt. Pour over each layer. Dot with butter. Peel oranges and cut into sections, making sure that all the white portion of skin and membrane is removed. Arrange in a circular pattern over the top. Sprinkle with white sugar. Cover. Bake 30 minutes in a preheated moderate oven (375° F.). Remove cover and bake 10 minutes longer. *Serves 6.*

BELGIAN ENDIVE IN CREAM SOUCE

The average family thinks of endive as a salad ingredient, but it is unusually delicious as a hot vegetable, simply prepared.

4 heads endive	1½ cups medium white sauce with ¼ cup sliced mushrooms
1 cup beef bouillon	
⅛ lb. butter	or
4 Tbsp. buttered bread crumbs (if desired)	1 10-oz. can condensed cream of mushroom soup with ⅓ cup milk

Crisp the endive in ice water. Drain on paper towel. Arrange in single layer in deep skillet. Melt butter over low heat, add bouillon, pour over endive. Cover tightly and simmer until endive is tender but not mushy. Heat the white sauce and mushrooms (or the soup and milk), and pour over endive. Sprinkle with buttered crumbs (if desired). Place under broiler flame 1 minute. *Serves 4.*

BAKED SPINACH AND EGGS

1½ lbs. fresh spinach	¼ tsp. pepper
2 Tbsp. finely chopped onion	⅛ tsp. salt (extra)
3 Tbsp. butter	⅛ tsp. pepper (extra)
1 tsp. salt	4 eggs

Wash spinach in cold water. Drain well. Sauté onion in butter in a saucepan. Add spinach, 1 tsp. salt and ¼ tsp. pepper. Cover. Cook slowly, until tender (4–5 minutes). Chop spinach, and place in 4 individual casseroles. Break an egg over each. Sprinkle with the remaining salt and pepper. Cover with aluminum foil. Bake in a preheated moderate oven (350° F.) until eggs have set. Serve at once. *Serves 4.*

CUCUMBER, HAM, TOMATO CASSEROLE

3 medium length cucumbers (2½ cups sliced)	½ cup grated sharp cheese
½ cup boiling water	½ tsp. salt (extra)
½ tsp. salt	⅛ tsp. pepper
1 cup diced, cooked ham	1 Tbsp. lemon juice
1 cup medium white sauce	3 small tomatoes, cut in half
	½ cup buttered bread crumbs

Slice cucumbers ¼-inch thick and place in a saucepan. Add boiling water and ½ tsp. salt. Cover and cook until tender. Place half the cucumbers in a 1-qt. casserole. Cover with diced ham. Cover with remaining cucumbers. Combine white sauce with cheese, remaining salt, pepper and lemon juice. Pour over the cucumbers. Top with tomato halves. Bake 30–40 minutes in a preheated moderate oven (350° F.). *Serves 6.*

BLUEBERRY PANCAKES

Nearly everyone loves pancakes, but the task of making old-fashioned ones has no place in the stepped-up tempo of modern living. Pancake mixes do a fine job of taking away the labor and leaving the goodness. Fresh or quick-frozen blueberries give pancakes a gourmet look and taste.

1 pkg. pancake mix	1 cup blueberries

Prepare pancake mix according to package directions. Rinse berries in cold water, dry on paper towel. Stir the blueberries into the mix. Drop batter from the tip of a large spoon onto a lightly greased hot griddle (griddle is hot when 2 to 3 drops of water dance in small beads when dropped on the surface. Cook on both sides, turning when the cakes are covered with bubbles. Serve with butter, maple syrup or honey. Yield: 2 dozen.

DATE AND APPLE GELATIN MOLD

1 pkg. lemon gelatin
1 cup sliced unpeeled apples
½ cup dates, chopped
½ cup nuts, chopped
¼ cup raisins
½ cup cream, whipped

Refreshing fruit mold is decorated on top with apple slices.

Prepare gelatin according to package directions. Arrange a few apple slices in fancy mold. Add enough gelatin mixture to hold apples in place. Chill until set. Chill the remaining gelatin mixture until syrupy. Combine remaining apples, dates, nuts and raisins. Fold in whipped cream, add to syrupy gelatin. Turn into mold on clear gelatin layer. Chill until ready to serve, turn out and garnish. *Serves 8.*

PEAR AND GRAPE SUNDAE

2 Bartlett pears
2 tsp. lime juice
1 cup sugar
2 cups water
1 Tbsp. lime juice (extra)

1/16 tsp. salt
½ cup green seedless grapes
½ cup Malaga or Tokay grapes
  (remove seeds)
4 scoops lime, lemon or orange
  ice or sherbet

Wash pears. Cut in half, lengthwise, cutting through stem but leaving it attached to pear. Remove center core. Brush cut surface with lime juice to prevent discoloration. Heat sugar, water, the remaining lime juice and salt, to boiling point. Add pears. Cover. Cook until tender (20–25 minutes). Remove pears to serving dish. Add grapes to the syrup. Pour over pears and chill. Top each serving with a scoop of fruit ice or sherbet just before serving. *Serves 4.*

MINCE MEAT MERINGUES WITH COGNAC

For the hostess who wants to serve a glamorous dessert, and take the fewest possible minutes to prepare it, this is a smart, sophisticated finale to a dinner.

6 meringue shells (from bakery)	¼–½ cup cognac
1 18-oz. jar ready-prepared mince meat	1 Tbsp. sugar

Heap mince meat into shells. Moisten with 1 Tbsp. of cognac over each portion.

Flaming Desert

Moisten sugar in spoon with cognac. Warm spoon with a lighted match under bowl of spoon. As soon as it flames, tip it over into a heavy pan in which ¼ cup cognac has been gently warmed. Stir until flame dies down. Pour hot cognac over mince meat. The alcohol burns off and the delightful flavor remains. *Serves 6.*

QUICK JAM TARTS

12 thin slices white bread	⅛ lb. butter
½ tsp. almond extract	6 Tbsp. apricot jam
½ tsp. vanilla extract	½ cup cream, whipped
	1 Tbsp. confectioners' sugar

Cut 6 slices bread with a 3-inch round cookie cutter, and 6 slices with a 2-inch round cutter. Cut centers from the 2-inch rounds with a ¾-inch round cutter (to form hollow centers). Cream the butter, add flavorings. Spread on the 12 small rounds, on one side only. Cover the larger rounds with jam. Press onto each a smaller round (with cut-out center) with the butter side down. Fill the center with more jam. Bake in moderate oven. Cool. Top with sweetened whipped cream. *Serves 6.*

NEW CHIFFON PIE MIXES

The new chiffon pie mixes have opened up a whole new world to the housewife of today. The new mixes enable both the new bride and the busy older woman to turn out a parfait, a chiffon pie or a pudding in quick time and with little labor.

Festive meringues are assembled in no time thanks to ready-prepared ingredients.

CHOCOLATE CHIFFON PARFAIT

1 pkg. chocolate chiffon pie mix	¼ cup sugar
1 cup scalded milk	1 pt. heavy cream, whipped
	1 tsp. vanilla

Place the mix in an electric mixer and add milk. Turn to high speed for 3–6 minutes. (The mix must stand in peaks.) Add sugar, beat 3 minutes. Flavor the whipped cream with vanilla. Rinse tall parfait glasses in cold water. Start at the bottom of each glass with part of the mixture. Add whipped cream. Then more mixture, and continue to alternate with whipped cream until the glass is filled, ending with the cream at the top. Chill until set.

PINEAPPLE COMPANY DESSERT

1 whole pineapple	¼ cup cognac
1 cup seedless white grapes	¼ cup sugar
1 cup fresh orange bits	6–8 maraschino cherries, cut in
1 cup grapefruit bits	bits
Blanched almonds	1 sliced banana

Cut pineapple lengthwise, and keep crown. Make an incision through the length of the pineapple with a sharp knife. Cut core on each side. Slip knife underneath core to loosen it. Cut pineapple into bite-size pieces and mix with other fruits (except banana). Sprinkle with sugar. Add cognac. Pour over the mixed fruit. Cover, chill until serving. Wrap pineapple shell halves in metal foil. At serving time, take the shells from the foil. Fill them with mixed fruit and liquid. Garnish with banana, cherries and almonds. (This looks very handsome and is easy to do.) *Serves 8.*

ANGEL'S BREATH LEMON DESSERT

1 envelope unflavored gelatin	centrate
½ cup sugar	½ cup cold water
1 6-oz. can frozen lemon con-	1 cup very cold evaporated milk,
	whipped

For toppings

Chocolate sprinkles	Thinly flaked coconut
Crushed lemon hard candies	Grated lemon rind with apricot
Crushed peppermint candies	preserves

Combine gelatin, sugar and water in saucepan. Place over low heat, stirring constantly until ingredients are dissolved. Remove from heat. Stir in concentrate until blended. Cool until the mixture holds its shape when dropped from a spoon. Fold in the whipped milk. Turn into individual molds, which are first rinsed in cold water. Serve with any desired topping. *Serves 4.*

FRESH PEACH ROLL

8 peaches, peeled and halved	1 qt. lemon or lime sherbet
Lemon juice	½ cup cream, whipped
	2 tsp. grated lemon rind

Sprinkle peaches with lemon juice to prevent discoloration. Allow one peach for each serving. Arrange peach half on plate. Slice off a small piece of rounded half of peach, so that it will remain flat on plate. Cover peach with a scoop of sherbet. Place second peach half on top, garnish with cream, and sprinkle with grated rind. *Serves 8.*

GRAPES IN TODAY'S DIET

The modern housewife who is well-informed on the need of fresh fruit in the daily diet will find many uses for grapes. Some suggestions are listed here for quick and easy use:

AS TOSSED SALADS: Toss grapes with salad greens and French dressing for a delightfully different salad. This is especially delicious served in a menu in which poultry, pork or ham is the main dish.

IN CHICKEN OR HAM SALAD: Grapes add an interesting texture and flavor to these salads.

WITH FRUIT ICES OR SHERBETS: Grapes, two or three varieties, combined in sherbet glasses, topped with fruit ice or sherbet, is a delicious, light, cooling and colorful dessert to top off a heavy meal.

WITH SOFT CUSTARD: Grapes mixed with gelatin, allowed to become firm, and served in parfait glasses with soft custard, is an easy-to-make delicious dessert for guests or family.

27.

DIETS FOR INVALIDS,
ALLERGIES,
AND TEEN-AGERS

IN THE COURSE of a lifetime, a wife and mother is certain to find times when a mild or serious illness in the family requires special menus and diets for the invalid. In many instances, the diets will be carefully prescribed by the doctor. But when a small child is recovering from one of the usual childhood diseases, the physician often prescribes a "light diet" and leaves it to the mother's own judgment. Wise mothers take care that they know exactly what the doctor has in mind.

Often, too, an elderly member of the family requires special diets, and the young wife is puzzled as to what to cook. It is always important to ask the doctor for accurate orders, and not to depend on vague directions. But no matter what the illness, a convalescent, child or adult, counts his sickroom tray as the highlight of his day.

A large quantity of food at one meal is out of the question for the sick person. The stomach and digestive organs are relaxed and lack the usual vigor of good health. Therefore, five small meals, such as breakfast, luncheon, and dinner, with two in-between meal "snacks," are better both from a dietary and a social point of view. The patient has enough time between meals for the digestive juices to function, and a feeling of importance that the family is waiting on him hand and foot! As a patient comes closer and closer to regaining full health, the value of nourishing foods becomes more and more important. But appetite is usually capricious, and the appearance, taste, daintiness, and attractiveness of the meal take on the aspect of major interest.

TRAY SERVICE

As soon as the occasion arises, a homemaker will find the purchase of a light wooden tray with folding legs to be a sensible purchase. A few individual dishes, such as ramekins, custard cups, covered earthenware casseroles, and a sugar-and-creamer, are also good items to have set aside for invalid use only.

APPEARANCE OF FOOD

Use ingenuity to make invalid meals look attractive. Serve such dishes as a half cup of soup, a thin perfectly toasted slice of toast cut in strips and wrapped in a warm napkin, baked potatoes cut in half with contents scooped out, seasoned and replaced. All such aids to dainty eating help an invalid to regain appetite. If possible, put a single flower on the tray, or a tiny serving of fresh fruit.

A LIGHT DIET

Some of the foods a doctor may suggest are: toast, milk toast, coddled eggs, poached eggs, puréed green vegetables, fruit drinks, egg-nogs, and custards either baked or soft. Meats or fish are broiled, not fried.

Pay particular attention to the rules of good nutrition when planning invalid diets.

A SAMPLE DAY OF MEALS

BREAKFAST

Orange juice (serve with straws)
Coddled egg—parsley garnish
Thin buttered toast
Milk or coffee (if allowed by doctor)

MID-MORNING SNACK

Egg-nog or lemonade

DINNER

Consommé
Small piece of broiled beef—rare
Puréed green peas
Baked potato
Caramel custard

SUPPER

Oyster stew
Hot buttered whole wheat toast
Apple sauce

BEDTIME SNACK

Graham crackers
Hot cocoa

An invalid's delicate appetite is a challenge to all the homemaker's creative skill. In addition to offering light foods, and portions which are small enough, remember the appeal of beautiful color and texture combinations, dainty, special service.

INVALID-SIZE PORTIONS

OYSTER STEW

¾ cup milk

¼ cup oyster liquor

4 oysters

1 Tbsp. butter

Salt to taste

Heat oysters in liquor until edges curl. Drain well. Heat milk, add oysters, butter and salt. Serve at once.

SCRAPED BEEF

Purchase ¼ lb. fresh raw beef from upper round. Wipe beef with damp cloth, place on wooden board. Scrape meat with broad-bladed knife until tender pulp has been gathered up from tough fiber. Pat pulp lightly into small round cake, pan broil in hot ungreased skillet. Allow 2 minutes on each side.

ORANGE DRINK

1 Tbsp. sugar
1 Tbsp. water

1 tsp. lemon juice
Juice 1 orange
1 egg white

Beat egg white stiff. Mix all ingredients together in small bowl, add to egg white and pour into tall glass. Serve with 2 straws.

LEMON JELLY

1 Tbsp. cold water
2 tsp. gelatin

¾ cup boiling water
¼ cup sugar
2 Tbsp. lemon juice

Pour cold water on gelatin. Let stand until softened. Add boiling water and sugar, and let cool. Add lemon juice, strain and cool.

ORANGE JELLY

1 Tbsp. cold water
2 tsp. gelatin
¼ cup boiling water

½ cup orange juice
¼ cup sugar
1 tsp. lemon juice

Proceed as with Lemon Jelly.

FRUIT SPONGE

Lemon or Orange Jelly may be changed in texture by chilling until it starts to thicken, then whipping with egg beater until light and fluffy. A stiffly-beaten egg white may be folded in.

FOOD ALLERGIES

The importance of knowing the actual content of an individual food is readily recognized when we are told that an allergy is a complaint which affects about 68% of our population. Doctors say it is probable that many obscure complaints which defied medical assistance in the past were due to allergies.

About 10% of these allergies are food allergies. Among the most common offenders are wheat, milk, and eggs—and as they are the most commonly used foods, they are the most difficult to omit from meal planning.

An allergy to a certain food sometimes lasts an entire lifetime; so it is vital for the patient who cannot have wheat, milk or eggs, to consult with his physician to find a sound diet which will maintain health without them.

The following recipes are offered as suggestions for use, after the food allergy has been diagnosed by the physician.

WHEAT-FREE

CRACKLIN' BREAD

1 cup diced bacon or salt pork	1 egg, beaten
2 cups cornmeal (yellow or white)	2 cups buttermilk
½ tsp. salt	3 Tbsp. bacon or salt pork
1 tsp. soda	drippings

Fry bacon or salt pork in skillet until crisp and brown; strain fat. Sift together cornmeal, salt, and soda. Combine egg and buttermilk; pour into dry ingredients. Add melted drippings and crisp meat pieces, and stir only enough to dampen dry ingredients. Pour into greased baking pan or cast-iron skillet, which has been heated in the oven, and bake in hot oven (475° F.) 20 to 25 minutes.

A dainty salad with cut fruits and nuts on cottage cheese should rouse a finicky appetite.

CORN OR EGG BREAD

2 cups cornmeal (yellow or white)	1 egg, beaten
1 tsp. salt	2 cups buttermilk
1 tsp. soda	4 Tbsp. bacon drippings

Sift together cornmeal, salt and soda. Stir in egg and buttermilk. Fold in melted bacon drippings. Pour into greased baking pan or cast iron skillet, which has been heated in the oven. Bake in hot oven (475° F.) 20 to 25 minutes.

OATMEAL PORRIDGE

2 cups oats (quick or regular, uncooked)	4 cups water or 2 cups water and 2 cups milk, if not on milk-free diet
1 tsp. salt	

Slowly stir rolled oats into briskly boiling salted water. Cook, stirring occasionally for 2½ minutes (quick), 5 minutes (regular), or longer. Turn off heat and let stand for 5 minutes in pan before serving.

Double Boiler Method: Slowly stir rolled oats, quick or regular, into briskly boiling salted water in top part of double boiler. Cook over direct heat for 2 minutes, stirring occasionally. Cover and place over boiling water. Cook 10 minutes (quick), 15 minutes (regular), or longer. Let stand in pan until served.

PRUNE-OAT WHIP

1½ cups cooked prunes (½ lb. dried)	¼ cup milk or cream
	¼ tsp. cinnamon
¾ cup cooked oats (quick or regular)	Dash of salt
	3 Tbsp. sugar
	1 egg white

Remove pits from prunes; mash the prunes. Add cooked and cooled oatmeal, milk, cinnamon, salt, and half the sugar. Beat egg white until stiff, add remaining sugar gradually; fold into prune mixture. Chill thoroughly and serve plain or with whipped cream.

RAISIN BREAD

2 eggs	½ tsp. soda
1¼ cups milk	2 tsp. baking powder
¼ cup mild molasses	1 tsp. salt
2½ cups oats (quick or regular, uncooked)	1 cup raisins, dates or chopped prunes
1 cup cornmeal	2 Tbsp. melted shortening

Beat egg until light and fluffy; add milk and molasses, mixing well. Grind oats with fine blade of food chopper. Measure 2 cups of the ground oats, and mix together with cornmeal, soda, baking powder, and salt; mix with raisins. Add to egg mixture, stirring only enough to combine. Fold in cooled shortening. Bake in a waxed paper-lined bread pan (4½ x 8½ inches), in moderate oven (350° F.) 1 hour. Cool on wire rack and store in bread box one day before slicing.

WHEAT- AND EGG-FREE

PRUNE PUDDING

½ cup barley	2 Tbsp. melted butter or fortified
1 qt. cold water	margarine
2 tsp. salt	¼ cup sugar
1 cup milk	1 tsp. cinnamon
	1 cup cooked prunes, chopped

Soak barley in cold water overnight. Add salt to barley and water, and bring to a boil. Cook for 45 minutes. Add milk, melted margarine, sugar, cinnamon and prunes. Pour into a greased baking dish and bake in moderate oven (350° F.) 45 minutes. Serve either hot or cold with cream.

WHEAT- AND MILK-FREE

GINGER PUDDING

2 eggs	2 cups oats (quick or regular,
⅓ cup sugar	uncooked)
½ cup mild molasses	½ tsp. salt
¼ cup shortening	¼ tsp. allspice
½ cup hot water	½ tsp. cinnamon
1 tsp. soda	½ tsp. ginger

Beat eggs until light; add sugar, continuing to beat until fluffy; add molasses. Melt shortening in hot water and add to egg mixture. Mix together oats, soda, salt, and spices until thoroughly blended; add to above mixture, stirring lightly. Place in a greased baking dish (1½ qt. size), and bake in a moderate oven (350° F.) 25 minutes. Serve warm or cold with lemon sauce.

BUTTERSCOTCH LACE COOKIES

2 Tbsp. shortening	¼ tsp. salt
1 cup brown sugar	1 Tbsp. baking powder
2 eggs	2 cups oats (quick or regular,
¼ tsp. vanilla	uncooked)
¼ tsp. nutmeg	½ cup chopped raisins

Cream shortening; add sugar gradually and cream well. Beat in eggs until light and fluffy. Add vanilla. Mix nutmeg, salt, and baking powder with oats, and add to first mixture. Add raisins. Drop from a tsp. into a greased baking sheet, 2 inches apart. Bake in moderate oven (350° F.) 10 to 12 minutes. Remove from sheets immediately.

OATMEAL GINGER COOKIES

½ cup mild molasses	¼ cup sugar
¼ cup shortening	1 tsp. ginger
2½ cups oats (quick or regular, uncooked)	½ tsp. salt
	¼ tsp. soda

Heat molasses to boiling point; pour over shortening in mixing bowl. Grind oats with fine blade of food chopper. Measure 2 cups of ground oats, and mix with sugar, ginger, salt, and soda until thoroughly blended. Add to molasses and shortening mixture, mixing well. Shape in rolls, in waxed paper, and chill in refrigerator. Cut in slices ¼ inch thick and bake on ungreased baking sheet, in moderate oven (375° F.) 10 to 12 minutes. Remove from sheets immediately.

CORNMEAL MUSH

1 cup cornmeal (yellow or white)	1 tsp. salt
1 cup cold water	3 cups boiling water

Mix 1 cup cornmeal with 1 cup cold water. Stir cornmeal mixture into 3 cups boiling salted water. Cook 5 minutes, stirring constantly. Cover, place over boiling water, and continue cooking for 30 minutes, stirring occasionally. Chill in greased bread pan, slice, fry in hot fat, and serve with syrup. Or, if not on milk-free diet, serve hot with milk and sugar.

HOMINY GRITS

1 cup hominy grits	5 cups boiling water
	1 tsp. salt

Slowly stir hominy grits into boiling salted water. Cover and cook slowly for 25 to 30 minutes, stirring frequently. Serve as a vegetable with gravy. Or, if not on milk-free diet, serve as a vegetable with butter, or as a breakfast cereal with milk and sugar.

Double Boiler Method: For 1 cup hominy grits use 4 cups boiling water. Add salt. Place in top of double boiler, and cook over boiling water for 45 minutes, stirring occasionally.

EGG- AND MILK-FREE

MOLASSES LACE COOKIES

⅔ cup sifted enriched flour
1 tsp. baking powder
½ tsp. soda
1 tsp. salt
1 tsp. cinnamon
1 tsp. nutmeg

½ tsp. cloves
2½ cups oats (quick or regular, uncooked)
½ cup shortening
¾ cup sugar
½ cup molasses

Sift together flour, baking powder, soda, salt and spices. Mix with rolled oats. Heat shortening, sugar, and molasses in saucepan, stirring constantly until mixture comes to a boil. Pour hot mixture over dry ingredients, stirring constantly. Drop from a teaspoon onto a well-greased baking sheet, 2 inches apart. Bake in moderate oven (350° F.) 15 minutes. Remove from sheets immediately.

A perfect luncheon is cottage cheese with fruit.

HINTS ON FOODS TO USE OR AVOID IN ALLERGY DIETS

Foods Allowed in Wheat-Free Diets

Beverages................	Tea, coffee, cocoa, fruit juices, ginger ale.
Breads..................	Only those made at home without wheat, or the Swedish type rye hard.
Cereals..................	Corn, rice, barley, rye, oats.
Cheese..................	All types.
Desserts................	Ice cream, ices, sherbets. If made at home, cakes, cookies, and pies prepared without wheat; custards, gelatins, fruits of all types; cornstarch puddings.
Eggs....................	As desired, but prepared without wheat.
Meats, Poultry and Fish.....	Prepared without wheat flour.
Salad Dressing............	Mayonnaise and French dressing (if home-made).
Vegetables...............	All kinds, but prepared without wheat flour.
Sauces..................	White sauce, with flour other than wheat as thickening agent.

Not Allowed

Breads..................	Except those made at home with special flours.
Cereals..................	Made from wheat.
Flour...................	Wheat, whole wheat, gluten, commercial rye.
Pastries................	Cakes, pies, cookies, doughnuts, rolls, etc.
Miscellaneous...........	Gravies, sauces, macaroni, spaghetti, noodles.

Food Allowed in Milk-Free Diets

Beverages................	Tea, coffee without milk or cream, fruit juices, ginger ale.
Breads..................	Made at home without the use of dairy products.
Candies.................	Made at home without dairy products.
Cereals.................	All types without milk or cream.
Desserts................	Fruit ices made with water, cakes and cookies without dairy products, fruits.
Eggs....................	Prepared without dairy products.
Meats, Poultry and Fish.....	Prepared without dairy products.
Salad Dressing............	Made without dairy products. .
Vegetables...............	Prepared without dairy products.
Fats....................	Meat or poultry fats, salad oils.

Soups.................... Meat stocks with vegetables.

Not Allowed

Beverages................. Chocolate, cocoa, malted milk.
Breads.................... Unless made at home without use of dairy products.
Candies................... Made with dairy products, fudge, caramels, milk chocolate.
Desserts.................. Cakes, cookies, custards, puddings, ice cream, sherbets.
Eggs...................... Omelets, scrambled, or any other type prepared with dairy products.
Salad Dressing............ All boiled dressings.
Miscellaneous............. Gravies and sauces, rarebits, escalloped and au gratin dishes, margarine.
Dairy Products............ Milk in all forms, buttermilk, cheese, cream, butter, whey.

TEEN-AGE PROBLEMS

Many a mother knows that the problem of diet is an acute one at the age of adolescence. Sometimes it is excessive overweight, which presents a social problem for boys or girls in their teens. The advice of a physician should be sought for adolescent problems such as overweight, listlessness, skin eruptions, and others.

In many instances, the advice given is to increase the quantity of foods rich in vitamins and minerals. For such a teen-age problem, the following recipes are offered.

Some of the foods which will be added to the weekly market order in greater quantity are: legumes, dark cereals, cheese, eggs, milk. Fish-liver oils are often recommended also.

NAVY BEAN SOUP

2 cups navy beans	½ tsp. sugar
3 qts. water	1 onion, minced
2 lb. ham bone	1 pt. milk

Wash beans and soak overnight in water. In morning, add ham bone, sugar, onion. Let simmer slowly 3 or 4 hours until beans are tender. Add seasoning and milk before serving.

PEANUT BUTTER SOUP

2 cups medium white sauce   ½ cup peanut butter

Prepare white sauce according to standard recipe. Add peanut butter, stir until well blended. Cook for 3 minutes.

VEGETABLE CHOWDER

½ cup chopped onions   2 tsp. salt
2 Tbsp. butter   ½ cup chopped carrots and
¼ cup rice   spinach
1 qt. water   2 cups milk

Melt butter, add onions, and cook until browned. Add rice and water, and boil about 10 minutes. Add carrots, spinach, and salt. Cook until vegetables are tender. Add milk and cook for a few minutes longer.

LIVER WITH RICE OR POTATOES

1 lb. liver   1 medium onion
2 cups canned tomatoes   3 cups cooked rice or potatoes
                             Salt to taste

Drop liver in boiling salted water and cook 5 to 10 minutes. Remove from water and cut in small pieces. Combine with tomatoes, onion, rice or potatoes. Cook a few minutes until flavor is blended.

SPINACH LOAF

2 eggs   1 No. 2 can spinach
2 slices bread   1 tsp. salt
3 Tbsp. onions, chopped   ⅛ tsp. pepper
                             1 Tbsp. melted butter

Beat eggs. Add crumbled bread, onion, spinach, and butter. Season with salt and pepper. Add enough liquid to make mixture of consistency to form into a loaf. Place in small greased loaf-pan, and bake in moderate oven (350° F.) 30 minutes.

DESSERTS

CHOCOLATE PUDDING

1 tall can evaporated milk   4 Tbsp. cornstarch or 8 Tbsp.
½ cup sugar   flour
4 Tbsp. cocoa   1 tsp. vanilla

Dilute milk with equal amount of water. Put in upper part of double boiler over hot water and scald. Put sugar, flour and cocoa in bowl. Add small amount of scalded milk to make smooth paste. Stir mixture into rest of milk, stirring constantly until smooth. Cook until thickened. Remove from fire. Cool and add vanilla. Serve cold.

BREAD PUDDING

4 cups dry bread crumbs	¾ cup sugar
4 cups milk	½ tsp. salt
2 eggs	Nutmeg

Soak bread crumbs in milk. Add beaten egg, sugar, and salt. Sprinkle top sparingly with nutmeg. Place pudding pan in hot water and bake in moderate oven (350° F.) until firm and browned on top.

MILK WITH FRUIT JUICE

½ cup fruit juice	½ cup milk

Orange juice, pineapple juice, or the juice of cooked dried apricots, peaches, or prunes. Have all liquids cold and combine just before serving.

Meatball-vegetable soup, a treat—full of vitamins.

28.

WEIGHT WATCHING

NEVER in the history of the country has there been such a lively and active interest in the food we eat. The study of diet on the process of aging, the research into the increased mortality rate due to heart-disease, the added years of life that older people can count on, all have made the study of the proper diet a subject of paramount interest to Americans. The average length of life in the United States is 68 years, whereas in 1850 it was estimated at 40 years.

The latest figures indicate that one out of every five Americans is overweight and that most of these people want to "do something about it."

HOW-TO-DIET

Many successful dieters attribute their slim, trim figures to eating less quantities of those foods to which they are accustomed. Others live by the calorie charts, and still a third group counts its success by hewing close to the line with recipes that use the new low calorie products on the market.

But, as stated in Chapter 2 (Good Eating and Good Health), a physician's advice should always be sought before making any radical change in food habits.

Any change in weight is a long-term plan, for the sake of good health, good morale and fine spirits. Sugar has its rightful place in the diet, but not to excess. At the same time, sugarless sweeteners are found helpful to many; but here, too, the doctor's advice should be sought as some of these products might contain materials which might not be good for the dieter.

Fat is the great "offender" in modern diets, as 1 lb. of fat equals 4000 calories. Therefore, the great variety of low calorie salad dressings, and other low calorie foods on the market, have a place on the pantry shelf of the thoughtful person interested in reducing weight.

People often ask, "But which calories are fattening?" and the briefest reply is, "The ones your body does not use up." All the calories that are used up

384

by your body are non-fattening. It's true, whether the calories come from broiled steak or lettuce or apple pie.

According to the National Research Council, a daily average allowance of 2300 calories is recommended if you are a 121-lb. moderately active woman. A man who weighs about 160 lbs., the Council states, expends about 2700 to 3500 calories a day, depending on whether he leads a sedentary or an active life.

Many people ask, "How can I lose weight without counting calories?" to which nutritionists reply, "Simply turn your regular diet into a reducing diet by eating the same foods you normally do, except cut down on all portions. Simply refuse second helpings and you will find that your appetite will get along on less food."

This might come as a surprise to you, but sugar helps to cut down and curb an oversized appetite quicker than any other food. And, incidentally, there are only 18 calories in a level teaspoonful of sugar. An important fact often overlooked is that sugar contributes to the basic nutritional needs. Carbohydrate foods, such as sugar, are a primary source of energy which you need in order to carry on every life process and activity.

WHENEVER YOU EAT

Fat is stored if you take in more food energy than your body uses. A little more food each day than you need and UP go the scales! A little less food each day than you need and DOWN go the scales! Calories measure the energy which foods give to the body.

It is safe to restrict calories if your food supplies the proteins, vitamins, minerals, fats and carbohydrates you need. It is safe to restrict the total calories in your daily diet in order to maintain your ideal body weight, or to lose excess pounds.

You can eat and control body weight. The best liked foods, those most commonly used in this country, if carefully selected and used in moderation, will supply you with all the nutriments you need in the quantities you require without supplying too many calories.

WHAT AND HOW MUCH SHOULD YOU EAT?

To lose weight successfully, the total energy in your daily food should be about 1000 calories less than your daily needs to lose 1½ to 2 lbs. per week. Your calorie needs depend upon your body build, height, state of health and physical activity.

If your doctor advises you to lose weight, discuss with him how many calories you need to lose weight at the rate he suggests, and what diet is best for you. Recheck with him as you lose pounds.

Most physically active adults lose body weight when they eat 1400 to 1800 calories per day. Small, moderately active women should keep food intake near the lower calorie level to reduce. Most men and larger, more active women can reduce at the higher level.

THE FOUR NECESSARY FOOD GROUPS

You are most apt to stick with your diet if you balance and vary your menus. This is easy when you select foods from the four broad categories of:

(1) *Milk Group:* Milk, cheese, ice cream
(2) *Meat Group:* Beef, veal, lamb, pork, poultry, eggs, fish
(3) *Vegetable-Fruit Group:* Vegetables and fruits rich in Vitamins A and C
(4) *Bread-Cereal Group:* Whole grains, enriched or restored

In addition you also need butter, margarine, fats or oils; but in all these foods the watchword is "moderation." Don't exceed your calorie quota.

WHAT ABOUT SPECIAL "DIET FOODS"?

These special low calorie foods can be helpful. They will give you a bit more food with fewer calories, and the non-calorie sweeteners and low calorie dressings may make your food taste more interesting. Their nutritional value is negligible.

WHAT ABOUT REDUCING SALONS?

Exercise is of value while dieting because it tones up your muscles and tissues, and helps burn your stored calories. The regimen and support of group work-outs in a salon may give you moral support in keeping to your progam, but if you cannot afford it don't do it. Thump and bump at home, but beware of over-exertion.

HELPING HINTS FOR REDUCERS

Use cottage cheese or stiffly beaten egg whites instead of flour.

Have butcher trim off all fat before he grinds beef for hamburgers.

Choose low calorie gelatin and pudding desserts, skim milk ice cream, dietetic fruit jellies and jams, and dietetic canned fruits.

Instead of adding butter to cooked fresh, canned or quick-frozen vegetables, dissolve 1 beef or chicken bouillon cube in ¼ cup boiling water.

Use this same liquid for cooking onions until they are soft and golden.

Broil meat under broiler instead of pan-frying in butter or other fat. Or, brush a heavy frying pan or electric skillet with a film of vegetable oil.

Use 4 oz. well-chilled evaporated milk (175 calories) to replace 4 oz. of heavy cream (414 calories).

Buy low calorie cake mixes and pancake mixes.

Take time to eat and get full satisfaction from your food. You are less likely to overeat if you savor each morsel.

Eat vegetables raw or cooked in a small amount of salted water.

Eat fresh fruits or those packed without sugar. Otherwise, reduce size of serving accordingly.

Add flavor and zest to food with salt, pepper, spices, vinegar, lemon or non-caloric sweeteners. Parsley or a bit of onion improve the flavor of food.

Include foods that contain few calories: bouillon, sugar-free gelatin, plain coffee (with or without caffeine) and plain tea.

Restrict gravies, candy, cream, oils, fats, cream sauces and salad dressing.

Later in this chapter is given a week's sample menu list, to help you in planning your own menus.

LOW CALORIE SNACKS

The serious dieter has many choices at a party these days, and the thoughtful hostess provides low calorie snacks for the guests who are weight-watchers. Here are some of the appetizing snacks that look pretty on a tray:

Long, slender, crisp carrot sticks
Hearts of celery
Celery stuffed with cottage cheese
Melba toast rounds
Hard-cooked eggs cut in half, filled with cottage cheese
Fresh pineapple chunks
Cucumber slices
Tomatoes, unpeeled, cut in wedges
Red apples, unpeeled, quartered
Cauliflower flowerets, raw
Red radishes

CANAPES FOR CALORIE COUNTERS

1 pt. cottage cheese	Melba toast rounds
1 Tbsp. chipped chives	Wheat thin crackers
2 tsp. prepared mustard	Triangle thin crackers

Garnishes
Raw carrot rounds, thinly sliced	Raw onion rounds, thinly sliced
Green pepper finely chopped	Tomato rounds, thinly sliced
	Hard-cooked eggs, sliced

Mix cheese with seasonings. Spread mixture on assorted crackers. Place them in center of large serving platter. Garnish with the various ingredients.

APPETIZERS WITH MUSHROOMS DE LUXE

Low calorie French dressing	Tomatoes, cut in wedges
1 lb. mushrooms	Celery hearts
Hard-cooked eggs, quartered	Skim-milk cottage cheese

Pour dressing into small saucers, to use as a dip. Wipe mushrooms with damp towel, chill. Cut in quarters. On large serving platter arrange 5 small bowls, put ingredients separately into the bowls. In center of the platter, place the "dip" saucers with dressing.

DEVILED HAM AND CHEESE RING MOLD

1 Tbsp. low calorie lemon
   gelatin
¼ cup cold water
½ cup boiling water
2 cups creamed cottage cheese
½ tsp. salt
¼ tsp. pepper
1 Tbsp. grated onion
1 cup finely diced celery
½ cup crumbled blue cheese
2 4½-oz. cans deviled ham
Crisp salad greens
Low calorie salad dressing

Low calorie ham and cheese mold is made with spicy deviled ham, blue cheese, and seasonings. Pretty ring mold is filled with crunchy raw vegetables for texture contrast.

Soften gelatin in cold water. Add boiling water and dissolve gelatin thoroughly. Chill until slightly thickened. Mix in cottage cheese, salt, pepper, onion, celery and blue cheese. Pour half the mixture into 5-cup ring mold. Chill until set. Spread a layer of deviled ham evenly over cheese. Spoon the remaining cheese mixture over ham. Chill until set. Unmold on salad greens. Fill center of the ring with any crisp raw vegetables you desire. Serve with dressing.

COTTAGE CHEESE AND FRUIT

½ pt. cottage cheese	Crisp greens
1 tsp. minced parsley	½ banana, peeled
1 bunch grapes in season	1 cup chunks canned pineapple,
Low calorie salad dressing	drained
	1 cup grapefruit sections, drained

Arrange greens on chilled plates. Place scoop of cottage cheese in center, arrange fruits around cheese. Serve well chilled. Pass dressing separately.

COTTAGE CHEESE SALAD DRESSING

(¼ pt. equals 215 calories)

1 cup cottage cheese	½ cup water
	Chopped chives or minced parsley

In electric blender beat cheese and water. Turn to high speed for 1 minute. Season with chives or parsley.

VEGETABLE SALAD, COTTAGE CHEESE DRESSING

1½ cups canned peas	½ cup cooked corn kernels
1½ cups quick-frozen whole	½ cup sliced beets
string beans	2 cups celery, sliced

Drain vegetables. Place each vegetable in a separate bowl. Add low calorie salad dressing to each bowl. Season each vegetable as follows:

Peas: ½ tsp. each minced onion and basil
Beans: ½ tsp. each basil, thyme, marjoram
Corn: 1 Tbsp. minced parsley
Beets: 2 Tbsp. vinegar
Celery: 1 tsp. poppy seeds

Blend each bowl of vegetables, dressing and seasonings lightly with two forks.

Colorful vegetable salad arranged artistically in your best salad bowl pleases dieters and non-dieters. Try cottage cheese dressing on top.

Cover. Chill until ready to serve. In large salad bowl arrange vegetables in separate mounds. Serve with cottage cheese salad dressing.

GELATIN LUNCHEON PLATE

1 pkg. low calorie fruit-
    flavored gelatin
2 cups cottage cheese
4 melon rings, in season

8 peach halves
Crisp greens
Low calorie salad dressing
4 Tbsp. blueberries

Prepare gelatin according to package directions, and jell in separate portions in 4 custard cups. Chill salad plates. Arrange greens on each plate. Cut one canteloupe or honeydew melon into four wide slices, scoop out seeds, peel. Place a slice on each plate on top of the greens. Turn one cup gelatin out on each plate. Arrange spoonfuls of cheese around melon ring, add peach halves. Sprinkle blueberries over each serving. *Serves 4.*

BAKED PEACHES WITH PANCAKES

6 whole peaches
6 tsp. sugar
½ cup hot water

2 Tbsp. lemon juice
2 Tbsp. butter
1 pkg. low calorie pancake mix

Cut peaches in half, peel, remove stones. Mix together other ingredients (except pancake mix) to make a syrup. Place peaches in glass baking dish. Pour syrup over peaches, cover. Bake in moderate oven (350° F.) for 30 minutes. In the meantime, prepare pancake mix in accordance with package directions. After peaches have been in oven 30 minutes, remove cover and bake 5 minutes longer. Serve peaches with pancakes, either on one dish or separately as you prefer.

COTTAGE CHEESE, APPLE, CELERY SALAD

2 cups diced, unpeeled
    red apples
1 cup sliced celery
2 cups diced, peeled cucumbers
2 cups cottage cheese
½ cup low calorie salad dressing
Crisp lettuce
4 black olives

Apples, celery and cucumber neatly diced make crisp salad. Serve on lettuce. Pile on cottage cheese and a black olive to complete.

Combine apples, celery and cucumber. Mix with dressing. Arrange salad greens in 4 bowls, top with ½ cup cheese in each bowl. Divide apple mixture into 4 portions, cover cheese, and garnish each bowl with an olive.

LOW CALORIE SAUCE

(51 calories per cup)

2 Tbsp. cake flour	2 cups cold water
4 Tbsp. dry skim milk	¼ tsp. pepper
½ tsp. seasoning salt	1 Tbsp. sharp cheddar cheese,
½ tsp. monosodium glutamate	grated, or 2 Tbsp. sherry wine

Pour water into electric blender or mixer. Add rest of ingredients except cheese or wine. Turn to high speed for 1 minute. Pour into heavy saucepan, over high heat. Cook, stirring constantly, for 2 minutes. Add cheese or sherry. Serve at once.

CREAMED CELERY

4 cups celery, cut into	saucepan
1-inch pieces	1 cup low-calorie sauce
1 onion, sliced	4 Tbsp. grated cheddar cheese
½ inch boiling water in heavy	Salt, pepper to taste

Cook celery and onion covered in boiling water, over low heat, until just tender. Save liquid, and use as part of liquid in sauce. Serve as creamed, or pour into well-greased casserole, sprinkle cheese on top, brown in oven. *Serves 4.*

CREAMED CUCUMBERS

4 cups cucumbers, peeled, cut	1 cup low-calorie sauce
into chunks	1 Tbsp. hot vinegar

Cook cucumbers in small amount of lightly salted water, until just tender. Add vinegar. Place in vegetable dish. Pour sauce over. Serve hot.

MACARONI AND CHEESE

1 ½-lb. pkg. elbow macaroni	¼ tsp. pepper
¼ lb. cheddar cheese, grated	Paprika
½ tsp. salt	3 cups low-calorie sauce

Cook macaroni according to package directions. Cook sauce and add cheese, remove from heat, stir well. Pour macaroni into well-greased casserole. Pour cheese sauce over top, allow to run down sides. Bake in preheated moderate oven (350° F.) for 20-30 minutes. *Serves 4-6.*

ELECTRIC SKILLET

The type of utensil used has a great bearing on the problem of weight reduction. There is probably no one single kitchen appliance which offers more value to weight-watchers than the electric skillet with its built-in thermostatic control.

It lends itself to a variety of dishes and to a simplicity of preparation that is hard to excel. It broils meat with little fat needed for cooking, also does the

An electric skillet uses little fat, keeps meat juicy.

same for broiled chicken, hamburgers, frankfurters and low-calorie hot breads. A cook book of tested recipes is included in the package with each appliance.

LAMB CHOPS

4 loin lamb chops (½-1   Salt and pepper
inch thick)   ½ Tbsp. shortening

Preheat electric skillet to 350° F. Melt shortening. Arrange chops in skillet. Cook on one side until brown, about 8 minutes. Turn chops, season with salt and pepper, and cook and brown the second side. Continue cooking until the desired degree of doneness (about 8-12 minutes). If fat collects during cooking pour off as necessary. *Serves 4.*

HAMBURGERS

1 lb. ground beef   1 onion, chopped
Salt and pepper   ½ Tbsp. shortening

Add onion to meat. Mix lightly. Divide meat evenly into four parts. Shape into balls, then flatten out to ½-inch thick. Preheat electric skillet to 350° F. Brush skillet lightly with shortening. Arrange hamburgers in skillet. For rare hamburgers cook 3 minutes, sprinkle with salt and pepper, turn and cook 3 minutes on other side. For medium-cooked hamburgers cook 4 minutes on each side. For well-done brown meat on both sides, cover skillet and cook 5 minutes or until done. The time for cooking hamburgers is approximate. Actual cooking time depends on the size and thickness of patties. *Serves 4.*

LOW CALORIE MENUS

As a guide for you to plan your own menus, here is a week's list of approximately 1500 calories a day. Your physician will tell you how many calories you need for reducing your weight and then for sustaining it; however, these sample menus show how it is possible to make up a full week's list without producing a monotonous diet.

MONDAY (1516 calories for day)

BREAKFAST

½ cup tomato juice
Soft boiled egg
2 slices enriched toast
2 tsp. butter
Black coffee

LUNCH

Chicken-watercress bouillon
Fresh fruit salad:
    ½ small orange sections
    ½ small grapefruit sections
    ½ small banana
    3 sweet cherries
    Lettuce leaf
1 oz. processed cheese
1 slice enriched toast
⅙ medium custard pie
Black coffee

DINNER

Pot roast with mushrooms
1 small boiled potato
½ cup green peas
Tossed salad with vinegar:
    Lettuce
    Cucumber
    Green pepper
1 slice enriched bread
1 tsp. butter
2-3 medium fresh apricots
1 cup skim milk

TUESDAY (1479 calories for day)

BREAKFAST

1 small orange, sliced
¾ cup farina
⅜ cup milk
1 slice whole wheat toast
1 tsp. butter
Black coffee

LUNCH

Beef bouillon
Liverwurst sandwich:
    2 slices liverwurst
    2 slices rye bread

Lettuce leaf
1 tsp. low-calorie salad dressing
Celery sticks
1 medium chocolate cupcake with fudge icing
1 cup skim milk

DINNER

1 small broiled hamburger
1 small parslied potato
½ cup cooked cabbage
Spring salad:
    Lettuce wedge
    Tomato
    Cucumber
    Green pepper
    Lemon wedge
1 slice enriched bread
1 tsp. butter
1 medium fresh pear
1 cup skim milk

WEDNESDAY (1499 calories for day)

BREAKFAST

½ small grapefruit
1 soft boiled egg
1 slice enriched toast
1 tsp. butter
Black coffee

LUNCH

2 slices French toast:
    1 beaten egg
    2 Tbsp. milk
    2 slices enriched bread
Melon ball salad with mint garnish:
    ¼ canteloupe
    ⅛ honeydew melon
    Lettuce leaf
2 large oatmeal cookies
1 cup skim milk

DINNER

Tomato bouillon
2 slices roast pork
1 medium baked potato
1 tsp. butter
½ cup baked acorn squash
Asparagus-pimiento salad
1 slice enriched bread
1 tsp. butter
½ cup unsweetened cinnamon apple sauce
1 cup skim milk

THURSDAY (1452 calories for day)

BREAKFAST

½ cup orange juice
1 poached egg
1 slice whole wheat toast
1 tsp. butter
Black coffee

LUNCH

Bologna sandwich:
    2 slices bologna
    2 slices enriched bread
    Lettuce leaf
    1 tsp. low-calorie salad dressing
Shredded cabbage salad with vinegar
⅙ medium cherry pie
1 cup skim milk

DINNER

Broiled calves' liver
1 small parslied potato
½ cup cooked carrot rings
Iceberg lettuce with lemon wedge
1 slice enriched bread
1 tsp. butter
2 medium fresh plums
1 cup skim milk

FRIDAY (1560 calories for day)

BREAKFAST

1 large tangerine
¼ cup cooked whole wheat cereal
½ cup milk
1 slice enriched toast
1 tsp. butter
Black coffee

LUNCH

Peanut butter-jelly sandwich:
      2 scant Tbsp. peanut butter
      ½ Tbsp. jelly
      2 slices enriched bread
Fresh pineapple-orange salad:
      ⅓ cup pineapple
      ½ small orange
      Lettuce leaf
3 small vanilla wafers
1 cup skim milk

DINNER

Broiled brook trout
½ cup canned sweet potatoes
½ cup green snap beans
Tomato salad with parsley garnish
1 slice enriched bread
1 tsp. butter
⅙ qt. vanilla ice cream
Black coffee

SATURDAY (1479 calories for day)

BREAKFAST

½ cup chilled prune juice
1 soft boiled egg
1 slice enriched toast
1 tsp. butter
1 doughnut (no jelly center, no sugar-topped)
Black coffee

LUNCH

Frankfurter on enriched bun
Mustard
Dill pickle
Green pepper strips
½ slice watermelon
1 cup skim milk

DINNER

2 slices roast leg of lamb
Mint sauce:
    Chopped mint
    Vinegar
    Non-caloric sweetener
½ cup rice
1 large stalk broccoli
Celery hearts and radish roses on lettuce leaf
1 slice enriched bread
1 tsp. butter
1 slice golden pound cake
1 cup skim milk

SUNDAY (1508 calories for day)

BREAKFAST

½ small canteloupe
1 plain omelet (1 egg)
1 broiled bacon strip
1 enriched sweet roll
Black coffee

DINNER

2 slices roast chicken
½ cup mashed potatoes
6 medium asparagus stalks
1 slice enriched bread
1 tsp. butter
Tomato salad on watercress
Baked apple with 1 tsp. sugar
1 cup skim milk

SUPPER

Bouillon with chopped parsley
Corned beef sandwich:
    2 slices corned beef
    2 slices rye bread
    1 tsp. butter
Dill pickle
½ large carrot, cut into sticks
1 slice dark fruit cake
1 cup skim milk

WANT TO GAIN WEIGHT?

For the member of the family who needs additional pounds, it is some-times a simple matter of merely adding whole milk to the meals, extra but-ter on the vegetables, cream and sugar in coffee and tea, gravy on the meat, and leaving the border of fat on the meat. Instead of the low-calorie salad dressing you may need the rich mayonnaise on salads, and perhaps whipped cream on your desserts.

However, just as the one who wants to reduce should first consult the doc-tor, the weight-gainer needs to get proper medical advice as well because some people do not need or cannot tolerate as much additional fat in the foods as others. Normally, and unless the physician directs otherwise, some fat is essential in the diet, especially to the one who desires to add pounds. The authorities in the field of nutrition think it is better to omit the fat in cooking, and enjoy the daily allowance where the fat *shows;* for instance, as on the vegetable after it is cooked, or on the bread or toast as a spread.

Pointers an gaining weight were discussed earlier in this book, and we re-fer you to the information on page 34.

Take it easy. The best homemaker is definitely not the one who runs around most. With a little planning, you can even ease the chore of doing dishes after a big meal.

29.

KOSHER COOKING

FOLLOWERS of the dietary laws of Jewish cooking have always adapted their dishes to the lands of their birth or choice, so that their traditional cooking has been enriched by the flavors of many other countries. It is possible to keep strictly in accord with the dietary laws, yet have an interesting and varied list of menus and recipes.

In the past few years, in this country, there has come about a fine spirit of cooperation between the large food and dairy companies and the housewives who adhere to kosher cooking. Over a period of time, these firms have adapted many of their products to the special needs of the kosher kitchen. Not only are bottled and packaged foods made available, because of strict supervision, but they have also added "kosher soap" to enable the housewife to attain maximum cleanliness of her kitchen utensils and dishes. Most important, the advent of vegetable shortening which is *parva* (adaptable to both "meat" and "milk" dishes) has opened up new fields for the kosher cook, and made it possible for her to use many recipes interchangeably.

Most of the recipes throughout this book may be adapted to kosher cooking; where some other fat is called for in a "milk" dish, butter or margarine might be substituted to make it suitable. Where it is desired to keep the recipe *parva,* then vegetable shortening could be substituted for either the fat or butter listed in the ingredients.

SELECTION OF FOODS

Meat and poultry, in order to be strictly kosher, must be purchased in a kosher butcher shop. In many localities, the law is stringent about this, and any butcher who professes to deal in kosher meat, but sells substitutes, is penalized. Thus, the reliability of the butcher will be the standard by which you will judge the suitability of the meat, from the standpoint of the dietary law.

Of course, there are some meats which are not permitted in kosher meals, such as pork or any product of the pork family. There are also some fowl not permitted, which your butcher will not carry in his shop. Fish has many stipulations: the kosher cook must not use shellfish (such as oysters, clams, lobsters, shrimp), nor any fish which does not have scales or fins, such as the eel.

For the strict observer of kosher rules, there are certain canned and packaged foods which might be questionable. In that case, it is best to find out from the company what the foods contain, and to discuss it with an authority on dietary laws in your vicinity.

Fish (except those not on the kosher list) is an adaptable food when you do not want to limit the meal to either a strict "meat" or strict "dairy" menu, as fish is *parva*. The same applies to fruits and vegetables, and to cereals—provided they are not cooked with some definite "meat" or "dairy" product, such as chicken fat, meat, milk, butter, or cheese. In the case of these foods, the only kosher observance is that they be clean—and that is a universal law which should apply to all food and all cooking everywhere. Eggs, too, may be used flexibly, as they are *parva*.

Meats and poultry are the foods which must follow a definite ritual, to make them suitable for kosher cooking. There may even be certain regional regulations adhered to by people of different countries, and if any such question arises, it is best to consult a local religious authority. However, following are given the basic *kashering procedures* which are generally observed.

KASHERING MEAT

To *kasher* means to remove or let out the blood. After you have bought your meat from the butcher (who buys it from a kosher slaughterhouse which observes the strict rules), you must make it fit for cooking. The meat is soaked in a pan of cold water for half an hour. This pan is used exclusively for this purpose, and no other! At the end of the half hour, the meat is taken from the water, washed off, then laid on a salting board, which is also used for this exclusive purpose. The board, if flat, should be perforated; or if a solid board, it should be propped up at one end and kept in a sloping position so that it drains off the blood. The best place for the board, therefore, is right next to the sink. Using coarse salt, sprinkle all sides and folds of the meat generously. After salted meat has drained on board for one hour, wash it thoroughly under running cold water. The meat is now ready for cooking.

The head and feet may be *kashered* while the hair and skin are still on them. But the head must be cut open first, the brain removed and *kashered separately*.

If meat, after delivery from the butcher, has been allowed to remain for three days without being soaked or salted, then it is not fit to be cooked by the usual methods of boiling, stewing or frying. It must only be broiled, over an open flame, to keep within the kosher bounds.

KASHERING LIVER

The foregoing rules for meat do not apply to liver. Cut the liver open in both directions, so that the blood will run out of the many openings, then wash under running cold water. Sprinkle it with salt, and broil over an open fire (or by gas flame). When it is seared on all sides, again let the cold water run over it to wash away any remaining blood. It is now ready to be used in any recipe calling for liver.

KASHERING CHOPS AND STEAKS

If they are to be broiled under or over the open flame, they are *kashered* by the same method as liver. But if they are to be cooked in any other way (except broiling) they must be *kashered* the same as other meats.

KASHERING FAT (OR SUET)

Remove the skin which adheres to the fat. Then *kasher* in the same way as meat.

KASHERING POULTRY

There are certain conditions which may render a fowl unfit for kosher cooking; for instance, it may have an abnormal growth in some part of its body; or it may have a damage such as a broken bone; or some organ (like the gall bladder) may be missing; or it might have swallowed a foreign object (such as a pin or needle) which is discovered inside the bird, especially when opening the gizzard. When such questionable factor is present, it is necessary to take the fowl to the nearest dietary authority who passes judgment as to whether it is kosher and may be used.

When no such question exists, proceed with *kashering* the fowl by removing the jugular vein which is found on the under-side of the neck. As the vein was severed in two (in the slaughtering process), it is important that you find both parts and pull them out. Cut off the claws of the feet, also the tips of the wings. After opening the fowl, remove the entrails. Slit the gizzard open lengthwise and discard its contents. If the heart is used, cut the tips off both ends, then cut it open, and make a further criss-cross slit over it.

After the fowl is cleaned, proceed to *kasher* it, using the same method as with any other meat. The liver is *kashered* in the same way as the liver from other animals, as described previously.

Fruit compote profits considerably from the addition of kosher honey. A fruit dessert of an attractive color and refreshing texture.

EGGS

By the time they come to your table, in their shells, they are *parva*. But eggs found within the fowl, with or without shells, are considered in the "meat" class exclusively. They, too, must be *kashered* by soaking and salting, and on the board they should be so placed that the blood flowing from the meat does not touch them.

An egg, when opened, must be clear. If there is a drop of blood in it, the egg is forbidden for use.

SETS OF DISHES

In order to comply fully with the separation of the "meat" and "milk" foods, the kosher home has two complete sets of dishes, cooking utensils, and silverware. Separate dish cloths and dish towels are, of course, a necessity in this instance. Those who are extremely strict have separate table linens; or even a third set of dishes—the *parva* set.

Soap made of animal fat is strictly forbidden in washing dishes and utensils, as it is not kosher. However, the vegetable soap which you can now buy is *parva*, and is the answer to getting greasy dishes clean.

FAVORITE RECIPES

All over the world live kosher cooks, so we cannot say that everyone uses the same recipes, even though observing the same laws of *kashering* and dietary. Luckily, for the sake of dispelling monotony in menus, kosher cooks show flexibility in adopting new recipes, and those which have become popular in certain localities. Here are some of the kosher dishes which have withstood time and geography, and are universal favorites:

CHOPPED HERRING

1 salt herring	1 sour apple
1 slice stale bread (soaked in water or mild vinegar)	1 tsp. salad oil
	Dash of pepper
1 medium onion	Hard-boiled egg for garnish

Soak herring in cold water at least two hours. Wash herring, then remove and discard head, tail, skin and bones. Place all ingredients except the oil in a wooden chopping bowl. Chop fine as possible. Remove from bowl. Add oil and mix to make a smooth consistency. Serve as appetizer, or in a salad, or as a sandwich spread. Garnish with chopped or sliced hard-boiled egg.

PICKLED HERRING

6 salt herrings (milch)	1 Tbsp. black peppercorns
2 onions, sliced	1 Tbsp. mustard seed
1 Tbsp. sugar	6 bay leaves
	1½ cups white vinegar

Soak herring in cold water at least 10 hours. Remove from water. Remove and discard entrails from herring, except the milch which is kept separate. Put herring into an earthen pot, alternating in layers with the other ingredients. Pour vinegar over all. Force milch through a fine sieve, or mash with a fork, and add to the liquid. Keep pot covered, in a cool place, for several days, or until it reaches the stage of pickling you desire. (Herring may be pickled whole, or in slices, or fillets.) Serve as appetizer, or in a salad, or in a sandwich.

CHOPPED CHICKEN LIVER

2 or 3 broiled chicken livers	Dash of salt and pepper
1 egg, hard-boiled	Chicken fat
1 small onion	Radish for garnish

Place all ingredients, except the fat, in a wooden chopping bowl. Chop fine as possible. (If you do not wish to use the chopping method, put all the ingredients into the meat grinder and grind together.) Take out of bowl, and add sufficient fat to work the chopped liver into a smooth consistency. Serve as appetizer, or in a salad, or as a sandwich spread. Garnish if desired with a slice of white radish, or with small red radishes.

STUFFED DERMA

Skin from neck of poultry (chicken, duck or goose)

Stuffing

½ cup flour	2 Tbsp. fat
2 Tbsp. chopped onion	¼ tsp. salt
	⅛ tsp. pepper

Remove skin from neck of bird, keeping it whole in one piece. Clean and wash thoroughly. Make a mixture of all the ingredients and fill the neck with this stuffing. Do not pack it tightly, as the stuffing expands during cooking. With heavy needle and coarse white thread, sew up neck at both ends with a close overcast stitch. Immerse in bowl of hot water, and when neck expands scrape off any remaining stubs of feathers. Then include neck with other poultry which is cooking, either by boiling it in the soup, or by roasting it in the oven until browned. Serve it sliced, as an appetizer, or with the meat course.

GEFILTE (STUFFED) FISH

2 medium-sized fish (Combine two different kinds: trout, pike, whitefish, pickerel, carp, or other fish you desire)	2 eggs, slightly-beaten
	¼ to ½ cup cold water
	3 additional onions, sliced but not peeled
2 slices stale bread	2 carrots, peeled, sliced
1 large onion, peeled	3 celery stalks, sliced
Salt and pepper to taste	Parsley sprigs
	3 potatoes, if desired

Scale fish, slit the under-side, and remove entrails. Wash thoroughly. Slit fish open along backbone. With small knife scrape out all the meat of the fish which clings to the skin. (Caution: do not cut into the skin.) If you want to keep fish whole, leave head and tail on, but remove backbone and save it for cooking. If fish has small bones, remove them carefully from the meat which you have taken out. Put meat into wooden chopping bowl. Soak bread in water, and when soft, take from water and squeeze dry. Add bread to fish in bowl, together with one peeled onion, salt and pepper. Chop fine. Add eggs and water gradually, during process of chopping, until they are absorbed into the smooth mixture. (To save time, fish and onions may be ground in meat grinder, then put into bowl, and other ingredients added and chopped together.) When finished, moisten hands with cold water and insert the mixture into the skin of the fish, molding it into the original shape of the fish. Cover mixture with skin.

You may prefer to arrange individual servings instead of stuffing entire fish. In that case, after preparing fish, remove head and tail (but save them); cut the fish into slices, then stuff the skin and mold each individual slice separately.

To cook, use a heavy pot. Put the 3 sliced onions, celery, carrots, and parsley, with the backbone, in bottom of pot. Include head and tail in bottom of pot, if you removed them from fish. Lay the fish on top of vegetables. Add boiling water to cover. Simmer on low fire 2 hours, with pot uncovered. Cover pot, and simmer 1 additional hour, or until fish is tender. During cooking, do not mix, but shake the pot every 15 minutes to prevent fish from sticking to pot. (If you include potatoes, peel and cut them in half, and place lightly on top of fish about ½ hour before the cooking is completed.) Taste the liquid in pot, during cooking, and add more salt if needed. Fish may be served hot, or served next day cold. It is good as an appetizer, or entrée, or in a salad.

SOUR GRASS SOUP

1 lb. sour grass (sorrel)	½ tsp. salt
2 cups raw diced potatoes	1 piece of sour salt
1 bunch scallions, minced fine	2 Tbsp. sugar
1 qt. water	1 egg yolk, well-beaten
	1 cup sour cream, if desired

Remove and discard stems from the sour grass. Wash leaves thoroughly, cut into small pieces. Put the potatoes, scallions, and salt into water. When it comes to a boil, add the grass and cook until tender. Add sour salt and sugar. Simmer 5 minutes. Cool soup, then add egg yolk and mix. Serve cold. Add sour cream before serving, if desired.

FARFEL

1 egg yolk	¼ tsp. salt
	Flour

Add salt to egg and beat lightly. Slowly add flour to mixture until dough becomes stiff and can be held in the hand like a ball. Rub the ball of dough on a grater with coarse teeth, which will produce small, unevenly-shaped farfel. Dry by spreading them on a towel or a board. 10 minutes before you are ready to serve, drop the farfel into the soup, and let it boil.

KASHE

2 cups kashe (buckwheat groats)   1 egg
1/4 tsp. salt

1 1/2 cups boiling water
1 1/2 Tbsp. fat (or butter)

Rub together the kashe, salt, and unbeaten egg. Place in a greased pot, in a moderate oven (350° F.) until browned. Add the fat. Then pour in the boiling water slowly and keep stirring. Cover and bake 20 minutes, or until it has the consistency of steamed rice. Serve in hot consommé, or as a cereal, or a vegetable.

Variation

For a main dish, combine hot kashe with sautéd mushrooms and gravy. Or prepare a three-in-one dish combination of the kashe, mushrooms and boiled lima beans.

BLINTZES, CHEESE

Batter

1 egg, lightly-beaten
1/2 tsp. salt
1 cup cold water
1 cup flour

Cheese Mixture

1 lb. cottage cheese
1 Tbsp. butter, melted
1 egg, lightly-beaten
1 tsp. sugar
1/4 tsp. cinnamon
1/4 tsp. salt

Cheese blintzes are a favorite dish. The busy homemaker can save time by preparing blintzes ahead of time, filling them with cheese mixture, and refrigerating until time to cook and serve.

Mix egg, salt and water lightly with a fork. Sift flour, and stir in slowly until a light, smooth consistency. Use small frying pan (about 6 inches) to make individual blintzes. Melt butter in bottom of pan, and when it is hot pour in 2 Tbsp. batter. Tilt the pan so that the batter will spread over its bottom surface. Do not turn batter over; let it cook only on under-side, over a low heat. Do not let it brown. When it is cooked enough to hold its shape, slide it out of the pan onto a clean towel with the cooked side down. Repeat this with batter, greasing pan with butter each time, until all batter is used up. On each blintze, place 1 1/2 Tbsp. of cheese mixture. Bend edges over the mixture, forming an oblong shape. Fold up the two narrow ends at each side. Press down tightly. Put into hot frying pan in which a generous amount of butter has been melted. Brown lightly on one side, then turn blintze over and brown on other side. Because of oblong shape, several may be cooked together in pan. If desired, 1 Tbsp. of sour cream may be placed on top of each blintze, or sour cream served separately in a dish. Provide sugar for those who like to sprinkle more sugar on top of blintze.

To save time, blintzes may be prepared and filled with cheese mixture, and kept in refrigerator, until it is time to cook and serve them.

Nowadays many markets carry excellent frozen blintzes filled with cherries, blueberries, etc., in lieu of the more classic cheese mixture.

KREPLACH, MEAT

Dough

1 egg	¼ tsp. salt
	¾ cup flour

Meat Mixture

2 to 3 cups cooked meat, ground	Salt and pepper to taste
	Dash onion juice, if desired

Add salt to egg and beat slightly. Slowly add flour to mixture until dough becomes stiff. Knead. When dough becomes smooth, roll it out thin, on a board. (Have a thin layer of flour on board, to keep dough from sticking to it.) Cut dough into 2½ inch squares. In each square put 1 Tbsp. meat mixture. Fold square over into a triangular pocket. Pinch edges of dough tightly together. Let dry ½ to 1 hour. If to be served in soup, drop into soup and boil 15 minutes. If to be used as an entrée, cook in boiling salted water 15 minutes.

KREPLACH, CHEESE

Prepare dough in the same way as given in the foregoing recipe, and fill the squares with this mixture:

1 lb. cottage cheese	½ tsp. cinnamon
1 egg, lightly-beaten	¼ tsp. salt
1 tsp. sugar	2 Tbsp. butter, melted
	Sour cream, if desired

Pinch edges of the folded stuffed kreplach tightly together. Place them in pan of boiling water. Boil 15 minutes. Serve hot, with melted butter, or with sour cream. Provide bowl of sugar for those who like to sprinkle it on kreplach.

Tuna fish macaroni salad is a delightful picnic dish of kosher tuna fish mixed with macaroni, chopped onion, and lemon juice. Each portion is garnished with sliced olives and a sprig of parsley.

KNISHES, MEAT

Dough

2 cups flour	1 Tbsp. fat
1 tsp. baking powder	2 eggs, well-beaten
¼ tsp. salt	2 Tbsp. cold water

Meat Mixture

2 cups cooked meat, ground	½ cup mashed potatoes
	Salt and pepper to taste

Sift dry ingredients together. Add fat and mix well. Add eggs and water.

Make into dough and knead until smooth. Roll dough until thin, on a board which has a thin layer of flour over it. Cut the sheet of dough into 4 parts. Divide the meat mixture into 4, and place on each square of dough. Bring dough together on top of mixture and pinch edges together. Melt fat in a shallow heated pan, and lay the knishes into pan. (In a square or oblong pan, may be laid side by side. If you use a round pan, make a circle of the knishes, inside one another.) Bake in moderate oven (350° F.) 40 minutes, or until crust is browned.

Variation

Potato Knishes are made in the same way. The stuffing, however, does not include the ground meat. Instead, increase the quantity of mashed potatoes to 2 cups and add to the mixture ½ cup of fried onions chopped into small pieces.

POTATO PANCAKES

4 large potatoes, grated	1 egg, well-beaten
For each cup of grated pulp, include:	½ Tbsp. flour
	¼ tsp. salt
	Pinch of pepper

Soak peeled potatoes in cold water about 2 hours. Make pulp by rubbing potatoes on medium grater. Drain off excess water. Add all ingredients in proportion given for each cup of potato pulp. Mix together thoroughly. (If you feel more flour is needed, add to batter gradually.) Melt shortening in a frying pan, and onto this hot greased pan drop the batter with a large spoon to form pancake. When brown on under-side, turn pancake over to brown on other side. Serve at once. Apple sauce makes a good accompaniment to this dish.

NOODLE PUDDING

4 cups noodles (broad preferred)	3 eggs, well-beaten
½ cup chicken fat	Raisins, if desired
	Sugar to taste, if desired

Cook noodles in boiling water 15 minutes. Drain. Add fat and eggs. Put into a well-greased pan. Bake in moderate oven 1 hour, or until pudding is browned on top. Sugar or raisins may be added to the ingredients, if desired. Serve hot. A hot fruit sauce is a good accompaniment.

POTATO PUDDING

4 cold boiled potatoes, peeled	3 eggs, well-beaten
	Salt to taste

Rub potatoes on grater. Mix thoroughly with eggs and salt, and put into a well-greased pan. Place pan in a wider pan, into which water is poured to reach about half way up around the pudding pan. Bake in moderate oven (350° F.) 40 minutes, or until top of pudding is brown. Serve hot.

THE WEEK OF PASSOVER

The observers of this holiday find a good deal of pleasurable excitement in changing the sets of dishes, preparing special menus, cooking traditional foods. Passover, beside its religious significance, has come to mean the marking of a new season, the advent of spring in the life of the household, and its meals bring a spirit of gayety to the family.

During the Passover, the orthodox observants change their cooking utensils, dishes, and silverware, and use those which they pack away from year to year just for this one week. However, there are certain dishes, and certain ways of *kashering* them, which make them fit for use during Passover as well as the rest of the year. This depends on the extent to which certain conditions are carried out, and each housewife would do well to get complete information on the subject from her nearest authority on ritual.

Matzos accompany this cottage cheese and fruit salad during the week of Passover.

Generally speaking, however, those foods which are leaven (or *chometz*) are not permitted on the menu during Passover, nor even in the home. This does not mean yeast bread alone, but includes other leaven foods such as those made with baking soda or baking powder, also starches and many cereal foods. Even some foods which are not *chometz* may be taboo, because they may have been in contact with leaven foods during the year.

In recent years, Passover meals have widened in scope and are not as limited as they used to be. Food companies, especially the milk and dairy food companies, and the canners and packers of certain fruits and vegetables, have set up special departments, under strict supervision, for Passover purposes. These reliable commercial firms are a great boon to the housewife who does not want her meals to become monotonous.

There are, of course, these delectable "one-week-a-year" dishes which will always hold first place in the household during Passover, and we give some of the recipes here. But the woman who takes pride in serving the unusual as well as the usual, will be able to find suggestions suitable for Passover throughout this book, and can use them to expand the limitations of the menu during this week in the spring.

BORSCHT

This is prepared in advance of Passover; that is, about 20 days ahead. Peel the beets. Place them (whole) into an earthenware pot or crock, and pour in cold water to cover the beets. Set the container in a warm spot, and by the time Passover arrives you will have at your disposal the Passover Borscht. To cook the borscht, measure out as much liquid as you will need, and heat it. For each pint of soup you allow 1 egg. Beat the yolk of the egg lightly, in a deep bowl or pan. Over this pour the hot borscht slowly, and stir. Some people prefer to include sugar, when heating the borscht, and the amount depends on your own taste. A boiled potato (hot or cold) is also favored by some as an addition to the hot soup.

FRIED MATZOS

3 matzos	¼ tsp. salt
3 eggs, lightly-beaten	Fat, for frying

Break matzos into large pieces. Dip in water for 2 minutes, to soften slightly. Drain water. Dip pieces in mixture of beaten eggs and salt. Fry in hot fat, stirring occasionally with fork to prevent egg adhering to pan. Remove when lightly-browned.

MATZO MEAL KNADLACH (BALLS)

½ cup matzo meal	1 Tbsp. chicken fat
2 eggs, lightly-beaten	Pinch of salt

Mix all ingredients together, stirring carefully. When right consistency, form into small balls. Let stand ½ to 1 hour in cool place or refrigerator. Drop in boiling salted water, and boil 15 minutes. Serve in soup, or as a vegetable with a roast (same as rice). Balls are also served as a separate dish, with hot chicken fat or gravy over them.

A truly engaging relish is cranberry relish mixed with kosher honey and grapefruit.

MATZO MEAL PANCAKES

1 cup matzo meal	½ tsp. salt
1 cup cold water	3 eggs, lightly-beaten

Mix thoroughly matzo meal, water and salt. Add to eggs, stir thoroughly until smooth. (If batter seems too thin, add more matzo meal, slowly and carefully.) On a well-greased, heated frying pan drop the batter slowly with a large spoon. When it becomes lightly brown on under-side, turn it to other side and brown lightly. Serve with jam or sprinkle with sugar, as a dessert. Or serve with a roast as vegetable, with gravy over it.

MATZO PUDDING

4 matzos	1 Tbsp. grated lemon or orange peel
1 cup matzo meal	Salt to taste
4 eggs, well-beaten	Fat for frying
1 apple, chopped fine	Sugar to taste, if desired

Place matzos in cold water for 5 minutes. Remove and drain, then squeeze dry. Melt fat in frying pan, add matzos, and stir thoroughly. Take pan off fire, and slowly add the other ingredients, one at a time, mixing carefully. Remove mixture from pan, and place it into a well-greased deeper pan. Bake in a moderate oven (350° F.) 45 minutes, or until top is browned. Serve at once. Hot fruit sauce goes well with this.

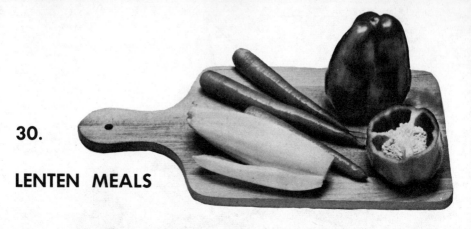

30.

LENTEN MEALS

MOST housewives look upon the preparation of meals during Lent as an extra burden and responsibility. This is largely because we are meat eaters, and the cooks of the nation have neglected the art of fish cookery. Therefore, with the advent of Lent, meals tend to become monotonous.

But this is unnecessary in our modern age. Not only is fish in season easily available, but there are also innumerable quick-frozen delicacies and canned products, which are both thrifty in price and luxurious in flavor.

Dried codfish makes wonderful fish cakes. Canned smoked oysters combine well with rice or noodles. Creamed codfish is old-fashioned, but wonderfully good, and it's definitely budget priced.

For families who have a prejudice against fish for dinner, a cheese soufflé can be prepared, or egg cutlets with mushroom sauce, or countless other cheese or egg dishes. Lent is a good season to serve hearty baked puddings with hot spicy sauces. Other good mealtime ideas center around a satisfying salad bowl.

Lenten menus may be made much more appetizing by the addition of home-made yeast breads, made from a basic sweet dough recipe.

It is a simple matter to work out a satisfying menu by using the many meat-less recipes in this book. However, for a special Lenten touch, here are a few additional menus and recipes which are colorful, nutritious and thrifty.

LUNCHEON

Tomato and Clam Juice
Baked Corn Pudding
String Beans, Baked Potatoes
Popovers
Cherry Whip with Custard Sauce

DINNER

Cream of Asparagus Soup
Fillet of Fish with canned Oyster Stuffing
Tomato, Cucumber and Lettuce Salad
Dried Apricot Pie

414

DINNER

Clam Chowder
Salmon Steak with Egg Sauce
New Potatoes with minced Parsley
Broccoli
Broiled Grapefruit with Honey

DINNER

Relish Tray: Celery, Carrot Sticks, Radishes
Stuffed Baked Fish
Broiled Tomatoes, Creamed Potatoes
Peaches in Lemon Jelly

The following recipes are planned to make approximately *4 servings.*

LENTEN VEGETABLE SOUP

1 No. 2½ can tomatoes	1 cup celery pieces
2 cups raw potato cubes	½ tsp. soda
3 onions	Salt and pepper
	Hot milk

Cook together until soft. Put through sieve. Return to saucepan and add hot milk until thin enough.

Lobster makes the Lenten luncheon a delightful affair, especially when the casserole is lobster shaped to become the conversation piece of your dinner table.

CHEESE AND TOMATO FONDUE

1 Tbsp. butter	¾ lb. soft yellow cheese
2 Tbsp. chopped green pepper	2 Tbsp. tomato juice
1½ Tbsp. chopped onion	½ of tomato pulp from No. 1 can
Dash of cayenne	¾ tsp. salt
	1 egg, slightly-beaten

Cook butter with pepper and onion for 3 minutes, stirring constantly. Add tomatoes, from which liquid has been drained. Cook 5 minutes. Add cheese, cut into small pieces, salt and cayenne. When cheese is melted, add tomato juice. Add egg. Cook for 1 minute, stirring constantly. Serve on hot rice or noodles.

OYSTERS AND NOODLES WITH CHEESE SAUCE

1 pt. oysters	2 cups medium white sauce
1 pkg. wide noodles	1 cup grated cheese
	Dash of paprika

Drain oysters from can, pick over for bits of shell. Cook noodles in boiling, salted water until tender. Add cheese to white sauce, and stir until melted. Cook oysters in sauce, over low heat, until edges curl. Pour over hot noodles, dust with paprika, and serve.

WELSH RAREBIT VARIATIONS

These recipes all combine with basic Welsh Rarebit (given in Chapter 9). However, in the following recipes, there are certain omissions from that basic Welsh Rarebit recipe, and they are explained in each case.

SARDINE RAREBIT

3 slices bread	Rarebit
1 can (3¾ oz.) sardines	2 Tbsp. chives or parsley, chopped

Make rarebit (but omit from basic recipe the salt, eggs and light cream). Toast slices of bread on one side. Butter untoasted side of bread, and arrange drained sardines on that side. Place under hot broiler, until sardines are heated and bread is toasted, about 1 minute. Place in individual serving dishes and pour hot rarebit over each. Garnish with chopped chives or parsley.

TOMATO RAREBIT

1 Tbsp. butter	Parsley sprigs
½ tsp. Worcestershire sauce	1⅓ cups condensed tomato soup
Rarebit	(No. 1 picnic can)

Make rarebit (but omit from basic recipe the salt, eggs and light cream). Melt butter in top of double boiler. Add rarebit, sauce, and soup. Heat and serve at once. Garnish with sprigs of parsley.

Baby whole carrots, cooked until just tender and then drained, are glazed in 3 Tbsp. butter or salad oil, ¾ cup brown sugar, 1 tsp. Angostura, and ¼ tsp. salt. Garnish center of platter with parsley.

Shrimp stuffed peppers form a hearty course, accompanied tartly by a fresh fruit salad.

BAKED BEAN RAREBIT

1 Tbsp. butter	style baked beans
2 Tbsp. onion, chopped fine	½ tsp. Worcestershire sauce
2 Tbsp. green pepper, chopped fine	Rarebit
1⅔ cups (1 lb. can) vegetarian	1⅓ cups condensed tomato soup (No. 1 picnic can)

Make rarebit (but omit from basic recipe the salt, cayenne, eggs and light cream). Melt butter in top of double boiler. Add onion and green pepper. Cook until tender but not browned, about 3 minutes. Add remaining ingredients. Heat and serve at once.

MUSHROOM RAREBIT

1⅓ cups condensed mushroom soup (No. 1 picnic can)	¼ tsp. powdered soluble coffee Rarebit

Make rarebit (but omit from basic recipe the salt, eggs and light cream; reduce mustard to ¼ tsp.). Add soluble coffee to rarebit. Heat soup and rarebit together. Serve at once.

CORN AND TOMATO RAREBIT

2 Tbsp. butter	1 cup drained whole kernel corn
2 Tbsp. onion, chopped fine	⅛ tsp. pepper
4 Tbsp. green pepper, chopped fine	½ tsp. Worcestershire sauce
1 cup stewed or canned tomatoes	Rarebit

Make rarebit (but omit from basic recipe the light cream and mustard). Melt butter in top of double boiler. Add onion and pepper, cook until tender but not browned, about 3 minutes. Add remaining ingredients. Heat together and serve at once.

BROILED SALMON STEAK

Salmon steaks average in size from ½ to 1 inch thick. Preheat oven and broiling pan for 10 minutes at full flame (or 500° F.). Dip salmon steak quickly in and out of cold salt water. Drain on absorbent paper or wipe dry with a damp cloth. Brush top-side evenly with shortening or oil, and place steak on preheated broiler pan 2 inches from flame. Broil 3 minutes on first side. Add seasoning, if you desire, and turn steak. Brush second side with shortening or oil; broil 3 minutes if a ½ inch steak, or 5 minutes if a 1 inch steak. When done, add seasoning, remove from pan. Garnish with slices of lemon. Serve at once.

CRABMEAT SALAD IN GRAPEFRUIT RING

3 Tbsp. gelatin	¾ cup orange juice
¼ cup cold water	¼ cup lemon juice
3 cups sweetened grapefruit juice	2 cups crabmeat

Add gelatin to cold water. Dissolve in boiling grapefruit juice. Add remaining fruit juices. Pour into 8-inch ring mold. Chill in refrigerator until firm. Unmold, and fill center with crabmeat. Garnish with crisp lettuce.

Note: Add mayonnaise, or whatever seasoning you prefer, to crabmeat, before putting into mold center.

Variations

Instead of crabmeat, you may substitute shrimp cut into small pieces, lobster, or any other cold flaked fish.

RED BEAN SALAD

1 can red kidney beans	3 sweet pickles, cut fine
¼ cup celery, diced	¼ tsp. salt
½ cup mayonnaise	Vinegar
1 hard-boiled egg, diced	Lettuce

Drain well the beans from the can. Lightly mix all ingredients. Add vinegar to taste. Serve with crisp lettuce.

COTTAGE CHEESE PINEAPPLE SALAD

1 pkg. gelatin (lime or lemon flavored)	½ cup evaporated milk
	⅔ cup drained, crushed pineapple (frozen, or canned—No. 1 flat can)
1½ cups hot water	
1 cup (8 oz.) cottage cheese	
½ cup mayonnaise	Watercress sprigs

Dissolve gelatin in the water. Cool. Blend together cheese and mayonnaise. Gradually stir in evaporated milk. Add pineapple and mix well. Combine cheese mixture and gelatin. Pour into 8 individual molds which have been rinsed in cold water. Chill in refrigerator until firm. Unmold on individual beds of lettuce. Garnish with watercress, if desired.

COTTAGE CHEESE SPRING SALAD

1 cup (½ lb.) cottage cheese	¾ cup cucumbers, diced
½ tsp. salt	¼ cup scallions, chopped
⅛ tsp. pepper	4 medium-sized green peppers
Dash garlic powder, if desired	Lettuce and other salad greens
½ cup radishes, sliced thin	Radish flowers
	Olives

Season cheese with salt, pepper, and garlic powder. Combine with radishes, cucumbers and scallions. Chill. Cut off tops of peppers and remove seeds and centers. Pile cheese mixture lightly into green pepper cups. Place top of green pepper over mixture. Arrange stuffed peppers on bed of salad greens. Garnish with radish flowers and olives. Serve with sour cream dressing (Chapter 14).

Note: For delicious variation, add 2 Tbsp. crumbled Roquefort cheese to cottage cheese.

CORN AND COTTAGE CHEESE PUDDING

4 eggs	1 tsp. Worcestershire sauce
2½ tsp. salt	1 cup cottage cheese
¼ tsp. pepper	1½ cups (12 oz. can) whole corn
1 Tbsp. sugar	kernels, chopped
1 tsp. onion juice	2 cups milk, scalded

Beat eggs slightly. Add salt, pepper, sugar, onion juice, and Worcestershire sauce; mix well. Mix together cheese and chopped corn kernels. Stir cheese and corn mixture into beaten eggs. Slowly add scalded milk, stirring constantly. Pour into lightly-greased 1 qt. casserole, and place casserole in pan of warm water. Bake in slow oven (325° F.) 1½ hours. Pudding is done when knife blade inserted comes out clean.

APRICOT NUT BREAD

½ cup dried apricots
1 egg
1 cup sugar
2 Tbsp. butter, melted
2 cups flour
3 tsp. baking powder
¼ tsp. soda
1 tsp. salt
½ cup orange juice
¼ cup cold water
¾ cup chopped Brazil nuts

Banana quick bread is another fruited bread.

Soak apricots in cold water ½ hour. Drain and cut into small pieces. Beat egg until light, stir in sugar, mix well, add butter. Sift together dry ingredients, and add alternately with liquids. Then add nuts. Mix well. Pour batter into well-greased loaf pan. Bake in moderate oven (350° F.) 1¼ hours.

SWEET DOUGH FOR HOT BREADS

½ cup sugar
½ cup shortening
1 Tbsp. salt

2 cups milk, scalded
2 yeast cakes
2 eggs, unbeaten
6 to 8 cups bread flour

Place sugar, salt and shortening in large bowl. Add scalded milk. Cool until lukewarm. Add yeast and eggs. Add flour. Cover tightly and let rise until double in bulk.

SALLY LUNN

Roll out sweet dough. Cut into rounds. Brush with butter. Let rise until very light. Just before baking, make a depression in center with end of a heavy spoon. Fill depression with butter and jelly. Bake in hot oven (400° F.) 15 minutes.

CRUMB CAKE

After sweet dough has risen, and been kneaded, shape dough into a shallow oblong pan, greased. Cover with crumb topping (recipe follows). Let rise. Bake in moderate oven (375° F.) 15 to 20 minutes.

TOPPING FOR CRUMB CAKE

3 Tbsp. flour

1 Tbsp. butter
2 Tbsp. sugar

Rub together all ingredients until of smooth consistency.

MY HUSBAND'S FAVORITE CAKE

6 Tbsp. flour
2 tsp. baking powder
¾ cups sugar
½ tsp. salt

1 cup chopped nut meats
½ lb. dates
4 eggs
1 tsp. vanilla
Powdered sugar

Sift and measure flour. Sift again with baking powder. Add salt, sugar, and nuts. Add eggs one at a time, beating after each addition. Add vanilla. Bake in greased and floured pan (9 x 9 inches), in a moderate oven (350° F.) 30 minutes. Cut in squares while warm and roll in powdered sugar.

LENTEN PIE

Prepare baked pie shell and meringue topping, according to instructions in Chapter 19. Then mix together the following ingredients:

1 cup heavy sour cream	2 egg yolks, beaten
1 cup sugar	⅛ tsp. salt
⅔ cup raisins	¼ tsp. cinnamon
	¼ tsp. cloves

Cook ingredients in double boiler, until thick. Cool, then pour into baked pie shell. Cover with meringue. Bake in slow oven (325° F.) 15 minutes.

ICE BOX TORTE

½ lb. butter	½ lb. macaroons
½ lb. powdered sugar	½ lb. lady fingers
4 eggs	2 cups fresh berries or other cut-up fruit
¼ lb. chopped nuts	½ pt. cream, whipped

Cream butter and sugar well. Add 2 eggs (one at a time) and beat well. Beat yolks of 2 remaining eggs with about one-fourth of chopped nuts. Add vanilla and beaten whites of the 2 eggs. Line pan with macaroons. Stand lady fingers around edge. Pour in mixture and place in refrigerator overnight. Spread fruit on top. Cover with whipped cream and remainder of nuts. Serve at once.

LENTEN STEAMED PUDDING

1¼ cups flour	½ cup molasses
1 tsp. soda	1 cup strong coffee
1 tsp. cinnamon	1 Tbsp. butter, melted
⅛ tsp. nutmeg	1 cup seedless raisins, chopped
1 pt. stale cake crumbs	¼ cup citron, chopped fine

Sift dry ingredients together, and mix with crumbs. Mix molasses, coffee, and melted butter together. Add to dry mixture. Mix raisins and citron together, and add to mixture. Pour into well-greased mold, cover with waxed paper, tie securely, and steam for 4 hours. (See Fruit Roly Poly, Chapter 20.)

SAVORY COTTAGE CHEESE CREAM PIE

1 unbaked 9-inch pie shell	1 tsp. salt
2 cups (1 lb.) cottage cheese	3 Tbsp. onion, chopped fine
¾ cup sour cream	4 Tbsp. pimiento, chopped
2 cups hot mashed potatoes	2 eggs, well-beaten
	1½ Tbsp. butter

Combine cheese with sour cream. Beat in mashed potatoes, blending thoroughly. Add salt, onion and pimiento; mix well. Fold in beaten eggs. Turn into unbaked pie shell. Dot with butter. Bake in moderate oven (350° F.) 1¼ hours, or until brown. Serve hot or cold as main dish with mixed green salad.

Fresh celery and fish chowder provides sturdy supper fare. It takes 1 cup chopped onion, 2 Tbsp. butter, 2 cups each diced celery and diced potatoes and boiling water, 4 tsp. salt, 1 lb. fish fillets, 3 cups milk, ½ tsp. ground thyme, ¼ tsp. ground black pepper. Sauté onion in butter or margarine. Add celery, potatoes, water, and salt. Cover and cook 10 minutes or until vegetables are tender. Add fish 5 minutes before cooking time is up. Stir in balance. Heat.

31.

FOREIGN FOODS

HOW FORTUNATE we Americans are! Not only do we have the regional dishes of our own country to enjoy—from New England chowder to California avocados, from Southern fruitcake to the Mid-West's corn pudding—but we also eagerly add the famous dishes of other countries to our cooking. And what a wealth of delightful and appealing dishes they are! No dinner need suffer from monotony when the whole world offers us their specialties to choose from.

CHOW MEIN

(China)

There are many discussions concerning the recipe for Chow Mein. Many Americans think it a typical Chinese dish, and the Chinese themselves offer stories concerning its origin. One of the most frequently heard stories explains it thus: "A Chinese cook came to America and was asked to prepare a meal. Knowing nothing of the American way of cookery, he struggled to create a dish out of the ingredients he found available in the nearby markets." Read the recipe given here, and form your own opinion.

1 Tbsp. peanut oil	12 water chestnuts, sliced thin
1 head Chinese cabbage, shredded	1 tsp. salt
¾ cup cooked shrimp	¾ tsp. seasoning powder
⅔ cup bamboo shoots, sliced thin	2¾ cups chicken stock
	1 Tbsp. cornstarch dissolved in 2 Tbsp. cold water

Heat oil in skillet. Fry cabbage for 2 minutes. Add all ingredients. Cover tightly and cook 5 minutes. Add cornstarch paste, cook 2 minutes longer. Serve with canned fried noodles, well-heated.

AMANDINE (ALMOND CAKES)

(France)

2½ cups almonds, chopped
1½ cups powdered sugar

3 eggs, separated
½ cup flour, sifted
¼ cup citron, cut in fine slivers

Mix almonds and sugar together. Add unbeaten egg yolks and 2 egg whites. Add flour and citron. Mix all together, and at last add the remaining egg white. Beat thoroughly. Bake in 12-inch round pan, in slow oven (300° to 325° F.) 30 minutes, or until a toothpick inserted in center comes out clean and dry.

CHOCOLATINE DESSERT

(France)

½ cup butter
¼ cup powdered sugar
4 sq. chocolate, melted

3 eggs, separated
½ tsp. vanilla extract
½ tsp. almond extract

Cream butter and sugar, add chocolate. Add egg yolks one at a time beating

Chow mein is a popular dish in America despite the argument over whether it is actually Chinese or not. It is easy to make at home with canned Chinese vegetables, easy to season.

well after each addition. Fold in stiffly-beaten egg whites, and flavorings. Line a mold with waxed paper. Pour in mixture, cover and place in refrigerator for 24 hours. Turn out of mold, remove paper. Serve with whipped cream, but in tiny servings—it's as rich as can be.

CRÊPES SUZETTE

(France)

This foreign dish is usually regarded as a glamorous dessert, yet it is very simple to prepare. Use a prepared pancake mix, and follow directions on the label. Put your pancake griddle on the stove and preheat it. Then pour the batter on the hot griddle, making very thin pancakes about 3 to 4 inches in diameter. Meanwhile heat a large platter, and as each pancake is baked place it on this platter. Sprinkle pancakes lightly with sugar, and keep the platter hot until all the pancakes are done.

The liquor sauce is the important "trimming" of this dessert. Into a hot skillet pour ½ cup brandy, 1 to 3 Tbsp. orange curacoa, and 1 Tbsp. sugar. Stir. When the sugar is melted, apply a flaming match to the hot liquid in the skillet, and quickly add the pancakes to the liquid. Keep shaking the skillet lightly with one hand, while with the other hand you are "spooning" the burning liquor over the pancakes. As the flame dies down, quickly form each pancake into a roll with the spoon. Transfer the pancakes to individual, well-heated serving plates, and pour any remaining liquor over the pancakes. Serve at once.

French onion soup will give you indescribable eating pleasure.

QUICHE LORRAINE (BACON PIE)

(France)

1½ cups flour
½ cup shortening
½ tsp. salt
½ cup ice water

3 eggs, well-beaten
½ cup cream
¼ lb. bacon, fried crisp,
    crumbled in pieces

Sift; measure flour. Cut in shortening until mixture resembles coarse corn meal, add salt. Make a hollow in center, slowly add water, stirring mixture with silver fork until dough forms ball. Turn out on lightly-floured board, roll out to fit large pie plate. Flute edges, sprinkle bacon over crust, add mixture of cream and eggs. Pour over bacon. Bake in hot oven (450° F.) 5 minutes. Reduce heat (350° F.). Bake until silver knife, inserted in center, comes out clean.

QUICK ONION SOUP

(France)

2 cups onion, sliced
3 Tbsp. butter
5 cups boiling water

4 bouillon cubes
Croutons or toasted ½ slices of
    bread
Parmesan cheese, grated

Fry onion in butter about 10 minutes, or until tender but not browned. Dissolve bouillon cubes in ¼ cup of the boiling water. Add this, and the rest of the water to the onions. Stir well. Toss croutons or toast into soup plate, pour hot soup over it. Sprinkle with grated cheese, if desired.

ESCALOPES EN MAUVIETTES (VEAL LARKS)

(France)

4 thin slices raw veal (6x3x½
    inch)
4 eggs, hard-cooked
4 thin slices raw smoked ham
    (same size as veal)

1½ cups cream of mushroom soup
½ cup light cream
¼ cup green olives, chopped
2 Tbsp. candied citron, sliced
    fine

Place an egg on slice of veal; roll up like a jelly roll. Wrap slice of ham around roll. Skewer through with 2 toothpicks. Place 4 "larks" in greased casserole, add soup, cream, olives, and citron. Cover, and bake in moderate oven (350° F.) 45 minutes.

STEAK À LA SHERRY

(France)

2 lb. piece of bottom round (cut ½ inch thick)
4 Tbsp. dry mustard
1 to 2 Tbsp. wine vinegar
4 Tbsp. onion, chopped fine

Salt, pepper, paprika
1 cup boiling water
Flour
¼ cup salad oil or butter or bacon fat
¾ cup sherry wine

Cut steak into 4 portions and spread with paste of mustard and vinegar. Sprinkle with onion and seasonings. Roll up like jelly roll; skewer securely with toothpicks, or tie with string. Fill shallow plate with flour seasoned with salt and pepper. Roll each steak in flour, brush off excess. Melt fat in heavy skillet, brown steaks on all sides. Add water, cover tightly, and simmer over low flame 45 minutes to 1 hour, or until tender. Add sherry wine and cook 10 minutes longer. Serve with candied sweet potatoes.

SIROP DE FRAMBOISE

(France)

1 pt. white wine

1 pt. fresh red raspberries
1 lb. granulated sugar

Pour wine over berries. Let stand 24 to 48 hours. Pour off wine, measure. Add 1 lb. sugar to 1 qt. liquor. Place in enamelware saucepan over low heat. Stir until sugar is dissolved. Bring to boil. Pour into clean, hot sterilized jars. Seal, cool. Drink as a hot weather beverage.

TIMBALE DE HOMARD (LOBSTER ON A PLATTER)

(France)

4 Tbsp. butter
4 Tbsp. flour
1 qt. milk, scalded
2 Tbsp. onion, minced fine
1 Tbsp. parsley, minced fine
2 Tbsp. tomato paste

½ tsp. salt
¼ tsp. pepper
1 lb. lobster meat
¼ lb. cooked mushrooms
1 cup white wine
1 egg yolk

Melt butter, add flour, and blend well. Add milk slowly, stir until smooth. Add chopped onions and parsley, tomato paste, salt, and pepper. Set aside. Cover lobster with wine, let stand 30 minutes, then pour off wine. Add lobster and mushrooms to sauce. Heat wine and add. Pour a little of sauce over egg yolk, return to saucepan, cook 1 minute.

SAUSAGES WITH BEER

(Germany)

1 lb. pork sausages	½ pt. beer
1 to 2 Tbsp. butter	Pinch of salt

Prick skin of sausages with fork. Melt butter in skillet until hot. Put in sausages, and when they are brown pour off the fat. Add beer and salt, and bring to boil. Cover tightly and simmer 15 to 20 minutes.

RUSK DESSERT

(Holland)

Rusk Crust

1 box Holland rusk	1 tsp. cinnamon
½ cup sugar	½ cup melted butter

Crush rusks into crumbs with rolling pin. Set aside 1 cup of crumbs for topping. Mix sugar, cinnamon, and butter together and combine with rest of crumbs. Grease a round cake pan and press crumb mixture down on bottom and sides. Place in refrigerator for 1 hour.

Filling

2 cups milk	4 eggs yolks
½ cup sugar	1 tsp. vanilla
2 Tbsp. flour	4 egg whites
¼ tsp. salt	½ cup sugar

Scald milk in upper part of double boiler over hot water. Mix sugar, flour, and salt. Blend with hot milk to make smooth paste. Return to double boiler, cook until thickened. Pour hot liquid over slightly-beaten egg yolks. Cook 1 minute longer, add vanilla. Cool, pour over crumb crust. Beat egg whites until stiff, fold in sugar. Pile lightly over custard, sprinkle with crumbs (which were set aside). Bake in slow oven (325° F.) 25 minutes. Serve cold.

GOULASH

(Hungary)

¼ cup butter	2 tsp. salt
1 Spanish onion, sliced	1 green pepper, minced
1 No. 2 can tomatoes	1½ lbs. boneless chuck, cubed
1 Tbsp. caraway seeds	1 cup celery, chopped
1 tsp. sugar	1 cup carrots, diced
4 peppercorns	1 cup potatoes, diced

Melt butter in skillet, add onion, and cook until yellow. Add tomatoes, car-

Chicken curry (India) is often seasoned with Tabasco.

away seeds, sugar, peppercorns, salt, green pepper, meat. Cover and simmer 2 to 3 hours. Add celery, carrots, potatoes. Cook 30 minutes. If too thick, add small amount of boiling water.

CHICKEN CURRY

(India)

1 chicken (cut in portions)	1 to 2 Tbsp. curry powder
½ cup butter	1 tsp. salt
2 onions, minced fine	½ tsp. pepper
2 cups canned tomatoes	¼ tsp. cayenne pepper
	1 cup light cream

Melt butter in deep saucepan, add onions, and cook slowly until onions are yellow in color. Wipe pieces of chicken with damp cloth, add to mixture, and stir well. Add tomatoes and seasonings. Cover tightly, and let simmer 1 hour or until tender. Stir occasionally. Add cream, let come to boil. Make a border of hot cooked rice on platter, place chicken in center.

Variations

2 lbs. of veal, mutton, or lamb may be prepared in the same manner. Length of cooking time is 2 hours.

CURRIED LAMB AND RICE

(India)

2½ lbs. lamb shoulder	1½ Tbsp. curry powder
2 Tbsp. shortening	2 Tbsp. flour
1 tsp. salt	2 Tbsp. water
¼ tsp. pepper	3 cups boiled rice

Cut lamb into 1-inch cubes and remove fat. Melt shortening in frying pan, add lamb, and sauté until brown. Cover with boiling water. Add salt, pepper, and curry powder mixed with a little cold water. Cover and simmer about 2½ hours, or until lamb is tender. Make a smooth paste of the flour and water, and add enough to stew to thicken liquid. Make a mound of hot rice in center of a hot platter, and pour curried lamb around it.

MINESTRONE

(Italy)

1 cup dried beans	¼ tsp. thyme
¼ lb. salt pork, diced	1 qt. soup stock
1 cup carrots, diced	1 cup elbow macaroni
1 cup celery, chopped	1 cup tomatoes, canned or fresh
½ cup onions, chopped	½ cup grated cheese
1 clove garlic, chopped	¼ cup parsley, chopped
1 bay leaf	(boiling water, if needed)

Soak dried beans overnight. Drain, cover with fresh water, bring to boil and cook 30 minutes. Drain. Fry salt pork for few minutes, add carrots, celery, onion, garlic; simmer 5 minutes. Add soup stock and seasonings; cook 15 minutes more. Add macaroni, cook until tender. Add boiled beans, tomatoes (add boiling water if more liquid is needed). Add parsley. Sprinkle cheese over each portion.

SPAGHETTI, MEAT BALLS AND SAUCE

(Italy)

Toss cooked spaghetti lightly with sauce. Add meat balls if desired. Serve on big platter. This is the best recipe imaginable.

Note: It is more efficient to fry onions and garlic for sauce and for meat balls at the same time. When they are cooked, divide into 2 portions and proceed as directed.

Sauce

2 Tbsp. salad oil	1½ Tbsp. grated Parmesan cheese
1 large onion, minced	1 Tbsp. sugar
1 clove garlic, minced	½ cup raisins
1 No. 2½ can Italian tomatoes	1 tsp. salt
1 7-oz. can tomato paste	½ tsp. pepper
	1 bay leaf

Heat oil in skillet, add onion and garlic. Fry gently until yellow. Add tomatoes, paste, cheese, sugar, raisins, seasonings. Stir well. Cook 15 minutes. Add meat balls, and cook over low heat 3 to 4 hours.

Meat Balls

4 Tbsp. salad oil	½ tsp. allspice
1 onion, minced	2 Tbsp. grated Parmesan cheese
1 clove garlic, minced	1 egg, well-beaten
4 slices bacon, cut fine	1 Tbsp. parsley, minced
1 tsp. salt	¾ cup soft, fine bread crumbs
¼ tsp. pepper	2 lbs. ground beef
	¼ lb. sausage meat

Heat ½ of oil in skillet, add onion and garlic. Fry gently until yellow. Place in large bowl. Fry bacon in same pan until crisp. Drain on brown paper, add to onion mixture in bowl. Add seasonings and cheese, mix well. Add egg, bread crumbs and meat, mix all ingredients until thoroughly blended. Form into small round balls about 2 inches in diameter. Chill for 1 hour in refrigerator. Heat remaining salad oil in skillet, gently brown meat balls on all sides. Add to sauce, after sauce has cooked 15 minutes.

ANTIPASTO

(Italy)

It is the custom in Italy to serve separate cruets of olive oil and wine vinegar, with a plate of appetizers. The plates are arranged with an assortment

Meat balls and spaghetti can be made even more flavorful when teamed with green salad and breadsticks.

of foods such as pickled beets, salami and bologna, sardines, celery hearts, olives, radishes, pimiento, scallions, and any other crisp foods. As an accompaniment, bread sticks are often served, rather than the usual bread or rolls.

VEAL SCALLOPINI

(Italy)

1½ lb. leg of veal, cut in ¼ inch slices	1 Tbsp. butter Flour

Dredge veal lightly with flour, shake off extra flour. Using the edge of a heavy saucer as a mallet, pound the veal until the flour is absorbed well into the meat. Melt butter in a skillet, add the veal, and pan-broil the pieces until they are golden-brown on each side. Meanwhile, prepare the sauce.

Sauce

1 to 2 Tbsp. butter	1 tsp. parsley, minced fine
1 small onion, minced fine	1 bay leaf, crumbled
1 garlic clove, minced fine	½ cup white wine
6 mushrooms, minced fine	½ cup clear chicken or beef
1 small carrot, grated	consommé

Melt butter in skillet. Cook onion and garlic in butter until yellow. Add mushrooms. Simmer 1 to 2 minutes. Add other ingredients. Simmer 10 to 15 minutes. When the sauce is done (and the veal is golden brown), pour the sauce over the meat, and simmer gently until the meat is tender (15 to 25 minutes).

Lasagna is an Italian treat now easily available to the American housewife by virtue of a wide Italian noodle now on the market. The noodles are boiled for about 35 minutes, then packed in layers in a baking dish, the filling between layers consisting of beaten egg, cottage cheese, tomato meat sauce, and mozzarella cheese. Parmesan cheese is sprinkled over the top before the dish is popped into the oven.

MEXICAN CORNBREAD

(Mexico)

Part I

1 No. 2 tin cream style corn	½ tsp. salt
1 cup yellow cornmeal	4 tsp. baking powder
1 cup milk	1 Tbsp. sugar

Mix and sift dry ingredients together; add milk slowly to make smooth batter. Add corn, shortening, and beat well. Grease oblong baking dish. Pour ½ of batter in dish.

Part II

½ lb. grated cheese	1 7-oz. tin green chili peppers,
1 cup fresh tomatoes, cut in pieces	cut in pieces

Mix ingredients in Part II together. Spread over mixture in dish. Cover with remaining ½ of cornmeal batter. Bake in moderate oven (350° F.) 45 minutes. Takes the place of a vegetable and potatoes, all in one.

BIGOS

(Poland)

4 Tbsp. bacon fat	1 can tomato soup
3 onions, sliced	4 boiled potatoes, sliced
½ lb. sauerkraut	4 frankfurters, cut in 1-inch slices
	1 to 2 cups boiling water

Melt bacon fat in skillet, add onions, and cook until soft, but not brown. Rinse sauerkraut in cold water, and drain. Add sauerkraut, and cook slowly for 5 minutes. Add soup, potatoes, frankfurters, and water. Stir well. Cover and cook slowly for 10 minutes. If mixture becomes too thick, add more water occasionally. Serve as a one-dish meal.

STEAK A LA NELSON

(Poland)

2 lbs. cross rib of beef, cut into 8 thin slices	½ cup cooked carrots, diced
	2 Tbsp. bacon fat
2 cups rye bread, crusts removed	½ tsp. salt
½ cup cold water	¼ tsp. pepper
1 onion, chopped	¼ tsp. sage
½ cup mushrooms, chopped	½ cup boiling water

Pound beef with potato masher to flatten meat. Soak bread in cold water 15 minutes. Squeeze bread between hands to remove excess water. Fry onions and mushrooms in fat. Add carrots, bread, and seasonings, mix well. Spread on slices of meat. Roll up each slice and tie with string, like a sausage roll. Brown meat lightly in skillet. Place in greased casserole, add boiling water, cover tightly. Roast in moderate oven (350° F.) 1 hour or until tender.

BORSCHT (BEET SOUP)

(Russia)

1 cup raw beets, shredded	1 Tbsp. butter
1 cup onions, minced	2 cups beef consommé
1 cup canned tomatoes, strained	1 Tbsp. lemon juice

Cover beets and onions with boiling water. Cover tightly and simmer gently for 20 minutes. Add butter, consommé and tomatoes. Cook 15 to 20 minutes longer. Add lemon juice. Dish of sour cream and platter of hot boiled potatoes may be served separately, for those who wish to put them into their plates of soup after being served.

Variations

Cabbage Borscht: To the above recipe, add 1 cup shredded cabbage.
Vegetarian Borscht: Substitute water for beef consommé, and add salt to taste.
Sweet and Sour Borscht: Substitute citric acid and sugar (to please individual taste) for lemon juice.
Cold Borscht: Place in refrigerator. Chill before serving.

RUSSIAN SALAD

3 small beets, diced	½ cup button mushrooms
3 Tbsp. green peas	1 Tbsp. capers
1 potato, cubed	2 sweet pickles, sliced
3 carrots, diced	1 Tbsp. parsley, minced fine
	12 cooked shrimp

Blend cooked vegetables together lightly with French dressing. Use two silver forks for mixing. Arrange on crisp lettuce, garnish with shrimp. Pour dressing over salad.

Dressing

½ cup sour cream	1 tsp. lemon juice
1 hard-cooked egg yolk	½ tsp. sugar
1 tsp. olive oil	½ tsp. salt
	¼ tsp. pepper

Mash egg yolk with oil, add other ingredients.

SAND KAKE

(A delicious little cake from Scandinavia)

2½ cups flour	1 egg yolk
½ lb. butter	2 Tbsp. cream
1 cup sugar	½ tsp. almond extract

Sift; measure flour. Cream butter, add sugar slowly, cream until fluffy. Add flour. Roll out lightly on floured board, cut into rounds with cookie cutter, and press down into fluted tin cup-cake molds. Bake in hot oven (400° F.) 12 minutes. These little cakes may be eaten plain, as they are very rich; or they may be filled with sweetened whipped cream, fresh strawberries, or cooked custard filling.

BOILED BANANAS

(South America)

6 bananas

Drop 6 firm whole unpeeled bananas into kettle of boiling water, cover tightly and boil gently 3 minutes. Lift out and cut a lengthwise slit in each. Serve in the peel, as a vegetable, with baked ham; also excellent with fried chicken.

Swedish dessert. Serve canned Lingonberry preserves with thin pancakes.

32.

COOKING WITH
HERBS AND SPICES

TO add interest, new flavors and new taste to old favorites, nothing takes the place in the cook's repertory of the knowledgeable use of herbs and spices.

To the novice, a word of caution: do not use too much quantity of these flavorings, do not use too many varieties of herbs and spices in one dish, and do not use them in more than two dishes served at the same meal.

HOW TO SELECT FLAVORINGS

The discriminating cook chooses the right herb or spice to go with the right menu and its individual dishes. The "spice chart" which is given in this chapter lists suggestions for adding interest to your cooking. There are many other uses to which these may be put, and you will keep adding to this list as you discover the fun of cooking with herbs and spices.

SEASONING SALTS

Every kitchen shelf should have these three stand-bys in constant supply: garlic, onion and celery salt. Their flavor is true to that of the vegetables themselves, thanks to modern methods of manufacture. They add zest to the simplest dish, even to slices of bread which are served at the family table or in picnic sandwiches. Just sprinkle the bread with one of these seasoning salts, or a combination of two of them, and see how you add sparkle to your meals.

VARIETY IN RECIPES

While in this chapter we give recipes for main dishes, salads, and desserts, we also refer you to the recipes using curry on pages 92, 95, 162, 305 and 430, as well as the recipes using spices listed on pages 208, 209, 219 and 326.

For some go-together hints in herbs and spices for everyday meals, you will find these of interest:

CURRIED PEA SOUP

Add ¼ tsp. of curry to a can of condensed pea soup.

CURRIED CHEESE CRACKERS

Spread salted crackers with a square of plain yellow cheese. Sprinkle lightly with curry powder. Place under broiler for 1 minute.

CURRIED RICE-MUSHROOM SOUP

2 cups cooked rice	4 hard-cooked eggs, sliced
1 can condensed cream of mushroom soup	1 tsp. curry powder

Fill casserole (or 4 individual ones) with layer of rice. Heat soup (undiluted), stirring constantly. Add curry powder. Stir. Pour over rice. Cover with egg slices. Serve at once. *Serves 4.*

MAIN DISH RECIPES

The following dishes have a touch of glamor to them, yet make fine meals for family eating as well as for guests.

BAKED FISH FILLETS AND CELERY

2 fish fillets, 1 lb. each	1½ cups finely chopped celery
¾ tsp. salt	2 cups soft bread crumbs
⅛ tsp. ground black pepper	⅛ tsp. pepper
1 Tbsp. lemon juice	½ tsp. salt
¼ cup butter, melted	½ tsp. ground thyme leaves
3 Tbsp. finely chopped onion	1 tsp. lemon juice

Wipe fish with damp cloth. Mix the ¾ tsp. salt and ⅛ tsp. pepper with 1 Tbsp. lemon juice, and rub over both sides of the fish. Let stand 20 minutes. In the meantime, melt butter in a saucepan, reserving 1 Tbsp. for later use. Add onions and celery, and sauté until vegetables are limp but not brown. Stir in remaining ingredients to form the stuffing. Butter a shallow baking dish and place one of the fillets on the bottom. Spread with the stuffing. Top with the remaining fillet. Use toothpicks to keep the top piece of fish in place. Brush with remaining Tbsp. melted butter. Cover and bake in a preheated moderate oven (350° F.) 30 to 40 minutes. Remove cover and place under broiler to brown lightly. Garnish with lemon slices and fresh parsley, if desired. *Serves 6.*

Spice Chart

HOW MUCH SPICE TO USE: When trying a new idea, it is safest to start with 1/4 teaspoon of spice (excepting the red pepper spices) to a pint of sauce, soup or vegetable or a pound of meat, fish or fowl.

ABOUT PEPPER: Our most important spice deserves special attention. So versatile is its flavor, it could play a welcome role in any dish on this chart (except desserts). Good cooks always remember pepper as a seasoning corrector, often adding a final dash to taste regardless of the other seasonings used.

SPICE	APPETIZER	SOUP	MEAT and EGGS	FISH and POULTRY	SAUCES	VEGETABLES	SALAD and DRESSING	DESSERTS
ALLSPICE	Cocktail Meatballs	Pot Au Feu	Hamsteak	Oyster Stew	Barbecue	Eggplant Creole	Cottage Cheese Dressing	Apple Tapioca Pudding
BASIL	Cheese Stuffed Celery	Manhattan Clam Chowder	Ragout of Beef	Shrimp Creole	Spaghetti	Stewed Tomatoes	Russian Dressing	
BAY LEAF	Pickled Beets	Vegetable Soup	Lamb Stew	Simmered Chicken	Bordelaise	Boiled New Potatoes	Tomato Juice Dressing	
CARAWAY Seed	Mild Cheese Spreads		Sauerbraten		Beef a la Mode Sauce	Cabbage Wedges		
CINNAMON	Cranberry Juice	Fruit Soup	Pork Chops	Sweet and Sour Fish	Butter Sauce for Squash	Sweet Potato Croquettes	Stewed Fruit Salad	Chocolate Pudding
CAYENNE	Deviled Eggs	Oyster Stew	Barbecued Beef	Poached Salmon Hollandaise	Bearnaise	Cooked Greens	Tuna Fish Salad	
CELERY Salt and Seed	Ham Spread (Salt)	Cream of Celery (Seed)	Meat Loaf (Seed)	Chicken Croquettes (Salt)	Celery Sauce (Seed)	Cauliflower (Salt)	Cole Slaw (Seed)	
CHERVIL	Fish Dips	Cream Soup	Omelet	Chicken Saute	Vegetable Sauce	Peas Francaise	Caesar Salad	
CHILI Powder	Seafood Cocktail Sauce	Pepper Pot	Chili con Carne	Arroz con Pollo	Meat Gravy	Corn Mexicali	Chili French Dressing	
CLOVES	Fruit Punch	Mulligatawney	Boiled Tongue	Baked Fish	Sauce Madeira	Candied Sweet Potatoes		Stewed Pears
CURRY Powder	Curried Shrimp	Cream of Mushroom	Curry of Lamb	Chicken Hash	Orientale or Indienne	Creamed Vegetables	Curried Mayonnaise	
DILL Seed	Cottage Cheese	Split Pea	Grilled Lamb Steak	Drawn Butter for Shellfish	Dill Sauce for Fish or Chicken	Peas and Carrots	Sour Cream Dressing	

SPICE	APPETIZER	SOUP	MEAT and EGGS	FISH and POULTRY	SAUCES	VEGETABLES	SALAD and DRESSING	DESSERTS
GARLIC Salt or Powder	Clam Dip	Vegetable Soup	Roast Lamb	Bouillabaisse	Garlic Butter	Eggs and Tomato Casserole	Tomato and Cucumber Salad	
GINGER	Broiled Grapefruit	Bean Soup	Dust lightly over Steak	Roast Chicken	Cocktail	Buttered Beets	Cream Dressing for Ginger Pears	Stewed Dried Fruits
MACE	Quiche Lorraine	Petite Marmite	Veal Fricassee	Fish Stew	Creole	Succotash	Fruit Salad	Cottage Pudding
MARJORAM	Fruit Punch Cup	Onion Soup	Roast Lamb	Salmon Loaf	Brown	Eggplant	Mixed Green Salad	
MINT	Fruit Cup	Sprinkle over Split Pea	Veal Roast	Cold Fish	Lamb	Green Peas	Cottage Cheese Salad	Ambrosia
MUSTARD Powdered Dry	Ham Spread	Lobster Bisque	Virginia Ham	Deviled Crab	Cream Sauce for Fish	Baked Beans	Egg Salad	Gingerbread Cookies
NUTMEG	Chopped Oysters	Cream DuBarry	Salisbury Steak	Southern Fried Chicken	Mushroom	Glazed Carrots	Sweet Salad Dressing	Sprinkle over Vanilla Ice Cream
ONION Powder, Salt, Flakes and Instant Minced Onion	Avocado Spread (Powder)	Consommés (Flakes)	Meat Loaf (Instant Minced Onion)	Fried Shrimp (Salt)	Tomato (Powder)	Broiled Tomatoes (Salt)	Vinaigrette Dressing (Instant Minced Onion)	
OREGANO	Sharp Cheese Spread	Beef Soup	Swiss Steak	Court Bouillion	Spaghetti	Boiled Onions	Sea Food	
PAPRIKA	Creamed Seafood	Creamed Soup	Hungarian Goulash	Oven Fried Chicken	Paprika Cream	Baked Potato	Cole Slaw	
PARSLEY Flakes	Cheese Balls	Cream of Asparagus	Irish Lamb Stew	Broiled Mackerel	Chasseur	French Fried Potatoes	Tossed Green Salad	
ROSEMARY	Deviled Eggs	Mock Turtle	Lamb Loaf	Chicken a la King	Cheese	Sauteed Mushrooms	Meat Salad	
SAGE	Cheese Spreads	Consommé	Cold Roast Beef	Poultry Stuffing	Duck	Brussels Sprouts	Herbed French Dressing	
SAVORY	Liver Paste	Lentil Soup	Scrambled Eggs	Chicken Loaf	Fish	Beets	Red Kidney Bean Salad	
TARRAGON	Mushrooms a la Greque	Snap Bean Soup	Marinated Lamb or Beef	Lobster	Green	Buttered Broccoli	Chicken Salad	
THYME	Artichokes	Clam Chowder	Use Sparingly in Fricassees	Poultry Stuffing	Bordelaise	Lightly on Sauteed Mushrooms	Tomato Aspic	

LUNCHEON MEAT CHEESE LOAF

2 cans (12 oz.) luncheon meat
⅛ lb. cheddar cheese
2 cups soft bread crumbs

2 eggs, lightly beaten
¼ cup milk
1 tsp. dry mustard
Mustard Raisin Sauce

Dice luncheon meat and cheese. Add bread crumbs, eggs, milk and mustard. Mix well. Turn into a greased 8x4x2½-inch loaf pan. Bake ½ to 1 hour, in a preheated moderate oven (350° F.). If glass baking dish is used, bake at 325° F. for one hour. Serve with Mustard Raisin Sauce. Or, for variety, serve with Tomato Sauce.

MUSTARD RAISIN SAUCE

2 Tbsp. sugar
1 Tbsp. flour
¼ tsp. salt
2 tsp. dry mustard

⅓ cup seedless raisins
1 cup milk
2 egg yolks
2 Tbsp. lemon juice

Combine first 5 ingredients in a saucepan or in the top part of a double boiler. Beat milk and egg yolks together and gradually stir into the dry mixture. Cook over low heat or over hot water (not boiling) until medium thickness, stirring constantly. Remove from heat. Stir in lemon juice. Serve over

Cold-weather fare. Company will relish this dish on a cold night. It is made with plenty of meat and a good amount of chili powder.

Luncheon Meat Cheese Loaf, or over baked ham or ham patties. Yield: 1⅓ cups.

MUSHROOM AND TURKEY PIE

4½ cups sliced fresh mushrooms	⅓ cup flour
½ cup chopped onion	2 cups turkey stock
⅛ tsp. minced garlic	1½ cups milk
⅔ cup sliced celery	2 cups diced cooked turkey
2 tsp. lemon juice	1¾ tsp. salt
⅓ cup butter	½ tsp. pepper
	Potato Pastry

Sauté mushrooms, onions, garlic and celery in lemon juice and butter. Blend in flour. Gradually stir in turkey stock and milk. Cook until slightly thickened. Add diced turkey, salt and pepper. Turn into a 2 qt. casserole. Cover with Potato Pastry (recipe follows) ⅛ inch thick. Bake in a preheated hot oven 30 minutes or until potato crust is brown. *Serves 6 to 8.*

POTATO PASTRY

1 cup sifted all-purpose flour	½ tsp. salt
1½ tsp. double-acting baking powder	⅓ cup shortening
	½ cup cold mashed potatoes
	About 2 tsp. milk

Sift first 3 ingredients together into mixing bowl. Cut in shortening and potatoes until the mixture resembles coarse cornmeal. Stir in just enough milk to form a stiff dough. Roll to ⅛ inch thickness ½ inch larger than the diameter of the 9-inch casserole. Place over casserole. Trim, turn under, flute the edge, and make slits to allow steam to escape.

CHILI WITH MEAT BALLS

1 lb. ground lean beef	2 Tbsp. shortening
⅓ cup fine dry bread crumbs	½ cup chopped green pepper
1 egg, lightly beaten	3-4 tsp. chili powder (extra)
1 tsp. salt	1 tsp. oregano
2 tsp. chili powder	¼ tsp. garlic powder
¼ tsp. pepper	2 8-oz. cans tomato sauce
2 Tbsp. instant minced onion	1-lb. can kidney beans
¼ cup tomato juice	5 cups cooked rice

Combine first 8 ingredients. Shape into balls. Brown in the shortening over low heat. Remove meat balls. Add the onions, green pepper, extra chili powder, oregano, and cook until peppers are limp. Add garlic powder, tomato sauce and beans. Cook 5 minutes or until thickened. Add meat balls. Heat and serve over hot cooked rice. *Serves 6.*

SWEET AND PUNGENT FRANKFURTERS

1½ lbs. frankfurters, sliced
2 Tbsp. butter
¼ cup sweet pickles, sliced
1 18-oz. jar mince meat
¾ cup pineapple juice
3 Tbsp. soy sauce
½ tsp. oregano
¼ tsp. basil
2 Tbsp. cornstarch
3 cups hot cooked rice
1 3½-oz. can chow-mein noodles

Frankfurters are exotic if made with mince meat, pineapple juice, pickles and seasonings.

Brown frankfurter slices in fat. Add pickles, mince meat, pineapple juice, herbs, soy sauce and 1 cup water. Bring to boil. Mix cornstarch with a few tablespoonfuls of cold water, stir into frankfurter mixture. Cook until thickened, stirring constantly. Serve over bed of rice. Serve noodles in separate dish. *Serves 6.*

MUSHROOMS STUFFED WITH HAM

(Serve as an hors d'oeuvre or with main dish)

15-20 small fresh mushrooms
1 Tbsp. butter
1 Tbsp. finely chopped onion
3 Tbsp. fine dry bread crumbs
¼ cup finely chopped tomato
2 Tbsp. deviled ham

1 Tbsp. grated sharp cheese
1 Tbsp. chopped fresh parsley
1 tsp. lemon juice
½ tsp. salt
⅛ tsp. pepper
½ tsp. thyme
Fresh parsley for garnish

Wash mushrooms, remove stems from the caps. Chop stems very fine and sauté in butter and onion. Combine with bread crumbs, tomatoes, ham, cheese, chopped parsley, lemon juice, salt, pepper and thyme. Fill mushroom caps with the mixture. Place on baking sheets. Broil 5 to 10 minutes with oven regulator set to broil. Garnish with parsley. Serve hot as an hors d'oeuvre, or stuff large mushrooms and serve with the main course. (Stuffing is sufficient for 15-20 small mushrooms or 8-10 large ones.)

BROCCOLI IN BROWNED BUTTER

1½ lbs. (1 bunch) fresh broccoli	3 Tbsp. butter
1 inch boiling water in saucepan	3 Tbsp. lemon juice
1 tsp. salt	⅛ tsp. pepper
	½ tsp. tarragon

Wash broccoli and trim off the tough portion of each stalk. Place in a saucepan with the boiling water and salt. Cover. Bring to boiling point. Boil 15 minutes or only until crisp-tender, lifting the cover 2 or 3 times to retain the bright, green color of the broccoli and to give a milder flavor. Drain. Place on serving dish. In the meantime, brown butter in a saucepan. Remove from heat and add lemon juice, pepper and tarragon. Pour over broccoli. *Serves 6.*

BROCCOLI AND SHRIMP CASSEROLE

1½ lbs. (1 bunch) broccoli	1¼ cups milk
1 inch boiling water in saucepan	1 cup grated sharp cheddar
1 tsp. salt	cheese
1 cup cooked de-veined shrimp	1 tsp. salt
2 Tbsp. butter	⅛ tsp. pepper
2 Tbsp. flour	½ tsp. tarragon

Wash broccoli and trim off the tough portions of each stalk. Place in saucepan with boiling water and 1 tsp. salt. Cover. Bring to boiling point. Boil 15 minutes or only until crisp-tender, lifting the cover 2 or 3 times to retain the bright, green color of the broccoli and to give it a milder flavor. Drain. Arrange half the broccoli in the bottom of a greased 10x5x2 inch baking pan. Top with the shrimp. Cover with remaining broccoli. In the meantime, melt the butter in a saucepan. Remove from heat and blend in flour. Gradually stir in milk. Cook until medium thickness. Stir in ½ cup of cheese, salt, pepper and tarragon. Pour over broccoli and shrimp. Sprinkle top with remaining cheese. Bake in preheated moderate oven (350° F.) 20 minutes or until browned. *Serves 6.*

BROCCOLI ON TOAST WITH EGG SAUCE

1½ lbs. (1 bunch) broccoli	2 cups medium white sauce
1 cup boiling chicken broth*	2 hard-cooked eggs
6 slices toast	2 tsp. toasted sesame seed

Wash broccoli. Trim off the tough portion of the stems. Place in saucepan with boiling chicken broth. Cover. Bring to boiling point. Boil 15 minutes or only until crisp-tender, lifting the cover 2 to 3 times to retain the bright green color of the broccoli and to give a milder flavor. Drain. Place on toast. Combine white sauce with 1 chopped, hard-cooked egg. Spoon over broccoli. Sprinkle with toasted sesame seed. Slice the remaining egg and place a slice on each serving. *Serves 6.*

* If desired, substitute 1 cup boiling water and 1 chicken bouillon cube.

CHICKEN STUFFED AVOCADO

3 avocados
4 whole pimientos
2 cups diced, cooked chicken
½ cup mayonnaise
¼ tsp. rosemary
⅛ tsp. thyme
1 Tbsp. lemon juice

Stuffed avocados look fancy, but are simple to fix. Lemon juice keeps them green. Herbed chicken salad is the filling.

Blend mayonnaise, seasonings and lemon juice together. Add to chicken. Cut avocados in half lengthwise, remove seed, sprinkle with lemon juice. Line each half avocado with a whole pimiento pod, and fill the pod with salad mixture. Garnish with bits of pimiento. *Serves 6.*

CURRIED SHRIMP STUFFED AVOCADOS

2 Tbsp. minced onion	1/16 tsp. garlic powder
2 Tbsp. butter	1 tsp. curry powder
2 Tbsp. flour	4½ oz. can whole shrimp*
1½ cups milk and shrimp broth*	2 avocados
1/16 tsp. ground black pepper	Parsley and paprika for garnish

Sauté onion in butter. Add flour. Stir in milk and shrimp broth drained from the can of shrimp. Cook until smooth. Add seasonings and shrimp. Cut avocados in half. Remove seed. Fill with creamed shrimp. Garnish with paprika and parsley. *Serves 4.*

* Cooked, diced chicken may be substituted for shrimp, and chicken broth for shrimp broth.

SWEET POTATOES, BACON, APPLE RINGS

4 medium-cooked (not peeled) sweet potatoes	4 slices of bacon
	2 Tbsp. sugar
4 raw apple rings, ¾ inch thick	½ tsp. ground cinnamon
	⅓ cup fresh orange juice

Remove skins from sweet potatoes. Place an apple ring over each and wrap with a strip of bacon. Place in an 8x8x2-inch greased baking dish. Mix sugar with cinnamon. Add orange juice. Pour over potatoes and apples. Bake 45 minutes or until done in a preheated moderate oven (375° F.). *Serves 4.*

SOUTHERN SWEET POTATO PIE
(Served as main dish or may be a dessert)

¾ cup sugar	sweet potatoes
½ tsp. salt	2 Tbsp. butter
1 tsp. ground cinnamon	3 eggs, unbeaten
1 tsp. ground ginger	1 tsp. grated lemon rind
⅛ tsp. ground cloves	1¼ cups milk
2 cups mashed hot cooked	9-inch unbaked pastry shell

Mix the first 5 ingredients. Add sweet potatoes and butter. Mix well. Cool. Beat in eggs. Stir in lemon ring and milk. Pour into unbaked pie shell. Bake 40-50 minutes, or until done in a preheated hot oven (400° F.). *Serves 6.*

FIRST COURSE AND SALAD

Herbs and spices are not limited to heavy main dishes alone; they can add a new touch to simple salads, soups, as well as appetizers. A few basic recipes are given, but your imagination need not stop at these when you are adding the extra fillip of flavoring.

CHILLED CUCUMBER SOUP

3 cucumbers	½ tsp. salt
1 small onion	¼ tsp. pepper
2 cups water	1 cup cream
3 Tbsp. flour	Paprika

Peel, seed and slice cucumbers. Grate onion. Add water and cook until very soft. Blend flour in slowly. Press through fine sieve. Add salt, pepper and cream. Chill. Serve ice cold, garnished with paprika just before serving. *Serves 6.*

AVOCADO SHRIMP COCKTAIL

½ cup ketchup	1 tsp. salt
4 tsp. lemon juice	¼ tsp. red-hot sauce
3 tsp. horseradish	1/16 tsp. pepper
2 tsp. grated onion	2-4½ oz, cans shrimp
1 tsp. powdered dry mustard	1½ cups diced ripe avocado
	Lettuce (torn into pieces)

Combine first 8 ingredients and chill. Into each of six long-stem sherbet glasses put a bed of lettuce, and place on top of the lettuce 3 shrimp and ¼ cup avocado. Top with 1½ tsp. cocktail sauce.

PIMIENTO BEANS IN SOUR CREAM

1 can or 4-oz. jar pimientos, cut in strips	4 Tbsp. butter, melted
	¼ tsp. rosemary
1 lb. can whole green beans or 1 pkg. quick-frozen beans	¼ tsp. thyme
	1 cup sour cream

Drain and combine the green beans and pimientos. Mix together the remaining ingredients, and pour the sour cream mixture over the beans and pimientos. Bake in a casserole at 350° F. for 30 minutes. *Serves 4.*

HEARTY HERB VEGETABLE SALAD

1 cup diced cooked potatoes	½ tsp. powdered dry mustard
1 cup cooked string beans	¼ tsp. pepper
1 cup cooked sliced carrots	2 Tbsp. chopped green pepper
1 Tbsp. cider vinegar	2 Tbsp. chopped onion
1 Tbsp. salad oil	1 cup sliced celery
1 tsp. garlic salt	2 Tbsp. mayonnaise
	Paprika and parsley for garnish

Combine first 8 ingredients in a mixing bowl. Cover. Chill 2 to 3 hours. Add the green peppers, onion, celery and mayonnaise. Toss lightly. Place on lettuce in a salad bowl. Garnish with chopped parsley and paprika. *Serves 6.*

SUMMER SALAD TREAT

Cucumbers diced fine and mixed with sour cream make a delicious stuff-

Fresh
Fruit Salad

Make-A-Meal
Salad

Shrimp
a la New Orleans

Dressed-up green beans cooked with herbs and rich sour cream go well with broiled meats and plain potatoes.

ing for garden-fresh ripe tomatoes. Add ground black pepper and salt to taste. Sprinkle with chives and add a rosy blush of paprika. This is delicious served as an accompaniment to fish.

FRESH VEGETABLE RING SALAD

Cut thick slices of fresh red tomatoes, rings of white onion and cucumbers, rings of green peppers. On a bed of lettuce arrange the four vegetables in alternating rows. Pass a French dressing well laced with ground basil leaves.

SPICED FRENCH DRESSING

2 Tbsp. mixed whole pickling spices	1 tsp. salt
¾ cup cider vinegar	1½ tsp. sugar
1 cup salad oil	½ tsp. onion salt
1¼ tsp. dry mustard	1 tsp. paprika
	Dash garlic powder

Heat pickling spices and vinegar in a saucepan for 3 minutes. Cover. Let stand 2 minutes. Strain and combine vinegar with remaining ingredients. Beat with rotary beater. Chill. Stir thoroughly before serving. Yield: 1¼ cups.

COOKED MUSTARD DRESSING

1 tsp. dry mustard	Dash ground cayenne pepper
2 Tbsp. flour	2 egg yolks
1 Tbsp. sugar	¾ cup water
1 tsp. salt	2 Tbsp. salad oil
	¼ cup fresh lemon juice

Combine first 5 ingredients in the top of a double boiler. Combine egg yolks and water, gradually stir into the dry mixture. Blend in salad oil. Cook until thick. Add lemon juice.

COOKIES AND DESSERTS

The old phrase "sugar 'n spice" is nowhere more fitting than in the use of spice in making tasty cookies and interesting desserts which top off a good meal. The addition of spice turns what might be an ordinary concoction into a taste-tempting delicacy.

ROLLED CHRISTMAS COOKIES

4 cups sifted all-purpose flour	1½ cups butter
1¾ cups sugar	2 eggs, lightly beaten
2 tsp. ground allspice	3 Tbsp. cold water

Sift the first 3 ingredients together. Cut in butter until the mixture resembles coarse corn-meal. Stir in eggs and water. Mix well. (This dough is stiff, so do not add more water.) Chill until the dough can be easily handled, about 1 hour. Roll to ⅛ inch thickness on a lightly floured board. Shape with assorted cookie cutters. Bake on ungreased cookie sheets in a preheated hot oven (400° F.) 7 to 8 minutes or until lightly brown around the edges. Decorate before baking with glazed fruit or colored sugar, or decorate with confectioners' sugar and water icing after baking. Yield: 9 dozen assorted sizes and shapes.

RAISIN AND NUT FUDGE SQUARES

⅔ cup sifted all-purpose flour	1 cup brown sugar
⅛ tsp. soda	1 tsp. vanilla extract
½ tsp. salt	2 eggs
1 tsp. ground allspice	2 Tbsp. milk
⅓ cup shortening	½ cup chopped nuts
2 sq. unsweetened chocolate	¼ cup seedless raisins

Sift the first 4 ingredients together. (Set aside for later use.) In the top of a

Allspice goes into these Christmas cookies. This recipe yields many dozen; use different cutters and varied decorations.

double boiler, large enough for mixing batter, melt shortening and chocolate over hot water. Stir in sugar and vanilla extract. Beat in eggs. Add milk and flour mixture. Blend in nuts and raisins. Turn into a well-greased, lightly-floured 9x9x2-inch square pan. Spread uniformly over bottom of pan. Bake in a preheated moderate oven (350° F.) 45 minutes or until done. Turn out on wire rack to cool. Cut into squares. Store in a tightly closed container. Yield: 32 squares.

GERMAN COOKIES

2½ cups sifted all-purpose
    flour
½ tsp. soda
½ tsp. ground cloves
¾ tsp. ground cinnamon
1 tsp. ground allspice
1 cup strained honey
¾ cup light brown sugar

1 egg, lightly beaten
1 Tbsp. lemon juice
1 tsp. grated lemon rind
½ cup chopped nuts
½ cup chopped glacé citron
Blanched almonds for garnish
Diced candied lemon peel for
    garnish

Sift the first 5 ingredients together, and set aside for later use. Mix honey with brown sugar in a saucepan large enough for mixing cookies. Heat to boiling point. Cool. Stir in egg, lemon juice and grated lemon rind. Gradually add flour mixture. Blend in chopped nuts and citron. Chill dough until stiff enough to roll (or chill overnight). Roll to ¼ inch thickness on a lightly-floured board. Shape with 2-inch cookie cutters. Place on greased cookie sheets. Decorate to resemble a daisy with a piece of diced citron placed in the center and strips of almond and candied lemon peel as the petals. Bake in a preheated moderate oven (350° F.) for 10 minutes. Store in a tightly-covered container 3 or 4 days before eating. They improve with age! Yield: 5½ dozen cookies.

SOFT GINGER COOKIES

2½ cups sifted all-purpose flour
1 tsp. double-acting baking
    powder
½ tsp. soda
¾ tsp. salt

1½ tsp. ground ginger
½ tsp. dry mustard
¾ cup shortening
1 cup light brown sugar
¼ cup light molasses
1 egg

Sift the first 6 ingredients together. (Set aside for later use.) Cream shortening and sugar together. Blend in molasses. Beat in egg. Stir in flour mixture. Drop from a teaspoon onto lightly greased cookie sheets. Bake 12 minutes or until lightly brown in a preheated moderate oven (375° F.). Yield: 3 dozen cookies.

GUM DROP GINGER COOKIES

½ cup shortening
1½ cups light brown sugar
¾ tsp. soda
1 tsp. salt
1½ tsp. ground ginger

1 tsp. ground cinnamon
1 egg
2½ cups sifted all-purpose flour
¼ cup sour milk
1 cup tiny gum drops

Cream first six ingredients together. Beat in egg. Stir in flour alternately with milk. Add gum drops. Drop dough onto lightly greased cookie sheets. Top each with a slice of gum drop. Bake 17 minutes or until edges have browned in a preheated moderate oven (375° F.). Yield: 3 dozen cookies.

SPICED LEMON CREAM WITH CHOCOLATE SAUCE

1 pkg. lemon gelatin	¼ tsp. grated lemon rind
2 cups hot water	⅛ tsp. salt
⅔ cup sugar	½ cup heavy cream, whipped
¼ cup lemon juice	¼ cup graham cracker crumbs
	⅛ tsp. ground cloves

Dissolve gelatin in hot water. Add sugar, lemon juice, lemon rind and salt. Mix well. Chill until mixture begins to thicken. Beat until fluffy. Fold in whipped cream. Lightly butter individual gelatin molds. Combine graham cracker crumbs and cloves. Sprinkle over the bottoms and sides of buttered molds. Pour in gelatin mixture. Cover with remaining crumbs. Place in freezing compartment of refrigerator. Just before serving, turn out onto dessert dishes. Top with Spiced Chocolate Sauce. *Serves 8.*

SPICED CHOCOLATE SAUCE

2 sq. unsweetened chocolate	⅛ tsp. salt
1 Tbsp. butter	⅛ tsp. ground cloves
1 cup sugar	¾ cup boiling water
½ Tbsp. cornstarch	¾ tsp. vanilla extract

Melt chocolate and butter over hot water. Mix sugar, cornstarch, salt and ground cloves together, and blend with melted chocolate and butter. Stir in boiling water. Boil until slightly thickened, about 3 minutes. Cool. Add vanilla extract. Serve over Spiced Lemon Cream, ice cream or plain cake. Store in covered jar in refrigerator and use as needed. Yield: 1¼ cups.

SPICED CHOCOLATE FROSTING

1 pkg. semi-sweet chocolate pieces	1 can (15 oz.) sweetened condensed milk
1 sq. unsweetened chocolate	¼ tsp. ground cinnamon
	⅛ tsp. ground cloves

Melt chocolate over hot water. Stir in milk and spices. Cook over low heat 5 minutes. Cool. Spread between layers and over top and sides of cake. Yield: Sufficient frosting for two 8- or 9-inch layer cakes.

Spicy fig pudding is a good idea at Christmas time. Maraschino sauce is the unusual extra touch.

SPICED APPLE CRUMB CAKE

¼ cup butter, melted
2 cups graham cracker crumbs
¼ tsp. ground cloves
2 Tbsp. sugar

4 cups apple sauce
¼ tsp. ground mace
⅓ cup heavy cream, whipped
2 tsp. sugar

Combine butter with graham cracker crumbs, cloves and 2 Tbsp. sugar. Lightly grease an 8x8x2-inch pan with butter. Sprinkle sides with some of the graham cracker crumbs. Fill with alternate layers of crumbs and apple sauce mixed with mace, having the crumbs as bottom and top layers. Chill overnight or 10 to 12 hours. Cut into squares. Top with whipped cream sweetened with the 2 tsp. sugar. *Serves 6-8.*

APPLES BAKED IN ORANGE JUICE

6-8 large tart baking apples
½ cup sugar
½ tsp. ground cinnamon

1/16 tsp. salt
1 cup orange juice
½ cup heavy cream, whipped

Heat oven to 375° F. (moderate). Peel a 1-inch strip around the stem-end of the apples. Core, being careful not to cut through the blossom-end. Place in a 12x8x2-inch baking pan. Mix sugar, cinnamon and salt, and spoon into the centers of the apples. Pour orange juice over apples. Cover. Bake 30 minutes. Uncover. Bake 20 minutes or until apples are soft. Baste occasionally (about every 15 minutes). Baking time depends upon the kind of apples used. *Serves 6.*

FRESH PEAR BETTY

6 cups peeled, sliced pears	⅓ cup brown sugar
¼ cup hot water	¼ tsp. salt
¼ cup brown sugar	¼ tsp. ground ginger
½ tsp. grated lemon rind	1½ cups soft bread crumbs
1 Tbsp. lemon juice	2 Tbsp. butter

Parboil pears in hot water in covered saucepan 5 minutes over medium heat. Add the ¼ cup sugar, lemon rind and juice to the pears. Pour half in a 5x 10x2-inch casserole. Mix remaining sugar, salt, ginger and bread crumbs. Sprinkle half over pears. Dot with half the butter. Repeat with the remaining ingredients. Bake 20 minutes or until pears are soft in a preheated moderately hot oven (375° F.). *Serves 6-8.*

HOLIDAY FIG PUDDING

1 cup butter, softened	3 tsp. baking powder
2 cups light brown sugar	1 tsp. cinnamon
4 eggs	½ tsp. ground cloves
3 cups sifted flour	½ cup milk
½ tsp. salt	1½ cups chopped light figs
1 cup raisins	½ cup chopped walnut meat

Cream butter and sugar together until light and fluffy, stir in eggs, and mix thoroughly. Sift dry ingredients and stir into butter mixture. Blend in milk, and fold in figs, raisins and nuts. Spoon into a well-greased 2-qt. melon mold. Bake in pan of hot water at 325° F. for about 2 hours. Take mold from pan of water and bake an additional 25 minutes or until excess moisture is removed. Serve with maraschino cherry sauce. *Serves 4.*

MARASCHINO SAUCE

¼ cup maraschino juice	6 cherries, chopped
2 Tbsp. lemon juice	2 cups confectioners' sugar

Mix fruit juices and cherries. Add sugar and beat well. Yield: 1¼ cups.

33.

WINE FOR SERVING
AND IN COOKERY

AMERICA'S new approach to wine with meals and in cookery has come about quite naturally; the number of men overseas in service had a definite bearing on wine's steadily increasing popularity; but more important, perhaps, is the improvement in our own American vineyards. Much credit is due to the wine-growers themselves and their years of research to improve the quality of American wine.

A final step in wine's everyday acceptance is the discarding of the rituals, rules and mumbo-jumbo that formerly waited upon serving a bottle of wine, such as the insistence on the "best" year, the "right" wine and the "right" glass. The variety of wines available for enjoyment is infinite and, to the novice, confusing. But they need no longer be bewildering if one remembers that of all the wines in the world, each one falls into one of the six different classifications as follows:

COCKTAIL AND REFRESHMENT	Sherry (dry, pale dry, cream) Vermouth (dry, sweet) Special natural pure fruit-flavor wines	Serve chilled—straight, in mixed drinks or on-the-rocks. Especially good with appetizers and soups, and when friends drop in.
DESSERT AND REFRESHMENT	Port (ruby, tawny, white) Muscatel Cream sherry Tokay Sweet sauterne Sweet semillon Sweet sauvignon blanc	Serve cool or chilled. Especially good with fruit, nuts, cheese, cakes, desserts; or when friends drop in; and as nightcaps.

RED DINNER	Burgundy Claret Chianti "Vino" red types	Serve at cool room temperature. Especially good with steaks, chops, game, cheese, spaghetti.
WHITE DINNER	Sauterne Rhine wine Chablis	Serve chilled. Good with white meats, salads, fish and seafoods, cheese and mushroom dishes, chicken, goose.
ROSÉ	Rosé (the light, gay all-purpose pink wine)	Serve well chilled; all occasions; good with any food.
SPARKLING	Champagne Pink champagne Sparkling burgundy	Serve well chilled. Gay, perfect, and correct for all occasions and every food.

HOW MANY SERVINGS IN A BOTTLE?

The average serving of dinner wine or champagne is
3 to 3½ fluid ounces; of cocktail or dessert wine, 2 to 2½ ounces. These bottles
give you these approximate servings:

Size	Ounces	Dinner Wine— Champagne	Cocktail— Dessert Wine
FIFTH (⅘ qt.)	25.6	8 servings	8-12 servings
TENTH (⅘ pt.)	12.8	4 servings	4-6 servings
SPLIT	6.4	2 servings	
QUART	32.	10 servings	10-14 servings
PINT	16.	5 servings	5-7 servings
½ GALLON	64.	20 servings	20-30 servings
GALLON	128.	40 servings	40-60 servings

WINE PARTY PUNCH

2 6-oz. cans frozen orange juice
2 6-oz. cans frozen
    lemonade concentrate
2 bottles (⅘ qt. each)

sauterne, chilled
2 large bottles sparkling
    water, chilled
Berries or sliced fruit for garnish

Mix frozen juices with wine and blend until smooth. Just before serving pour in sparkling water. Add ice cubes or block of ice. Garnish with berries, cherries, or slices of orange, lemon or pineapple. Makes about 40 servings.

RUBY WINE PUNCH

1 bottle (⅘ qt.) claret or
  burgundy, chilled
3 cups orange juice, chilled

⅓ cup lemon juice
½ cup sugar
1 qt. ginger ale, chilled

In a punch bowl combine wine, orange juice, lemon juice and sugar. Stir until sugar is dissolved. Add ice cubes or a block of ice, then pour in ginger ale just before serving. Makes 25 servings.

GOLDEN CHAMPAGNE PUNCH

1 6-oz. can frozen orange
  juice
1 cup lemon juice

1 No. 2 can pineapple juice
1 cup sugar
1 bottle (⅘ qt.) sauterne
2 bottles (⅘ qt. each) champagne

Mix fruit juices and sugar. Stir to dissolve sugar. Cover. Chill in refrigerator several hours. Just before serving pour mixture over block of ice in punch bowl. Add chilled sauterne and champagne. Garnish with orange slices, maraschino cherries or strawberries, if desired. Makes 3½ quarts.

PINK PARTY PUNCH

4 12-oz. pkgs. frozen sliced
  strawberries, thawed
1 cup sugar
4 bottles (⅘ qt. each) rosé wine

4 6-oz. cans frozen lemonade
  concentrate
2 large bottles sparkling
  water, chilled

Combine strawberries, sugar and 1 bottle of wine. Let stand for an hour, covered. Strain into punch bowl. Add lemonade concentrate, stir until thawed. Add 3 more bottles wine, then the sparkling water. Add block of ice or tray of ice cubes, and serve at once. Makes 60 servings.

BURGUNDY PITCHER PUNCH

2 bottles (⅘ qt. each) burgundy
  or other red dinner wine

2 large bottles ginger ale

Pour wine and ginger ale over ice. Stir well to blend. Transfer to pitcher. Serve in punch cups or small glasses. *Serves 20-24.*

WINE IN COOKERY

The field of cookery is greatly enhanced, the variety of flavors greatly expanded, and subtle flavors of various foods are accented by a judicious addition of wine.

WINE COOKERY CHART

	FOODS	AMOUNT	WINES
SOUPS	Cream Soups	1 tsp. per serving	Sauterne or Sherry
	Meat and Vegetable Soups	1 tsp. per serving	Burgundy or Sherry
SAUCES	Cream Sauce and Variations	1 tbsp. per cup	Sherry or Sauterne
	Brown Sauce and Variations	1 tbsp. per cup	Sherry or Burgundy
	Tomato Sauce	1 tbsp. per cup	Sherry or Burgundy
	Cheese Sauce	1 tbsp. per cup	Sherry or Sauterne
	Dessert Sauces	1 tbsp. per cup	Port or Muscatel
MEATS	Pot Roast—Beef	¼ cup per lb.	Burgundy
	Pot Roast—Lamb and Veal	¼ cup per lb.	Sauterne
	Gravy for Roasts	2 tbsps. per cup	Burgundy, Sauterne or Sherry
	Stew—Beef	¼ cup per lb.	Burgundy
	Stew—Lamb and Veal	¼ cup per lb.	Sauterne
	Ham, Baked—Whole	2 cups (for basting)	Port or Muscatel
	Liver, Braised	¼ cup per lb.	Burgundy or Sauterne
	Kidneys, Braised	¼ cup per lb.	Sherry or Burgundy
	Tongue, Boiled	½ cup per lb.	Burgundy
FISH	Broiled, Baked or Poached	½ cup per lb.	Sauterne
POULTRY & GAME	Chicken, Broiled or Sauté	¼ cup per lb.	Sauterne or Burgundy
	Gravy for Roast or Fried Chicken and Turkey	2 tbsps. per cup	Sauterne, Burgundy or Sherry
	Chicken, Fricassee	¼ cup per lb.	Sauterne
	Duck, Roast—Wild or Tame	¼ cup per lb.	Burgundy
	Venison, Roast, Pot Roast or Stew	¼ cup per lb.	Burgundy
	Pheasant, Roast or Sauté	¼ cup per lb.	Sauterne, Burgundy or Sherry
FRUIT	Cups and Compotes	1 tbsp. per serving	Port, Muscatel, Sherry, Rosé Sauterne or Burgundy

WINE MARINADE

½ cup finely chopped onion
¼ tsp. garlic powder or
2 finely crushed cloves garlic

½ cup red or white table wine
1 8-oz. can tomato sauce
1 tsp. salt
½ tsp. paprika

Combine all ingredients. Pour over meat in a large bowl and marinate for several hours or overnight. This is suitable for pot roast, steaks or hamburger patties.

WINE BARBECUE

OR

BASTING SAUCES

(Read recipes downward,
from top to bottom.)

USE THESE INGREDIENTS	FOR BEEF OR VEAL
WINE VINEGAR	¼ cup
WINE OR BROTH (or other liquid)	1 cup red dinner wine 1 cup consommé
HERBS AND SPICES	2 teaspoons mixed thyme, rosemary, marjoram
GARLIC	1 clove, crushed
ONION.	¼ cup, grated
MUSTARD (dry or prepared)	2 teaspoons
CATSUP OR CHILI SAUCE	¼ cup
BROWN SUGAR OR HONEY	1 tablespoon brown sugar
SALT	1 teaspoon
PEPPER OR PAPRIKA	½ teaspoon pepper
SOY SAUCE	. . . . . .
WORCESTERSHIRE SAUCE	1 tablespoon
OIL	½ cup

Chicken takes to wine barbecue sauce. Serve a big salad with the spicy chicken and lots of French bread to soak up the sauce.

FOR PORK	FOR CHICKEN, TURKEY OR LAMB	FOR FISH
⅓ to ½ cup	⅓ cup	¼ cup
1 (8 oz.) can tomato sauce 1 cup chicken broth	1 cup white dinner wine 1 cup chicken broth	¾ cup sherry ¾ cup broth
1 teaspoon powdered ginger	2 teaspoons mixed rosemary and oregano 1 teaspoon dried dill	½ teaspoon powdered ginger
. . . . . .	1 clove, crushed	1 clove, crushed
¼ cup, grated	2 tablespoons, grated	. . . . . .
1 teaspoon	. . . . . .	. . . . . .
. . . . . .	¼ cup catsup (optional)	2 tablespoons (optional)
3 tablespoons brown sugar or honey	2 tablespoons brown sugar or honey	. . . . . .
1 teaspoon smoked salt	1 teaspoon	. . . . . .
¼ teaspoon pepper	½ teaspoon paprika	¼ teaspoon paprika
1 tablespoon	1 teaspoon	¼ cup
1 tablespoon	1 teaspoon	1 teaspoon
¼ cup	½ cup	½ cup

These easy sauce recipes make from 2½ to 3¼ cups. Heat each sauce to blend ingredients, and baste meat with warm sauce. You'll find each one simply delicious, used on its proper meat, whether barbecued or oven-baked.

STEAK WITH BANANAS

2-3 lb. rump, hip or round steak	Wine marinade
4 peeled bananas	2 Tbsp. lemon juice
	Watercress or parsley

Broil steak after it has remained in marinade 24 hours. Brush whole bananas with lemon juice and place on broiler rack with steak 10 minutes before steak has finished broiling. Before serving, cut bananas in half diagonally. Garnish warm platter with greens. *Serves 4.*

SHERRIED SHELLFISH DRESSING

1 cup mayonnaise	3 Tbsp. sherry
½ cup chili sauce	½ tsp. Worcestershire sauce
	Salt, pepper to taste

Combine all ingredients and chill thoroughly before serving. Excellent as a dressing for crab, shrimp or lobster. Makes about 1½ cups dressing. Keeps well in refrigerator.

JAMBALAYA CALIFORNIA

1½ cups tomato juice	Salt, celery salt, pepper to taste
½ cup sauterne or other white table wine	1 cup uncooked rice
1 chicken bouillon cube	1 cup slivered cooked ham
1 Tbsp. butter	1 cup cooked or canned shrimp
1 Tbsp. minced onion	

Combine tomato juice, wine, bouillon cube, butter and onion in a saucepan. Bring to a boil and stir until bouillon cube is dissolved. Season. Gradually add uncooked rice to the boiling mixture. Stir in ham and shrimp. Cover and cook very gently for about 25 minutes, or until rice is tender and all liquid is absorbed. Stir gently before serving. *Serves 4.*

WESTERN BARBECUED TURKEY

1 turkey (4-6 lbs. ready-to-cook weight), cut into pieces for serving	1 Tbsp. wine vinegar
1 cup catsup	½ cup butter or oil
1¼ cups water	½ cup minced onion
½ cup burgundy or other red table wine	⅛ tsp. garlic powder
	2 tsp. Worcestershire sauce
	1 Tbsp. sugar
	2 tsp. paprika
	½ tsp. salt

Place turkey, skin side down, in a roasting pan. Combine in a saucepan remaining ingredients, heat to boiling, pour over turkey. Cover and bake in a moderately hot oven (375° F.) 1 hour, basting occasionally. Remove cover, and turn turkey skin side up. Continue baking, uncovered, about ¾ to 1¼ hours, or until turkey is tender, basting and turning turkey occasionally. (Thin with more wine if necessary.) *Serves 4-6.*

WILD DUCK BURGUNDY

1 clean, dressed duck	4 celery slices
4 onion slices	½ clove garlic
4-6 apple slices	1 Tbsp. soy sauce
4-6 orange slices	1 Tbsp. salad oil
	½ cup burgundy

Stuff duck with slices of onion, orange and apple, garlic and celery. Rub breast with soy sauce and salad oil. Roast in uncovered baking pan in very hot oven (400° F.), basting often with burgundy. Roasting time: rare, 15-20 minutes per pound; well-done 45 minutes per pound. Remove stuffing before serving. *Serves 2.*

LEMON PORK CHOPS

4-5 shoulder pork chops	1 medium-sized onion
Salt and pepper	¾ cup catsup
4-5 slices lemon	¾ cup sauterne or other white dinner wine

Trim excess fat from chops and sprinkle with salt and pepper. Heat heavy skillet and rub with bit of fat trimmed from meat. Brown chops slowly on both sides. Place a lemon slice on each. Peel and slice onion, and separate into rings. Sprinkle over meat. Combine catsup and wine, pour over all. Cover closely, and cook very slowly about 1 hour, until meat is very tender. If necessary add a little additional wine or water the last half hour. *Serves 4-5.*

BARBECUED CHICKEN, NAPA VALLEY STYLE

1 frying chicken (3½ lbs.), cut in pieces for serving	2 Tbsp. butter or bacon drippings
Flour	2 Tbsp. salad oil
Salt, pepper to taste	Wine barbecue sauce

Dust pieces of chicken in flour seasoned with salt and pepper. Heat butter and salad oil in a large, heavy skillet. Add chicken and sauté until nicely browned on all sides. Transfer chicken to a casserole or roasting pan. Pour sauce over chicken. Cover and bake in a moderately slow oven (325° F.) for 1½ hours, or until chicken is tender. Rice goes well with this dish. *Serves 3-4.*

HAMBURGER STROGONOFF WITH WINE

2 Tbsp. salad oil
1½ lbs. hamburger
1 large onion, thinly sliced
3 Tbsp. flour
1 10½-oz. can condensed
    consommé
1 cup evaporated milk or
    top milk
3 Tbsp. tomato paste
1 Tbsp. Worcestershire sauce
Salt, garlic salt, pepper to taste
¼ cup sauterne or sherry

Inexpensive version of beef Strogonoff calls for chopped meat and a little sauterne or sherry.

Heat oil in a large skillet, add hamburger and onions. Cook, stirring with a fork, until hamburger is nicely browned. Sprinkle flour over meat and onion, stir until well-blended. Add consommé, milk and tomato paste. Cook, stirring constantly, until sauce is thickened and smooth. Add seasonings, simmer 10 minutes longer, stirring frequently. Just before serving, stir in wine. Serve with baked potatoes, rice or noodles. *Serves 4-5.*

HAM STEAK FRANÇOIS

1 (1 inch) center cut
    slice uncooked ham
1 cup apricot jam
1 cup sauterne or other white table wine

Ham lovers will appreciate this different topping for thick ham steak. Simply combine equal parts of apricot jam and any white table wine. Baste often.

Trim rind from ham. Slice and slash fat on edge in several places to prevent curling. Place ham in shallow baking pan. Combine jam and wine. Pour over ham. Bake in moderate oven (350° F.) for 1 hour. Baste frequently. *Serves 4.*

SHERRY, CHERRY AND HAM CASSEROLE

1-lb. can red sour cherries,
   pitted
¼ cup sugar
4 tsp. cornstarch
½ cup sherry
1½ tsp. lemon juice
1 18-oz. can whole sweet
   potatoes (dry pack)
1 Tbsp. butter
4-6 slices cooked ham, pork
   or tongue

Sherry, sour cherries, ham, lemon, sweet potatoes—all these flavors blend together in a savory casserole. Red coloring for the cherries makes for a pretty dish.

Drain cherries. Combine sugar and cornstarch in saucepan. Stir in sherry. Cook, stirring constantly, until mixture comes to a boil. Boil ½ minute. Remove from heat, add cherries and lemon juice. Place potatoes in shallow baking dish. Dot with butter. Place slices of meat in center. Pour cherry mixture over all. Bake in moderate oven (350° F.) 45 minutes. *Serves 4-6.*

LIMA BEANS WITH BURGUNDY

2 1-lb. cans lima beans
1 onion, sliced
¼ cup unsulphured molasses
1 tsp. dry mustard

1 Tbsp. sugar
2 tomatoes, peeled, cut into
   large pieces
1 12-oz. can kernel corn
1 cup burgundy

Drain beans. Cook onion in wine until liquid is reduced to half the amount. Remove from heat. Add molasses, mustard and sugar, stir well. Add beans, tomatoes and corn. Turn into well-greased casserole. Bake in moderate oven

(375° F.) for 30 minutes. *Serves 6-8*. (If preferred, dried lima beans may be used instead of canned. Cook beans according to package directions.)

BANANAS IN CHAFING DISH

4 ripe bananas	2 Tbsp. brown sugar
2 Tbsp. apricot jam	2 Tbsp. muscatel or sherry
2 Tbsp. butter	1 Tbsp. lemon juice

Sherried bananas keep warm in an electric skillet or lend a touch of elegance in a chafing dish.

Peel bananas, sprinkle with lemon juice. Combine all ingredients, heat slowly until butter is melted in chafing dish or electric skillet. Add bananas, spoon sauce up and over bananas. Cook uncovered until just tender, 10-15 minutes. *Serves 4*.

LIVER PATÉ IN SHERRIED ASPIC

1 envelope unflavored gelatin	2 hard-cooked eggs, sliced
10½-oz. can beef consommé	or
1 tsp. Worcestershire sauce	10 stuffed olives, sliced
½ tsp. soy sauce	or
½ cup sherry	2 pimientos cut into strips

Soften gelatin in ¼ cup consommé. Add remaining consommé and cook over hot water until gelatin melts. Stir in seasoning and sherry. Pour a small amount of the aspic mixture into a lightly greased 1-qt. mold. When aspic is slightly thickened, decorate with slices of eggs or olives or pimiento, then pour on another thin layer of aspic and let thicken slightly before adding the paté.

LIVER PATÉ

1 lb. chicken livers	2 tsp. salt
4 hard-cooked eggs	¼ tsp. pepper
4 large onions	2 Tbsp. lemon juice
	½ cup butter, melted

Cook livers for 5 minutes in small amount of boiling water. Drain. Grate onion. Add livers. Add salt, pepper, lemon juice and eggs. Chop fine with chopper, or put in blender and mix until smooth. Add butter and mix well. Garnish with parsley. Serve with saltine crackers.

NORMANDY FRUIT CUP

½ cup granulated sugar
¼ tsp. ground cloves
½ cup water
¾ cup port wine
1 cup melon balls
1 cup sliced seeded Tokay grapes
1 cup sliced bananas

Continental dessert of fresh fruits and port wine is becoming an American favorite for summer evenings. Touch up with a bit of mint.

Combine sugar, cloves and water, and bring to boil. Boil five minutes. Cool. Add wine. Pour over melon and grapes and place in refrigerator for several hours. Add bananas just before serving. *Serves 4-5.*

FROSTY ORANGE CUP

½ cup light corn syrup

½ cup white port wine

¼ cup orange juice

1 Tbsp. lemon juice

1 Tbsp. grated orange rind

3 cups orange sections

1 pt. orange sherbet

Place corn syrup, wine, orange juice, lemon juice and grated orange rind in a saucepan. Bring to a boil, then simmer gently for 15 minutes. Let sauce cool, then chill thoroughly in the refrigerator. At serving time, place ½ cup orange sections in each of 6 sherbet glasses or dessert dishes. Top with sherbet. Pour sauce over all. *Serves 6.*

COCONUT CREAM DESSERT

1 pkg. coconut cream
pudding and pie filling

2 cups milk

Place pudding mix in saucepan. Add milk gradually, blending well. Cook and stir over medium heat until mixture comes to a full boil and is thickened. Turn hot pudding at once into custard cups, which have first been dipped in cold water. Chill. Unmold. Serve with cranberry sauce. *Serves 4.*

CRANBERRY SAUCE

1½ cups maple-blended syrup   4 cups (1 lb.) fresh cranberries
½ cup water   ¼ cup port wine

Combine syrup and water in saucepan. Add cranberries, bring to a boil. Cook, covered, for 5 minutes. Do not stir. Remove from heat and let stand, covered, for 5 minutes. Remove to heat and cook 5 minutes longer. Add wine. Cool without stirring, then chill. Makes 3½ cups.

RASPBERRY SAUCE

1 No. 2 can red raspberries   1 Tbsp. butter
4 tsp. cornstarch   2 Tbsp. lemon juice
¼ cup sugar   ¼ cup port wine

Press raspberries through sieve to remove seeds, makes a thick purée. Mix cornstarch and sugar until thoroughly blended. Stir in raspberry purée, cook over low heat until mixture comes to boil (about 5 minutes). Remove from heat. Add butter, lemon juice and wine. Chill before serving in a separate sauce dish. Makes 2 cups.

INDIAN PUDDING WITH WINE

It is easy to change an old familiar dessert into a new exciting one with the addition of muscatel or sherry poured around hot Indian pudding. Use recipe given on page 256, allow 1-2 Tbsp. wine to each portion. Place scoop of ice cream on each serving, or serve with Zabaglione sauce.

ZABAGLIONE

6 eggs   6 Tbsp. sugar
½ tsp. salt   1½ cups sherry
                                    Grated nutmeg

Beat eggs with a rotary beater. Add the salt. Dissolve sugar in wine and add to eggs, beating constantly. Place over hot water and cook very, very slowly, stirring constantly to maintain a smooth consistency. Cook until mixture is as thick as a thick cream. Serve hot or cold in tall glasses and sprinkle with nutmeg. *Serves 6-8.* (Zabaglione may also be used as a thick, rich pudding sauce.)

34.

HOMEMADE CANDIES

LET the professional candy-makers delight you with their elaborate dipped chocolates, and all manner of fancy centers. These have no place in the home kitchen. But when it comes to old-fashioned popcorn balls, chocolate fudge, divinity fudge, and a number of other easily-made candies, then everyone within sniffing distance of the cooking sweetness joins in anticipation of pleasures to come. If, after many successful ventures with the simpler confections, the candy-maker wants to try dipping chocolates, it is necessary to purchase a special dipping chocolate from a wholesale house which caters to candy-makers.

Once the fact is established that candy made at home is going to be a regular part of family life, the purchase of a candy thermometer is advised, since the exact degree of "doneness" spells the difference between success and failure in candy-making. The bulb of a candy thermometer must be entirely covered with the boiling syrup, and the saucepan must be carefully removed from the heat, while the testing is being done.

If there is no candy thermometer at hand, then a small amount of the syrup may be dropped into a saucer of ice cold water; as soon as the syrup begins to form a small ball, lift it up in the fingers. There are four degrees of "doneness," known as:

1. *Soft ball*. The hot syrup will stay together in one mass and can be lifted out of the water, but flattens when laid upon the fingers.
2. *Firm ball*. The hot syrup will hold its shape when lifted out of the water, yet feels plastic.
3. *Hard ball (or crack)*. The hot syrup separates into threads when it strikes the water, but can be shaped into a hard ball with the fingers.
4. *Brittle*. The hot syrup separates into threads which remain brittle and break easily when removed from the water.

CANDY POINTERS TO SUCCESS

If syrup shows a tendency to stick to bottom of pan, draw spoon across

470

bottom. The smaller the sugar crystals, the smoother and creamier the candy. Keep the pan covered as much as possible to avoid sugar crystals forming on sides of pan. Wash sides of pan with clean wet cloth to catch excess crystals.

OLD-FASHIONED FUDGE

3 cups granulated sugar	½ cup water
3 sq. unsweetened chocolate	3 Tbsp. white corn syrup
1 cup milk or	3 Tbsp. butter
½ cup evaporated milk	1 Tbsp. vanilla extract

Combine sugar, chocolate, milk, and corn syrup in heavy saucepan. Stir over low heat until sugar is dissolved and chocolate melted. Cook without stirring until soft-ball stage (232° F.) is reached. Remove from heat, add butter and vanilla extract. Set aside to cool. Do not beat until fudge is cool. (This is the secret of a smooth, creamy fudge.) Grease a square pan with butter. Beat fudge until mixture thickens and begins to "fudge" at edges. Pour out quickly. Cut in squares. *Note:* Add ½ cup water only if evaporated milk is used.

Variations

Brown Sugar Fudge: Substitute half the amount of brown sugar for white sugar.

Nut Fudge: Add ½ cup finely cut nut meats as candy begins to thicken.

Maple Sugar Fudge: Substitute half the amount of maple sugar for white sugar.

Marshmallow Fudge: Add 1 cup marshmallows, cut in pieces, just before pouring in pan.

UNCOOKED FUDGE

4 sq. unsweetened chocolate	1 lb. sugar or confectioner's sugar
¼ cup butter	1 Tbsp. vanilla extract
	2 to 4 Tbsp. cream

Melt chocolate and butter in upper part of double boiler over hot water. Remove from heat, and gradually add sugar, alternating with cream, until mixture is thick enough to pour. Add vanilla extract, beat well and pour into well-buttered square pan. Let stand several hours to ripen. Cut in squares.

Variations

Mocha Fudge: Substitute strong, hot coffee for cream.

Nut Fudge: Decorate each square with one-half nut meat. Or add ½ cup cut nut meats to mixture.

Candied Fudge: Decorate each square with cut piece of candied or glacé pineapple or cherry.

PENUCHE

This is an immensely popular candy with the college girl. It is spelled in different ways, but it tastes just as good in any spelling.

3 cups brown sugar	1 Tbsp. vanilla extract
1 cup light cream	3 Tbsp. butter
¼ tsp. salt	1 cup chopped nut meats

Combine sugar, cream and salt in heavy saucepan and stir over low heat until sugar is dissolved. Cook without stirring; just an occasional careful scraping across the bottom of the pan is all that is necessary. Cook until soft-ball stage is reached. Set aside to cool, add butter and vanilla extract. When mixture is cool, beat well and proceed as for fudge.

MOLASSES TAFFY

2 cups molasses	2 Tbsp. butter
1 Tbsp. vinegar	Few drops of oil of
½ tsp. soda	peppermint or wintergreen

Combine molasses and vinegar in heavy saucepan. Cook without stirring until hard-ball stage (270° F.) is reached. Remove from heat. Add soda, butter, and flavoring and pour at once into well-buttered oblong pans. Let cool until edges begin to crinkle. Grease hands lightly with butter. Pick up a portion of the taffy, as much as can be handled. Pull candy out to length that can be managed without strands falling. Fold candy back onto itself, and pull out. Continue process of pulling and folding until taffy is firm. Have a pair of sharp scissors at hand. Dip scissors into boiling water, and snip off pieces of candy onto a piece of waxed paper.

CANDIED ORANGE OR LEMON PEEL

Peel 3 naval oranges or 6 lemons	2 Tbsp. light corn syrup
1 cup sugar	¾ cup water
	½ tsp. salt

Cover peel with water. Add salt. Boil ½ hour. Drain. Cover again with water and boil until tender. (A longer period is required to tenderize lemon peel than orange peel.) Drain. Cut peel in strips. Bring sugar, corn syrup, and water to boil. Cook peel at low temperature in this, to gently absorb most of the syrup. Cover. Cool overnight in the syrup. Reheat slowly to simmering point the following day. Cool again in syrup. Reheat and continue this heating and cooling process until most of the syrup is absorbed, which will probably take four days. Drain. Spread out to dry on rack or waxed paper until surface syrup has been absorbed—one day or more. Roll in granulated sugar, or shake peel in paper bag with a little sugar. Store in covered container.

Variations

Colored Peel: Add red or green vegetable coloring to syrup.
Spiced Peel: Add a little cinnamon or clove to syrup. Tie spices in cloth to prevent darkening peel.

DIVINITY FUDGE

2 cups sugar	1 tsp. vinegar
½ cup dark corn syrup	2 egg whites
¼ cup water	¾ cup chopped nuts
	1 tsp. vanilla extract

Mix sugar, syrup, water, and vinegar. Cook slowly, without stirring, until mixture forms a firm ball (265° F.). Pour gradually over stiffly-beaten egg whites, beating continuously, with a wire whip, until thick and creamy. Add nuts and vanilla, continuing to beat until fudge thickens and begins to lose its gloss. Pour into a buttered pan. Cut in squares.

FRUIT ROLL

1 lb. prunes	½ cup chopped nut meats
½ lb. seedless raisins	2 Tbsp. confectioner's sugar
	1 Tbsp. cocoa

Steam prunes for 5 minutes. Remove pits from prunes. Grind raisins and prunes in a food chopper. Add nuts, and mix thoroughly. Grease hands lightly with butter, and shape fruit mixture into 3 rolls about 1½ inches in diameter. Wrap rolls in waxed paper and place in refrigerator for several hours. Immediately before serving, remove fruit roll from refrigerator, and roll in combined sugar and cocoa. Cut into ¼ inch slices.

POPCORN BALLS

1 pkg. corn for popping	1 Tbsp. vinegar
2 cups molasses	3 Tbsp. butter

Popcorn

Prepare popcorn according to directions on package. Pop the corn, salt lightly. Remove any unpopped kernels.

Syrup

Combine molasses and vinegar in heavy saucepan. Cook over low heat until the soft-ball stage is reached. Continue cooking at reduced heat until hardball stage is reached. Remove from heat, add butter, and slowly pour over big bowl of popped corn. Grease hands lightly with butter. Pick up syrup-coated popcorn and press into balls, being careful not to crush corn. Cool, and wrap each ball in waxed paper. Tie with scarlet ribbon for holiday season.

TURKISH DELIGHT

2 pkgs. gelatin dessert (any flavor)	2 cups sugar
	½ cup cold water
⅔ cup boiling water	Powdered sugar

Add boiling water to gelatin. Allow to stand 15 minutes. Boil sugar and cold water without stirring, to 238° F., or until syrup spins thread. Remove from heat. Slowly add hot syrup to gelatin, stirring constantly. Pour into shallow pan rinsed in cold water. Chill overnight. Turn out on board with powdered sugar. Cut into oblong pieces with sharp knife. Cover thoroughly with sugar.

STUFFED FRUITS

1 lb. dried prunes or figs	1 lb. dates
	Granulated sugar

Steam prunes or figs over hot water for 15 minutes, or until fruit plumps out and feels soft to touch. Make a lengthwise slit on prunes and dates, remove pit. Make opening in figs. The dried fruits may be stuffed with any kind of nut meat, peanut butter, candied ginger, marshmallow, or fudge. Dates are usually rolled in granulated sugar.

FRUIT BARS

1 cup figs	1 cup chopped nut meats
1 cup raisins	Orange juice
1 cup dates	Lemon juice
	Granulated sugar

Put fruits through food grinder. Add chopped nut meats, and enough fruit juice to moisten. Press mixture in small square pan. Pat down to make a

Candy-making at home is definitely in order when there are children in the family. Making candy for themselves, the family, and guests offers them an opportunity to march right into the kitchen and make themselves at home.

smooth surface. Cut in bars, 1 inch by 2 inches. Sprinkle with granulated sugar.

MICHIGAN CREAM CANDY

3 cups granulated sugar
1 cup light corn syrup
1 cup light cream

Pinch of salt
1 cup broken nut meats
1 Tbsp. vanilla extract

Combine all ingredients (except nuts and vanilla) in heavy saucepan. Stir over low heat until sugar is dissolved. Cook until soft-ball stage is reached. Remove from heat. Cool without stirring until cool. Beat until creamy. Add nuts and vanilla extract. Turn into a well-buttered square pan. Cut into squares. This candy is truly delectable.

BITTERSWEET SPRINKLES

2 cups sugar or confectioner's
    sugar
4 Tbsp. boiling water
½ cup cocoa

Cream to moisten
1 tsp. vanilla extract
1 tsp. almond extract
1 cup chocolate sprinkles

Combine sugar with paste made of cocoa and boiling water. Blend until smooth. If mixture is too thick, moisten with a little cream. Add extracts. Shape with fingers into tiny balls, about 1 inch big. Pour sprinkles into shallow plate. Roll balls in coating until well-covered. These are dainty and very rich.

Variations

The chocolate balls may be rolled in Dutch cocoa, finely-chopped nut meats, or finely-shredded coconut.
A candied cherry may be placed in center of ball.

SPICED NUTS

2 cups shelled nut meat halves	¼ tsp. cinnamon
¼ cup sweet butter	¼ tsp. allspice

Melt butter in heavy skillet, add nut meats. Stir gently over low heat. Sprinkle with spices, and stir until nuts are well-coated. Turn out on brown wrapping paper. Cool, store in covered tin box.

PEANUT CLUSTERS

Package of semi-sweet chocolate (7½ oz.), melted	2 cups shelled peanuts
	Pinch of salt

Melt chocolate over hot water. Remove from heat, add salt and peanuts. Drop by spoonfuls on waxed paper. Cool, store in covered tin box.

Variations

Raisin: Substitute light raisins for peanuts.
Coconut: Substitute shredded coconut for peanuts.
Marshmallow: Substitute marshmallows for peanuts.

UNCOOKED FONDANT

(Christmas Mint Patties)

1 lb. sugar or confectioner's sugar, sifted	1 egg white, unbeaten
	Few drops of oil of peppermint
	Vegetable coloring: red, green

Mix the egg white in a bowl with small portion of sugar. Gradually add remainder of sugar and oil of peppermint, until mixture is soft enough to drop from spoon, but firm enough to hold shape, as mint patty flattens out on waxed paper. When mixture is right consistency, divide into separate portions. Color one portion red and the other green.

Variations

Chocolate Mints: Color white mixture with small quantity of melted bitter chocolate.
Coconut Mints: Mix with shredded coconut and drop from spoon.
Fruit Mints: Mix fondant with small quantities of candied cherries, candied pineapple. Drop from teaspoon or shape with fingers into long roll. Wrap in waxed paper and store in refrigerator until firm. Slice down like jelly roll.

SALTED NUTS

1 lb. shelled nuts, blanched   Salad oil
                                    Salt

Pour salad oil into a heavy skillet to the depth of ¼ to ½ inch. Dry nuts thoroughly, after blanching. Heat oil, but not to smoking. Add a portion of nuts at a time, stir gently over low heat until a delicate brown. Lift out with perforated spoon, and place on brown wrapping paper. Drain well and transfer to clean paper, sprinkle lightly with salt. Cool. Store in covered tin box.

BLANCHED ALMONDS

Pouring boiling water over shelled almonds. Let nuts stand until skins begin to wrinkle. Lift out with perforated spoon and remove skins by rubbing between fingers.

SUGARED NUT MEATS

1 lb. shelled walnuts or pecans   1 tsp. cinnamon
½ cup granulated sugar   2 Tbsp. butter

Pour nut meats into heavy skillet. Add butter and cinnamon. Stir until nut meats are thoroughly coated. Remove from heat, and sprinkle with sugar. Turn out on waxed paper. Store in covered tin box.

CREAM CARAMELS

1 cup granulated sugar   1 cup light cream
1 cup light corn syrup   ¼ cup sweet butter
                             1 Tbsp. vanilla extract

Combine sugar and corn syrup in heavy saucepan. Stir until sugar is dissolved, and cook until it forms a thick syrup. Add butter and cream with extreme care, so that syrup continues to boil. Stir constantly until it forms a firm ball. Add vanilla extract. Pour into well-buttered pan. Do not permit sugar crystals on sides of pan to be scraped off. Cool. Cut into squares.

CHOCOLATE CREAM CARAMELS

1 cup granulated sugar   ¼ tsp. salt
¾ cup light corn syrup   1½ cups cream
3 sq. unsweetened chocolate   1 Tbsp. vanilla extract

Combine sugar, chocolate, corn syrup, salt, ½ cup cream in heavy saucepan. Cook over low heat, stirring constantly, until sugar is dissolved. Cook slowly

Welcome Christmas gifts are assorted candies and cookies, attractively packed.

until soft-ball stage is reached. Add another ½ cup of cream, and again bring to soft-ball stage. Slowly, so that mixture does not stop boiling at any time, add final ½ cup of cream and cook to firm-ball stage. Add vanilla extract. Pour into well-buttered square pan. Cool and let stand for several hours to dry. Cut in squares.

Variations

Any kind of broken nut meats are delicious added to all caramel candies.

CARAMEL FUDGE ROLL

1 recipe chocolate fudge   1 recipe chocolate caramels

Pour caramel mixture into 2 well-buttered pans. When cold, remove from pans. Place on board lightly dusted with powdered sugar.

Prepare fudge mixture, beating until thick but only until it loses its gloss. Spread evenly on sheets of caramel, using ½ of fudge for each. (If fudge becomes too firm, knead until soft and creamy.) Roll tightly as for jelly roll and wrap in waxed paper. Let stand several hours to harden. Cut crosswise in ¼ inches slices.

ALMOND BUTTER CRUNCH

1 cup butter	½ cup finely chopped blanched
1 cup sugar	almonds, lightly toasted
	4 sq. unsweetened chocolate

Add butter to sugar in heavy saucepan. Place over low heat, stir constantly until sugar is dissolved. Cook until a small amount of mixture becomes brittle in cold water, stirring occasionally to prevent scorching. Add ¼ cup nuts. Pour into lightly-buttered pan. Cool. Heat chocolate over boiling water until partly melted, then remove from boiling water and stir it rapidly until entirely melted. Spread ½ of chocolate over top, and sprinkle with ½ of remaining nuts. Cool until chocolate is firm. Turn out on board and spread remaining chocolate over top. Sprinkle with final portion of nuts. Cool until chocolate sets. Break up lightly with handle of silver knife.

CANDY BARS

The goodness of these bars depends upon melted chocolate—which is always melted in a double boiler, over hot, *not boiling,* water.

NUT BARS

¾ cup halves salted cashew nuts,	blanched almonds
roasted peanuts, or toasted	1 pkg. semi-sweet chocolate

BRAZIL NUT BARS

1 cup Brazil nut meats	½ lb. unsweetened chocolate

Line bottom of loaf pan with waxed paper, letting paper extend in 2-inch tabs at each end. Melt chocolate, turn out into pan. Arrange nuts in rows over chocolate. Let stand in cool place to harden. Lift out of pan with paper tabs. Cool, cut in bars, 1 by 2 inches.

COCONUT BARS

1 can moist coconut	6 sq. unsweetened chocolate

Arrange coconut in lined pan and cover with melted chocolate. Stir lightly with fork until well mixed. Cool and cut in bars.

RAISIN NUT BARS

⅔ cup seedless raisins

⅔ cup broken walnut meats
½ lb. unsweetened chocolate

Wash raisins in hot water and dry thoroughly. Arrange raisins in lined pan; then sprinkle with nuts. Cover with melted chocolate. Cool and cut in bars.

FIG, DATE, NUT BALLS

½ cup dried figs
½ cup dates

1 cup nut meats, chopped
1 Tbsp. lemon juice
Powdered sugar

Put figs and dates through food grinder. Add nut meats. Combine all ingredients, mix until blended. Shape into balls about ¾ inch in diameter. Roll in powdered sugar.

OPERA CREAMS

2 cups sugar
⅔ cup heavy cream
1 cup milk
¼ cup light corn syrup

¼ tsp. salt
1 tsp. vanilla
1 cup pecan meats
1 pkg. semi-sweet chocolate

Combine sugar, cream, milk, corn syrup, and salt in heavy saucepan. Stir until sugar is dissolved, and mixture comes to boil. Continue cooking, stirring occasionally, until a small amount of syrup forms a soft ball in cold water. Cool to lukewarm and add vanilla extract. Beat until mixture begins to thicken; then add nuts and continue beating only until mixture loses its gloss. Turn at once into well-buttered pan. Heat chocolate over boiling water until partly melted; then remove from boiling water and stir rapidly until entirely melted. Pour over candy. Cool until firm. Cut in squares.

CHOCOLATE COCONUT KISSES

1 pkg. semi-sweet chocolate
    (14 oz.)

⅔ cup condensed milk
½ can moist coconut
1 Tbsp. vanilla extract

Heat chocolate over boiling water until partly melted; then remove from boiling water and stir rapidly until entirely melted. Add milk and blend; then add coconut and vanilla. Drop from spoon on waxed paper to form small mounds. Cool until firm.

35.

A HOSTESS IN

HER OWN HOME

WHAT does every bride seek when she sets up a home of her own? She craves to be known as a charming hostess. This instinct has been handed down from generation to generation, and it is as natural for a new bride to want to be a lovely hostess as it is for her to breathe.

But it isn't a particularly simple part to play; in fact, it may take a good many social occasions before a bride learns the art of being gracious and friendly when the burden of responsibility rests upon her shoulders. And many tears have been shed by inexperienced brides before this role of hostess has been mastered.

Fortunately, there are certain fundamental rules to guide a brand-new homemaker, and it is well worth her while to study these principles and apply them to her social obligations. As soon as they are really a part of her life, she is ready to play her role of hostess without strain.

Basically, every human being craves companionship. The young men and women who marry, and bring up their children in this new world of ours, are apt to spend a great share of their leisure time in informal entertaining at home. The young years are the years in which to make new friends, who belong to both husband and wife and are proudly called "our friends."

These new families are the nucleus of America's pattern of social life, and it's a wise bride who learns how to handle her share of entertaining at home gracefully and easily. The business success of many a young husband depends in large part upon the role his wife plays in their social life. Entertaining is an important factor in a young man's career, and a wife's ability to further her husband's advancement is often dependent upon her ability to cook a first-rate meal and appear to advantage as a hostess. The promise of contributing to her husband's future is something well worth her effort.

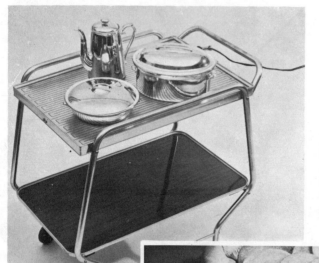

Movable tables find many uses in the home. As a double-decker the table can be loaded in the kitchen and rolled out to guests.

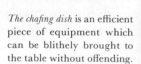

The chafing dish is an efficient piece of equipment which can be blithely brought to the table without offending.

These fundamental principles of social success are easily learned; they may be listed briefly as follows:

1. The art of bringing congenial people together.
2. The ability to introduce people tactfully.
3. Pre-planning for the occasion.
4. The practice of cookery to achieve a perfect meal.
5. The budgeting of the money.
6. Enjoying the party.

Sunday "brunch" is a pleasant custom for people who like the relaxation of friendly rather than formal entertaining. Serve plenty of piping hot coffee.

Hot broth is a surprise first course for brunch.

1. The Art of Bringing Congenial People Together

A party must have a sound reason for existence. Inviting everyone in town may make a large and noisy occasion, but it is a party without a purpose, and the guests are not particularly honored by the invitation. The new hostess is better advised if she invites two or three couples with mutual interests—definite hobbies or sports—to create an atmosphere of congeniality.

When a hostess issues her invitations, it is a courtesy to each guest to mention the names of the other guests. Perhaps some unfriendly social situation exists, and embarrassment could be avoided by such forehandedness. This is especially true if the bride is a newcomer in a community and knows little of the social background of her new acquaintances. Often a bride is called upon to be hostess to guests many years her senior. In such instances it is flattering to select a guest of honor and build the party around that individual.

2. The Ability to Introduce People Tactfully

Volumes could and should be written on the great American fault of mumbling introductions. When new friends are meeting under your roof for the first time, see to it that you speak their names clearly. Invest the introduction with dignity, and make all guests feel that you are honored to have them in your home. It is a good idea to make out a list of their names, and learn it by heart ahead of time. As the evening wears on, keep an eye on the small groupings that form. If people are happily chatting, leave them alone; but if an individual is sitting apart, make an opportunity for a personal visit with the solitary one. Don't clutch a victim and drag him to a group which is already formed. Rather, ask one or more persons to join you. Make a point of a personal visit with each guest before the evening is over. Don't attempt bridge or other games if you are a novice. Find out in advance if each guest plays, or wants to play, or expects to play, and arrange your program accordingly. The same thing holds true for literary games. Always keep a party on a light-hearted casual note.

3. Pre-planning the Occasion

Many hostesses feel that parties which just happen are the most fun. When everything is at hand "to do with," and there's enough leisure during the day to plan the details, this is often the case. But today's social picture includes many young women who work and whose social life is concentrated on weekends.

Careful planning gives a charming, casual air to the party. How to plan? Make out a written guest list to make sure that the guest will take to each other. Make out a list of supplies. Polish the silver, wax the furniture, or do whatever special jobs are necessary. Careful planning means menu-planning also. Are the groceries in the house well in advance of the party, so that there is no last-minute rush? Has each dish been cooked for the family a time or two, so that the results will be perfect? Is the menu one which can be largely prepared in advance?

Avoid dishes which require fussing-over during the last half hour. Avoid dishes which aren't fit to eat if a guest is late—there's always *one* late arrival. A hostess must be calm, gracious, and make each guest feel welcome, no matter what time he makes his appearance.

The beauty and elegance of this table setting is reflected in the sparkling glassware and sterling silver, which will heighten the pleasure of the meal itself.

Informal buffet service is a "natural" for the inexperienced hostess or for the professional woman who must budget her time. Create that party air by decorating the table with lovely, fresh flowers or plants.

Trays, large, small, square, round, whatever you can acquire, are indispensable aids to the hostess. Plain or sectionalized relish dishes are also essential for those who do much casual entertaining.

A large wooden tray, polished and gleaming, offers a brilliant setting for an array of cheese and crackers.

A *punch bowl and punch cups* will say "It's a grown-up party" to any youngster.

Individual shells plus this stylish tall pepper mill on a platter give a party atmosphere to this luncheon of creamed crab and salad.

Individual cocktail trays are a boon to both hostess and guests. They permit guests to balance refreshments neatly in one spot, and lessen the possibility of grease stains and alcohol spots on the hostess' treasured furnishings.

Cheese is the common denominator on this appetizer tray: in balls, in wedges, with nuts, on crackers and in a spread.

4. The Practice of Cookery to Achieve a Perfect Meal

Is it your first party? Are you a novice in the art of cookery? If the answer is "yes" to these questions, give a buffet supper party. The essentials for the meal may be purchased from fresh, canned, and quick-frozen foods available in every grocery store. It is then a simple matter to plan the menu, prepare the foods, arrange the flowers, set the table, and generally create a party air.

A party is a show. The hostess plays the lead, and the guests are the cast.

When the preliminaries are whipped into shape, take time to perfect an entrée, a salad, and a dessert. Serve them to the family two or three times, tucked into other menus, until the dishes are letter-perfect. Be smart. The wise hostess holds her rehearsals in her own kitchen.

5. The Budgeting of the Money

Many a budget has gone on the rocks because the thrifty young housewife suddenly becomes weary of thrift and decides to give a party. The food budget for a week is spent on luxury foods for a hasty, extravagant party. Smart food budgeteers include parties in their plans. It is the simple, well-thought-out social affairs of a home which make it the center of the family's universe.

One clever way to manage for party money is to buy one or two canned specialties each week, and set them aside on a special party shelf. Another plan is to set aside a small sum of money for the same purpose. Whichever method is used, the important thing is to find a system which is practical and stick to it.

6. Enjoying the Party

A new homemaker needs more than help on table-setting, menus, and recipes. A new team needs practice to be successful. A husband's advice about the guest list and his opinion of the menu are of genuine value. The party is given for mutual happiness. Plan the party together; a man's counsel is important. So talk things over together, and work together to make the party the hit of the season.

Nearly unbreakable melamine dinnerware lovely enough even for a party for a bride.

36.

APPETIZERS—

SANDWICHES

A NEW development in the American hospitality scene may possibly be traced to the appeal of the decorative tid-bits of food known as canapés or hors d'oeuvres. Canapés are usually served on bread, toast or crackers, and hors d'oeuvres separately. Their variety is endless, and the number of recipes available rather bewilders a novice.

As the greater part of our social life is carried on today without maid service, so the increasing popularity and use of appetizers served in the living room before dinner may be due to the fact that it simplifies home entertaining. An essential part of the fun and gayety of a party is the dressed-up appearance of the food. Appetizers give the hostess a free field in which to let her imagination run riot.

The chief reason for serving appetizers is to stimulate appetite and conversation; also, to simplify table service. The portions are finger-size, to enable them to be eaten in one or two neat bites. The flavor is sharp, tart, or piquant; it should never be bland or cloying. A hostess can soon learn the trick of making these gay nothings, whether the food selected be simple or elaborate.

When several varieties of superlatively good appetizers are served, the party is off to a flying start. Some special equipment is needed in the way of tools; a sharp knife for cutting, a stout wooden cutting-board, a set of cutters for fancy shapes, tiny molds for aspics, a really good can-opener, an egg-slicer, and a small pastry bag. If you keep this party equipment in a special place, ready for use, interesting and colorful appetizers are a matter of minutes.

Service: use an attractive large tray of wood, glass or metal, small plates and napkins, and small dishes for extra relishes.

Food: practically any food may be used for appetizers; meat, fish, poultry, eggs, cheese, raw vegetables, pickles, olives, and relishes are good choices.

Container: the appetizer base may be bread, toast, crackers, fancy puff paste shapes, even tiny cream puff shells and tart shells.

490

When planning an assortment for a party a good rule to follow is: 1 meat, 1 fish, 1 egg or cheese, 2 raw vegetables, and 3 relishes. If it is a large party, a greater variety may be made, to fill an enormous tray of "thingamabobs."

APPETIZERS WITH BREAD AS A BASE (CANAPÉS)

Have all ingredients ready at hand. Place utensils on large utility tray convenient for use. Arrange bread on cutting-board, remove crusts, and cut bread in desired shapes. Thin-sliced bread is good for this purpose. If bread is unsliced cut in ¼ inch slices and then into fancy shapes. Sharp cutters are sold singly and in sets for this purpose.

TO SAUTÉ BREAD

Place skillet over low heat on stove, melt butter, margarine, or salad oil in pan, enough to cover bottom of pan. When fat is hot, place bread in pan, being careful to handle it so pieces remain whole. A spatula is good for this. Place a sheet of brown paper on a flat cookie sheet. When bread is golden brown on one side, lift out and drain on paper. Quickly spread with canapé mixture, place on covered dish, and serve immediately. If dish has no cover, place clean napkin on warm plate, and fold it over the canapés.

Or the bread may be buttered, placed on rack in oven, and toasted on both sides under broiler flame. For a very small party, the electric toaster may be utilized. But nothing is quite as delicious as the sauté method in the skillet.

Another method of serving canapés is the "spread to order" variety. In this case, the hostess arranges a bowl of unsweetened crackers or potato chips, and places close at hand several small bowls of canapé mixtures and small knives for spreading. The guests choose the mixtures they like, and spread the crackers themselves. For an informal party this type of service is popular.

SOME POPULAR CANAPÉS

(Finger Service)

ANCHOVY AND CREAM CHEESE

1 pkg. cream cheese	1 Tbsp. lemon juice
1 Tbsp. anchovy paste	1 doz. sautéd bread crescents
	Hard-cooked egg yolk

Mash cheese, anchovy paste, and lemon juice together until smooth. Spread on crescents, and garnish with tiny pieces of hard-cooked egg yolk. Serve hot. Anchovy paste is sold in tubes.

ANCHOVY CANAPÉS

| 1 2½-oz. tin rolled fillets | Hard-cooked egg |
| of anchovies | Sliced stuffed olives |

Cut bread in fancy shapes, sauté and drain on brown paper. Lay two fillets on toast with slice of olive on top. Remove egg yolk and rub through a fine sieve. Garnish with tiny portion. Cut egg white in ornamental pieces, lay on top.

AVOCADO PEAR BUTTER

1 avocado	1 tsp. lemon juice
1 tsp. mayonnaise	Dash red pepper
¼ tsp. curry powder	1 tsp. onion juice
¼ tsp. dry mustard	Clove of garlic
	½ tsp. salt

Cut the avocado in half lengthwise. Remove stone and scoop out pulp carefully. Rub a bowl with clove of garlic cut in half. Mix pulp with other ingredients and refill shells. Dust lightly with paprika. Serve with crisp toasted crackers.

CHICKEN LIVERS

| ½ lb. cooked chicken livers | 1 Tbsp. mayonnaise |
| | 1 tsp. grated onion |

Mash livers with fork. Blend with mayonnaise and onion, until a smooth consistency. Spread on bread or crackers. Garnish with slices of stuffed olive.

DEVILED HAM

| 1 3½-oz. tin deviled ham | ¼ tsp. dry mustard |
| 1 Tbsp. sour cream | 1 Tbsp. salad oil |

Blend all ingredients together. Spread on bread, cut in squares, or rolled. Also excellent on crackers. Decorate with slice of sweet pickle.

DEVILED CHEESE

¼ lb. cheddar cheese	¼ tsp. dry mustard
¼ tsp. curry powder	1 Tbsp. mayonnaise
	1 egg yolk

Beat all ingredients together until mixture is smooth. Spread on crisp crackers at last minute. Light broiler oven and brown under flame until cheese melts. Serve at once.

DEVILED TOMATO

Slices of Spanish onion
Ripe tomatoes
Hard-cooked egg

Mayonnaise with dash of dry
mustard
Salt, paprika
Crisp crackers

Peel onions, slice thin. Slice tomatoes. Slice eggs in wire slicer. Spread seasoned mayonnaise on cracker, place slice of onion on top, sprinkle lightly with salt and paprika, place slice of tomato on top of onion, place egg on top of tomato. Garnish with tiny dab of mayonnaise.

SARDINE CANAPÉS

1 tin sardines

1 Tbsp. lemon juice
2 Tbsp. mayonnaise

Open tin of sardines, drain oil. Remove all skin and bone. Mash sardines with

Canapé trays filled with an array of delectable appetizers increase the enjoyment of any party.

silver fork and mix with lemon juice and mayonnaise. Spread on toast or crackers.

SARDINE IN EGG CUPS

6 hard-cooked eggs	Sardine mixture
	(see recipe above)

Cut eggs in half crosswise, slice a thin slice from each half so egg will stand upright on circle of toast. Remove egg yolks and blend with sardine mixture. Add salt to taste. Fill cups with mixture and serve each egg on its own circle of toast. Garnish plate with parsley.

SARDINE AND EGG SPREAD

1 4-oz. tin sardines	2 Tbsp. canned mushroom pieces
2 hard-cooked eggs	2 Tbsp. mayonnaise
	1 Tbsp. lemon juice

Prepare sardines as above. Chop eggs fine. Drain mushrooms, chop fine. Mix all ingredients together and use as spread, or on rolled sandwiches.

COTTAGE CHEESE CANAPÉS

Cottage cheese has many possibilities. The thrifty hostess will find this an excellent stand-by for many a party.

COTTAGE CHEESE BOWL

½ lb. cottage cheese	½ cup sour cream, whipped
1 3-oz. pkg. cream cheese	½ tsp. salt
	1 tsp. lemon juice

Blend all ingredients together and beat until smooth and creamy. Pile high in a pretty dish and dust lightly with paprika. Serve well-chilled. Spread on potato chips or crackers.

COTTAGE CHEESE MIX

½ lb. cottage cheese	1 Tbsp. mayonnaise
1 small cucumber	Salt to taste
	Pumpernickel bread

Peel cucumber, slice, and chill in ice water until crisp. Drain, chop cucumber fine. Mix with cheese and mayonnaise. Serve on fingers of bread, sliced thin.

COTTAGE CHEESE AND CHIVES

½ lb. cottage cheese	2 Tbsp. chives, chopped fine
1 Tbsp. sour cream	1 Tbsp. onions, chopped fine
	Salt to taste

Mix all ingredients and spread on rounds of bread. Garnish with thin slice of stuffed olive on top.

Bread for tea sandwiches should be sliced as thin as possible. Always leave butter at room temperature for a time before attempting to spread it on these thin slices.

COTTAGE CHEESE AND CELERY

½ lb. cottage cheese	¼ tsp. curry powder
1 3-oz. pkg. cream cheese	½ tsp. salt
¼ tsp. Worcestershire sauce	1 Tbsp. mayonnaise
¼ tsp. dry mustard	Stalk of celery

Clean celery, crisp it in a bowl of ice water. Drain, and dry well in clean towel. Make a mixture of cheese and seasonings. Stuff each stalk, and smooth evenly with knife. Wrap in damp cloth and place in refrigerator until ready to serve. Cut in 2-inch lengths. Serve on lace-doily-covered plate.

ROLLED SANDWICH

STEP 1

STEP 2

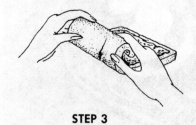

STEP 3

STEP 4

SHAPED SANDWICHES

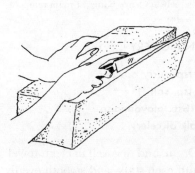

STEP 1

STEP 2

RIBBON LOAF SANDWICHES

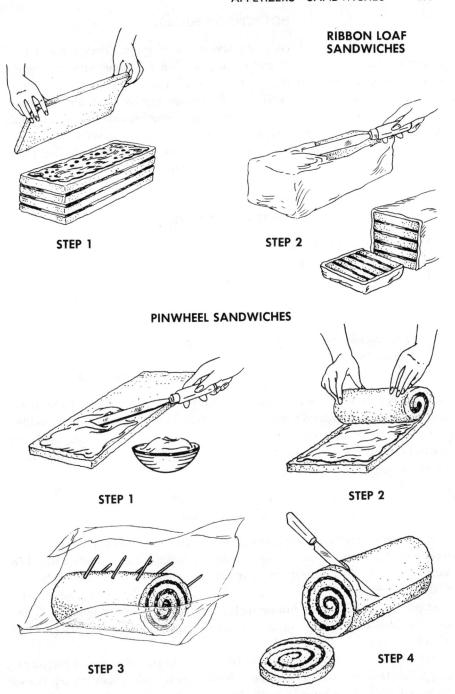

STEP 1

STEP 2

PINWHEEL SANDWICHES

STEP 1

STEP 2

STEP 3

STEP 4

The best tea parties are those at which the hostess provides a generous assortment of fancy sandwiches with intriguing fillings.

HOT HORS D'OEUVRES

These delicacies have become the favorite of everyone. They are served in most elaborate style at hotels and restaurants, but the home party may enjoy them in a more simplified form.

Cocktail sausages and cocktail frankfurters are usually available. The ever-popular "hot franks" may be cut into 2-inch lengths, brushed lightly with melted butter or bacon fat, and pan-broiled in a heavy iron skillet over a low flame. Serve on a hot plate, with a toothpick skewered in each portion. Place a small glass of mustard in the center of the plate, and pass tiny hot buttered rolls.

HOT MUSHROOMS

Mushrooms sautéd in butter are sold in tins. It is only necessary to heat, drain and skewer with toothpicks so that each mushroom may be picked up easily. Or each mushroom may be skewered to a toast round.

HOT CHICKEN LIVERS

½ lb. chicken livers
2 Tbsp. flour

1 tsp. salt
4 Tbsp. butter or salad oil
6 triangles buttered toast

Roll chicken livers in flour and salt, in soup plate. Place on clean paper towel and shake well to remove excess flour. Heat butter or salad oil in skillet. Brown livers on both sides, reduce heat to low, and sauté until livers are cooked through. Serve on buttered toast at once. Or serve with toothpicks to be eaten "as is."

SANDWICHES

If a hostess entertains frequently, there is no branch of party food which pays better dividends than an assortment of delectable fancy sandwiches. The same special kitchen utensils used for canapés are needed for sandwiches.

The bakeries offer a variety of breads, which include: nut bread, cheese, orange, raisin, cinnamon, pumpernickel, white, whole wheat, and rye. If unsliced sandwich bread is used, it is usually necessary to order it a day or two ahead of time.

Bread for tea sandwiches should be as thin as possible. Bread for picnic and lunch box sandwiches should be about ¼ inch thick, crusts left on. Bread for rolled sandwiches must be fresh that day, otherwise the slice cracks as the sandwich is being rolled. Bread should be one day old for making all other sandwiches. Wrap tightly in waxed paper and leave in refrigerator overnight.

Hearty sandwich fare is this hamburger topped with onion ring.

HOW TO SPREAD SANDWICHES

Place a large wooden cutting-board on table. Place slices of bread in pairs, just as they come from loaf. Leave butter at room temperature to soften, and rub with spoon until creamy enough to spread easily. Butter one slice of bread only for cheese, egg, or meat fillings. Butter each slice of bread for soft fillings. For afternoon tea sandwiches, it is better to butter the bread on the loaf, before cutting or removing slice from loaf.

READY-TO-USE FILLINGS

Stop at the grocer's and get acquainted with the variety of sandwich spreads offered. There are many of them today, and they offer the hostess the benefits of convenience and simplicity of preparation. Some of the more popular ones are:

Anchovy paste
Anchovy fillets, flat or rolled
Cheese spreads: pineapple, olives, pimientos (wine or brandy added)
Smoked cheese
Cheddar cheese
Meat spreads
Liver pastes
Salmon, tuna fish, herring, fish roe, sardines, caviar
Seedless jams, guava, grape, or apple jelly

CUTTING SANDWICHES

Have waxed paper and clean linen napkins on hand. Put the cutting-board in place, arrange butter and fillings at hand for efficient work.

ROLLED SANDWICHES

Cut off crusts with sharp knife, spread bread with soft butter to within ½ inch from end of slice, spread with soft filling, such as cream cheese or deviled ham. Roll up sandwich exactly as a sheet of paper is rolled up, and press ends together. As the bread is rolled, the filling tends to spread so it is not neces-

Picnic sandwiches need to be sturdy. There's something about open-air eating combined with a hike or a swim that whets the appetite.

sary to spread filling to end of slice. Skewer the sandwich with two toothpicks. As each sandwich is rolled and skewered, lay it on plate covered with waxed paper. When one plate is finished, cover tightly with paper, wrap in damp towel, and store away in refrigerator until ready to use. For a garnish, a tiny sprig of parsley in each end makes a good appearance.

SHAPED SANDWICHES

For afternoon tea parties, these continue to head the list in popularity. Cutters come in sets appropriate for bridge, special holidays, and children's parties. Cut all crusts from the entire unsliced loaf, then proceed to cut the slices lengthwise of the loaf to avoid excessive waste. Butter, cut and spread with filling. If the shape selected is round, it is attractive to cut a small hole in the top round, and insert a garnish of olive or pimiento.

RIBBON LOAF

This is a good choice if a dozen or more are apt to be served. The procedure is the same as for fancy sandwiches. After the bread is sliced lengthwise of the loaf, the slices are buttered. The bottom slice is spread with a filling, a buttered slice placed on top, and a different filling is selected for each slice, until four or more slices are placed one on top of the other. The top slice is buttered only, ready for frosting.

A frosting is made by softening three cakes of cream cheese mixed with top milk or light cream. Dip a silver knife in hot water and spread the "frosting" evenly over top, sides and ends. Garnish with a design of slices of stuffed olives.

Wrap loaf in waxed paper and then in a damp cloth. Place in refrigerator for several hours. When ready to serve, slice down as if slicing a loaf of bread.

PINWHEELS

Remove all crusts from sandwich loaf. Cut in slices, lengthwise of loaf. Spread each slice with any one of the sandwich butters (or any smooth, creamy filling). Start at the long end and roll up, just as for a jelly roll. Skewer with toothpicks, wrap in waxed paper, cover with damp coth; chill in refrigerator for several hours, and when ready to serve, lay on cutting-board and slice in thin slices crosswise.

SUGGESTED SANDWICH FILLINGS

Afternoon Tea or Bridge Club Sandwiches

Cream cheese and crushed, drained pineapple.
Cream cheese and finely chopped cucumber.

Cream cheese and chopped walnuts and olives.
Cream cheese and orange marmalade.
Cream cheese and chopped unsalted almonds.
Cream cheese and chives.
Minced mushrooms sautéd in butter, rolled up.
Minced chicken and finely chopped celery and mayonnaise.
Cheddar cheese, rolled and toasted.
Chopped shrimp and mayonnaise.
Flaked salmon with diced celery and mayonnaise.
Minced ham with sweet pickle and mayonnaise.
Chopped dates and walnuts.

SANDWICH BUTTERS FOR PINWHEELS

Soften butter at room temperature. Beat with spoon until creamy, and season with any one of the following:

Anchovy paste	Chutney
Curry powder	Minced chives
Chili sauce	Parsley
	Watercress

FILLINGS FOR FOUR-LAYER RIBBON LOAF

Flaked salmon with mayonnaise.
Cream cheese and chopped olives.
Deviled ham, with dash of dry mustard, and moistened with cream.

SCHOOL LUNCH BOXES AND PICNICS

Peanut butter and strained honey.
Sliced cold meat, crisp lettuce.
Sliced hard-cooked eggs with mayonnaise and lettuce.
Crisp bacon and sliced eggs.
Cole slaw and sliced eggs.
Jam or jelly.
Flaked salmon, tuna, or sardine with lemon juice and mayonnaise.
Cottage cheese and chopped cucumbers.
Cream cheese and chopped stuffed olives.
Cream cheese and chopped nuts.
Deviled ham and minced sweet pickle.
Egg salad and lettuce.
Nut bread and cream cheese.
Cheddar cheese and sliced ham.

37.

TV SNACKS
AND
SUPPER TRAYS

THE ADVENT of the television screen into the home has probably had more effect on the eating habits of the modern family than any other single influence. When the family's favorite show starts at the dinner hour, there is only one thing to do and that is to move the dinner in front of the TV set. And that is precisely what millions of families have done and will continue to do.

This in turn does away with formal table settings, large tables and tablecloths, and three to four course dinners. The demand today is for a hearty soup or entrée, a dessert that is easily made and, of course, snacks to appease hunger during a long evening of watching television.

TV BEEF STEW

¼ cup dried onion flakes
¼ cup dried celery flakes
1 16-oz. can mixed vegetables, drained
1 10½-oz. can condensed tomato soup
½ 10½-oz. can condensed beef

broth
1 16-oz. can tiny potatoes, drained
2 4-oz. cans mushrooms
1 12-oz. can roast beef
¼ tsp. Tabasco
Biscuit mix

Add onion and celery flakes to liquid drained from mixed vegetables. Bring to boil in a saucepan, and simmer 6-8 minutes. Transfer mixture to baking dish, and add mixed vegetables, tomato soup and ½ can of condensed beef broth. Mix well. Add all remaining ingredients except biscuit mix. Cut beef into bite-size pieces, blend in thoroughly. Bake in 425° F. oven for 30 minutes. Remove dish from oven. Top with dropped biscuits made according to package directions, and bake for 15 minutes or until biscuits are well browned. *Serves 6.*

JIFFY CHICKEN À LA KING

1 cup sliced fresh or canned mushrooms	2 Tbsp. sherry
½ cup chopped green pepper	2 cups diced, cooked chicken
¼ cup butter	2 Tbsp. chopped pimiento
¼ cup flour	1 cup water and 1 cup evaporated milk, or 2 cups cream
2 tsp. chicken bouillon	¼ tsp. rosemary
	¼ tsp. marjoram

Lightly brown mushrooms and green pepper in butter. Add flour, bouillon, herbs, water and milk (or cream). Cook until thick, stirring constantly. Bring to a boil, add chicken and pimiento and sherry. Serve on toast or in pastry shells. *Serves 6.*

Cold supper. Arrange ham-cheese rolls, fruit, greens and tiny bread and butter sandwiches prettily on individual plates. Set plates in ice box to chill until serving time.

QUICK ONION SOUP

3 Tbsp. butter	1 10-oz. can water
3 Tbsp. instant minced onion	1 tsp. lemon juice
2 10½-oz. cans consommé or bouillon	Toasted rounds of French roll
	Grated Parmesan cheese

Melt butter over low heat. Add onion and heat slowly, stirring until golden brown. Add consommé, water and lemon juice. Bring to boil and simmer about 5 minutes. Place a round of toasted French roll in bottom of each dish, fill with hot soup, and serve with grated cheese. *Serves 3-4.*

PARTY STUFFED EGGS

2 tsp. instant minced onion	¼ cup sour cream or mayonnaise
1 Tbsp. water	½ tsp. seasoning salt
6 hard-cooked eggs	Few grains cayenne
¼ cup liverwurst sausage, mashed	1 Tbsp. finely chopped parsley

Stir onion into water. Peel eggs, cut in half lengthwise. Remove and mash yolks. Blend all ingredients except egg whites, until smooth. Refill whites with mixture, and refrigerate. *Serves 12.*

LUNCHEON MEAT AND PATTY-CAKE SHELLS

Patty-Cake Shells*

16 thin slices white bread	2 Tbsp. butter, softened

Trim bread crusts. Butter each slice lightly. Press down into muffin tins. Preheat oven to moderate (350° F.). Bake shells until golden brown.

Filling

2 cups diced luncheon meat	1 Tbsp. minced onion
1 cup diced boiled potatoes	2 Tbsp. minced sweet pickles
1 cup diced hard-cooked eggs	½ cup mayonnaise
	2 cups shredded cole slaw

Combine ingredients (with exception of slaw). Blend lightly with mayonnaise. Cover, refrigerate until ready to serve. Arrange two patty-cakes on each plate. Divide meat mixture into 4 portions, also cole slaw into 4 portions. On each serving plate, fill one patty-cake with the meat mixture, and the other one with the cole slaw. *Serves 4.*

* The extra 8 shells may be reserved for a dinner several days later. Simply reheat when ready to serve. Creamed salmon, tuna fish or chicken are excellent in these shells or patty-cakes. Green peas in the other shell make a pretty and attractive TV tray supper.

GLAZED VEGETABLE MACARONI PLATE

Two or three different vegetables could be combined in the serving plate or TV tray, and macaroni and cheese added (or omitted if not desired). The macaroni and cheese could be bought in a quick-frozen package or a can, and just heated before serving, thus saving time in preparation. The vegetables, however, are glazed in this manner:

GLAZED CARROTS

1 lb. carrots, cooked	½ tsp. salt
2 Tbsp. melted butter	½ tsp. paprika
6 Tbsp. brown sugar	2 tsp. water

Cut cooked carrots into halves. Dip into melted butter. Place in a heavy skillet over low flame. Sprinkle with sugar, salt and paprika. Add water. Cook until well glazed, spooning sugar mixture over carrots occasionally. *Serves 4.*

GLAZED ONIONS

2 Tbsp. melted butter	½ tsp. paprika
6 Tbsp. sugar	2 tsp. water
½ tsp. salt	1 lb. small onions, boiled, or
	1 jar ready-cooked

Blend first five ingredients in large skillet over low flame. Add onions. Cook, turning often, until onions are golden and glazed. *Serves 4.*

QUICK BEET SUPREME

1 No. 2 can whole beets	½ tsp. salt
¼ cup sliced onions	⅛ tsp. pepper
2 Tbsp. butter	2 Tbsp. lemon juice
2 Tbsp. sugar	⅓ cup beet liquid

Pour off liquid from beets, and reserve. Sauté onions in butter until onions are tender. Stir in sugar, salt, pepper, lemon juice and beet liquid. Add beets and cook until beets are thoroughly heated, about 5 minutes, stirring occasionally. *Serves 4.*

FILLED HAM ROLLS

3 3-oz. pkgs. cream cheese	8 slices boiled ham
3 tsp. mayonnaise	4 slices canned pineapple,
1 cup celery, diced	drained, chilled
	2 doz. cooked prunes, pitted

Mix cheese, mayonnaise and celery together. Divide evenly into 8 portions. Spread each portion on ham slice. Roll up, skewer with toothpicks. Chill. On serving plate arrange ham roll, pineapple and prunes. *Serves 4.* For picture see page 504.

TV PIZZA PIE

4 English muffins, split, toasted, buttered	4 slices mild brick cheese
1 cup canned or quick-frozen pizza sauce or tomato sauce	¼ tsp. oregano
	¼ tsp. basil
	4 tsp. minced onion

Add herbs and onion to sauce, cook 5 minutes. Place split muffins on sheet of heavy-duty metal foil. Spoon hot sauce over the toasted muffins. Cover each half of muffin with one-half slice of cheese. Place in preheated hot oven (400° F.). Bake 15 minutes or until cheese is bubbly and golden brown. *Serves 4.*

STUFFED MUSHROOM SNACKS

24 medium size mushrooms	6 Tbsp. blue cheese
6 Tbsp. cream cheese	6 Tbsp. heavy cream
	¼ tsp. paprika

Remove mushroom stems and wipe caps with damp cloth. Cream the two cheeses together with the cream, add paprika, and beat until mixture is smooth. Stuff mushroom caps with mixture. May be served raw, or the stuffed mushrooms may be sautéed in a covered saucepan in 2 Tbsp. butter for 3-5 minutes. Serve with fork as first course or as an appetizer.

SARDINE AND VEGETABLE SUPPER

4 Tbsp. butter	1 tsp. salt
3 medium sized onions, thinly sliced	¼ tsp. pepper
1½ cups finely diced raw carrots	½ cup dry bread cubes
1 cup chopped green pepper	2½ cups diced raw tomatoes
¾ cup chopped celery	2 cans (3¼-4 oz.) sardines
	¼ cup grated Parmesan cheese
	3 Tbsp. butter (extra)

Melt butter in heavy skillet. Add onions, carrots, green pepper and celery; sprinkle with salt and pepper. Cover tightly and cook gently for 15 minutes. Stir in bread cubes, tomatoes and herbs. Place vegetable in bottom of greased 2-qt. baking dish. Arrange sardines on top, sprinkle with cheese and dot with remaining butter. Brown slowly under broiler (approximately 8-10 minutes). *Serves 6.* For picture see page 508.

Hot sardines. Sprinkle Parmesan cheese on sardine and vegetable casserole and place under broiler for a short time.

SAN FRANCISCO SEAFOOD PLATE DINNER

4 peeled tomatoes

Salt to taste

2 cups canned shrimp, tuna fish
  or crabmeat

1 cup sliced celery

½ cup mayonnaise

2 Tbsp. French dressing

2 Tbsp. lemon juice

¼ cup sliced stuffed olives

½ cup chopped walnuts

Cut tomatoes into 6 slices, starting at the top and coming down within one inch of (but not through) the stem end, to form an open rosette. Sprinkle with salt. Cover. Chill until serving time. Rinse fish, drain, combine lightly with celery. Mix mayonnaise, French dressing and lemon juice. Chill. Just before serving, blend lightly into the dressing mixture the olives and nuts. Pour over the fish mixture. Fill spaces in tomatoes with the mixture. Serve on crisp greens. *Serves 4.*

PRUNE AND NUT RING MOLD

1 envelope unflavored gelatin

¼ cup cold water

2 cups prunes, plus 6 prunes set aside for garnish, soak in hot water 1 hour

1 cup hot prune juice (from cooked prunes)

½ cup sugar

¼ tsp. salt

1 Tbsp. lemon juice

1 cup grapefruit sections, diced

1 cup walnuts, chopped

Filling for center

2 3-oz. pkgs. cream cheese

1 cup cream, whipped

1 Tbsp. sugar

1 tsp. almond extract

Healthy salad mold combines gelatin, prunes and grapefruit. Center contains fluffy cheese filling.

Soften gelatin in water. Add hot prune juice, sugar, salt and lemon juice, stirring until sugar is dissolved. Chill mixture until syrupy. Pit prunes, cut into pieces. Add prunes, grapefruit and nuts to syrupy gelatin. Pour into ring mold. Chill until ready to serve,. Turn out on serving dish. Mix the 4 ingredients for the center filling, blend together lightly. Fill center of mold with cheese mixture. Garnish with greens, prunes or grapefruit sections.

ORANGE BUTTER SANDWICH FILLING

¼ lb. butter

4 Tbsp. grated orange rind

1 Tbsp. orange juice

Soften butter at room temperature. Cream together with orange juice until it is of spreading consistency. Add rind. Spread on thinly sliced white bread. Cover with a second slice. Trim crusts, cut in triangles.

These are good accompaniments to salads, or for nibbling snacks with a beverage.

GAZPACHO

3 lbs. tomatoes cut in chunks	3 cups tomato juice, chilled
2 cucumbers, diced	½ cup olive oil
1 green pepper, seeded, diced	¼ cup wine vinegar
1 small onion, diced	2 cloves garlic, crushed
1 cup pitted black olives	½ tsp. salt
	¼ tsp. pepper

Place all ingredients into large bowl, allow to stand 30 minutes. Add tomato juice, stir well, season to taste. Fill 8-10 soup plates, add ice cube to each plate. *Serves 8-10.* Serve with hearty sandwiches and a beverage.

OPEN HAM-CHEESE SANDWICH

4 thin slices white bread	Pickles
4 thin slices whole wheat bread	4 slices boiled ham
⅛ lb. butter	4 slices Swiss, cheddar or
Crisp greens, shredded	Munster cheese
Salad dressing	4 tomatoes, cut in wedges
Mustard	4 hard-cooked eggs, sliced

Soften butter, spread bread slices to edges. (Trim crusts if desired.) Arrange 2 slices of bread on plate (one of each), cover one slice with shredded lettuce, top with slice of ham. Cover other slice of bread with a slice of cheese, top with sliced egg. Garnish each plate with tomatoes and pickles. Complete with 2 tiny fluted paper cups, mustard in one and mayonnaise in the other. *Serves 4.*

SLICELETS (DATES AND CHEESE)

2 8-oz. pkgs. cream cheese	¼ cup commercial sour cream
	½ lb. fresh dates, cut finely

Soften cheese at room temperature, blend at low speed on electric mixer for 1 minute. Moisten with cream gradually. Add dates. Yield: 3 cups.

(This mixture is a delicious spread on slices of bread. When it is mixed, it may be wrapped well and chilled until ready to serve. It may also be used as a filling for stuffed dates.)

Useful spread of cream cheese and dates is kept moist by sour cream. The mixture is good on bread or crackers or as a filling for dates.

A dozen spicy apple sauce turnovers can be prepared ahead of time and kept in the freezer. Quickly reheat before dessert and supply sauce or wedges of cheese.

SPICED APPLE TURNOVERS

2 cups canned apple sauce	¼ tsp. nutmeg
¼ cup brown sugar	2 tsp. lemon juice
½ tsp. allspice	½ cup seedless raisins
½ tsp. cinnamon	1 pkg. prepared pie crust mix

Combine all ingredients except the mix, and blend well. Prepare the mix according to directions on the package. Roll out a portion of the mix. Cut into 5-inch squares. Moisten edges with cold water. Place a heaping spoonful of the apple sauce mixture in the center of each square. Fold edges of the dough over and press together with tines of fork. Cut a small slit in the top of the dough to allow steam to escape. Bake in hot oven (425° F.) 20-25 minutes. *Serves 12.* (Good when served with cheese, hard sauce or cream.)

SWEET POTATO SPICE BREAD

2 cups sifted all-purpose flour
3 tsp. baking powder
¾ cup granulated sugar
¼ tsp. salt
1 tsp. cinnamon
¼ tsp. allspice
¼ tsp. cloves
1 cup raisins, chopped

1 cup chopped nuts
1 cup mashed, canned sweet
   potatoes
2 eggs
⅓ cup evaporated milk
Grated rind of ½ orange
⅓ cup orange juice
⅓ cup melted butter

In a large bowl mix all dry ingredients, raisins and nuts. Put mashed sweet potatoes into a 1-qt. bowl. Beat in eggs, one at a time. Add milk, then orange rind and juice, then melted butter. Beat to combine. Pour this mixture over dry ingredients. Stir until blended. Beat 25 strokes. Pour into a well-greased 9x9 inch square pan. Bake in oven at 375° F., 35-40 minutes. Yield: 18 pieces 1½x3 inches. (This is delicious served with a hearty soup supper.)

PIMIENTO CHEESE BREAD

3¾ cups prepared biscuit mix
1 egg, beaten
1½ cups milk
1 cup grated cheddar cheese
1 4-oz. can pimientos, drained
   and chopped

Hot breads go well with hot or cold meals. Add pimientos and grated cheddar cheese to bread, rolls or biscuit mix and in no time you have a real treat ready.

Preheat oven to 350° F. Mix all ingredients together. Pour into a well-greased loaf pan. Bake 50-60 minutes.

Individual Salads with French Dressing

Stuffed Baked Potatoes

PIMIENTO PARTY LOAF

1 loaf brown 'n' serve bread

⅛ lb. softened butter
1 4-oz. jar pimientos

Slice through bread, at 2-inch intervals, to within 1 inch of (but not through) the bottom crust. Spread inside the cuts with butter. Cut pimientos into thin strips and place them between the bread cuts. Bake 7-10 minutes.

PIMIENTO HOT BREADS

1 pkg. brown 'n' serve rolls

1 4-oz. can pimientos
⅛ lb. cheddar cheese

Preheat oven to 425° F. Pull rolls apart at top. Cut pimientos and cheese into thin strips. Insert into opening of roll strips of pimiento and cheese. Fasten with toothpicks. Bake 5 minutes. *Serves 4.*

CHEESE BALL

3 3-oz. pkgs. cream cheese
½ lb. Roquefort cheese
½ lb. cheddar cheese, grated
½ tsp. paprika

3-4 Tbsp. heavy cream or
mayonnaise
¼ cup finely minced chives
1-2 drops green for coloring
2 Tbsp. toasted sesame seeds

Soften cheese at room temperature. Mix together with cream or mayonnaise. Add coloring and cheese. Shape into ball, sprinkle with seeds. Chill. Cut into individual portions when serving. *Serves 8-12.*

CHEESE SPREAD

2 3-oz. pkgs. cream cheese
¼ lb. cheddar cheese, grated
coarsely

¼-½ cup condensed tomato
soup
1 Tbsp. Worcestershire sauce

Place all ingredients at once in electric blender. Turn to low speed for 2 minutes. Chill and serve with potato chips or crackers or melba toast. *Serves 8.*

SHERRIED CHEESE MULTI-MIX

1 lb. cheddar cheese
½ lb. blue cheese
¼ cup softened butter
½ cup sherry

1 Tbsp. Worcestershire sauce
1 tsp. prepared mustard
Dash of Tabasco sauce
Onion salt and garlic salt, to taste

Have cheese at room temperature. Grate cheddar cheese. Crumble blue cheese.

Combine cheese and butter in a bowl. Blend well with a fork. Gradually beat in wine. Add seasonings. Continue beating, preferably with an electric beater, until mixture is smooth and fluffy. Store, covered, in the refrigerator. Bring to room temperature before serving. Yield: 5 cups.

This cheese multi-mix may be used in these ways:

1. Party dip. Serve with potato chips, crackers or melba toast.
2. Sandwich spread. For canapés, rolled tea sandwiches, and as an extra filler in man-size meat sandwiches.
3. Hors d'oeuvre filling. May be stuffed in celery stalks, or rolled in slices of dried beef.
4. Dessert cheese. Serve with crisp crackers and a tray of fresh fruit.

QUICK CHEESE MIX SNACK

5-oz. jar cheddar cheese spread
2 Tbsp. of wine, either sherry or sauterne

Nothing could be simpler to mix than this. It can be done at a minute's notice when unexpected guests drop in. Serve with potato chips or crackers or melba toast.

PEAR AND CHEESE SALAD DESSERT

8 Bartlett pear halves, drained
   from can, chilled
1 cup blue cheese, crumbled
2 3-oz. pkgs. cream cheese
1 cup nut meats, finely chopped
2-4 Tbsp. heavy cream
¼ tsp. salt

Pears with nutted cheese balls do double duty —act as a salad course and a dessert.

Mash cheese, cream and salt together. Shape into balls the size of a walnut. Chill. Roll in chopped nut meats. At serving time, arrange crisp greens on platter. Place pear halves with hollow side up. Fill each pear with cheese balls. Serve with lemon mayonnaise cream dressing, or with lemon juice instead of the dressing.

Speedy dessert is made by topping canned fruit cocktail with a large dab of almond-flavored whipped cream.

LEMON MAYONNAISE CREAM DRESSING

1 cup mayonnaise

½ cup heavy cream, whipped

1 Tbsp. lemon juice

Beat all ingredients together to a smooth consistency.

FRUIT COCKTAIL DESSERT

1 No. 2½ can fruit cocktail

½ pt. heavy cream, whipped

2 Tbsp. powdered sugar

1 tsp. almond extract

Heap fruit high in glass sherbet dishes. Into the whipped cream sift the sugar and add the extract. Top the fruit with the cream mixture. *Serves 4.*

ORANGE CUP CAKES

1 pkg. gold cake mix

Bake according to package directions in small, fluted cake tins. Turn out, cool. Turn upside down. Frost with the delectable orange frosting.

ORANGE BUTTER CREAM FROSTING

¼ lb. butter	1 lb. pkg. confectioners' sugar
¼-½ cup orange juice, strained	Grated rind thin-skinned orange

Cream butter until soft and white around edges, soften with juice, 1 table-spoonful at a time, alternating with sugar. When it is at spreading consistency, add rind. Place each cup cake on a form, allow soft frosting to spread over top and sides. Garnish with bit of fresh orange. This will cover 2 dozen cakes.

Variation

3 egg whites, unbeaten	Grated rind thin-skinned orange
1 lb. confectioner's sugar	¼-½ cup orange juice, strained

Place egg whites in deep bowl, adding sugar gradually. As it thickens, add juice. When it is of spreading consistency, add rind.

(If preferred, lemon juice and rind may be used instead of orange.)

BANANA STRAWBERRY WHIP

1 cup quick-frozen strawberries	½ cup sugar
3 bananas	¼ cup lemon juice
	½ pint heavy cream

Measure strawberries. Peel bananas and force both fruits through sieve. Place in saucepan. Add sugar and lemon juice. Cook just to boiling point. Chill until ready to serve. Whip cream. Fold cream into mixture just before serving. *Serves 6.*

ORANGE AND BANANA AMBROSIA

2 navel oranges, cut into chunks	2 peeled bananas, thinly sliced
½ cup thinly flaked coconut	2 Tbsp. lemon juice
¼ cup sugar	Maraschino cherries

Sprinkle orange pieces with coconut and sugar. Cover. Chill. Sprinkle banana slices with lemon juice to prevent discoloration. When ready to serve, blend banana lightly with orange mixture. Garnish with maraschino cherry. *Serves 4.*

POPCORN NIBBLER

¼ lb. butter	3 qts. hot popcorn
1½ Tbsp. instant minced onion	1 tsp. salt

Melt the butter in a skillet. Add minced onion. Cook over very low heat, stirring constantly, until onion is pale gold. Pour this hot mixture over the popcorn which you placed in a deep pan. Mix lightly. Sprinkle with salt.

ICED GINGER TEA

1 cup sugar	10 whole cloves
1 cup water	½-inch sq. fresh ginger (peeled,
1 stick of cinnamon	sliced thin)

Bring water to boil in a small pan. Add sugar, cinnamon, cloves and ginger. Stir over low heat until sugar is dissolved. Bring to boil for 7 minutes. Cool. Remove cinnamon stick and cloves. Prepare iced tea in your favorite manner add 1-2 Tbsp. of this ginger syrup according to taste. Garnish glasses with lemon slices.

SPICED ICED COFFEE

2 cinnamon sticks	3 cups double-strength coffee,
4 cloves	cold
4 allspice berries	⅓ cup sugar

Pour coffee over cinnamon sticks, cloves and berries. Let stand one hour. Drain and pour coffee over ice in 4 tall glasses. Add sugar and cream.

Fruit whip goes over big with young and old. Pile into pretty glass dessert dishes and bring out on a tray with lady fingers. Watch them be grabbed up.

38.

BEVERAGES

A GOOD CUP of coffee; clear, fragrant, strong! That is the dream of every coffee lover. But, how are you to make a perfect cup of coffee every time? That is an art, dependent upon well-known factors.

A good cup of coffee begins at the grocery counter, and a new housekeeper can only experiment with the great variety of blends until she finds the one her family likes best. Some prefer a light, delicate blend. Others prefer a richer, "heavier" coffee. The next step is to match the grind of coffee with the type of coffee-maker at home; finely-ground for glass coffee-maker, drip-grind for a drip coffee pot, all-purpose grind for a percolator or an old-fashioned coffee pot. In many stores, the coffee may be purchased in the bean and ground to order, or carried home in the bean and ground in a home-style grinder just before the coffee is made.

The tendency on the part of many coffee blenders is to sell only two grinds —a fine-grind for glass coffee-makers, and an all-purpose grind for other methods. Here again the novice will want to experiment to find the coffee-maker which best suits her needs. Finally, the directions for making coffee and for the care of the coffee-maker need to be scrupulously carried out. These rules have been drawn up by a group of experts, and if faithfully followed will insure a perfect cup of coffee every time.

1. Measure coffee and water accurately. Use 2 level Tbsp. of coffee to each 6 or 8 oz. of water (¾ to 1 standard measuring cup).
2. Use fresh water for making coffee. Water which has been preheated or drawn from the hot water faucet may impart an undesirable taste to the brew.

518

3. Serve coffee as soon as possible after brewing. If necessary to let brewed coffee stand any length of time, hold at serving temperature by placing pot in pan of hot water or over very low heat on asbestos pad. Keep the coffee hot, but do not let it boil. Coffee that has cooled cannot be reheated without loss of flavor.

4. For best results, always brew coffee at full capacity of the coffee-maker.

5. Never re-use coffee grounds.

6. Never allow cloth filters to become dry. Keep immersed in cold water. Never use soap in washing the cloth filters.

7. Keep coffee-maker immaculately clean. Wash thoroughly after each use, and rinse with clear hot water. Always scald coffee-maker before using.

8. Buy fresh coffee—enough for a week's supply.

DRIP COFFEE

Preheat pot by scalding with hot water. Measure required amount of ground coffee into filter section. Measure required amount of fresh boiling water into upper container, then cover. When dripping is completed, remove upper section immediately. Stir brew and serve.

VACUUM COFFEE

Follow directions which are enclosed with new coffee-maker. Measure required amount of fresh cold water into lower bowl; place on heat. Place filter

Fragrant, hot coffee breathes hospitality. Some folks like it with plenty of cream and sugar. Others substitute saccharine for sugar, and still others like nothing better with coffee than a twist of lemon peel.

Iced coffee does very well on its own, but for special enjoyment try it with vanilla ice cream topping.

in upper bowl and add measured quantity of finely-ground or drip-grind coffee, but do not insert in lower bowl. When water in lower bowl boils, turn gas low. If electricity is used, turn off heat. Insert upper bowl with a slight twist to insure a tight seal. When the water has risen into upper bowl (some water will always remain in the lower bowl) stir water and coffee thoroughly. In 1 to 3 minutes (finer grinds require the shorter time) turn off gas. If electricity is used, remove coffee-maker from heat. When all coffee has been drawn into lower bowl, remove upper bowl. Serve at once.

PERCOLATED COFFEE

Measure freshly-drawn water from cold water faucet, place in bottom con-

Tea and roast beef: Typical English food.

tainer. Place coffee in upper perforated section, cover, and place pot over heat. When water begins to percolate up over coffee, turn heat down so that percolating will continue slowly. Coffee takes on a bitter taste, and its delicate aroma is lost, if percolating goes on at a rapid pace. 8 to 12 minutes is the usual length of time required. When coffee is amber in color, remove upper section, replace cover on percolator, and pour at once.

CHOOSING COFFEE-MAKING EQUIPMENT

1. *Vacuum types made of glass:* some have a metal rod, and some are entirely of glass. Follow directions given by manufacturer for care of coffee-maker, for making coffee, and for buying correct grind.

2. *Percolator:* some are equipped to plug into electric outlet.
3. *Drip pot:* simplest to use; preferred by many.

A well-stocked pantry contains two coffee pots; an average-sized pot to serve the family's daily needs, also a large drip-grind, vacuum type of coffee pot to be used for entertaining.

ICED COFFEE

This popular beverage needs twice as much coffee per cup as does hot coffee. Prepare in usual way, but allow 4 Tbsp. per cup instead of 2 Tbsp. Pour the strong, hot coffee over ice cubes in a tall glass, and serve at once.

TEA

Again, as in the case of coffee, individual taste is the best guide. The basic teas are black, or fermented tea; and green, or unfermented. Oolong tea is a semi-fermented type. Tea as sold today is a blend of several grades and varieties. Orange Pekoe is not a variety of tea, but a name which describes the size of the tea leaf.

The commonly accepted rules for making tea include:

1. Use freshly boiling water.
2. Scald pot before making tea.
3. Use china, glass or pottery teapot.
4. Use 1 to 2 tsp. tea to 2 cups water.
5. Brew tea by letting the boiling water remain in pot for 2, 3, or 5 minutes. The longer the tea "steeps" in the water, the stronger it becomes. A bitter taste develops from the tannic acid if tea steeps too long.
6. Have a warm pot at hand, and pour the freshly-made tea into the serving pot. Cover with a quilted tea cozy for added charm in serving. Have an extra pot of boiling water at hand if weaker tea is preferred by some.

TEA ACCESSORIES OR ACCOMPANIMENTS

Many tea lovers prefer tea with milk; others like tea with lemon and sugar. Still others like their tea clear, or with a slice of lemon or slice of orange in which a few cloves have been stuck.

At feminine tea parties, the tea table often has a plate of candied cherries, stick cinnamon, or peppermint drops to be put into tea cups. No doubt this would be regarded as sacrilege by an Englishman, but it amuses American hostesses.

ICED TEA

Iced tea may be made several hours ahead of time. The tea is prepared as usual, strained, and allowed to stand in room temperature. Just before serving, ice is added. This method is apt to make a cloudy glass of tea.

If tea is prepared with a double amount of tea leaves, strained and poured hot over ice in tall iced-tea glasses, the beverage is clear.

Plenty of lemon cut in wedges, fine sugar, sprigs of mint, and long-handled spoons are necessary to make this beverage just right.

COCOA

3 Tbsp. cocoa	2 cups milk, scalded
2 Tbsp. sugar	Pinch of salt
½ cup water	½ tsp. vanilla extract

Combine cocoa and sugar. Stir well, and add water to make smooth paste.

Iced chocolate is a grand warm weather beverage. In a party mood, serve it with scoops of sherbet.

Simmer gently until mixture thickens. Slowly pour into hot milk. Keep hot over a pan of hot water. Just before serving, beat with egg beater until frothy. Add salt and vanilla extract. Pour into warmed tea cups or chocolate cups. Serve with whipped cream or a marshmallow.

HOT CHOCOLATE

3 sq. chocolate	3 cups milk, scalded
3 Tbsp. sugar	Pinch of salt
½ cup boiling water	½ tsp. vanilla extract

Melt chocolate over hot water, add sugar, and stir until well-mixed. Add water, and cook slowly over hot water until thickened. Pour into milk, stir well and beat with egg beater until frothy. Add salt and vanilla. Pour into chocolate cups. Garnish with sweetened whipped cream or marshmallow.

For gracious service of beverages without a disturbing and distracting scramble to and from the kitchen, a bar takes high honors.

PARTY BEVERAGES

The parties which are spoiled by too-sweet punches! How guests hate them! A good punch should quench the thirst; should have enough of a tang so that the first cup immediately makes the second cup imperative; should have enough body so that one recognizes the flavor; should have jewel-tone colors, so that it is a picture to look at in the gleaming glass bowl. Keep the recipe a bit on the tart side; and be sure the beverage is continually ice cold, and strong enough to be good. (Of course, children prefer the punch sweeter than adults do.)

Strong tea is an excellent base for many a fruit punch, and simple syrup is the best sweetening to use, since it utilizes all the sweetness of the sugar without wasting it.

SIMPLE SYRUP

Combine equal parts of granulated sugar and water. Place in saucepan over low flame. Stir until sugar is dissolved. Simmer for 5 minutes without stirring. Cool, put into clean jar, cover. Keep in refrigerator. This is a good way to save sugar when making hot weather drinks frequently, or preparing punch for a crowd. Saves time, too.

ORANGE PUNCH

1 cup strong tea	¼ cup lemon juice
1 qt. orange juice	½ cup simple syrup

Brew tea, cool, mix with syrup, add fruit juices. Mix well. Fill tall glasses with ice cubes, pour mixture over ice. Garnish with maraschino cherry and slice of unpeeled orange.

PINEAPPLE PUNCH

1 pt. pineapple juice	1 cup grapefruit juice
1 pt. ginger ale	½ cup lemon juice
	½ to 1 cup simple syrup

Prepare in tall glasses as above, or place cake of ice in large bowl. Mix syrup, lemon juice and grapefruit juice together. Pour over ice, add other liquids, mix and serve. Garnish with lemon and orange slices, unpeeled.

FRUITED PUNCH

3 cups orange juice	3 cups pineapple juice
1½ cups lemon juice	1 pt. to 1 qt. simple syrup
3 cups grapefruit juice	1 pt. to 1 qt. ginger ale
	1 qt. carbonated water

Mix simple syrup with lemon juice and grapefruit juice and let stand 1 hour. Stir occasionally. Place in refrigerator. Chill all ingredients for several hours.

Place cake of ice in punch bowl. Pour all juices over ice. Just before serving, add ginger ale and carbonated water. Decorate with cherries and slices of orange and lemon.

PUNCH FOR CHILDREN'S PARTY

A good party punch, which is inexpensive and easy to make, consists in mixing equal quantities of grape juice and ginger ale together in a large bowl. Place a cake of ice in bottom of bowl, and pour liquid over ice. Serve at once.

Another drink for the youngsters is made by putting 1 qt. of orange ice (sherbet) in the bottom of the punch bowl, and pouring 1 qt. of ginger ale over it. In about 5 minutes, you have a deliciously flavored, cold punch. In making more or less quantity, just remember to use equal quantities of each ingredient.

MULLED GRAPE JUICE

1 qt. grape juice	2 lemons
1 pt. water	1 stick cinnamon, 2 to 3 inches
½ cup sugar	12 cloves

Put spices in loosely-tied muslin bag. Add grape juice, sugar, and water. Slowly heat until steam rises. Stir well, and let stand 10 minutes. Add juice of lemons and rind of 1 lemon, bring to boiling point. Remove lemon peel and muslin bag. Serve hot as a winter beverage.

EGGNOG

4 eggs	2 tsp. vanilla
8 Tbsp. sugar	2 qts. milk
½ tsp. salt	Nutmeg

Separate egg yolks from whites. Beat yolks until thick and lemon-colored. Add sugar, salt, vanilla and milk. Beat until thoroughly blended. Beat egg whites separately, then fold into mixture. Pour into tall glasses or eggnog cups, and sprinkle with nutmeg.

A punch bowl is pretty as a picture. Guests love milk punch when it's made the right way— not too sweet. It can be varied—as here— with cucumbers floating in it.

→

39.

COOKING
FOR A CROWD

THE social life of any American community includes every variety of "meeting" under the sun. There are women's clubs, church groups, men's clubs, Boy Scouts, Girl Scouts, and a hundred and one special occasions where the women are called upon to serve a meal to a group of people.

Many communities boast a Community House. Others have a club auditorium, and still others have modern kitchens installed in church buildings. But whatever the facilities available, sooner or later a woman is called upon to be head of a committee for some affair where refreshments are to be served. Her first task is to draw up an over-all picture of the situation. Just as she plans the details of china, silver, linen, marketing and serving for a small party, so she must give the same careful planning to a large party. The selection of a menu must be governed by the amount of cooking space available, the pieces of equipment on hand, and the number of people who will assist in the actual work. A large party requires more physical effort than the average woman is used to expending, so simple foods are the most successful.

The recipes in this chapter serve fifty.

The following suggestions will enable the refreshment chairman to do her job capably:

PRACTICAL PLANNING

1. Plan menus with reference to the equipment available and size of stove on which to cook and bake.

2. Do as much preparation as possible the day before party.
3. Use large shallow pans for baking, for perfect results.
4. Bake cakes in large sheets—cool in the pans, frost, and cut in squares for serving.
5. Store partially prepared foods in refrigerators. Do not depend upon open windows for cooling food overnight.
6. Divide up work among assistants. Do not attempt to do too much single-handed.
7. Plan menu by following references in Chapter 1. Use guide for color, texture, flavor.
8. Plan foods which hold up well when allowed to stand. For example:

Molded salads	Hearty salads
Deviled eggs	Baked macaroni and cheese
Mousses	Baked beans

VEGETABLE SOUP

10 lbs. of bones with meat on them	2 qts. potatoes, diced
	1 qt. celery, chopped
¼ cup salt	2 cups onions, chopped
3 gal. water	1½ qts. canned tomatoes
1 Tbsp. pepper	1 cup raw rice
2 qts. carrots, diced	2 qts. cabbage, chopped

Soak soup bones several hours in water to which salt has been added. Bring to boil and simmer 2 hours. Strain to remove bones, and add enough water to make 3 gal. stock. Add pepper, carrots, potatoes, celery, onions, tomatoes, and rice. Cook slowly for 2 hours, stir frequently. Add chopped cabbage, boil gently for 7 minutes. Serve immediately. If soup must stand, omit cabbage.

BAKING POWDER BISCUITS

6 qts. flour	¾ cup baking powder
¼ cup salt	3 cups shortening
	2 qts. milk

Sift flour, measure. Add salt, baking powder, and sift again. Cut in the shortening with pastry blender or two knives. Add milk slowly, to make a soft dough. Roll out on slightly-floured board to ¾ inch thickness, and cut with a biscuit cutter. Put on a greased baking sheet, and bake in hot oven (425° F.) 10 to 15 minutes. Makes 100 biscuits.

MEAT LOAF

6 lbs. raw beef, ground	2 qts. soft bread crumbs
½ lb. raw pork, ground	3 large onions, chopped
6 eggs	3 Tbsp. salt
5 cups milk	1 tsp. pepper

Beat eggs well, add milk and bread crumbs. Mix with onions and seasonings. Add to meat and blend thoroughly. Pack into well-greased loaf-pans. Bake in moderate oven (350° F.) 40 minutes.

BOSTON BAKED BEANS

4 qts. dried beans	2 tsp. dry mustard
4 tsp. salt	2 cups dark molasses
4 qts. water	2 lbs. salt pork, sliced

Wash beans, cover with cold water, and soak overnight. Drain, measure 4 qts. of water, add salt, and simmer until beans are tender. Add mustard and molasses to beans. Pour into shallow baking pans. Lay slices of pork on top. Bake

Sizzling macaroni and cheese is a good inexpensive dish for a crowd.

A portable grill is the answer to a prayer for those who want to do outdoor entertaining but have no outdoor fireplace. The model shown here has a charcoal fire box for flat grilling. When you are through using the grill it can be rolled into a storage space until the next time you plan to entertain outdoors.

in slow oven (300° to 325° F.) 4 hours. If the beans become dry, add more hot water from time to time.

MACARONI AND CHEESE

3 lbs. macaroni	4 qts. milk
3 gal. boiling salted water	2 Tbsp. salt
1½ cups flour	3 lbs. American cheese
1½ cups butter	3 cups soft bread crumbs

Break macaroni in pieces and cook in boiling salted water. Drain. Rinse in cold water. Make a white sauce of butter, flour, milk and 2 Tbsp. salt (see Chapter 13). Cut cheese in pieces and melt in sauce. Grease baking dishes. Place macaroni and sauce in alternate layers, with sauce as final layer. Sprinkle with bread crumbs. Dust with paprika. Bake in moderate oven (350° F.) until crumbs are brown.

SCALLOPED POTATOES

8 qts. raw potatoes	2 tsp. pepper
½ lb. butter	½ cup flour
3 Tbsp. salt	3 qts. milk

Place layers of thinly-sliced potatoes in 6 shallow greased baking dishes. Dot each layer with butter, sprinkle with salt, pepper, and flour. Pour milk over potatoes. Bake in slow oven (300° F.) until potatoes are tender, about 1½ to 2 hours. Cook covered until last half hour.

CHICKEN A LA KING

6 qts. cooked chicken, removed from bones	2 tsp. pepper
1 small tin pimientos, chopped	4 Tbsp. parsley, chopped
2 Tbsp. salt	2 lbs. mushrooms, sliced
	½ cup butter
	3 qts. medium white sauce

Cut chicken in cubes before measuring. Add pimiento, salt, pepper, and parsley. Heat in white sauce. Peel mushrooms, slice thin and sauté in butter. Add to the white sauce and chicken mixture. Keep hot over boiling water until ready to serve. Serve on hot toast or in patty shells.

CHICKEN SALAD

4 qts. cooked chicken, removed from bones	1 Tbsp. salt
4 qts. celery, diced	1 tsp. pepper
	2 qts. salad dressing
	8 hard-cooked eggs, sliced

Cut chicken in cubes before measuring. Mix chicken, celery, salt, and pepper together. Mix lightly with salad dressing. Serve on crisp lettuce leaves, and garnish with hard-cooked eggs.

POTATO SALAD

8 to 9 qts. (18 lbs.) cooked potatoes, cut in cubes	1 pt. French dressing
1 pt. onions, minced fine	2 tsp. celery salt
1 qt. celery, diced	¼ cup salt
	1 tsp. pepper
	1 tsp. paprika

Blend all ingredients lightly, a portion at a time. Place in large mixing bowls, cover tightly. Chill in refrigerator for several hours. Just before serving add 1 qt. cooked salad dressing. Blend, turn out on crisp lettuce. Garnish with minced parsley.

COLE SLAW

10 qts. shredded raw green cabbage	1½ cups of lemon juice
1½ qts. mayonnaise	1½ cups sugar
	¼ cup salt

Add mayonnaise, lemon juice, and salt to shredded cabbage, and toss together until well-mixed. Keep cool until ready to serve.

COCOA

½ lb. cocoa	½ tsp. salt
1 lb. sugar	1 gal. boiling water
	2½ gal. hot milk

Mix cocoa, sugar, and salt together. Add ½ of boiling water slowly. Stir gently to keep smooth. Cook this cocoa mixture over low heat 10 minutes, stirring occasionally. Add remainder of water to the milk, and heat over boiling water or over slow direct heat to prevent scorching. When ready to serve, add cocoa syrup to the hot milk.

Indoor entertaining for a group can often be wearing on the hostess if she has too much to coordinate at the last moment. Plan to serve tempting appetizers shortly before the meal is to be served. You can then leave guests nibbling while you go off to take care of arrangement and service of the meal.

COFFEE

Select a large round pot. Cut a generous square of unbleached muslin and lay flat on table. For 50 people, use 1 lb. of drip-grind coffee. Pour coffee onto muslin. Tie loosely but firmly with clean string to form a bag. Drop into clean, scalded pot. Pour on 8 qts. boiling water. Cover with lid, turn heat low and

Sturdy fare for a gang are frankfurters, pineapple cole slaw, and cokes.

let coffee steep for 15 minutes. Once in a while, lift cover and move bag around a bit. At conclusion of 15-minute period, lift out bag, and dash ½ cup cold water into coffee to settle any loose grounds. Pour through fine cheesecloth into heated coffee pot and serve at once.

FRUIT PUNCH

2 cups water	2 cups orange juice
2 cups sugar	2 cups pineapple juice
2 cups fruit syrup (strawberry	Ice water
or loganberry)	1 cup maraschino cherries
1 cup lemon juice	4 qts. ginger ale

Boil water and sugar together for 5 minutes. Add fruit syrup, lemon juice, orange juice, and pineapple juice. Let stand for 30 minutes. Strain and add enough ice water to make 1½ gal. of liquid. Add cherries and ginger ale. Serve in punch bowl, with large piece of ice.

APPLE PIE FILLING

14 lbs. tart apples	6 lbs. sugar
2 Tbsp. cinnamon	2 cups flour
1 Tbsp. nutmeg	½ cup shortening

Pare, core, and cut apples in thin slices. Add cinnamon, nutmeg, sugar and flour, and mix well. Line pie pans with pastry and fill with apple mixture. Dot with shortening. Cover with top crust, trim and press edges together to make a fancy edge. Prick top to permit steam to escape. Bake in hot oven (425° F.) 10 minutes. Reduce heat to moderate oven (350° F.), and bake 20 to 30 minutes. This recipe makes 12 two-crust pies.

PIE CRUST

5 lbs. flour	5 cups shortening
5 tsp. salt	Cold water

Sift; measure flour, add salt, and sift again. Cut in shortening with 2 knives or pastry blender. Moisten with just enough water to hold the mixture together. Chill thoroughly. Divide into 12 portions. Roll out on lightly-floured board. This makes 12 two-crust pies.

CHOCOLATE CAKE

6 cups flour	8 eggs, separated
4 tsp. baking powder	10 sq. chocolate, melted
1 tsp. salt	2 cups milk
4 cups sugar	2 cups hot water
1½ cups shortening	4 tsp. vanilla

Sift; measure flour, add baking powder and salt, sift again. Cream shortening, add sugar slowly, and cream until fluffy. Add beaten egg yolks, and beat well. Add milk and dry ingredients alternately. Beat well after each addition. Add chocolate and vanilla extract. Beat well. Fold in stiffly-beaten whites. Bake in 4 pans (10x10x2 inches), in moderate oven (350° F.) 20 to 30 minutes.

ORANGE CUP CAKES

8 cups cake flour	1 Tbsp. grated orange rind
3 Tbsp. baking powder	4½ cups sugar
1½ tsp. salt	6 eggs
1½ cups shortening	1½ cups milk
	1 cup orange juice

Sift; measure flour, add baking powder and salt, sift again. Cream shortening with orange rind. Add sugar slowly, and cream until fluffy. Add eggs, one at a time, and beat well. Add flour alternately with milk and orange juice; begin and end with flour. Fill well-greased muffin tins ⅔ full. Bake in moderate oven (350° F.) 20 minutes. Ice with Orange Frosting.

Cheese, crackers, and fruit make the best dessert for a crowd, if the main part of the meal has been especially heavy. But—if you are going to serve cheese, go in for it in the grand manner. Offer your guests a variety of cheeses.

CHOCOLATE FROSTING

4 sq. chocolate

¼ lb. butter

1 Tbsp. vanilla extract

¾ cup milk

2 lbs. sugar

Cream butter, add ½ of milk slowly, and cream until smooth. Add 1 cup sugar, beat well. Melt chocolate. Add chocolate and vanilla. Beat again, add remainder of sugar alternately with milk. Spread on cake. This amount will frost 4 cakes in 10x10x2 inch pans.

ORANGE FROSTING

3 lbs. sugar

¾ cup milk

6 Tbsp. orange juice

1 Tbsp. orange rind, grated

Sift sugar into bowl. Add milk, orange juice, and rind. Stir until smooth and thick. More orange juice may be added if mixture is too thick to spread. This amount will frost 100 cup cakes.

MOLASSES COOKIES

3 cups cake flour

3 cups graham flour

2 tsp. baking powder

1 tsp. soda

2 tsp. cinnamon

1 tsp. ginger

1 cup shortening

1 cup sugar

1¼ cups molasses

1 cup hot water

2 eggs, well-beaten

Sift; measure flour, add graham flour, baking powder, soda, salt, cinnamon, and ginger. Sift again. Cream shortening, add sugar slowly, and cream until fluffy. Add molasses and hot water. Beat well, add eggs, beat again. Add dry ingredients gradually. Beat thoroughly. Drop by teaspoonfuls onto well-greased cookie sheet. Bake in moderate oven (350° F.) 15 minutes. Remove from pan at once. Place on wire rack. Makes 100 cookies.

CHOCOLATE BROWNIES

12 cups cake flour	8 cups sugar
1 Tbsp. baking powder	8 eggs, well-beaten
1 Tbsp. salt	1 lb. chocolate, melted
3 cups shortening	6 cups nut meats, chopped
	1 Tbsp. vanilla extract

Sift; measure flour, add baking powder and salt, sift again. Cream shortening, add sugar slowly, and cream until fluffy. Add eggs and beat well, melt chocolate. Add chocolate and flour. Beat again. Add nut meats and vanilla extract. Bake in 4 well-greased cake pans (8x8x2 inches), in moderate oven (350° F.) 30 to 35 minutes. Cut in squares while still in pan. Makes 48 Brownies.

40.

OUTDOOR
COOKERY

THE new leisure in America, the surge to suburban living and outdoor summer living has brought about a quiet and pleasant revolution in family and company meals. A large share of the credit belongs to the many new developments in the use of aluminum foil. Unheard of not too many years ago, its use has made possible a whole new field of outdoor cookery.

No longer is the homemaker or the man of the house confined to broiling expensive steaks, chickens and the more humble hamburger. Now there may also be cooked fruit, vegetables, spareribs; in fact, nearly everything except salads and ice cream.

The right fire is the first essential, along with the right broiler equipment and a few good long-handled utensils. Add a pair of heavy cotton gloves and the summer stretches ahead invitingly to every family who enjoys outdoor living.

TIPS FOR USING BARBECUE GRILLS

You may have built a fireplace in your garden or backyard, which is stationary. Or, you may use a portable outdoor grill. In either case, these are good tips to follow:

1. Build the fireplace (or wheel the portable grill) in a position where it is protected from the wind, and where the breezes will blow the smoke away from the chef.

2. Line the bottom of the fireplace or portable grill with one or more layers of heavy-duty aluminum foil. This reflects the heat back up on the food, speeds cooking, and uses a smaller amount of briquets. It also evens out the temperature on the grid over the fire, so that the food will not burn in one spot and undercook in another.

3. Be sure to use dry briquets. If purchased ahead, store them in a dry place. Space the briquets ½ inch apart for medium-heat cooking fire.

4. Start the fire 20 to 30 minutes before cooking time. Briquets ignite in several places when the starter material is touched with a match. The fire spreads until all are burning. If the day is windy they ignite more quickly.

5. Use a safe starter material, such as the impregnated granulated charcoal starter which comes packaged in foil. With no dangerous liquid involved, you avoid the danger of spilling with consequent flare-up.

6. Remember that briquets do not glow red when burning. Instead, they are spotted gray. Use tongs if it is necessary to move them. DO NOT TOUCH THEM WITH YOUR FINGERS. The briquets will burn for an hour or longer, giving a good cooking fire. If more briquets are to be added, simply shake them on. They will ignite from those already burning.

7. Have food at least 4 inches above the fire. Keep handy a container of baking soda, so that if any grease or fat flames up or catches fire you can extinguish it by throwing soda on the fire.

8. When your cooking is finished, and the briquets have burned themselves out, gather them up in the foil with the ashes and deposit in trash can. The grill will be left clean, since the foil will protect it from dripping fat.

BARBECUE BEEF BUNDLES

Try cooking individual dinners in metal wrap on your outdoor grill. Beef Bundles are whole meals of beef, vegetables and sauce, sealed into a package of foil. Prepare them ahead of time. Let them chill in the refrigerator until you are ready.

2 large zucchini, sliced	2 large potatoes, peeled and
1 lb. tender beef (round steak)	quartered
cut in ¾ inch cubes	2 large tomatoes, halved (or
12 small onions, peeled (or No. 2	small can tomato sauce)
can onions)	Salt and pepper, to season

Tear off 4 12-inch sheets of foil wrap. Onto each piece of foil pile portions of zucchini, beef cubes, 3 onions, 2 potato pieces, and half fresh tomato or 3 Tbsp. tomato sauce. Season to taste. Bring edges of foil together and seal with double folds to make airtight packages. Place on grill and cook for 50

Each foil bundle unwraps to reveal a complete meal—tender cubes of beef with colorful juicy vegetables plus potatoes.

minutes to 1 hour, turning packages occasionally. Ten minutes before dinners are cooked, split hard rolls and toast on grill. *Serves 4.*

CALIFORNIA BARBECUED SPARERIBS

4 to 5 lbs. spareribs (in 2 pieces)	Salt, to season
	Pepper, to season
	California Barbecue Sauce

Salt and pepper spareribs and brown on grill over moderate fire, turning them once or twice. Prepare pan from double thickness of heavy duty aluminum foil to fit the spareribs, by turning up the edges of the foil 1½ inches all around. Mitre the corners so the pan will be secure. As soon as spareribs have browned on grill, transfer them to the foil pan and spoon over the meat about 1 cupful of California Barbecue Sauce. Place the foil pan on the center of the grill, and continue cooking for about 1½ hours longer. Baste with the sauce occasionally. To serve, transfer the foil pan with spareribs to a platter. Ribs separate easily when cut with a sharp knife. *Serves 6-8.*

CALIFORNIA BARBECUE SAUCE

½ cup honey	½ tsp. tabasco sauce
⅔ cup soy sauce	1 clove garlic, finely mashed
⅔ cup ketchup	1 tsp. salt
1 tsp. dry mustard	1 cup orange juice
1 tsp. paprika	1 cup wine vinegar

Combine ingredients. Mix well.

CHICKEN BASKETS

1 broiler-fryer chicken
1 envelope dehydrated onion
   soup
4 tsp. butter
½ lb. fresh mushrooms
½ cup milk or cream

Basket meal. Each hungry person gets a basket full of chicken, and bread to lap up the tasty mushroom-onion gravy.

Rinse chicken, dry and remove small protruding bones. Tear off 4 large squares (12x14 inches) of heavy duty foil wrap. Shake out onion soup into a small bowl and stir to blend evenly. Place dab of butter and 1 Tbsp. of the dry onion soup in center of each square of foil wrap. Arrange chicken quarters over this. Sprinkle each with 2 additional Tbsp. of the dry onion soup, and dot with butter. Add the mushrooms, dividing them evenly, and top each serving with 2 Tbsp. of milk or cream. No additional seasonings needed. Bring foil up over food, sealing the edges with a tight double fold. Seal the ends in the same fashion, turning them up, so the juices will not run out. Cook for 45-50 minutes on a grill over medium heat. Serve the packages in baskets or on paper plates. Use the delicious gravy which forms from the juices of the chicken mingled with all the other ingredients.

CHICKEN, SWEET POTATO, APPLE

Prepare chicken according to recipe given for Chicken in Foil (Basic Pattern). Place on foil, season with salt and pepper. Prepare other ingredients as follows:

2 sweet potatoes, fresh cooked   ½ tsp. grated lemon rind
2 unpeeled apples   4 Tbsp. brown sugar
2 Tbsp. lemon juice   1 Tbsp. softened butter

Peel and slice sweet potatoes (or yams), and arrange around chicken. Slice apples into ½-inch slices. Add 4 slices to chicken. Mix lemon juice, rind, sugar and butter. Spread over apples and potatoes. Wrap in foil and cook over open grate, as described in Basic Pattern recipe. *Serves 4.*

"PIG IN POKE" DINNER

4 pork chops
2 sweet potatoes
2 tart apples
8 onion slices
1 tsp. thyme
Salt and pepper to season

Hearty pork chop dinner combines the flavors of sweet potatoes, tart apples, onions and thyme. Use good thick pork chops.

Lightly brown pork chops in a skillet. Tear off four large squares of heavy-duty aluminum foil, and in center of each place a chop. Add two or more thick slices of apple, sweet potato and onion to each. Season each well with salt, pepper and ¼ tsp. thyme. Bring foil up over the food, and seal into tight packages by double-folding edges together. Place on grill over medium heat and cook about 1 hour.

CHICKEN IN FOIL

(Basic Pattern)

Many combinations may be made, depending on seasonable vegetables, personal taste and family budget. Basically this is the method to follow:

1 chicken (for 4 people)
or
Quick-frozen chicken parts
4 Tbsp. butter
Salt
Pepper

Inexpensive chicken and seasonal vegetables are cooked together over the coals for a good budget meal.

Cut chicken into 4 parts (or use quick-frozen parts). Pull out the small protruding bones. Rinse, dry with paper towel. Tear off large squares of heavy-duty aluminum foil. Place single portion of chicken, skin side down, on the foil. Add 1 Tbsp. butter, salt and pepper. Bring the foil up over chicken, seal the edges together with a tight double fold. Seal the ends in the same way, finishing with upturn to hold the juices intact. Place on outdoor grill and cook over medium heat for about 40 minutes. Have fire at good heat before starting.

This basic pattern for cooking in foil is used for any number of appetizing variations. The method and preparation of the chicken portions is the same, and different vegetables are added as follows:

Variations

1. *Zucchini and Tomato Sauce:* Before wrapping chicken, place 4-5 one-inch slices of raw tender zucchini around each portion of chicken. Add 1 Tbsp. canned tomato sauce. Complete seal in foil and cook as described in basic pattern.
2. *Rice and Tomatoes:* Before wrapping chicken, combine 1 cup canned tomatoes (drained), 1 cup cooked rice, 2 Tbsp. butter and 1 Tbsp. minced onion. Season with ½ tsp. salt and ¼ tsp. pepper. Divide mixture into 4 portions, spoon a single portion over each chicken portion. Complete seal and cook as described.

VEGETABLES IN A POKE

Thaw frozen vegetables just until they can be broken apart. (You may choose peas, corn, lima beans, string beans or asparagus.) Place in center of large square of heavy-duty aluminum foil. Add a generous pat of butter, and season with salt and pepper. Seal the foil tightly. Cook about 40 minutes over medium heat.

French bread, sliced and buttered (and wrapped in foil) can heat during the last 15 minutes while the vegetables are cooking.

GARDEN VEGETABLES

(Cooked Over The Coals)

Garden vegetables are simply wonderful when cooked out-of-doors, and so easy on the hostess! Heavy-duty foil is used. The squares of foil are torn off, brought up over the food, and twisted at top to seal the wrapping. When cooking in foil it is necessary to test for doneness. The most satisfactory way is to pierce the foil with a sharp, long-handed steel skewer. Do not turn the package after it is pierced.

Garden vegetables taste sensational when cooked out-of-doors. Experiment with different herbs and combinations of vegetables.

WHOLE ONIONS

Leave skins on, rinse and dry. Place each onion in square of foil, and wrap and seal. Cook over grill for 40-50 minutes, turning occasionally. When done, push back foil. Push open onion skins. Season with salt and pepper.

WHOLE BEETS

Remove stems and leaves. Scrub well. Place 4-6 beets on a large square of foil. Add 3-4 tsp. water and ¼ tsp. salt. Wrap in foil, and seal. Place over medium heat on grill. Cook 50-60 minutes, turning occasionally. Test for doneness.

CORN ON THE COB

Place each husked ear on a square of foil. Brush corn with melted butter, sprinkle lightly with salt. Wrap in the foil, and seal. Cook over a medium fire on grate for 20-30 minutes.

NEW POTATOES

Scrub well. Place 3-4 potatoes on a good-sized square of foil. Add 2-3 Tbsp.

Baked eggs "team up" with ham and pineapple for breakfast or brunch.

water, 1 sq. butter, and ¼ tsp. salt. Wrap in foil, and seal. Cook 40-50 minutes. Test for doneness.

STRING BEANS, TOMATOES AND ONIONS

Use string beans alone, or in combination with tomatoes and onion. Sliver the beans, add tomato wedges and wafer-thin slices of onion. Place individual portions on squares of heavy-duty foil. Add salt, pepper and butter. Basil is a good herb seasoning for all vegetable combinations with tomatoes included. Wrap in foil, and seal. Cook on grate over medium heat for 35-40 minutes, turning over once or twice.

ZUCCHINI, TOMATOES AND ONIONS

Slice zucchini. Cut peeled tomatoes in quarters. Slice onions very thin. Place the combined three vegetables on a large square of foil. Season with salt, pepper, and basil. Dot with butter. Wrap in foil, and seal. Place on grill over medium fire and cook about 30 minutes, turning once. This is also delicious when summer squash is used instead of zucchini.

CARROTS AND CELERY

Scrape carrots and cut into strips. Cut celery into small pieces. Combine both vegetables. Add butter and seasonings. Sprinkle with a little chopped parsley or mint. Wrap in foil, and seal. Place on grill over medium fire and cook 35-40 minutes, turning once.

HOT HORS D'OEUVRES

Form a shallow aluminum foil pan, and place it on grate over the fire. Broil

Start off your outdoor meal on a sophisticated note with a variety of hot appetizers. Bite sized meats cook together in heavy aluminum foil; sandwiches toast separately. Be sure to make enough.

in the foil pan any of your favorite cocktail snacks:

Chicken livers wrapped in bacon

Cocktail sausages

Shrimps dipped in garlic butter

Square bite-size sandwiches filled with deviled ham mixture

Or any other type of hot food you prefer to serve as an appetizer.

ROTISSERIES
AND HOW TO USE THEM

Outdoor barbecues sometimes mean a pleasant meal on a porch, terrace or patio. In such cases, portable rotisseries are used in place of the charcoal-burning portable or built-in grills. There are a great variety of rotisseries on the market, ranging from the moderately-priced to the very expensive ones.

The table-top type appliance is easy to use, does not throw off excessive heat, and may be used indoors if it rains. The appliance has three different methods of cooking:

1. Food may be broiled on a revolving spit
2. Food may be cooked on griddle on the top surface over the broiler
3. Food may be baked in the conventional manner by sliding the baking unit into place in the bottom, and closing glass door.

The use of heavy-duty aluminum foil catches the drippings when the revolving spit is used, and it also holds the vegetables being cooked. Extend the foil up around the edges, inside the rotisserie, about 2 inches in height. Corners of this foil liner may be securely mitered, so that a good pan is formed and later, when time to make a gravy or sauce to serve with the roto-broiled meat, the drip pan and foil pan containing the juices are placed on the top griddle, and the sauce prepared. The broiler heats the griddle.

ROTO-BROILED CHICKEN

4 16-oz. chickens	2 Tbsp. lemon juice
½ cup soft butter	1 tsp. powdered ginger (or 1 nutmeg)
1 tsp. grated lemon rind	Salt and pepper to season

Prepare the birds in the usual way (see page 136 "Broiled Chickens"). Insert the spit of the roto-broiler through the front and neck openings of the chickens, forcing them close together. Mix butter with all seasonings. Spread the butter mixture over the birds, and place them in position under the heat. Make a pan formed from aluminum foil, and place it in drip pan to catch the juices. Close the glass front of the broiler. Let chickens revolve under medium broiler heat for 40 minutes. (Larger birds may take 1 hour.) Once or twice during broiling, stop the revolving spit and brush the birds with the

Rotisseries magically prepare complete meals, are easily moved to porch or patio and save the day in case of rain.

soft, seasoned butter. When they are brown and tender, remove the chickens from the broiler, take them off the spit, and serve garnished with lemon slices. *Serves 4.*

ROTISSERIE COOKED VEGETABLES

2 whole, unpeeled tomatoes
4 Tbsp. butter, softened
1 kohlrabi or summer squash,
   medium size

2 cooking apples
2 Tbsp. brown sugar
4 Tbsp. buttered crumbs
   or
4 Tbsp. grated Parmesan cheese

Form 2 pans from heavy-duty aluminum foil and place on one of the rotisserie pans. Cut tomatoes in half, arrange in a foil pan. Spread tops with softened butter, sprinkle with salt and pepper. Peel kohlrabi, slice in thin slices, and cook in a saucepan in boiling salted water until just tender. Peel and core apples, slice in rings and steam 5 minutes in saucepan with kohlrabi.

Remove both from saucepan, draining them, and arrange in the second foil pan, alternating the slices. Sprinkle with light brown sugar and pour over a little melted butter. Place the two foil pans of vegetables under broiler, and allow to brown slowly. Top tomatoes with buttered crumbs or grated cheese during last 2 minutes of broiling. *Serves 4.*

BREAKFAST EGGS AND SAUSAGES

8 eggs	2 tsp. butter
½ lb. "Brown & Serve" sausages	Salt and pepper to taste

Make double thick squares of heavy-duty foil 5x7 inches. Turn up edges ¾ inch all around and mitre corners to hold firm. Brown sausages quickly right on the grill, over direct heat. Place little foil pans on grill, add a dab of butter to each. Place the sausages into pans and break in the eggs. Let eggs cook until firm. Sprinkle with seasonings. If the day is breezy, cover tops of pans with squares of foil so eggs will cook on top. *Serves 4.*

BREAKFAST APPLES IN FOIL

4 apples	4 Tbsp. walnuts, chopped
4 Tbsp. orange marmalade	2 tsp. lemon juice

Core large baking apples, peel skin from upper part. Place on squares of heavy-duty foil. Fill centers with marmalade, top with walnuts. Sprinkle with lemon juice to keep cut surface from discoloring. Wrap in foil, twisting at top to close. Store in refrigerator until ready to cook. Place on the grill over medium heat. Cook about 45 minutes. Test for doneness. To serve, turn back the foil attractively to form a foil dish. *Serves 4.*

POPPY SEED BREAD

1 loaf homestyle poppy seed bread, unsliced	1 Tbsp. poppy seeds
½ cup butter, softened	or
	4 Tbsp. sugar mixed with 1 tsp. cinnamon

Cut loaf into 10-12 thick slices, down to, but not through bottom crust. Stand on large sheet of aluminum foil. Mix butter with poppy seeds (or sugar and cinnamon mixture). Bring the foil up over the bread and wrap it, but leave an opening at top for the steam to escape. Heat for about 20 minutes on grill, over medium heat. Tip over on both sides for part of the time, for even heating. Serve from foil.

Breakfast out-of-doors (top) on sizzling sausage and fried eggs appeals to even the non-breakfasters in the family.

Apples baked in foil (bottom) are filled with marmalade and chopped nuts. Serve in the foil or transfer to individual dishes and pass a pitcher of milk or cream.

41.

PARTY AND
HOLIDAY MENUS

PARTIES, feast days, other gala affairs, are the highlights of a year. The routine of everyday life is happily interrupted by such holidays and festivals. Special occasions, children's parties and birthdays, are among a family's yearly celebrations. As has been the custom from time immemorial, special events are still marked by feasting. Each country has its own feast-day dishes, and in our country, each region has special ways of preparing holiday foods. Many recipes will be found in this book which a new homemaker may add to her collection of foods for her own family parties. Some party menus follow, which may be used as a guide for outstanding occasions.

NEW YEAR'S EVE

MIDNIGHT BUFFET SUPPER

Platter of Cold Baked Ham, thinly sliced
Garniture of Peach Halves
Center filled with cream cheese
Scalloped Oysters
Hot Buttered Rolls
Olives—Celery Hearts—Sweet Pickles
Bowl of Green Salad
Crescents of Orange and Avocado Pear
Lady Baltimore Cake
XII Marked in silver ornament on frosting
Lemon Sherbet
Coffee
Brandy

VALENTINE PARTY

Cream Puff Shells
Filled with Crab Meat and Pimiento Garnish
Buttered Green Peas
Currant Jelly   Stuffed Olives
Crescent Rolls
Vanilla Ice Cream
Crushed Raspberry Sauce
Petits Fours
Candy Heart Decorations
Coffee

Sentimental occasions call for special decorations. Heart motifs on cakes, napkins, and favors, will convey the festive mood.

Easter bunnies will enchant the young fry when they're made of molasses cup cakes, marshmallows, and colored candies.

EASTER BREAKFAST

Grapefruit and Orange Fruit Cup
Poached Eggs on Toast
Garnish of Watercress
Thin slices of Broiled Ham
Popovers   Butter
Strawberry Preserves
Coffee   Milk

FOURTH OF JULY DINNER

Jellied Tomato Madrilène
Celery Hearts
Roast Spring Lamb
New Potatoes   Parsley Garnish
New Green Peas in Cream
Currant Jelly   Mint Sauce
Lemon Sherbet   Glacé Cherry Garnish
Chocolate Cup Cakes (tiny ornamental flag in each cake)
Coffee   Milk

HALLOWE'EN PARTY FOR CHILDREN

Assorted Sandwiches
    Brown Bread and butter
    Cream Cheese   Sliced Olive Garnish
    Peanut Butter and Honey

Individual Cup Cakes
    Chocolate Frosting with Jack O'Lantern Face
    Marked in White Frosting
Glasses of Milk

Spooky Hallowe'en cake, made of ice cream and ginger snap crumbs, will highlight any child's Hallowe'en party.

THANKSGIVING DINNER

Pineapple and Orange Fruit Cup
Clear Consommé
(lemon slice garnish)
Toasted Crackers

Celery   Olives   Carrot Sticks

Roast Duckling
Orange Sauce
OR
Roast Turkey
Chestnut Stuffing
Brown Gravy

Creamed Onions   Candied Sweet Potatoes
Romaine Salad   French Dressing
Pumpkin Pie   Cheese

Demitasse

CHRISTMAS DINNER

Oysters on Half Shell
Tomato Juice Cocktail

Hearts of Celery   Ripe Olives
Carrot Strips   Currant Jelly

Roast Turkey
Giblet Gravy
Lancaster Stuffing

Green Beans   Yellow Turnips
Mashed Potatoes

Nesselrode Ice Cream   Petits Fours
Salted Pecans   Chocolate Mints

Demitasse

Plum pudding served with hard sauce tops off any winter holiday dinner with distinction.

42.

PARTIES AROUND
THE CALENDAR

AS A NATION of people given to sociability, we are particularly fortunate, for not only can we celebrate legal holidays, religious festivals, birthdays and anniversaries, but we also have a number of special-event occasions which call for observance of some sort or other. A comprehensive list from which to choose is given below:

January
    New Year's Day
    Robert E. Lee's Birthday

February
    Boy Scout Day
    Abraham Lincoln's Birthday
    St. Valentine's Day
    George Washington's Birthday

March
    Girl Scout Day
    St. Patrick's Day

Religious Festivals
    Easter
    Passover
    Russian Easter
    These festivals fall near each other in March or April, as a rule.

April
    April Fool's Day
    Army Day
    Pan-American Day

Election Day offers a grand time for having friends in.

May

    May Day

    Maritime Day

    Memorial Day

    American Indian Day

    Mother's Day

June

    Father's Day

    Jefferson Davis Day

    Flag Day

    Bunker Hill Day

July

    Independence Day—Fourth of July

August

    No national holidays, but midsummer festivals are given in many states.

September

    Labor Day

    Constitution Day

A cherry holiday pudding, with coffee and assorted nuts, spells Christmas festivity.

October
    Columbus Day
    Navy Day
    Hallowe'en

November
    Election Day
    Armistice Day
    Thanksgiving Day

December
    Christmas
    New Year's Eve

This chapter is tailor-made for the hostess who wants to give a party "just for fun." Such parties are distinguished by their casual air, imagination and ingenuity. To the guest, a party of this type should appear to have been whipped together quickly. And the way to create this desired effect is to plan it in advance, so that none of the behind-the-scenes hard work shows when the curtain goes up.

Table setting and table service are explained in detail in Chapter 43. Holiday menus are found in Chapter 41, and "Cooking for a Crowd" is in Chapter 39. These helpful aids save time and effort, but more than general information is necessary. A hostess needs to use her own original ideas.

It may be well to note that a party which includes a large number of guests should be served buffet style. Its informality puts the guests at ease immediately, and enables the hostess to mingle more freely with her guests.

THE YEAR STARTS

New Year's Eve—A good start to any party is the kind of invitation which is sent. Choose a card which conveys the spirit of the occasion, lively, cheerful and gay. Or make your own. Plain heavy cards with tiny figures pasted, painted or hand-drawn add individuality. The theme commonly chosen is a design which features The Old Year Goes Out—The New Year Comes In. The table setting is chosen with the same theme. Dolls appropriately dressed are attractive, so are large calendar pages torn off and used as tablemats.

Many people like to choose amusing favors from grab-bags. New Year's Resolutions make a popular game, with a prize given for the most amusing

"*Happy New Year*" with the first breakfast of the new year: waffles and pork sausage links.

or most original list. The smart hostess plans her games and entertainment ahead of time, being careful to keep it casual. Costume parties are great favorites for New Year's Eve, and there should be prizes enough for something to be given to practically everyone: unique, least costly, funniest, prettiest, etc., etc.

Twin hearts avocado salad molds star at St. Valentine's Day party. This old-fashioned holiday is a good time for formal service.

St. Valentine's Day—The theme for this party is that of the always romantic and popular "hearts and cupids." Witty and modern, or lovely and old-fashioned, the fact is that nearly everyone remembers this day. Table decorations and settings carry out the motif of the invitations. A big crepe-paper heart drawn snugly over a heavy cardboard base may be used as the centerpiece. Favors for the guests are placed inside the heart and each one tied with a narrow, red silk ribbon streamer, which is then stretched out to each place. Dinner and dancing partners are chosen by duplicate-numbered hearts. Old ballads may be sung; quiz games on famous lovers of history and fiction are usually popular. Food carries out the theme in color and shape.

George Washington's Birthday—The invitations usually carry the motif of the hatchet or cherry tree, or the silhouettes of George and Martha. The party itself may be a patriotic one, or it may stress Colonial ideas, such as the

Party idea. Invite company on Derby Day. Start off with mint juleps.

Minuet as a dance, the lovely costumes of the day. Here is an opportunity for quizzes concerning Colonial history. Charades is a good game for this party, too. A "Truth and Consequence" game, based on the famous old tale of "I cannot tell a lie," would be appropriate.

Hallowe'en—This is a holiday beloved by the young in heart. Parties for this date are among the highlights of the calendar year. The black witches flying through the air, or the grinning jack-o-lanterns, make appealing cardboard invitations. Heavy, colored paper, crepe-paper, scissors, paste pot, and a little ingenuity turn out eerie invitations for everyone. Table settings have the traditional pumpkin as a centerpiece, real or made of papier-maché. Black candles, alternating with white or orange-colored, cast a weird light. Paper bats or witches suspended from the ceiling add fun to the occasion. Black and orange crepe-paper, in long panels and ruffled at the edges, makes a good tablecloth. Weird costumes are usually worn at Hallowe'en parties. Ghost stories, telling fortunes, bobbing for apples, games in keeping with the "Witches' Night" are all in tune with a gay party. Cider and doughnuts are the usual refreshments served, plus a big bowl of brightly polished apples.

Other parties which have their ardent devotees are:

St. Patrick's Day—The shamrocks, the "wearin' of the green," the clay pipes—all belong to the 17th of March.

Pan-American Day—This calls for a gay fiesta, native costumes, wonderful music, and South-of-the-Border things to eat.

Fourth of July—America turns out en masse for backyard parties, picnics at the beach, barbecues, and fireworks. For an evening party, mass the country's colors in great bows of red, white and blue ribbon. Never use the flag for decorative purposes. Uncle Sam may preside as a centerpiece for the table, with streamers of ribbon falling to the floor at each corner of the table. Color hard-cooked eggs in red and blue, and combine with the white eggs, for use as a centerpiece instead of flowers.

Thanksgiving—One of our most important holidays, deeply-rooted in the very foundations of our country. Each family has its own traditional menu, based upon the original Thanksgiving Day feast. As a rule, this is a family party, observed with a spirit of fervor. Snowy-white linen, polished silver, the

Cranberry-fruit salad mold. Give guests wedges with the Thanksgiving turkey.

fine china, and a handsome centerpiece of fruit and flowers are the settings for this great day.

So, to our hostesses, we say: Have a fine party, and have a good time at your own party, secure in the knowledge that if you enjoy the occasion, so will your guests!

St. Patrick's Day mold made in shamrock shape.

Candied-apple ice cream is special for Hallowe'en.

43.

TABLE SERVICE

NOT SO many years ago, the ritual and ceremony with which a meal was served was elaborate, expensive and time-consuming. But modern living has brought a new sense of values, and it is no longer necessary for a hostess to suffer agonies of embarrassment because she lacks a maid.

Whether it be a party or a family meal, the appearance of the table is important—and an immaculate, neatly-set table is a pretty table. Fresh tablecloth or doilies, sparkling silver, china and glassware, and a flowering plant or a few fresh flowers will make any table a pleasing picture.

TABLE LINEN

Table linen is no longer limited to large tablecloths, heavily monogrammed. Today we also enjoy the use of luncheon cloths, runners, or doilies made of any material we prefer—rayon, cotton, linen, plastic, fiber, and even paper or cork. On their dinner tables, handsome doilies please many households.

THE INDIVIDUAL "COVER"

The silver, linen, china, and glass used by one person is called a "cover," and an area of 20 to 24 inches is allowed for each person, to give elbow room. If the table edge is straight, place the "cover" 1 inch from it. If it is rounded, the "cover" edge does not parallel it, but is a straight line, with the outer articles in the "cover" 1 inch from the edge of the table.

The plate is the center of the "cover." Silver pieces which are used with the right hand (including knives, spoons for fruit, dessert, cereal and soup, also the oyster fork) go to the right of the plate, in the order in which they are to be used, from the outside in. Silver pieces which are used with the left hand

BREAKFAST COVER FOR HOSTESS

LUNCHEON COVER

DINNER COVER

A table correctly set is one of the marks of a good hostess. Correct setting will also make for greater ease and enjoyment on the part of guests.

BUFFET FOR OBLONG TABLE AGAINST THE WALL

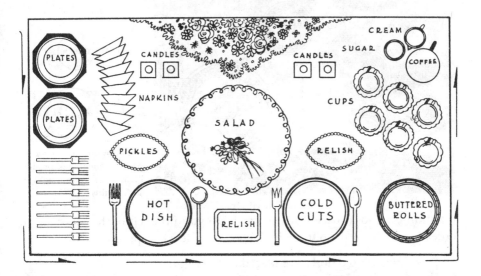

Lovely linen, tastefully selected silver and china, and a centerpiece of fruit and flowers make this a gracious table which will heighten the pleasure of the meal itself.

A baking dish you can bring to the table and use without embarrassment. Today's trend toward more informal entertainment has brought great favor to cooking ware such as this.

(including all forks except the oyster fork) go to the left of the plate, in the order of use, from the outside in. There are a few exceptions:

1. If no knife is used, forks are placed at the right.
2. Individual butter-spreaders are placed on the bread-and-butter plates, parallel to the edge of the plate.
3. The spoon for orange or grapefruit may be placed on the plate on which the fruit is served, parallel to the other silver.
4. The dessert silver is often placed with the dessert. Knife blades are turned toward the plate; forks are placed with tines up, and spoons with bowls turned up. Glasses are placed on the right hand, at the tip of the knife; the bread-and-butter plate is placed on the left at the tip of the fork. Individual salt and pepper shakers may be placed above the plate, in line with the glass for each "cover" or between two "covers."

Napkins are folded in squares and placed at the left of the forks, so that the lower right-hand corner is the open corner.

If your family includes a left-handed person, or if you know that a guest is left-handed, it is an appreciated gesture to reverse the setting of that particular "cover."

DISHES ADDITIONAL TO INDIVIDUAL "COVERS"

Serving silver may be placed to the right of the space provided on the table for the serving dish, or laid on the table with the dish.

The dishes needed vary with each meal, but in general the following articles will be used and placed as follows:

BREAKFAST

The coffee percolator or other container is put at the hostess's right, with the handle parallel to her silver. The cups and saucers are placed above her "cover."

Prepared cereal or eggs may be served individually, or placed on the table above the hostess's "cover" and then served by her.

LUNCHEON—DINNER

The salad or salad plates are placed at the left of the "covers," just beyond the napkins. The carving fork should be at the left of the space for the platter, the carving knife and a tablespoon at the right. The water pitcher is placed on a plate or on a tile at the right of one "cover" (other than that of the host or the hostess).

INFORMAL SERVICE

Practically every meal today is served informally. Even in the household which has a maid, her work is often too complex to enable her to serve elaborate meals. If a hostess plans a large formal luncheon or dinner, it might be necessary to engage extra maid service. But for daily living an informal service has been developed, to serve the food quickly while it is piping hot and appetizing. The first course is usually at each place on the table when the family enters the dining room. A tea cart, or a small table placed at the right of the hostess, should have on it the covered dishes which contain the next course. If the dessert is anything but ice cream or a hot soufflé, it may be placed on the cart ready to be served at the proper time. The tea cart or small table is also an excellent place for the hostess to put the used dishes from the previous course, so that she need not get up from the dining table.

ENTERTAINING GUESTS

LUNCHEON OR DINNER

Pleasant meals may be conducted with grace and charm, without a sign of a maid. If the first course consists of vegetable or fruit juices, or other cocktails, accompanied by canapés or salted crackers, the hostess can save a good deal of work by serving these in the living room. Juices or cocktails in attractive glasses, and appetizers arranged on a pretty plate, are placed on a large tray. Small cocktail-size napkins accompany this serving. The tray may be passed around, or placed on a table within convenient reach of the guests so that they can help themselves. This promotes a congenial atmosphere, and helps to bridge the first social gap, especially if someone is late in arriving. At the same time, the hostess can devote the last minutes to the main course before the guests are seated at the dining table.

Imaginative accessories, like the net, fisherman's basket, shells, and foil dishes lend a seashore atmosphere to this lobster dinner party.

The host serves the meal and vegetables. The hostess serves the soup, dessert, tea and coffee, and asks the guests to serve themselves from dishes which are convenient to them; also to help by passing plates or dishes to others, and passing the used dishes back to her. If there is no host (but only a hostess) another member of the family, or a best friend, may take the part usually played by the host.

The entire main course may be arranged on hot individual dinner plates in the kitchen, and brought to the table immediately after the guests are seated. Then with the use of a tea wagon or small table, the meal can be served with the minimum of confusion.

BUFFET SERVICE

A buffet meal is adaptable to any time of the day, such as breakfast or "brunch," luncheon, dinner, or after-theatre snack. It is an excellent way to provide refreshments at a large party, as it places much less strain upon the hostess, and the guests do have a good time when they can use the self-service method of selecting their own food and beverage. Buffet service is also a boon to the hostess when she cannot know beforehand the exact number of guests, or when some guests may be late in arriving.

The buffet table is most convenient when placed against the wall. However, if the room is large, and the table is in the center, it can remain there provided there is sufficient room for the guests to walk around it. The good hostess selects the tablecloth and decorations to suit the occasion—formal or informal. However, the buffet table is never cluttered with too much decoration. Room must be left on the table to stack the large plates, the folded napkins, and the silverware (forks are laid side by side, spoons are laid side by side).

The menu should be carefully planned so that there will be no need for knives or for small plates, as the meal is eaten on the one large plate. The buffet table should include one or two hot dishes, a salad bowl, and a plate of buttered sliced bread or rolls. If desired, a platter of mixed sandwiches, or crackers and cheese may also be included, as well as small dishes of candies, nuts or relishes, and a bowl of fruit.

To facilitate the self-service, and to keep the buffet table from being too crowded, you can place the beverages (hot and cold), together with glasses, cups, saucers and teaspoons, on a nearby small serving table, tea cart, or even a bridge table, so that the guests may help themselves.

Some people are quite graceful at balancing a laden plate on their laps; however, it is not especially recommended, and if possible it is best to have small tables on which the guests may place their plates. For this purpose coffee tables and end tables come into use; if you have a nest of tables, this is the proper time to separate and distribute them. Also the thoughtful hostess opens up her bridge tables so that the guests may bring their plates there.

For the hostesses who have no maid service, who have no dining room, and especially for people who go to business this buffet style of serving is a boon. It does not have to be saved just for a party—it is an excellent idea to try out on a family gathering occasionally, to imbue it with the "party spirit."

AFTERNOON TEA

Here is a gracious way of entertaining. A "tea" does not require strenuous preparation on the part of the hostess, and it is a pleasant way of introducing a newcomer to the family or a group of friends, or of getting acquainted with new neighbors. Even though it is thought of as a feminine pastime, actually men like tea, too, and one should not hesitate to invite them.

The tea table must be attractive. It should be covered with a lace or finely embroidered cloth, and a small bowl of flowers adds a charming touch. Use your prettiest china and silverware. Napkins should be small and of delicate pattern.

The hostess, or a member of the family, or a friend she has asked to pour the tea, sits at one end of the tea table on which is placed a tray holding the teapot, hot water, cream, lemon, and sugar. At the left of this service tray, the saucers are stacked, and the cups are placed with their handles toward the left. If the number of guests is large, and the table small, it may be necessary to stack the cups, but it is preferable to avoid this if possible.

Conveniently placed on the table, so that the guests may help themselves, are the folded napkins, teaspoons, and plates or trays containing cakes, or small sandwiches, or bread and butter slices. A doily is placed on each of these plates or trays before the refreshments are arranged on them.

An afternoon tea may be informal or formal, and the table setting and refreshments should be adapted to the particular occasion.

The whole matter of a pleasant, easily arranged party revolves around good planning in advance. For the hostess who takes pride in her parties, it is suggested that she keep abreast of entertainment ideas by reading good magazines which specialize in women's home activities.

44.

FURNISHING
THE KITCHEN

THE FAMILY kitchen is the heartbeat of the home. The first lesson which a bride learns about housekeeping is the importance of good equipment in the kitchen, and its relation to the use of the food she buys.

How vital it is that the dollars spent on heavy kitchen equipment, appliances, and cooking utensils be disbursed with the utmost intelligence! Many a housekeeper has found to her sorrow that cheap utensils are the most expensive in the long run. Good pans last for years, and are handed down from mother to daughter. Cheap ones burn the food, cook it unevenly, get marred and scarred by continual use, and have to be replaced frequently—a waste that is quite unnecessary.

When a family moves into a new house, it soon becomes apparent that major purchases are necessary. In homes which are rented, many landlords do not furnish range or refrigerator. If a new home is purchased outright, these expensive pieces of kitchen equipment are often included in the purchase price—but there is no hard-and-fast rule concerning it.

Many young couples who are not yet established in a permanent home wish to postpone the purchase of these major items. For them, the market offers a wealth of portable kitchen equipment. There are electric roasters, two-plate electric burners, deep casseroles, table grills, and table-top broilers. These modern appliances are a godsend to small families living in small quarters.

In addition to the array of portable cooking appliances designed to take the place of large cooking ranges, or serve as adjuncts to them, there are also a great number of small kitchen and dining room appliances which serve many useful purposes. These should be thoroughly examined before purchasing, to determine the current (AC or DC). Every appliance sold has the voltage and current clearly marked on the item, and the local utility company is one of the best sources of information for kitchen appliances which use electric current. These include such items as electric mixers, toasters, waffle irons, sandwich grills, coffee machines, juice extractors.

Heavy equipment has changed considerably, and a housewife is advised to study the new equipment being offered before coming to a decision. Household refrigerators are now available in portable sizes. One of the newer ones weighs only 55 lbs., yet has a capacity of 8 ice trays.

Get one that is large enough. Young families are going to grow. A 7-cubic-foot refrigerator is considered by many experts to be the minimum capacity for a family of two. Answer these questions to your own satisfaction before making a purchase. How much milk will be stored daily? How much quick-frozen food? How many soft-drink bottles?

Frequency of marketing has a very definite bearing on the size of the refrigerator required. So does the amount of regular entertaining a family must plan for. When a refrigerator is overcrowded, the operation is less satisfactory and increased operating costs are apt to result.

The third type of electric refrigerator is the home-freezer. This is specifically designed to serve the family who wants to quick-freeze fresh food and store it until ready to use. A wide variety of types is on the market. Some are simple single compartments, which are merely storage lockers and offer no way to quick-freeze the food. Others provide a quick-freezing compartment, plus one or several compartments for storage. The development of this type of refrigerator is so new that each type offered for sale should be scrutinized minutely before making the purchase.

There is no doubt in the minds of the experts that home-freezing is the latest development in good living. It offers greater food variety; surplus foods

The modern refrigerator is one of the housekeeper's greatest blessings. Treat yours well by reading the manufacturer's instructions and following them after buying a new refrigerator. Otherwise, use general common sense and get the most use by storing food intelligently.

"U" SHAPED KITCHEN UNIT

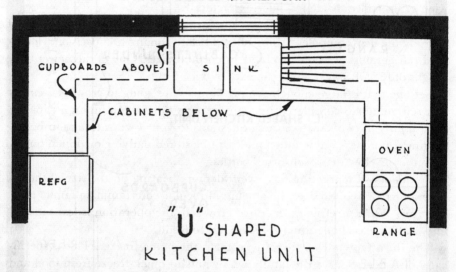

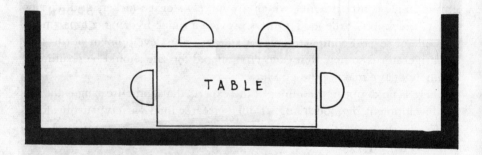

ONE WALL KITCHEN UNIT

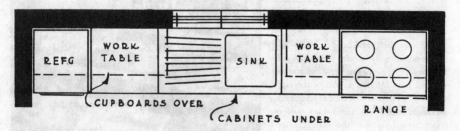

Kitchen plans vary with the amounts of space and money available. Here are several of the most typical as well as practical layout plans.

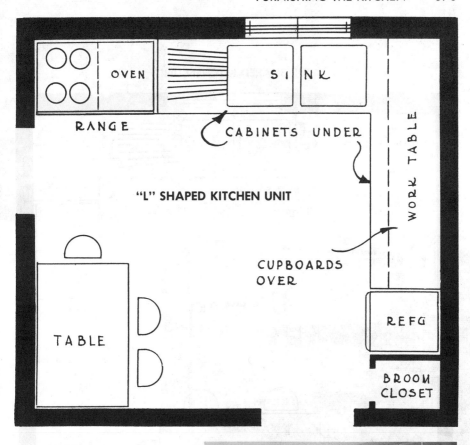

OVEN

SINK

RANGE

CABINETS UNDER

WORK TABLE

"L" SHAPED KITCHEN UNIT

CUPBOARDS
OVER

REFG

TABLE

BROOM
CLOSET

Your kitchen should be made as step-saving as possible. By careful planning, you will be able to work out certain patterns in your own kitchen to follow the patterns developed in this modern kitchen. In the picture below, three work centers have been laid out: the refrigeration and preparation center, the sink and dishwasher center, and the range and serving center.

A new horizontal refrigerator may be mounted wherever the owner wishes, eliminating stooping and reaching.

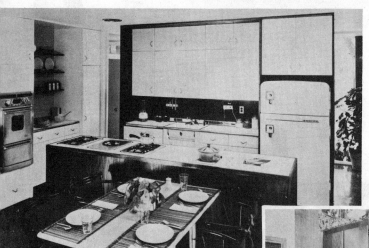

A modern gas kitchen groups appliances for flexible family living within easy reach of the family table.

A dining nook will save the housekeeper who does her own work an infinite amount of energy. If your kitchen room is spacious, try to adapt one corner or alcove so that you can serve breakfast and lunch with a minimum of fuss and steps.

An infrared lamp is put to practical use as a defroster for frozen foods, so that the busy housewife can get dinner on the table in no time at all.

Cooking versatility is achieved with this Rotiss-O-Mat, which fries eggs and bacon on top, while a chicken turns on the spit underneath.

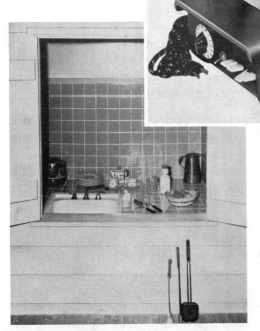

The new second kitchen is important, with to-day's emphasis on outdoor eating. This niche "pantry" facing outdoors will speed service and reduce clean-up chores, with ceramic tile's ability to come clean with the swish of a damp cloth.

may be quick-frozen and served later; foods in or out of season are available for the year around. Home-freezing means more meat and poultry for the family dinner table, at lower 'cost. More fruits and vegetables can be served, thus giving added nutrition at lower cost.

With a home-freezer, meals are easier to prepare and require less preparation in advance. Shopping trips may be less frequent. If a family is fortunate enough to have a garden, home-grown produce may be prepared, scalded, and packaged. Tedious old-time canning methods may be cut to a minimum. Small or large quantities may be prepared at a single session.

Home-freezing also means that, in the country where butchering takes place, meals from quick-frozen food supplies offer the maximum in appetite appeal and the minimum in waste. No food need be wasted when efficient home-freezing is part of the family's equipment.

The freezers available are:

Chest-Type Freezer. Usually square or oblong in shape, with a top opening.

The Walk-in Freezer. Usually used on small farms where storage area is required for quantities of apples, winter fruits, and vegetables.

The Well-Type. Similiar to the chest-type except for its round shape. The freezing and storage are usually done in the same compartment.

The Upright Design. Provided with front or side opening doors. It usually includes one compartment for sub-zero freezing, with several compartments for zero storage. A number of manufacturers are adopting this type for several reasons:

a. Research indicates better results with separate compartments at sub-zero temperature.
b. Users prefer to reach in for product when ready to defrost it.
c. Defrosting is simple. Simply put food in storage compartment.
d. It is serviced exactly like an electric refrigerator.

One piece of equipment, offered to the American public for the first time, appeared in 1947. This is an electric range with a "defrost-all" feature. The manufacturers say that this scientific addition to an electric range reduces the time-lag between the frozen state of food and its appearance on the table. This exciting new appliance cuts the time of defrosting to a minimum. A warm breeze is "wrapped around" the quick-frozen foods, so that their return to their natural state is speeded up and, consequently, the food values are retained to a greater degree.

The use of electric ranges has increased steadily since their introduction. Features have been added to make home cooking an art anyone can master. Some new ranges offer auxiliary ovens which may be used when the larger oven is not required. Two ovens for baking provide a feature which home-bakers like. Automatic timers, constant heat control, signal lights—each new

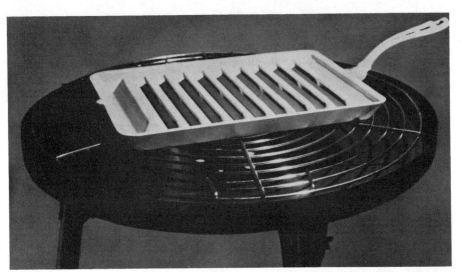

Auxiliary cooking fixtures permit you to broil, fry, or roast foods.

Two-oven ranges should be considered if you plan to buy a new stove. A week's baking can be done at one time in this type of range. All the meats for the week end or holiday can be done in advance, leaving the housekeeper time to be with her family and guests.

range has modern gadgets to simplify cooking. Some ranges offer built-in pressure cookers, others a deep-well or waterless cookery unit. One of the new ranges has a special burner for slow cooking.

Still another range which delights families in apartments or rented houses is a bantam-size affair which plugs into the electric outlet. The oven will hold a 20 lb. turkey; there's a broiler oven, and two units for surface cookery.

New portable washing machines, and ironers which permit the operator to sit comfortably while the sheets roll through, are among the household appliances which make other countries envy Mrs. America.

PLANNING THE KITCHEN

Modern kitchens are planned for efficiency, comfort, good looks, and the ultimate in convenience. The kitchens are designed to permit the worker to start her tasks at the end of the room, and step-by-step follow through in a direct line, without criss-crossing back and forth on her own footprints.

For easy deliveries, storage space is planned at the entrance or close to the entrance. A food-preparation work-center follows in order, with a cooking

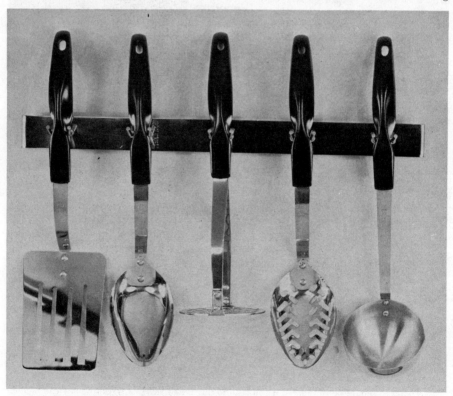

A utensil rack with shiny tools such as this one boasts will spur you on to organize your kitchen tasks in an efficient, workmanlike manner.

A grinder is a kitchen aid which will serve well in the preparation of countless dishes.

work-center in logical sequence, and a clean-up work-center as the final step. Each unit of space is arranged with correctly placed table work-surfaces, accompanying cabinets, and necessary shelves.

Pots and pans are arranged at proper heights, according to the needs of the individual housewife.

UTENSILS AND POTS AND PANS

Practically every material one can imagine is used to make kitchen furnishing a pleasure; heavy cast-iron, stainless steel, copper, aluminum, enamelware; earthenware, heat-proof glassware, and china to add variety and color.

A housewife may choose a cast-iron Dutch oven, and an earthenware casserole, or a whole collection of earthenware. She may choose copper-bottomed steel saucepans. The world is hers for the asking. She may select any color scheme she desires. Floor coverings are usually heavy-duty or lighter linoleum. The walls may be painted, or covered with washable wallpaper. The heavy-duty equipment is usually gleaming white porcelain on steel. And her colored cabinets may be selected from the shades in the rainbow.

ESSENTIAL KITCHEN UTENSILS

1 grater (4 sides)
1 glass orange-juice squeezer
1 coffee pot
1 can opener
1 apple corer
1 coarse wire strainer
1 set measuring spoons
2 measuring cups (½ pt.)
1 qt. measure
1 egg beater
1 pastry blender
1 biscuit cutter
1 rolling pin
1 bread board
1 flour sifter
1 sugar scoop
1 spatula
1 pancake turner
3 mixing spoons
1 set mixing bowls
1 set of jars for storing dry foods
1 set muffin tins (set of 6)
1 square cake pan
2 round layer-cake pans

2 oblong bread pans
1 cookie sheet
1 wire cake cooler
1 pie tin
1 set heat-resistant glass baking dishes
1 set kitchen knives
1 pair scissors
1 covered casserole
1 cake board and cover
1 set salt and pepper shakers
1 small skillet (5 inches in diameter, heavy iron, aluminum, or steel)
1 large skillet (10 inches in diameter)
1 tea kettle
1 saucepan (1 pt.)
1 saucepan (1 qt.)
1 saucepan (2 qt.)
1 double boiler
1 colander
2 wire strainers (1 coarse, 1 fine)
1 dish pan
1 drain rack for clean dishes
1 wastepaper basket
1 roaster pan

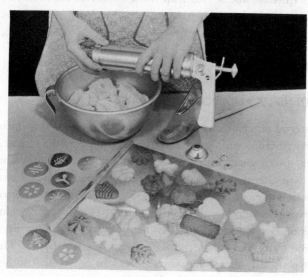

A cookie cutter is a handy gadget, especially if you have cookie-hungry small fry at home.

ACKNOWLEDGMENTS

The author acknowledges with appreciation the great number of individuals, firms, and associations who graciously contributed technical data, suggestions, and pictures.

Special thanks are due to:

Dorothy Sara, editor

Miriam B. Reichl, picture editor

Margot L. and Donald D. Wolf, designers

The picture editor gratefully credits the following firms and associations with the photographs they have so generously contributed to the following pages:

2–3 American Spice Trade Association
13 American Sheep Producers Council
17 United Fresh Fruit and Vegetable Association
20 (top left) Ocean Spray Fresh Cranberries
20 (bottom left) Knox Gelatine
20 (right) Sealtest Kitchens
25 Ewing Galloway
26 Campbell Soup Company
27 National Biscuit Company
30 Underwood Deviled Ham
33 National Biscuit Company
35 United States Department of Agriculture
37 American Dairy Association
40 American Spice Trade Association
42 National Biscuit Company
43 Tabasco
45 (top left) American Meat Institute
45 (top right) American Meat Institute
45 (bottom left) United States Department of Agriculture
45 (bottom right) Wear-Ever Aluminum, Inc.
48 Sealtest Kitchens
49 American Meat Institute
50 Pan-American Coffee Bureau
51 (top) Best Foods - Corn Products Company
51 (bottom) Best Foods - Corn Products Company
52 Bananas - The United Fruit Company
53 Angostura-Wuppermann Corp.

54 Sealtest Kitchens
55 National Biscuit Company
57 Best Foods - Corn Products Company
58 (top) The Borden Company
58 (bottom) Brer Rabbit Molasses
59 The Borden Company
60 United Fresh Fruit and Vegetable Association
63 The Borden Company
67 Angostura-Wuppermann Corp.
69 Angostura-Wuppermann Corp.
70 Ac'cent International
73 (top) Ac'cent International
73 (bottom) The Borden Company
75 (left) The Borden Company
75 (right) American Spice Trade Association
78 Best Foods - Corn Products Company
81 The Borden Company
84 United Fresh Fruit and Vegetable Association
89 United Fresh Fruit and Vegetable Association
90 The Borden Company
91 Gas Appliance Manufacturing Association
92 The Borden Company
93 Best Foods - Corn Products Company
94 (left) Chase and Sanborn Coffee
94 (right) Best Foods - Corn Products Company
96 The Borden Company
98 (top) National Biscuit Company
98 (bottom) Sealtest Kitchens

99 The Borden Company
100 (left) The Borden Company
100 (right) The Borden Company
101 National Biscuit Company
102 American Meat Institute
106 American Meat Institute
109 (top left) Pan-American Coffee Bureau
109 (top right) National Biscuit Company
109 (bottom) The Borden Company
110 Ac'cent International
111 American Meat Institute
117 Ac'cent International
118 American Lamb Council
120 National Biscuit Company
124 Wear-Ever Aluminum, Inc. - Alcoa Wrap
127 The United Fruit Company
132 Broiler Council
134 Broiler Institute
135 Wear-Ever Aluminum, Inc.
137 United Fresh Fruit and Vegetable Association
140 The Borden Company
141 Wear-Ever Aluminum, Inc.
143 Coca-Cola
144 Delmarva Poultry Industry
145 Delmarva Poultry Industry
146 Alcoa Wrap
147 South African Rock Lobster Association
149 Brer Rabbit Molasses
151 (top) Aluminum Company of America
151 (bottom) Alcoa Wrap
154 Aluminum Company of America
155 Best Foods - Corn Products Company
158 Sealtest Kitchens
159 Wear-Ever Aluminum, Inc.
160 Angostura-Wuppermann Corp.
163 (left) Campbell Soup Company
163 (right) The Borden Company
166 National Kraut Packers Association
169 (top left) Wear-Ever Aluminum, Inc.
169 (top right) American Blue Cheese Association
169 (bottom left) Sealtest Kitchens
169 (bottom right) Wear-Ever Aluminum, Inc.
170 National Kraut Packers Association
171 Ac'cent International
175 Evaporated Milk Association
176 United Fresh Fruit and Vegetable Association
179 The Underwood Kitchen
181 Switzerland Swiss Cheese Association
183 Sealtest Kitchens
186 Wheat Flour Institute
191 Pan-American Coffee Bureau
195 Blueberry Cooperatives of New Jersey and Michigan
199 National Cotton Council
201 Fleischmann Yeast Company
203 Blueberry Cooperatives of New Jersey and Michigan
205 National Biscuit Company
209 National Biscuit Company
211 National Biscuit Company
215 American Dairy Association
217 American Dairy Association
218 The Borden Company
223 United Fruit Company - Bananas
224 Nescafé
226 Brer Rabbit Molasses
227 Brer Rabbit Molasses
229 Nestlé
231 Cherry Growers and Industries Foundation
232 Nestlé
235 Karo Syrup
238 Sealtest Kitchens
240 National Biscuit Company
243 California Strawberry Advisory Board
246 Broiler Council
248 The Borden Company
249 Sealtest Kitchens
251 (top) American Sheep Producers Council
251 (bottom) The Borden Company
252 (top) California Strawberry Advisory Board
252 (bottom) National Biscuit Company
253 American Spice Trade Association
255 Sealtest Kitchens
260 The Borden Company
262 National Biscuit Company
269 National Biscuit Company
270 Sealtest Kitchens
271 California Strawberry Advisory Board
273 United States Department of Agriculture - Agricultural Research Service
274 Sealtest Kitchens
275 The Borden Company
278 Sealtest Kitchens
280 United Fresh Fruit and Vegetable Association
283 (top) Ocean Spray Fresh Cranberries
283 (bottom left) Sealtest Kitchens
283 bottom right) Bananas - United Fruit Company

285 (top) Ocean Spray Fresh Cranberries
285 (bottom) American Blue Cheese Association
287 U. S. Department of Agriculture-Agricultural Research Service
289 Wear-Ever Aluminum, Inc.
298 Angostura-Wuppermann Corp.
301 U. S. Department of Agriculture-Agricultural Research Service
304 Broiler Council
308 Libbey Glass Photo
314 United Fresh Fruit and Vegetable Association
319 U. S. Department of Agriculture
320 (top) U. S. Department of Agriculture
320 (middle) U. S. Department of Agriculture
320 (bottom left) U. S. Department of Agriculture
320 (bottom right) U. S. Department of Agriculture
321 (top) U. S. Department of Agriculture
321 (middle) U. S. Department of Agriculture
321 (bottom) U. S. Department of Agriculture
323 (top) U. S. Department of Agriculture
323 (middle) U. S. Department of Agriculture
323 (bottom) U. S. Department of Agriculture
329 (top left) U. S. Department of Agriculture
329 (top right) U. S. Department of Agriculture
329 (bottom left) U. S. Department of Agriculture
329 (bottom right) U. S. Department of Agriculture
331 U. S. Department of Agriculture
336 United Fresh Fruit and Vegetable Association
345 American Spice Trade Association
348 National Macaroni Institute
351 (top) Sealtest Kitchens
351 (bottom) American Lamb Council
352 Sealtest Kitchens
355 The Borden Company
356 U. S. Department of Agriculture
359 Minute-Rice
361 American Spice Trade Association
363 Brer Rabbit Molasses
367 National Apple Institute
368 The Mince Meat Institute
370 American Spice Trade Association
371 Fleischmann Yeast Company
373 The Borden Company
375 Sealtest Kitchens
379 Sealtest Kitchens
383 American Spice Trade Association
384 Best Foods - Corn Products Company
388 The Underwood Kitchen and Danish Blue Cheese
390 National Apple Institute
392 General Electric Corp.
399 U. S. Department of Agriculture - Agricultural Research Service
400 American Spice Trade Association
403 National Dietary Foods Association
407 Milady Food Products, Inc.
409 National Macaroni Institute
411 The Borden Company
413 Florida Citrus
414 United Fresh Fruit and Vegetable Association
415 Alcoa Wrap
417 (top) Angostura-Wuppermann Corp.
417 (bottom) National Biscuit Company
420 Bananas - United Fruit Company
423 United Fresh Fruit and Vegetable Association
424 Best Foods - Corn Products Company
425 Brer Rabbit Molasses
426 Campbell Soup Company
430 Tabasco
433 National Macaroni Institute
434 Sealtest Kitchens
437 Pan-American Coffee Bureau
438 American Spice Trade Association
442 American Spice Trade Association
444 Mince Meat Institute
446 Associated Pimiento Canners
449 Associated Pimiento Canners
451 American Spice Trade Association
454 Sugar Information, Inc.
456 Wine Institute
460 Wine Institute
464 (top) Wine Institute
464 (bottom) Wine Institute
465 Canned Red Cherries Association
466 United Fruit Company
467 Wine Institute
468 General Foods
470 National Biscuit Company
475 The Borden Company
478 The Borden Company
481 The Underwood Kitchen

482 (top) Hammacher Schlemmer
482 (bottom) South African Rock Lobster Association
483 (top) Pan-American Coffee Bureau
483 (bottom) Campbell Soup Company
485 (top) Libbey Glass Photo
485 (bottom) Delmarva Poultry Industry
486 (top) Sealtest Kitchens
486 (bottom) The Borden Company
487 (top) Sealtest Kitchens
487 (bottom) Angostura - Wuppermann Corp.
488 (top) Coca-Cola
488 (bottom) American Dairy Association
489 Melamine Dinnerware
490 The Underwood Kitchen
493 Coca-Cola
495 United Fruit Company - Bananas
496 Pan-American Coffee Bureau
499 Kentucky Bred Bourbon
500 Nestlé
503 Campbell Soup Company
504 Danish Chesse Association
508 Maine Sardine Council
509 Dried Prunes Association
511 (top) California Fresh Dates
511 (bottom) National Apple Institute
512 Associated Pimiento Canners
514 Danish Cheese Association
515 Danish Cheese Association
517 Sugar Information, Inc.
518 Sealtest Kitchens
519 Pan-American Coffee Bureau
520 Pan-American Coffee Bureau
521 Tender Leaf Tea
523 Sealtest Kitchens
524 Tip Top Equipment Company
527 Sealtest Kitchens
528 United Fresh Fruit and Vegetable Association
530 V. La Rosa & Sons, Inc.
531 Switzerland Cheese Association
533 Sealtest Kitchens
534 Coca-Cola
536 American Dairy Association
537 American Spice Trade Association
538 Canned Carbonated Beverages
540 Reynolds Metals Company
541 Reynolds Metals Company
542 (top) Reynolds Metals Company
542 (bottom) Reynolds Metals Company
544 Reynolds Metals Company
545 Reynolds Metals Company
547 Reynolds Metals Company
549 (top) Reynolds Metals Company
549 (bottom) National Apple Institute
551 Campbell Soup Company
552 Brer Rabbit Molasses
553 National Biscuit Company
554 National Biscuit Company
555 United Fresh Fruit and Vegetable Association
556 Pan-American Coffee Bureau
557 Cherry Growers and Industries Foundation
558 American Meat Institute
559 United Fresh Fruit and Vegetable Association
560 Cherry Growers and Industries Foundation
561 United Fresh Fruit and Vegetable Association
562 (top) Wear-Ever Aluminum, Inc.
562 (bottom) Sealtest Kitchens
563 "Williamsburg" cut Stemware by Libbey
565 Libbey Glass Photo
566 Campbell Soup Company
568 Alcoa Wrap
570 Kitchen - Maid Cabinets, Kitchen - Maid Corp.
571 Gas Manufacturing Appliance Company
573 Ceramic Tile Council
574 (top) American Gas Association
574 (middle) American Gas Association
574 (bottom) Ceramic Tile Council
575 (top) Sylvania Electric Products Inc.
575 (middle) Rotiss-O-Mat Corp.
575 (bottom) Ceramic Tile Council
577 (top) Hammacher Schlemmer
577 (bottom) Gas Manufacturing Appliance Company
578 Wear-Ever Aluminum, Inc.
579 Ocean Spray Fresh Cranberries
580 Wear-Ever Aluminum, Inc.

PICTURE INDEX

A variety of canapés, simply and attractively served, highlights a successful afternoon party.

INDEX TO RECIPES AND INSTRUCTIONS

Welsh rarebit and salad make a hearty snack.